# Century 21
# Accounting

## Advanced
### Working Papers
### Chapters 1-14

## 10e

**Claudia Bienias Gilbertson, CPA**
Retired
North Hennepin Community College
Brooklyn Park, Minnesota

**Mark W. Lehman, CPA, CFE**
Associate Professor Emeritus
Richard C. Adkerson School of Accountancy
Mississippi State University
Starkville, Mississippi

**Dan Passalacqua, MA**
Retired
Oak Grove High School
San Jose, California

SOUTH-WESTERN
CENGAGE Learning

Australia • Brazil • Japan • Korea • Mexico • Singapore • Spain • United Kingdom • United States

**SOUTH-WESTERN**
CENGAGE Learning·

© 2015, 2009 Cengage Learning

WCN: 01-100-101

For product information and technology assistance, contact us at **Cengage Learning Academic Resource Center, 1-800-423-0563.**

For permission to use material from this text or product, submit all requests online at **www.cengage.com/permissions**. Further permissions questions can be emailed to **permissionrequest@cengage.com**.

ISBN-13: 978-1-133-10368-4
ISBN-10: 1-133-10368-5

**Cengage Learning**
200 First Stamford Place, 4th Floor
Stamford, CT 06902
USA

Cengage Learning is a leading provider of customized learning solutions with office locations around the globe, including Singapore, the United Kingdom, Australia, Mexico, Brazil, and Japan. Locate your local office at: **www.cengage.com/global.**

Cengage Learning products are represented in Canada by Nelson Education, Ltd.

For your course and learning solutions, visit **www.cengage.com/school.**

Visit our company website at **www.cengage.com**.

Printed in the United States of America
2 3 4 5 6 7 20 19 18 17 16

## TO THE STUDENT

These *Working Papers* are to be used in the study of Chapters 1–14 of *Century 21 Accounting Advanced, 10E*. Forms are provided for the following:

1. Study Guides

2. Work Together Exercises

3. On Your Own Exercises

4. Application Problems

5. Mastery Problems

6. Challenge Problems

7. Source Documents Problems

8. Reinforcement Activities 1, 2, and 3

Printed on each page is the number of the problem in the textbook for which the form is to be used. Also shown is a specific instruction number for which the form is to be used.

You may not be required to use every form that is provided. Your teacher will tell you whether to retain or dispose of the unused pages.

The pages are perforated so they may be removed as the work required in each assignment is completed. The pages will be more easily detached if you crease the sheet along the line of perforations and then remove the sheet by pulling sideways rather than upward.

| Name | | Perfect Score | Your Score |
|---|---|---|---|
| | Identifying Accounting Terms | 24 Pts. | |
| | Analyzing Accounting Principles, Concepts, and Procedures | 20 Pts. | |
| | **Total** | 44 Pts. | |

## Part One—Identifying Accounting Terms

**Directions:** Select the one term in Column I that best fits each definition in Column II. Print the letter identifying your choice in the Answers column.

*Contains accounting terms for Lesson 1-1.*

| Column I | Column II | Answers |
|---|---|---|
| A. account | 1. Anything of value that is owned. (p. 7) | 1._____ |
| B. accounting equation | 2. An amount owed by a business. (p. 7) | 2._____ |
| C. asset | 3. Financial rights to the assets of a business. (p. 7) | 3._____ |
| D. controlling account | 4. The amount remaining after the value of all liabilities is subtracted from the value of all assets. (p. 7) | 4._____ |
| E. double-entry accounting | | |
| F. equities | 5. The owners' equity in a corporation. (p. 7) | 5._____ |
| G. file maintenance | 6. An equation showing the relationship among assets, liabilities, and owners' equity. (p. 7) | 6._____ |
| H. general ledger | 7. Business papers from which information is obtained for a journal entry. (p. 7) | 7._____ |
| I. journal | | |
| J. ledger | 8. The recording of debit and credit parts of a transaction. (p. 8) | 8._____ |
| K. liability | 9. A form for recording transactions in chronological order. (p. 8) | 9._____ |
| L. owners' equity | 10. A journal used to record only one kind of transaction. (p. 8) | 10._____ |
| M. source documents | 11. A record that summarizes all the information pertaining to a single item in the accounting equation. (p. 9) | 11._____ |
| N. special journal | |  |
| O. stockholders' equity | 12. A group of accounts. (p. 11) | 12._____ |
| P. subsidiary ledger | 13. A ledger that contains all accounts needed to prepare financial statements. (p. 11) | 13._____ |
| | 14. A ledger that is summarized in a single general ledger account. (p. 11) | 14._____ |
| | 15. An account in a general ledger that summarizes all accounts in a subsidiary ledger. (p. 11) | 15._____ |
| | 16. The procedure for arranging accounts in a general ledger, assigning account numbers, and keeping records current. (p. 11) | 16._____ |

*Accounting terms for Lessons 1-2 and 1-3 are presented on the following page.*

**Directions:** Select the one term in Column I that best fits each definition in Column II. Print the letter identifying your choice in the Answers column.

*Contains accounting terms for Lessons 1-2 and 1-3.*

| Column I | Column II | Answers |
|---|---|---|
| A. cash discount | 1. An accounting system showing accounting information for two or more departments. (p. 13) | 1._____ |
| B. contra account | 2. A business that purchases and sells goods. (p. 13) | 2._____ |
| C. debit memorandum | 3. Transferring transaction information from a journal entry to a ledger account. (p. 15) | 3._____ |
| D. departmental accounting system | 4. A form prepared by the customer showing the price deduction taken by the customer for a return or an allowance. (p. 18) | 4._____ |
| E. merchandising business | 5. An account that reduces a related account on a financial statement. (p. 18) | 5._____ |
| F. petty cash | 6. A deduction that a vendor allows on the invoice amount to encourage prompt payment. (p. 20) | 6._____ |
| G. posting | 7. A cash discount taken on merchandise purchased on account. (p. 20) | 7._____ |
| H. purchases discount | 8. An amount of cash kept on hand and used for making small payments. (p. 25) | 8._____ |

# Part Two—Analyzing Accounting Principles, Concepts, and Procedures

**Directions:** Place a *T* for True or an *F* for False in the Answers column to show whether each of the following statements is true or false.

**Answers**

1. The accounting equation may be stated as assets = owners' equity. (p. 7)  1. _____

2. A business with many daily transactions may use special journals. (p. 8)  2. _____

3. Owners' equity accounts have normal credit balances. (p. 9)  3. _____

4. A liability account has a normal debit balance. (p. 9)  4. _____

5. Revenue accounts have normal credit balances. (p. 9)  5. _____

6. Expense accounts have normal credit balances. (p. 9)  6. _____

7. Increases in asset accounts are recorded on the credit side. (p. 9)  7. _____

8. Increases in liability accounts are recorded on the credit side. (p. 9)  8. _____

9. Increases in owners' equity accounts are recorded on the debit side. (p. 9)  9. _____

10. Decreases in revenue accounts are recorded on the credit side. (p. 9)  10. _____

11. Decreases in expense accounts are recorded on the credit side. (p. 9)  11. _____

12. In a departmental accounting system, gross profit is calculated for each department. (p. 13)  12. _____

13. A departmental purchases journal should contain a Purchases Debit column for each department. (p. 14)  13. _____

14. Individual amounts in the Accounts Payable Credit column of the purchases journal are posted only at the end of each month. (p. 15)  14. _____

15. When a customer returns merchandise for credit, the customer issues a debit memorandum for the amount of the return. (p. 18)  15. _____

16. Using a vendor invoice as the source document for a cash payment transaction is an application of the accounting concept Objective Evidence. (p. 20)  16. _____

17. A purchases discount is usually stated as a percentage. (p. 20)  17. _____

18. A discount is calculated on the original purchase price, even if a purchase return or allowance has been granted. (p. 21)  18. _____

19. Replenishing the petty cash fund increases the Petty Cash account balance. (p. 25)  19. _____

20. Amounts in the General Debit and General Credit columns of a cash payments journal are posted individually. (p. 26)  20. _____

## 1-1  WORK TOGETHER, p. 12

**Determining the normal balance, increase, and decrease sides for accounts**

**1., 2., 3., 4.**

**Determining the normal balance, increase, and decrease sides for accounts**

**1., 2., 3., 4.**

|  |  |
|---|---|
| <br><br><br> | <br><br><br> |
| <br><br><br> | <br><br><br> |
| <br><br><br> | <br><br><br> |
| <br><br><br> | <br><br><br> |

## 1-2 WORK TOGETHER, p. 19

**Journalizing and posting purchases on account and purchases returns and allowances**

**1., 2.**

### PURCHASES JOURNAL

PAGE _____

| | DATE | ACCOUNT CREDITED | PURCH. NO. | POST. REF. | 1 ACCOUNTS PAYABLE CREDIT | PURCHASES DEBIT | | |
|---|---|---|---|---|---|---|---|---|
| | | | | | | 2 AUDIO | 3 VIDEO | |
| 1 | | | | | | | | 1 |
| 2 | | | | | | | | 2 |
| 3 | | | | | | | | 3 |
| 4 | | | | | | | | 4 |
| 5 | | | | | | | | 5 |
| 6 | | | | | | | | 6 |
| 7 | | | | | | | | 7 |
| 8 | | | | | | | | 8 |
| 9 | | | | | | | | 9 |

**1.**

### GENERAL JOURNAL

PAGE _____

| | DATE | ACCOUNT TITLE | DOC. NO. | POST. REF. | DEBIT | CREDIT | |
|---|---|---|---|---|---|---|---|
| 1 | | | | | | | 1 |
| 2 | | | | | | | 2 |
| 3 | | | | | | | 3 |
| 4 | | | | | | | 4 |
| 5 | | | | | | | 5 |
| 6 | | | | | | | 6 |
| 7 | | | | | | | 7 |
| 8 | | | | | | | 8 |
| 9 | | | | | | | 9 |
| 10 | | | | | | | 10 |
| 11 | | | | | | | 11 |
| 12 | | | | | | | 12 |
| 13 | | | | | | | 13 |
| 14 | | | | | | | 14 |
| 15 | | | | | | | 15 |
| 16 | | | | | | | 16 |
| 17 | | | | | | | 17 |

**1.**

## ACCOUNTS PAYABLE LEDGER

VENDOR Davis Corporation                                        VENDOR NO. 210

| DATE | | ITEM | POST. REF. | DEBIT | CREDIT | CREDIT BALANCE |
|---|---|---|---|---|---|---|
| 20-- June | 1 | Balance | ✔ | | | 1 0 3 4 23 |
| | | | | | | |
| | | | | | | |
| | | | | | | |

VENDOR National Industries                                      VENDOR NO. 220

| DATE | | ITEM | POST. REF. | DEBIT | CREDIT | CREDIT BALANCE |
|---|---|---|---|---|---|---|
| 20-- June | 1 | Balance | ✔ | | | 9 0 2 44 |
| | | | | | | |
| | | | | | | |
| | | | | | | |
| | | | | | | |

VENDOR TPC Supply                                               VENDOR NO. 230

| DATE | | ITEM | POST. REF. | DEBIT | CREDIT | CREDIT BALANCE |
|---|---|---|---|---|---|---|
| 20-- June | 1 | Balance | ✔ | | | 2 3 1 2 41 |
| | | | | | | |
| | | | | | | |
| | | | | | | |
| | | | | | | |

**1-2** **WORK TOGETHER (concluded)**

**1., 2.**                                    **GENERAL LEDGER**

ACCOUNT Accounts Payable                                    ACCOUNT NO. 2105

| DATE | ITEM | POST. REF. | DEBIT | CREDIT | BALANCE DEBIT | BALANCE CREDIT |
|------|------|-----------|-------|--------|---------------|----------------|
| 20--<br>June 1 | Balance | ✔ | | | | 4 2 4 9 08 |
| | | | | | | |
| | | | | | | |

ACCOUNT Purchases—Audio                                    ACCOUNT NO. 5105

| DATE | ITEM | POST. REF. | DEBIT | CREDIT | BALANCE DEBIT | BALANCE CREDIT |
|------|------|-----------|-------|--------|---------------|----------------|
| 20--<br>June 1 | Balance | ✔ | | | 38 4 8 9 10 | |
| | | | | | | |

ACCOUNT Purchases Returns and Allowances—Audio                                    ACCOUNT NO. 5115

| DATE | ITEM | POST. REF. | DEBIT | CREDIT | BALANCE DEBIT | BALANCE CREDIT |
|------|------|-----------|-------|--------|---------------|----------------|
| 20--<br>June 1 | Balance | ✔ | | | | 8 1 1 50 |
| | | | | | | |
| | | | | | | |

ACCOUNT Purchases—Video                                    ACCOUNT NO. 5205

| DATE | ITEM | POST. REF. | DEBIT | CREDIT | BALANCE DEBIT | BALANCE CREDIT |
|------|------|-----------|-------|--------|---------------|----------------|
| 20--<br>June 1 | Balance | ✔ | | | 28 4 8 9 08 | |
| | | | | | | |

ACCOUNT Purchases Returns and Allowances—Video                                    ACCOUNT NO. 5215

| DATE | ITEM | POST. REF. | DEBIT | CREDIT | BALANCE DEBIT | BALANCE CREDIT |
|------|------|-----------|-------|--------|---------------|----------------|
| 20--<br>June 1 | Balance | ✔ | | | | 6 2 1 70 |
| | | | | | | |
| | | | | | | |

**Journalizing and posting purchases on account and purchases returns and allowances**

**1., 2.**

PURCHASES JOURNAL

| | DATE | ACCOUNT CREDITED | PURCH. NO. | POST. REF. | 1 ACCOUNTS PAYABLE CREDIT | PURCHASES DEBIT | | |
|---|---|---|---|---|---|---|---|---|
| | | | | | | 2 CLOTHING | 3 SHOES | |
| 1 | | | | | | | | 1 |
| 2 | | | | | | | | 2 |
| 3 | | | | | | | | 3 |
| 4 | | | | | | | | 4 |
| 5 | | | | | | | | 5 |
| 6 | | | | | | | | 6 |
| 7 | | | | | | | | 7 |
| 8 | | | | | | | | 8 |
| 9 | | | | | | | | 9 |

**1.**

GENERAL JOURNAL

| | DATE | ACCOUNT TITLE | DOC. NO. | POST. REF. | DEBIT | CREDIT | |
|---|---|---|---|---|---|---|---|
| 1 | | | | | | | 1 |
| 2 | | | | | | | 2 |
| 3 | | | | | | | 3 |
| 4 | | | | | | | 4 |
| 5 | | | | | | | 5 |
| 6 | | | | | | | 6 |
| 7 | | | | | | | 7 |
| 8 | | | | | | | 8 |
| 9 | | | | | | | 9 |
| 10 | | | | | | | 10 |
| 11 | | | | | | | 11 |
| 12 | | | | | | | 12 |
| 13 | | | | | | | 13 |
| 14 | | | | | | | 14 |
| 15 | | | | | | | 15 |
| 16 | | | | | | | 16 |
| 17 | | | | | | | 17 |

## 1-2 ON YOUR OWN (continued)

**1.**                                    **ACCOUNTS PAYABLE LEDGER**

VENDOR  Ackerman Supply                                          VENDOR NO. 210

| DATE | | ITEM | POST. REF. | DEBIT | CREDIT | CREDIT BALANCE |
|---|---|---|---|---|---|---|
| 20--<br>July | 1 | Balance | ✔ | | | 2 0 6 8 00 |
| | | | | | | |
| | | | | | | |

VENDOR  Keller Corporation                                       VENDOR NO. 220

| DATE | | ITEM | POST. REF. | DEBIT | CREDIT | CREDIT BALANCE |
|---|---|---|---|---|---|---|
| 20--<br>July | 1 | Balance | ✔ | | | 1 5 2 4 50 |
| | | | | | | |
| | | | | | | |
| | | | | | | |
| | | | | | | |

VENDOR  Peters Company                                           VENDOR NO. 230

| DATE | | ITEM | POST. REF. | DEBIT | CREDIT | CREDIT BALANCE |
|---|---|---|---|---|---|---|
| 20--<br>July | 1 | Balance | ✔ | | | 3 1 5 4 75 |
| | | | | | | |
| | | | | | | |
| | | | | | | |

**1., 2.**                                              **GENERAL LEDGER**

ACCOUNT Accounts Payable                                          ACCOUNT NO. 2105

| DATE | | ITEM | POST. REF. | DEBIT | CREDIT | BALANCE DEBIT | BALANCE CREDIT |
|---|---|---|---|---|---|---|---|
| July 1 | | Balance | ✔ | | | | 18 4 4 9 20 |
| | | | | | | | |
| | | | | | | | |
| | | | | | | | |

ACCOUNT Purchases—Clothing                                       ACCOUNT NO. 5105

| DATE | | ITEM | POST. REF. | DEBIT | CREDIT | BALANCE DEBIT | BALANCE CREDIT |
|---|---|---|---|---|---|---|---|
| July 1 | | Balance | ✔ | | | 68 4 8 9 60 | |
| | | | | | | | |
| | | | | | | | |

ACCOUNT Purchases Returns and Allowances—Clothing                ACCOUNT NO. 5115

| DATE | | ITEM | POST. REF. | DEBIT | CREDIT | BALANCE DEBIT | BALANCE CREDIT |
|---|---|---|---|---|---|---|---|
| July 1 | | Balance | ✔ | | | | 1 0 8 5 15 |
| | | | | | | | |
| | | | | | | | |
| | | | | | | | |
| | | | | | | | |

ACCOUNT Purchases—Shoes                                          ACCOUNT NO. 5205

| DATE | | ITEM | POST. REF. | DEBIT | CREDIT | BALANCE DEBIT | BALANCE CREDIT |
|---|---|---|---|---|---|---|---|
| July 1 | | Balance | ✔ | | | 49 1 4 8 60 | |
| | | | | | | | |
| | | | | | | | |
| | | | | | | | |

ACCOUNT Purchases Returns and Allowances—Shoes                   ACCOUNT NO. 5215

| DATE | | ITEM | POST. REF. | DEBIT | CREDIT | BALANCE DEBIT | BALANCE CREDIT |
|---|---|---|---|---|---|---|---|
| July 1 | | Balance | ✔ | | | | 2 3 1 95 |
| | | | | | | | |
| | | | | | | | |
| | | | | | | | |

**1-3  WORK TOGETHER, p. 27**

**Journalizing and posting departmental cash payments**

**1., 2.**

## CASH PAYMENTS JOURNAL

PAGE 6

| DATE | ACCOUNT TITLE | CK. NO. | POST. REF. | GENERAL DEBIT 1 | GENERAL CREDIT 2 | ACCOUNTS PAYABLE DEBIT 3 | PURCH. DISCOUNT CR. CRAFTS 4 | PURCH. DISCOUNT CR. FRAMES 5 | CASH CREDIT 6 |
|---|---|---|---|---|---|---|---|---|---|
| 1 | | | | | | | | | |
| 2 | | | | | | | | | |
| 3 | | | | | | | | | |
| 4 | | | | | | | | | |
| 5 | | | | | | | | | |
| 6 | | | | | | | | | |
| 7 | | | | | | | | | |
| 8 | | | | | | | | | |
| 9 | | | | | | | | | |
| 10 | | | | | | | | | |
| 11 | | | | | | | | | |
| 12 | | | | | | | | | |
| 13 | | | | | | | | | |
| 14 | | | | | | | | | |
| 15 | | | | | | | | | |
| 16 | | | | | | | | | |
| 17 | | | | | | | | | |
| 18 | | | | | | | | | |
| 19 | | | | | | | | | |
| 20 | | | | | | | | | |
| 21 | | | | | | | | | |
| 22 | | | | | | | | | |

Chapter 1 Recording Departmental Purchases and Cash Payments • **13**

**1., 2.**                                    **ACCOUNTS PAYABLE LEDGER**

VENDOR  Fulton Corporation                                    VENDOR NO. 235

| DATE | | ITEM | POST. REF. | DEBIT | CREDIT | CREDIT BALANCE |
|---|---|---|---|---|---|---|
| 20--<br>June | 1 | Balance | ✔ | | | 3 6 7 4 22 |
| | | | | | | |

VENDOR  Harris Industries                                    VENDOR NO. 245

| DATE | | ITEM | POST. REF. | DEBIT | CREDIT | CREDIT BALANCE |
|---|---|---|---|---|---|---|
| 20--<br>June | 1 | Balance | ✔ | | | 2 9 5 3 30 |
| | | | | | | |

**1., 2.**                                    **GENERAL LEDGER**

ACCOUNT  Cash                                    ACCOUNT NO. 1105

| DATE | | ITEM | POST. REF. | DEBIT | CREDIT | BALANCE DEBIT | BALANCE CREDIT |
|---|---|---|---|---|---|---|---|
| 20--<br>June | 1 | Balance | ✔ | | | 16 4 3 5 34 | |
| | | | | | | | |

ACCOUNT  Supplies                                    ACCOUNT NO. 1405

| DATE | | ITEM | POST. REF. | DEBIT | CREDIT | BALANCE DEBIT | BALANCE CREDIT |
|---|---|---|---|---|---|---|---|
| 20--<br>June | 1 | Balance | ✔ | | | 6 4 3 2 54 | |
| | | | | | | | |

ACCOUNT  Accounts Payable                                    ACCOUNT NO. 2105

| DATE | | ITEM | POST. REF. | DEBIT | CREDIT | BALANCE DEBIT | BALANCE CREDIT |
|---|---|---|---|---|---|---|---|
| 20--<br>June | 1 | Balance | ✔ | | | | 16 4 6 2 27 |
| | | | | | | | |

ACCOUNT  Purchases—Crafts                                    ACCOUNT NO. 5105

| DATE | | ITEM | POST. REF. | DEBIT | CREDIT | BALANCE DEBIT | BALANCE CREDIT |
|---|---|---|---|---|---|---|---|
| 20--<br>June | 1 | Balance | ✔ | | | 164 3 2 6 74 | |
| | | | | | | | |

## 1-3 WORK TOGETHER (concluded)

ACCOUNT Purchases Discount—Crafts      ACCOUNT NO. 5110

| DATE | ITEM | POST. REF. | DEBIT | CREDIT | BALANCE DEBIT | BALANCE CREDIT |
|------|------|-----------|-------|--------|-------|--------|
| 20-- June 1 | Balance | ✔ | | | | 1 8 0 7 59 |
| | | | | | | |
| | | | | | | |

ACCOUNT Purchases—Frames      ACCOUNT NO. 5205

| DATE | ITEM | POST. REF. | DEBIT | CREDIT | BALANCE DEBIT | BALANCE CREDIT |
|------|------|-----------|-------|--------|-------|--------|
| 20-- June 1 | Balance | ✔ | | | 94 3 6 5 33 | |
| | | | | | | |
| | | | | | | |

ACCOUNT Purchases Discount—Frames      ACCOUNT NO. 5210

| DATE | ITEM | POST. REF. | DEBIT | CREDIT | BALANCE DEBIT | BALANCE CREDIT |
|------|------|-----------|-------|--------|-------|--------|
| 20-- June 1 | Balance | ✔ | | | | 6 7 9 43 |
| | | | | | | |
| | | | | | | |

ACCOUNT Advertising Expense—Crafts      ACCOUNT NO. 6105

| DATE | ITEM | POST. REF. | DEBIT | CREDIT | BALANCE DEBIT | BALANCE CREDIT |
|------|------|-----------|-------|--------|-------|--------|
| 20-- June 1 | Balance | ✔ | | | 7 5 9 0 00 | |
| | | | | | | |
| | | | | | | |

ACCOUNT Miscellaneous Expense      ACCOUNT NO. 7125

| DATE | ITEM | POST. REF. | DEBIT | CREDIT | BALANCE DEBIT | BALANCE CREDIT |
|------|------|-----------|-------|--------|-------|--------|
| 20-- June 1 | Balance | ✔ | | | 3 7 6 5 86 | |
| | | | | | | |
| | | | | | | |

**Journalizing and posting departmental cash payments**

**1., 2.**

## CASH PAYMENTS JOURNAL

PAGE 6

| DATE | ACCOUNT TITLE | CK. NO. | POST. REF. | GENERAL DEBIT (1) | GENERAL CREDIT (2) | ACCOUNTS PAYABLE DEBIT (3) | PURCH. DISCOUNT CR. CERAMIC (4) | PURCH. DISCOUNT CR. STONE (5) | CASH CREDIT (6) |
|------|---------------|---------|-----------|-------------------|--------------------|-----------------------------|----------------------------------|-------------------------------|------------------|
| | | | | | | | | | | 1 |
| | | | | | | | | | | 2 |
| | | | | | | | | | | 3 |
| | | | | | | | | | | 4 |
| | | | | | | | | | | 5 |
| | | | | | | | | | | 6 |
| | | | | | | | | | | 7 |
| | | | | | | | | | | 8 |
| | | | | | | | | | | 9 |
| | | | | | | | | | | 10 |
| | | | | | | | | | | 11 |
| | | | | | | | | | | 12 |
| | | | | | | | | | | 13 |
| | | | | | | | | | | 14 |
| | | | | | | | | | | 15 |
| | | | | | | | | | | 16 |
| | | | | | | | | | | 17 |
| | | | | | | | | | | 18 |
| | | | | | | | | | | 19 |
| | | | | | | | | | | 20 |
| | | | | | | | | | | 21 |
| | | | | | | | | | | 22 |

**1-3**    **ON YOUR OWN (continued)**

**1., 2.**                     **ACCOUNTS PAYABLE LEDGER**

VENDOR Marris Ceramics                         VENDOR NO. 260

| DATE | ITEM | POST. REF. | DEBIT | CREDIT | CREDIT BALANCE |
|---|---|---|---|---|---|
| 20-- July 1 | Balance | ✔ | | | 4 0 9 8 20 |
| | | | | | |

VENDOR Overland Stone                         VENDOR NO. 270

| DATE | ITEM | POST. REF. | DEBIT | CREDIT | CREDIT BALANCE |
|---|---|---|---|---|---|
| 20-- July 1 | Balance | ✔ | | | 3 5 6 0 50 |
| | | | | | |
| | | | | | |

**1., 2.**                     **GENERAL LEDGER**

ACCOUNT Cash                               ACCOUNT NO. 1105

| DATE | ITEM | POST. REF. | DEBIT | CREDIT | BALANCE DEBIT | BALANCE CREDIT |
|---|---|---|---|---|---|---|
| 20-- July 1 | Balance | ✔ | | | 12 5 3 2 12 | |
| | | | | | | |

ACCOUNT Supplies                           ACCOUNT NO. 1405

| DATE | ITEM | POST. REF. | DEBIT | CREDIT | BALANCE DEBIT | BALANCE CREDIT |
|---|---|---|---|---|---|---|
| 20-- July 1 | Balance | ✔ | | | 5 1 2 6 21 | |
| | | | | | | |

ACCOUNT Accounts Payable                   ACCOUNT NO. 2105

| DATE | ITEM | POST. REF. | DEBIT | CREDIT | BALANCE DEBIT | BALANCE CREDIT |
|---|---|---|---|---|---|---|
| 20-- July 1 | Balance | ✔ | | | | 22 1 5 6 75 |
| | | | | | | |

ACCOUNT Purchases—Ceramic                 ACCOUNT NO. 5105

| DATE | ITEM | POST. REF. | DEBIT | CREDIT | BALANCE DEBIT | BALANCE CREDIT |
|---|---|---|---|---|---|---|
| 20-- July 1 | Balance | ✔ | | | 175 4 6 3 33 | |
| | | | | | | |

ACCOUNT Purchases Discount—Ceramic                    ACCOUNT NO. 5110

| DATE | ITEM | POST. REF. | DEBIT | CREDIT | BALANCE DEBIT | BALANCE CREDIT |
|------|------|-----------|-------|--------|-------|--------|
| 20-- July 1 | Balance | ✔ | | | | 1 5 7 9 17 |
| | | | | | | |

ACCOUNT Purchases—Stone                              ACCOUNT NO. 5205

| DATE | ITEM | POST. REF. | DEBIT | CREDIT | BALANCE DEBIT | BALANCE CREDIT |
|------|------|-----------|-------|--------|-------|--------|
| 20-- July 1 | Balance | ✔ | | | 91 0 6 4 54 | |
| | | | | | | |

ACCOUNT Purchases Discount—Stone                     ACCOUNT NO. 5210

| DATE | ITEM | POST. REF. | DEBIT | CREDIT | BALANCE DEBIT | BALANCE CREDIT |
|------|------|-----------|-------|--------|-------|--------|
| 20-- July 1 | Balance | ✔ | | | | 7 2 8 52 |
| | | | | | | |

ACCOUNT Advertising Expense—Stone                    ACCOUNT NO. 6205

| DATE | ITEM | POST. REF. | DEBIT | CREDIT | BALANCE DEBIT | BALANCE CREDIT |
|------|------|-----------|-------|--------|-------|--------|
| 20-- July 1 | Balance | ✔ | | | 3 6 7 0 00 | |
| | | | | | | |

ACCOUNT Miscellaneous Expense                        ACCOUNT NO. 7125

| DATE | ITEM | POST. REF. | DEBIT | CREDIT | BALANCE DEBIT | BALANCE CREDIT |
|------|------|-----------|-------|--------|-------|--------|
| 20-- July 1 | Balance | ✔ | | | 4 6 4 2 87 | |
| | | | | | | |
| | | | | | | |

## 1-1 APPLICATION PROBLEM (LO3), p. 31

**Determining the normal balance, increase, and decrease sides for accounts**

**1., 2., 3., 4., 5.**

| 1 | 2 | 3 | 4 | 5 | 6 | 7 | 8 |
|---|---|---|---|---|---|---|---|
| Account Title | Account Classification | Account's Normal Balance | | Increase Side | | Decrease Side | |
| | | Debit | Credit | Debit | Credit | Debit | Credit |
| Prepaid Insurance | Asset | ✔ | | ✔ | | | ✔ |
| | | | | | | | |
| | | | | | | | |
| | | | | | | | |
| | | | | | | | |
| | | | | | | | |
| | | | | | | | |
| | | | | | | | |
| | | | | | | | |
| | | | | | | | |
| | | | | | | | |
| | | | | | | | |
| | | | | | | | |
| | | | | | | | |
| | | | | | | | |
| | | | | | | | |
| | | | | | | | |
| | | | | | | | |
| | | | | | | | |
| | | | | | | | |
| | | | | | | | |
| | | | | | | | |

Journalizing and posting departmental purchases on account and purchases returns and allowances

**1., 2.**

### PURCHASES JOURNAL

PAGE

| | DATE | ACCOUNT CREDITED | PURCH. NO. | POST. REF. | ACCOUNTS PAYABLE CREDIT | PURCHASES DEBIT | | |
| | | | | | | FLOWERS | GIFTS | |
|---|---|---|---|---|---|---|---|---|
| 1 | | | | | | | | 1 |
| 2 | | | | | | | | 2 |
| 3 | | | | | | | | 3 |
| 4 | | | | | | | | 4 |
| 5 | | | | | | | | 5 |
| 6 | | | | | | | | 6 |
| 7 | | | | | | | | 7 |
| 8 | | | | | | | | 8 |
| 9 | | | | | | | | 9 |

**1.**

### GENERAL JOURNAL

PAGE

| | DATE | ACCOUNT TITLE | DOC. NO. | POST. REF. | DEBIT | CREDIT | |
|---|---|---|---|---|---|---|---|
| 1 | | | | | | | 1 |
| 2 | | | | | | | 2 |
| 3 | | | | | | | 3 |
| 4 | | | | | | | 4 |
| 5 | | | | | | | 5 |
| 6 | | | | | | | 6 |
| 7 | | | | | | | 7 |
| 8 | | | | | | | 8 |
| 9 | | | | | | | 9 |
| 10 | | | | | | | 10 |
| 11 | | | | | | | 11 |
| 12 | | | | | | | 12 |
| 13 | | | | | | | 13 |
| 14 | | | | | | | 14 |
| 15 | | | | | | | 15 |
| 16 | | | | | | | 16 |

**1-2** **APPLICATION PROBLEM (continued)**

**1., 2.**                    **ACCOUNTS PAYABLE LEDGER**

VENDOR Carson Growers                                    VENDOR NO. 210

| DATE | | ITEM | POST. REF. | DEBIT | CREDIT | CREDIT BALANCE |
|---|---|---|---|---|---|---|
| 20-- Aug. | 1 | Balance | ✔ | | | 2 5 4 4 00 |
| | | | | | | |
| | | | | | | |

VENDOR Glade Arts Center                                 VENDOR NO. 220

| DATE | | ITEM | POST. REF. | DEBIT | CREDIT | CREDIT BALANCE |
|---|---|---|---|---|---|---|
| 20-- Aug. | 1 | Balance | ✔ | | | 4 9 8 1 25 |
| | | | | | | |
| | | | | | | |
| | | | | | | |

VENDOR Marlon Nursery                                    VENDOR NO. 230

| DATE | | ITEM | POST. REF. | DEBIT | CREDIT | CREDIT BALANCE |
|---|---|---|---|---|---|---|
| 20-- Aug. | 1 | Balance | ✔ | | | 3 1 0 4 70 |
| | | | | | | |
| | | | | | | |
| | | | | | | |

VENDOR Tennessee Crafts                                  VENDOR NO. 240

| DATE | | ITEM | POST. REF. | DEBIT | CREDIT | CREDIT BALANCE |
|---|---|---|---|---|---|---|
| 20-- Aug. | 1 | Balance | ✔ | | | 4 1 9 5 80 |
| | | | | | | |
| | | | | | | |
| | | | | | | |

**1., 2.** **GENERAL LEDGER**

ACCOUNT Accounts Payable      ACCOUNT NO. 2105

| DATE | ITEM | POST. REF. | DEBIT | CREDIT | BALANCE DEBIT | BALANCE CREDIT |
|------|------|-----------|-------|--------|-------|--------|
| 20-- Aug. 1 | Balance | ✔ | | | | 14 825 75 |

ACCOUNT Purchases—Flowers      ACCOUNT NO. 5105

| DATE | ITEM | POST. REF. | DEBIT | CREDIT | BALANCE DEBIT | BALANCE CREDIT |
|------|------|-----------|-------|--------|-------|--------|
| 20-- Aug. 1 | Balance | ✔ | | | 68 489 60 | |

ACCOUNT Purchases Returns and Allowances—Flowers      ACCOUNT NO. 5115

| DATE | ITEM | POST. REF. | DEBIT | CREDIT | BALANCE DEBIT | BALANCE CREDIT |
|------|------|-----------|-------|--------|-------|--------|
| 20-- Aug. 1 | Balance | ✔ | | | | 1 085 15 |

ACCOUNT Purchases—Gifts      ACCOUNT NO. 5205

| DATE | ITEM | POST. REF. | DEBIT | CREDIT | BALANCE DEBIT | BALANCE CREDIT |
|------|------|-----------|-------|--------|-------|--------|
| 20-- Aug. 1 | Balance | ✔ | | | 49 148 60 | |

ACCOUNT Purchases Returns and Allowances—Gifts      ACCOUNT NO. 5215

| DATE | ITEM | POST. REF. | DEBIT | CREDIT | BALANCE DEBIT | BALANCE CREDIT |
|------|------|-----------|-------|--------|-------|--------|
| 20-- Aug. 1 | Balance | ✔ | | | | 231 95 |

**1-3** **APPLICATION PROBLEM (LO7, 8), p. 32**

**Journalizing and posting departmental cash payments**

**1., 2.**

CASH PAYMENTS JOURNAL

PAGE ____

| | | | GENERAL | | ACCOUNTS PAYABLE DEBIT | PURCH. DISCOUNT CR. | | CASH CREDIT |
|---|---|---|---|---|---|---|---|---|
| DATE | ACCOUNT TITLE | CK. NO. | POST. REF. | DEBIT | CREDIT | | GUITARS | KEYBOARDS | |
| | | | | **1** | **2** | **3** | **4** | **5** | **6** |
| 1 | | | | | | | | | |
| 2 | | | | | | | | | |
| 3 | | | | | | | | | |
| 4 | | | | | | | | | |
| 5 | | | | | | | | | |
| 6 | | | | | | | | | |
| 7 | | | | | | | | | |
| 8 | | | | | | | | | |
| 9 | | | | | | | | | |
| 10 | | | | | | | | | |
| 11 | | | | | | | | | |
| 12 | | | | | | | | | |
| 13 | | | | | | | | | |
| 14 | | | | | | | | | |
| 15 | | | | | | | | | |
| 16 | | | | | | | | | |
| 17 | | | | | | | | | |
| 18 | | | | | | | | | |
| 19 | | | | | | | | | |
| 20 | | | | | | | | | |
| 21 | | | | | | | | | |
| 22 | | | | | | | | | |

Chapter 1 Recording Departmental Purchases and Cash Payments • **23**

**1., 2.**                              **ACCOUNTS PAYABLE LEDGER**

VENDOR Airways Music                                         VENDOR NO. 210

| DATE | | ITEM | POST. REF. | DEBIT | CREDIT | CREDIT BALANCE |
|---|---|---|---|---|---|---|
| Mar. 20-- | 1 | Balance | ✔ | | | 5 2 0 9 20 |
| | | | | | | |
| | | | | | | |

VENDOR Campbell Guitar                                       VENDOR NO. 220

| DATE | | ITEM | POST. REF. | DEBIT | CREDIT | CREDIT BALANCE |
|---|---|---|---|---|---|---|
| Mar. 20-- | 1 | Balance | ✔ | | | 4 2 0 9 90 |
| | | | | | | |
| | | | | | | |

**1., 2.**                              **GENERAL LEDGER**

ACCOUNT Cash                                                ACCOUNT NO. 1105

| DATE | | ITEM | POST. REF. | DEBIT | CREDIT | BALANCE DEBIT | BALANCE CREDIT |
|---|---|---|---|---|---|---|---|
| Mar. 20-- | 1 | Balance | ✔ | | | 20 4 5 2 53 | |
| | | | | | | | |

ACCOUNT Supplies                                           ACCOUNT NO. 1405

| DATE | | ITEM | POST. REF. | DEBIT | CREDIT | BALANCE DEBIT | BALANCE CREDIT |
|---|---|---|---|---|---|---|---|
| Mar. 20-- | 1 | Balance | ✔ | | | 3 6 4 3 21 | |
| | | | | | | | |

ACCOUNT Accounts Payable                                   ACCOUNT NO. 2105

| DATE | | ITEM | POST. REF. | DEBIT | CREDIT | BALANCE DEBIT | BALANCE CREDIT |
|---|---|---|---|---|---|---|---|
| Mar. 20-- | 1 | Balance | ✔ | | | | 28 5 4 6 27 |
| | | | | | | | |

ACCOUNT Purchases—Guitars                                  ACCOUNT NO. 5105

| DATE | | ITEM | POST. REF. | DEBIT | CREDIT | BALANCE DEBIT | BALANCE CREDIT |
|---|---|---|---|---|---|---|---|
| Mar. 20-- | 1 | Balance | ✔ | | | 95 6 4 2 87 | |
| | | | | | | | |

**24** • Working Papers

**1-3  APPLICATION PROBLEM (concluded)**

ACCOUNT Purchases Discount—Guitars                                   ACCOUNT NO. 5110

| DATE | ITEM | POST. REF. | DEBIT | CREDIT | BALANCE DEBIT | BALANCE CREDIT |
|---|---|---|---|---|---|---|
| Mar. 1 | Balance | ✔ | | | | 1 9 1 29 |

ACCOUNT Purchases—Keyboards                                          ACCOUNT NO. 5205

| DATE | ITEM | POST. REF. | DEBIT | CREDIT | BALANCE DEBIT | BALANCE CREDIT |
|---|---|---|---|---|---|---|
| Mar. 1 | Balance | ✔ | | | 104 2 5 6 89 | |

ACCOUNT Purchases Discount—Keyboards                                ACCOUNT NO. 5210

| DATE | ITEM | POST. REF. | DEBIT | CREDIT | BALANCE DEBIT | BALANCE CREDIT |
|---|---|---|---|---|---|---|
| Mar. 1 | Balance | ✔ | | | | 6 2 5 54 |

ACCOUNT Advertising Expense—Guitars                                 ACCOUNT NO. 6105

| DATE | ITEM | POST. REF. | DEBIT | CREDIT | BALANCE DEBIT | BALANCE CREDIT |
|---|---|---|---|---|---|---|
| Mar. 1 | Balance | ✔ | | | 3 6 0 0 00 | |

ACCOUNT Miscellaneous Expense                                       ACCOUNT NO. 7125

| DATE | ITEM | POST. REF. | DEBIT | CREDIT | BALANCE DEBIT | BALANCE CREDIT |
|---|---|---|---|---|---|---|
| Mar. 1 | Balance | ✔ | | | 5 2 4 7 23 | |

**Journalizing departmental purchases and cash payments**

**1., 3.**

## PURCHASES JOURNAL

PAGE

| | DATE | ACCOUNT CREDITED | PURCH. NO. | POST. REF. | ACCOUNTS PAYABLE CREDIT | PURCHASES DEBIT | |
|---|---|---|---|---|---|---|---|
| | | | | | 1 | 2 COSTUME | 3 FINE |
| 1 | | | | | | | | 1 |
| 2 | | | | | | | | 2 |
| 3 | | | | | | | | 3 |
| 4 | | | | | | | | 4 |
| 5 | | | | | | | | 5 |
| 6 | | | | | | | | 6 |
| 7 | | | | | | | | 7 |
| 8 | | | | | | | | 8 |
| 9 | | | | | | | | 9 |

**1.**

## GENERAL JOURNAL

PAGE

| | DATE | ACCOUNT TITLE | DOC. NO. | POST. REF. | DEBIT | CREDIT | |
|---|---|---|---|---|---|---|---|
| 1 | | | | | | | 1 |
| 2 | | | | | | | 2 |
| 3 | | | | | | | 3 |
| 4 | | | | | | | 4 |
| 5 | | | | | | | 5 |
| 6 | | | | | | | 6 |
| 7 | | | | | | | 7 |
| 8 | | | | | | | 8 |
| 9 | | | | | | | 9 |
| 10 | | | | | | | 10 |
| 11 | | | | | | | 11 |
| 12 | | | | | | | 12 |
| 13 | | | | | | | 13 |
| 14 | | | | | | | 14 |
| 15 | | | | | | | 15 |
| 16 | | | | | | | 16 |

## 1-M MASTERY PROBLEM (continued)

**1., 3.**

**CASH PAYMENTS JOURNAL**

| DATE | ACCOUNT TITLE | CK. NO. | POST. REF. | GENERAL DEBIT (1) | GENERAL CREDIT (2) | ACCOUNTS PAYABLE DEBIT (3) | PURCH. DISCOUNT CR. COSTUME (4) | PURCH. DISCOUNT CR. FINE (5) | CASH CREDIT (6) |
|------|---------------|---------|------------|---------|----------|-----------------|---------|------|-------------|
| | | | | | | | | | |
| | | | | | | | | | |
| | | | | | | | | | |
| | | | | | | | | | |
| | | | | | | | | | |
| | | | | | | | | | |
| | | | | | | | | | |
| | | | | | | | | | |
| | | | | | | | | | |
| | | | | | | | | | |
| | | | | | | | | | |
| | | | | | | | | | |
| | | | | | | | | | |
| | | | | | | | | | |
| | | | | | | | | | |
| | | | | | | | | | |
| | | | | | | | | | |
| | | | | | | | | | |
| | | | | | | | | | |
| | | | | | | | | | |
| | | | | | | | | | |
| | | | | | | | | | |

**1., 2.**                            **ACCOUNTS PAYABLE LEDGER**

VENDOR Austin Creations                                   VENDOR NO. 210

| DATE | ITEM | POST. REF. | DEBIT | CREDIT | CREDIT BALANCE |
|------|------|-----------|-------|--------|----------------|
|      |      |           |       |        |                |
|      |      |           |       |        |                |
|      |      |           |       |        |                |
|      |      |           |       |        |                |

VENDOR Destin Crafters                                    VENDOR NO. 220

| DATE | ITEM | POST. REF. | DEBIT | CREDIT | CREDIT BALANCE |
|------|------|-----------|-------|--------|----------------|
| Aug. 1 (20--) | Balance | ✔ |  |  | 2 6 4 3 63 |
|      |      |           |       |        |                |
|      |      |           |       |        |                |

VENDOR Jenkins Designs                                    VENDOR NO. 230

| DATE | ITEM | POST. REF. | DEBIT | CREDIT | CREDIT BALANCE |
|------|------|-----------|-------|--------|----------------|
|      |      |           |       |        |                |
|      |      |           |       |        |                |
|      |      |           |       |        |                |
|      |      |           |       |        |                |

VENDOR Ketler Krafts                                      VENDOR NO. 240

| DATE | ITEM | POST. REF. | DEBIT | CREDIT | CREDIT BALANCE |
|------|------|-----------|-------|--------|----------------|
| Aug. 1 (20--) | Balance | ✔ |  |  | 2 9 5 3 30 |
|      |      |           |       |        |                |
|      |      |           |       |        |                |

# 1-M  MASTERY PROBLEM (continued)

**1., 2., 3.**                    **GENERAL LEDGER**

ACCOUNT Cash                                              ACCOUNT NO. 1105

| DATE | | ITEM | POST. REF. | DEBIT | CREDIT | BALANCE | |
|---|---|---|---|---|---|---|---|
| | | | | | | DEBIT | CREDIT |
| 20-- Aug. | 1 | Balance | ✔ | | | 14 5 4 2 87 | |

ACCOUNT Supplies                                         ACCOUNT NO. 1405

| DATE | | ITEM | POST. REF. | DEBIT | CREDIT | BALANCE | |
|---|---|---|---|---|---|---|---|
| | | | | | | DEBIT | CREDIT |
| 20-- Aug. | 1 | Balance | ✔ | | | 3 2 5 6 37 | |

ACCOUNT Accounts Payable                                ACCOUNT NO. 2105

| DATE | | ITEM | POST. REF. | DEBIT | CREDIT | BALANCE | |
|---|---|---|---|---|---|---|---|
| | | | | | | DEBIT | CREDIT |
| 20-- Aug. | 1 | Balance | ✔ | | | | 6 4 3 2 34 |

ACCOUNT Purchases—Costume                               ACCOUNT NO. 5105

| DATE | | ITEM | POST. REF. | DEBIT | CREDIT | BALANCE | |
|---|---|---|---|---|---|---|---|
| | | | | | | DEBIT | CREDIT |
| 20-- Aug. | 1 | Balance | ✔ | | | 58 6 4 5 23 | |

ACCOUNT Purchases Discount—Costume                      ACCOUNT NO. 5110

| DATE | | ITEM | POST. REF. | DEBIT | CREDIT | BALANCE | |
|---|---|---|---|---|---|---|---|
| | | | | | | DEBIT | CREDIT |
| 20-- Aug. | 1 | Balance | ✔ | | | | 5 2 7 81 |

ACCOUNT Purchases Returns and Allowances—Costume         ACCOUNT NO. 5115

| DATE | | ITEM | POST. REF. | DEBIT | CREDIT | BALANCE | |
|---|---|---|---|---|---|---|---|
| | | | | | | DEBIT | CREDIT |
| 20-- Aug. | 1 | Balance | ✔ | | | | 8 2 3 44 |

ACCOUNT Purchases—Fine        ACCOUNT NO. 5205

| DATE | ITEM | POST. REF. | DEBIT | CREDIT | BALANCE DEBIT | BALANCE CREDIT |
|------|------|-----------|-------|--------|-------|--------|
| 20-- Aug. 1 | Balance | ✔ | | | 65 4 3 7 86 | |

ACCOUNT Purchases Discount—Fine        ACCOUNT NO. 5210

| DATE | ITEM | POST. REF. | DEBIT | CREDIT | BALANCE DEBIT | BALANCE CREDIT |
|------|------|-----------|-------|--------|-------|--------|
| 20-- Aug. 1 | Balance | ✔ | | | | 5 2 3 50 |

ACCOUNT Purchases Returns and Allowances—Fine        ACCOUNT NO. 5215

| DATE | ITEM | POST. REF. | DEBIT | CREDIT | BALANCE DEBIT | BALANCE CREDIT |
|------|------|-----------|-------|--------|-------|--------|
| 20-- Aug. 1 | Balance | ✔ | | | | 9 7 8 56 |

ACCOUNT Advertising Expense—Fine        ACCOUNT NO. 6205

| DATE | ITEM | POST. REF. | DEBIT | CREDIT | BALANCE DEBIT | BALANCE CREDIT |
|------|------|-----------|-------|--------|-------|--------|
| 20-- Aug. 1 | Balance | ✔ | | | 8 9 0 0 00 | |

ACCOUNT Miscellaneous Expense        ACCOUNT NO. 7125

| DATE | ITEM | POST. REF. | DEBIT | CREDIT | BALANCE DEBIT | BALANCE CREDIT |
|------|------|-----------|-------|--------|-------|--------|
| 20-- Aug. 1 | Balance | ✔ | | | 6 2 7 5 31 | |

ACCOUNT Rent Expense        ACCOUNT NO. 7140

| DATE | ITEM | POST. REF. | DEBIT | CREDIT | BALANCE DEBIT | BALANCE CREDIT |
|------|------|-----------|-------|--------|-------|--------|
| 20-- Aug. 1 | Balance | ✔ | | | 16 8 0 0 00 | |

ACCOUNT Utilities Expense        ACCOUNT NO. 7160

| DATE | ITEM | POST. REF. | DEBIT | CREDIT | BALANCE DEBIT | BALANCE CREDIT |
|------|------|-----------|-------|--------|-------|--------|
| 20-- Aug. 1 | Balance | ✔ | | | 5 2 7 7 94 | |

## 1-S SOURCE DOCUMENTS PROBLEM (LO4, 6, 7), p. 33

**Journalizing purchase and cash payment transactions**

**1., 2.**

PURCHASES JOURNAL                    PAGE

| | DATE | ACCOUNT CREDITED | PURCH. NO. | POST. REF. | ACCOUNTS PAYABLE CREDIT | PURCHASES DEBIT GOLF | PURCHASES DEBIT TENNIS | |
|---|---|---|---|---|---|---|---|---|
| 1 | | | | | | | | 1 |
| 2 | | | | | | | | 2 |
| 3 | | | | | | | | 3 |
| 4 | | | | | | | | 4 |
| 5 | | | | | | | | 5 |
| 6 | | | | | | | | 6 |
| 7 | | | | | | | | 7 |
| 8 | | | | | | | | 8 |
| 9 | | | | | | | | 9 |
| 10 | | | | | | | | 10 |
| 11 | | | | | | | | 11 |
| 12 | | | | | | | | 12 |
| 13 | | | | | | | | 13 |
| 14 | | | | | | | | 14 |
| 15 | | | | | | | | 15 |
| 16 | | | | | | | | 16 |
| 17 | | | | | | | | 17 |
| 18 | | | | | | | | 18 |
| 19 | | | | | | | | 19 |
| 20 | | | | | | | | 20 |
| 21 | | | | | | | | 21 |
| 22 | | | | | | | | 22 |
| 23 | | | | | | | | 23 |
| 24 | | | | | | | | 24 |
| 25 | | | | | | | | 25 |
| 26 | | | | | | | | 26 |
| 27 | | | | | | | | 27 |
| 28 | | | | | | | | 28 |
| 29 | | | | | | | | 29 |
| 30 | | | | | | | | 30 |

**1., 3.**

CASH PAYMENTS JOURNAL

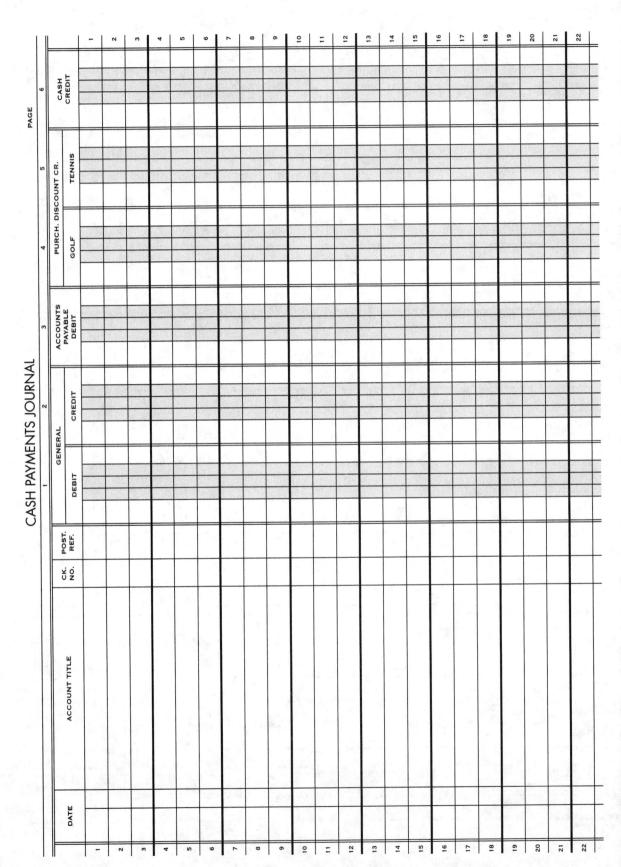

## 1-S    SOURCE DOCUMENTS PROBLEM (continued)

**1.**

GENERAL JOURNAL

PAGE

| | DATE | | ACCOUNT TITLE | DOC. NO. | POST. REF. | DEBIT | CREDIT | |
|---|---|---|---|---|---|---|---|---|
| 1 | | | | | | | | 1 |
| 2 | | | | | | | | 2 |
| 3 | | | | | | | | 3 |
| 4 | | | | | | | | 4 |
| 5 | | | | | | | | 5 |
| 6 | | | | | | | | 6 |
| 7 | | | | | | | | 7 |
| 8 | | | | | | | | 8 |
| 9 | | | | | | | | 9 |
| 10 | | | | | | | | 10 |
| 11 | | | | | | | | 11 |
| 12 | | | | | | | | 12 |
| 13 | | | | | | | | 13 |
| 14 | | | | | | | | 14 |
| 15 | | | | | | | | 15 |
| 16 | | | | | | | | 16 |
| 17 | | | | | | | | 17 |
| 18 | | | | | | | | 18 |
| 19 | | | | | | | | 19 |
| 20 | | | | | | | | 20 |
| 21 | | | | | | | | 21 |
| 22 | | | | | | | | 22 |
| 23 | | | | | | | | 23 |
| 24 | | | | | | | | 24 |
| 25 | | | | | | | | 25 |
| 26 | | | | | | | | 26 |
| 27 | | | | | | | | 27 |
| 28 | | | | | | | | 28 |
| 29 | | | | | | | | 29 |

| Marchese Manufacturing<br>725 Dreshertown Road<br>Fort Washington, PA 19034 | INVOICE | | REC'D 05/06/ -- P662 |
|---|---|---|---|
| | SOLD TO: Mike's Discount Golf<br>8520 N. Dale Mabry<br>Tampa, FL 33618 | DATE: | 5/2/-- |
| | | INV. NO. | 4818 |
| | | TERMS: | 2/10, n/30 |
| | | ACCT. NO. | 2450 |

| QUANTITY | CAT. NO. | DESCRIPTION | UNIT PRICE | TOTAL |
|---|---|---|---|---|
| 250 | 8186 | 3-Pack tennis balls | $ 2.19 | $ 547.50 |
| 30 | 4811 | 4-Pocket tennis bag, assorted colors | 25.65 | 769.50 |
| | | TOTAL | | $ 1,317.00 |

| Perfect Score, Inc.<br>809 E. 12th St.<br>Los Angeles, CA 90021 | SALES INVOICE | | REC'D 05/14/ -- P663 |
|---|---|---|---|
| | TO: Mike's Discount Golf<br>8520 N. Dale Mabry<br>Tampa, FL 33618 | NO. | 16548 |
| | | DATE: | 5/12/-- |

| CUSTOMER P.O. | ORDER RECEIVED | ORDER SHIPPED | SALES REPRESENTATIVE | TERMS | CUSTOMER ACCOUNT |
|---|---|---|---|---|---|
| 642 | 4/16/-- | 5/11/-- | MGE | 2/10, n/30 | 1420 |

| PART NO. | QUANTITY | DESCRIPTION | UNIT PRICE | TOTAL |
|---|---|---|---|---|
| 156 | 12 | Beginner short set, right | $ 69.99 | $ 839.88 |
| 184 | 10 | Terston brand set, right steel | 249.99 | 2,499.90 |
| 185 | 15 | Terston brand set, right graphite | 349.99 | 5,249.85 |
| | | TOTAL | | $ 8,589.63 |

| Altman Industries<br>1125 Fulton Ave.<br>San Antonio, TX 78201 | INVOICE | | REC'D 05/28/ -- P664 |
|---|---|---|---|
| | SOLD TO: Mike's Discount Golf<br>8520 N. Dale Mabry<br>Tampa, FL 33618 | NO. | 895 |
| | | DATE: | 5/25/-- |
| | | TERMS: | 2/10, n/30 |

| QUANTITY | PART | DESCRIPTION | UNIT PRICE | TOTAL |
|---|---|---|---|---|
| 60 | B-8015 | 80 Compression, 15-pack | $ 7.95 | $ 477.00 |
| 80 | B-9015 | 90 Compression, 15-pack | 8.25 | 660.00 |
| | | TOTAL | | $ 1,137.00 |

**1-S**　**SOURCE DOCUMENTS PROBLEM (continued)**

No. 57

## DEBIT MEMORANDUM

*Mike's Discount Golf*
8520 N. Dale Mabry
Tampa, FL 33618

TO: Marchese Manufacturing
725 Dreshertown Road
Fort Washington, PA 19034

DATE: May 7, 20--
ACCT. NO. 248

| QUANTITY | CAT. NO. | DESCRIPTION | UNIT PRICE | TOTAL |
|---|---|---|---|---|
| 2 | 4811 | 4-pocket tennis bag, assorted colors<br><br>damaged in transit | $　　25.65 | $　　51.30 |

No. 58

## DEBIT MEMORANDUM

*Mike's Discount Golf*
8520 N. Dale Mabry
Tampa, FL 33618

TO: Altman Industries
1125 Fulton Ave.
San Antonio, TX 78201

DATE: May 14, 20--
ACCT. NO. 206

| QUANTITY | CAT. NO. | DESCRIPTION | UNIT PRICE | TOTAL |
|---|---|---|---|---|
| 5 | B-9015 | 90 Compression, 15-pack<br>short shipment | $　　8.25 | $　　41.25 |

| NO. 738 | $ 2,690.77 | | |
|---|---|---|---|
| Date: May 4 | | 20-- | |
| To: Altman Industries | | | |
| For: Purchase invoice #660 for golf equipment, $2,745.68, less 2% discount | | | |
| BALANCE BROUGHT FORWARD | | 8,943 | 72 |
| AMOUNT DEPOSITED | Date | | |
| SUBTOTAL | | 8,943 | 72 |
| OTHER: | | | |
| _____ | | | |
| _____ | | | |
| SUBTOTAL | | 8,943 | 72 |
| AMOUNT THIS CHECK | | 2,690 | 77 |
| BALANCE CARRIED FORWARD | | 6,252 | 95 |

| NO. 739 | $ 103.18 | | |
|---|---|---|---|
| Date: May 6 | | 20-- | |
| To: | | | |
| For: Supplies | | | |
| BALANCE BROUGHT FORWARD | | 6,252 | 95 |
| AMOUNT DEPOSITED | 5 5 -- | 3,154 | 00 |
| SUBTOTAL | Date | 9,406 | 95 |
| OTHER: | | | |
| _____ | | | |
| _____ | | | |
| SUBTOTAL | | 9,406 | 95 |
| AMOUNT THIS CHECK | | 103 | 18 |
| BALANCE CARRIED FORWARD | | 9,303 | 77 |

| NO. 740 | $ 418.15 | | |
|---|---|---|---|
| Date: May 8 | | 20-- | |
| To: | | | |
| For: Utilities | | | |
| BALANCE BROUGHT FORWARD | | 9,303 | 77 |
| AMOUNT DEPOSITED | Date | | |
| SUBTOTAL | | 9,303 | 77 |
| OTHER: | | | |
| _____ | | | |
| _____ | | | |
| SUBTOTAL | | 9,303 | 77 |
| AMOUNT THIS CHECK | | 418 | 15 |
| BALANCE CARRIED FORWARD | | 8,885 | 62 |

| NO. 741 | $ 1,240.39 | | |
|---|---|---|---|
| Date: May 10 | | 20-- | |
| To: Marchese Manufacturing | | | |
| For: Purchase invoice #662 less debit memorandum 57, less 2% discount | | | |
| BALANCE BROUGHT FORWARD | | 8,885 | 62 |
| AMOUNT DEPOSITED | 5 8 -- | 1,485 | 18 |
| SUBTOTAL | Date | 10,370 | 80 |
| OTHER: | | | |
| _____ | | | |
| _____ | | | |
| SUBTOTAL | | 10,370 | 80 |
| AMOUNT THIS CHECK | | 1,240 | 39 |
| BALANCE CARRIED FORWARD | | 9,130 | 41 |

## 1-S SOURCE DOCUMENTS PROBLEM (continued)

| NO. 742 | $ 4,485.00 | | |
|---|---|---|---|
| Date: May 16 | | 20-- | |
| To: Eastern Tennis Mfg. | | | |
| For: Tennis merchandise | | | |
| BALANCE BROUGHT FORWARD | | 9,130 | 41 |
| AMOUNT DEPOSITED | | | |
| SUBTOTAL | Date | 9,130 | 41 |
| OTHER: | | | |
| SUBTOTAL | | 9,130 | 41 |
| AMOUNT THIS CHECK | | 4,485 | 00 |
| BALANCE CARRIED FORWARD | | 4,645 | 41 |

| NO. 743 | $ 1,900.00 | | |
|---|---|---|---|
| Date: May 20 | | 20-- | |
| To: Veteran Support Society | | | |
| For: Tournament sponsorship | | | |
| BALANCE BROUGHT FORWARD | | 4,645 | 41 |
| AMOUNT DEPOSITED | 5 18 -- | 3,164 | 18 |
| SUBTOTAL | Date | 7,809 | 59 |
| OTHER: | | | |
| SUBTOTAL | | 7,809 | 59 |
| AMOUNT THIS CHECK | | 1,900 | 00 |
| BALANCE CARRIED FORWARD | | 5,909 | 59 |

| NO. 744 | $ 2,482.50 | | |
|---|---|---|---|
| Date: May 28 | | 20-- | |
| To: Lake Michigan Fabrics | | | |
| For: Golf merchandise | | | |
| BALANCE BROUGHT FORWARD | | 5,909 | 59 |
| AMOUNT DEPOSITED | | | |
| SUBTOTAL | Date | 5,909 | 59 |
| OTHER: | | | |
| SUBTOTAL | | 5,909 | 59 |
| AMOUNT THIS CHECK | | 2,482 | 50 |
| BALANCE CARRIED FORWARD | | 3,427 | 09 |

| NO. 745 | $ 145.35 | | |
|---|---|---|---|
| Date: May 31 | | 20-- | |
| To: Sandy Adams, Petty Cash | | | |
| For: Petty cash | | | |
| BALANCE BROUGHT FORWARD | | 3,427 | 09 |
| AMOUNT DEPOSITED | 5 30 20-- | 5,486 | 18 |
| SUBTOTAL | Date | 8,913 | 27 |
| OTHER: | | | |
| SUBTOTAL | | 8,913 | 27 |
| AMOUNT THIS CHECK | | 145 | 35 |
| BALANCE CARRIED FORWARD | | 8,767 | 92 |

No. 69

**MEMORANDUM**

Attached Macon Office Supply invoice #6434 is for store supplies.

Signed: Sheila Manuel     Date: May 3,     20--

No. 70

**MEMORANDUM**

Declare dividend of $2.00 on 5,000 shares outstanding

Signed: Thomas Maloney     Date: May 31,     20--

*Macon Office Supply*
8125 N. Dale Mabry
Tampa, FL 33618

INVOICE

TO: *Mike's Discount Golf*
*8520 N. Dale Mabry*
*Tampa, FL 33618*

DATE: *5/3/--*
INV. NO. *6434*

| CUSTOMER P.O. | ORDER RECEIVED | ORDER SHIPPED | SALES REPRESENTATIVE | TERMS | CUSTOMER ACCOUNT |
|---|---|---|---|---|---|
| *629* | *4/10/--* | *Pick up* | *Danny S.* | *Net 30* | ——— |

| QTY | ITEM | ITEM DESCRIPTION | UNIT PRICE | TOTAL |
|---|---|---|---|---|
| *1* | *n/a* | *Custom printing of accounting documents* | $ *142.68* | $ *142.68* |
| | | TOTAL | | $ *142.68* |

---

*Davidson Office Center*
29780 Highway 19 North
Palm Harbor, FL 34684

INVOICE

TO: Mike's Discount Golf
8520 N. Dale Mabry
Tampa, FL 33618

DATE: May 6, 20--
INV. NO. 9484
TERMS: Cash

| QUANTITY | PART NO. | DESCRIPTION | UNIT PRICE | TOTAL |
|---|---|---|---|---|
| 2 | 9444 | Tape dispenser | $ 9.95 | $ 19.90 |
| 4 | 1648 | 8" × 11" Envelopes, box of 25 | 12.99 | 51.96 |
| 3 | 136-48 | Pens | 6.20 | 18.60 |
| 3 | 136-86 | White board marker, black | 1.99 | 5.97 |
| | | SUBTOTAL | | $ 96.43 |
| | | TAX | | 6.75 |
| | | TOTAL | | $ 103.18 |

---

Southern Electric
P.O. Box 1342
Tampa, FL 33602

**61564**
*May 8, 20 --*

TO: *Mike's Discount Golf*
*8520 N. Dale Mabry*
*Tampa, FL 33618*

| | This Month | Last Month | |
|---|---|---|---|
| *Kilowatts* | *2,488* | *2,348* | *Paid this amount* ⟶ $ *418.15* |
| *per Day* | *80* | *78* | |

*Serving Your Energy Needs Since 1948*

**1-S** **SOURCE DOCUMENTS PROBLEM (continued)**

| Eastern Tennis Mfg. | | INVOICE | | |
|---|---|---|---|---|
| 1633 NW 37th Ave. | | | | |
| Miami, FL 33125 | | | DATE: | 5/16/20-- |
| | | TO: Mike's Discount Golf | INV. NO. | 16489 |
| | | 8520 N. Dale Mabry | TERMS: | Cash |
| | | Tampa, FL 33618 | | |

| QUANTITY | CAT. NO. | DESCRIPTION | UNIT PRICE | TOTAL |
|---|---|---|---|---|
| 3 | 9448 | Tennis ball machine | $1,495.00 | $ 4,485.00 |
| | | TOTAL | | $ 4,485.00 |

---

**Veteran Support Society**

P.O. Box 1223
Brandon, FL 33619

TO: Mike's Discount Golf
  8520 N. Dale Mabry
  Tampa, FL 33618

May 20, 20--
Invoice No. 4688
Terms: Cash

| | |
|---|---|
| Hole sponsorship of golf tournament benefiting Veteran Support Society shelter project | $ 1,500.00 |
| Four-player green fee | 400.00 |
| | $ 1,900.00 |

Thank you for your support!

| Lake Michigan Fabrics<br>7542 Lakefront Avenue<br>Evanston, IL 60204 | | INVOICE | | | |
|---|---|---|---|---|---|
| | | | | DATE: | 5/28/-- |
| | TO: | Mike's Discount Golf<br>8520 N. Dale Mabry<br>Tampa, FL 33618 | | INV. NO.<br>TERMS: | 48942<br>Cash |
| QUANTITY | PART | DESCRIPTION | UNIT PRICE | TOTAL | |
| 15 | B164 | Golf netting | $165.50 | $ | 2,482.50 |
| | | TOTAL | | $ | 2,482.50 |

**PETTY CASH REPORT**

Date: ___May 31, 20—___          Custodian: ___Sandy Adams___

| | Explanation | | Reconciliation | | Replenish Amount |
|---|---|---|---|---|---|
| Fund Total | | | 250.00 | | |
| Payments: | Supplies | 64.21 | | | |
| | Advertising—Tennis | 50.00 | | | |
| | Miscellaneous | 31.14 | | | |
| Less: | Total payments | | 145.35 | →  | 145.35 |
| Equals: | Recorded amount on hand | | 104.65 | | |
| Less: | Actual amount on hand | | 104.65 | | |
| Equals: | Cash short (over) | | —— | →  | —— |
| **Amount to Replenish** | | | | | 145.35 |

## 1-C CHALLENGE PROBLEM (LO3), p. 33

### Establishing a departmental accounting system

| Number of Departments | | | Quantity | Description | Unit Cost | Sales Price |
|---|---|---|---|---|---|---|
| 4 | 3 | 2 | | | | |
| | | G | 3 | Guitar straps | $ 6.95 | $ 12.95 |
| | | G | 1 | 5-string banjo | 149.00 | 299.00 |
| | | G | 15 | 6-string nylon guitar strings | 5.95 | 12.95 |
| | | G | 1 | Acoustic guitar | 1,495.98 | 2,399.00 |
| | | O | 50 | Sheet music, recent publication mix | 3.99 | 6.99 |
| | | G | 25 | 20' electric guitar cable | 8.95 | 19.99 |
| | | O | 2 | Wireless microphone | 325.95 | 650.00 |
| | | G | 5 | Effects pedal | 99.99 | 209.95 |
| | | G | 6 | Beginner guitar package | 89.99 | 199.99 |
| | | O | 3 | Harmonica with case | 159.25 | 249.99 |
| | | G | 5 | Bass guitar package | 129.99 | 199.99 |
| | | O | 2 | Tom drums with stand | 109.95 | 189.99 |
| | | O | 6 | Digital metronome | 59.99 | 109.95 |
| | | O | 20 | 5B drumsticks | 4.95 | 9.99 |
| | | G | 3 | Acoustic electric guitar with gig bag | 219.99 | 379.99 |
| | | G | 4 | 12-string nylon guitar strings | 5.95 | 12.95 |
| | | O | 20 | Microphone wind screens | 2.99 | 4.95 |
| | | O | 4 | 100' 8-channel audio snake | 129.99 | 259.99 |
| | | G | 2 | Bass guitar with case | 799.99 | 1,799.99 |
| | | O | 15 | Ear plugs | 2.95 | 5.95 |
| | | G | 12 | 5-string bass guitar strings | 6.95 | 15.95 |
| | | O | 3 | Drum set | 495.95 | 795.95 |

Codes:

Two departments

G - Guitars _____

O - Other _____

Three departments

_____

_____

_____

Four departments

_____

_____

_____

_____

| Name | Perfect Score | Your Score |
|---|---|---|
| Analyzing Departmental Accounting Procedures | 15 Pts. | |
| Analyzing Departmental Sales and Cash Receipts | 13 Pts. | |
| Analyzing Transactions Recorded in Special Journals | 19 Pts. | |
| **Total** | 47 Pts. | |

**Study Guide 2**

## Part One—Analyzing Departmental Accounting Procedures

**Directions:** Place a *T* for True or an *F* for False in the Answers column to show whether each of the following statements is true or false.

**Answers**

1. Records of departmental operating expenses are necessary to determine departmental gross profit from operations. (p. 38)    1. _____

2. In a departmental business, each sales invoice shows the amount of merchandise sold by department. (p. 38)    2. _____

3. Preparing two copies of a sales invoice provides a copy for the customer and a copy for the business to use for journalizing the transaction. (p. 38)    3. _____

4. Each departmental sales journal entry is posted individually as a credit to the appropriate customer's account. (p. 41)    4. _____

5. After posting a line of a departmental sales journal, the customer number is recorded in the journal's Post. Ref. column. (p. 41)    5. _____

6. The vendor prepares a debit memorandum for a sales returns and allowances transaction. (p. 43)    6. _____

7. An account showing deductions from a sales account is known as a contra cost account. (p. 44)    7. _____

8. A cash discount on a sale taken by the customer is called a sales discount. (p. 47)    8. _____

9. A departmental cash receipts journal contains a Cash Debit column for each department. (p. 48)    9. _____

10. Both the debit part and the credit parts of a cash or credit card sales transaction are entered in special amount columns in a departmental cash receipts journal. (p. 49)    10. _____

11. Each amount in the Accounts Receivable Credit column of a departmental cash receipts journal is posted individually to the accounts receivable ledger. (p. 51)    11. _____

12. Each amount in the Accounts Receivable Credit column of a departmental cash receipts journal is posted when the transaction is recorded in the cash receipts journal. (p. 51)    12. _____

13. Each amount in the Cash Debit column of a departmental cash receipts journal is posted individually to the debit side of the Cash account. (p. 52)    13. _____

14. The total of each Sales Credit column of a departmental cash receipts journal is posted to a general ledger account. (p. 52)    14. _____

15. After the totals of special amount columns have been posted, the general ledger account numbers are written in parentheses below the totals of the special columns in the cash receipts journal. (p. 52)    15. _____

## Part Two—Analyzing Departmental Sales and Cash Receipts

**Directions:** For each item below, select the choice that best completes the sentence. Print the letter identifying your choice in the Answers column.

1. One item of information available through a departmental accounting system is the (A) net income or net loss for each department (B) gross profit from operations for each department (C) administrative expenses for each department (D) total operating expenses for each department. (p. 38)

   1. _____

2. The source document for recording a transaction in a departmental sales journal is (A) a cash register tape (B) a memorandum (C) a sales invoice (D) an adding machine tape. (p. 38)

   2. _____

3. Recording all sales at the time of sale, regardless of when payment is made, is an application of the (A) Going Concern concept (B) Realization of Revenue concept (C) Matching Expenses with Revenue concept (D) Historical Cost concept. (p. 38)

   3. _____

4. When audio equipment subject to sales tax is sold on account, Accounts Receivable is (A) debited for the amount of merchandise sold (B) debited for the amount of merchandise sold plus the sales tax on the merchandise (C) credited for the amount of merchandise sold (D) not affected. (p. 40)

   4. _____

5. In a departmental business, when audio equipment is sold on account, (A) Sales is debited (B) Sales—Audio is debited (C) Sales is credited (D) Sales—Audio is credited. (p. 40)

   5. _____

6. Each amount in the Accounts Receivable Debit column of a departmental sales journal is (A) posted as a debit to a customer's account (B) posted as a credit to a customer's account (C) posted to a controlling account (D) not posted. (p. 41)

   6. _____

7. The total of each column in a departmental sales journal is (A) posted daily (B) posted weekly (C) posted at the end of the month (D) posted when the page is filled or at the end of the month. (p. 42)

   7. _____

8. The account credited when a customer returns merchandise or is granted an allowance is (A) Accounts Payable (B) Sales Returns (C) the appropriate departmental sales account (D) none of these. (p. 43)

   8. _____

9. The source document for a sales returns and allowances transaction is (A) a sales invoice (B) a debit memorandum (C) a credit memorandum (D) none of these. (p. 43)

   9. _____

10. Sales returns and allowances are posted (A) monthly to a customer's account in the general ledger (B) frequently to a customer's account in the general ledger (C) monthly to a customer's account in the accounts receivable ledger (D) to the customer's account in the accounts receivable ledger and the general ledger when the transaction is journalized. (p. 45)

    10. _____

11. A business offers a sales discount (A) because of state laws (B) to encourage early payment (C) to get repeat business from the customer (D) none of these. (p. 47)

    11. _____

12. The terms 2/10, n/30 mean (A) a 2% sales discount may be deducted if sales on account are paid within 30 days of the invoice date (B) a 2% sales discount may be deducted if sales on account are paid within 10 days (C) all sales on account must be paid within 30 days (D) B and C. (p. 47)

    12. _____

13. Credit card sales are recorded in the cash receipts journal because (A) the cash is usually deposited in the cash account in two or three days (B) government policy requires immediate payment (C) credit card companies are not included in the accounts receivable ledger (D) this procedure is the first step in collecting from credit card companies. (p. 49)

    13. _____

# Part Three—Analyzing Transactions Recorded in Special Journals

**Directions:** In Answers Column l, print the abbreviation for the journal in which each transaction is to be recorded. In Answers Columns 2 and 3, print the letters identifying the accounts to be debited and credited for each transaction.

**SJ**—Sales journal; **CRJ**—Cash receipts journal; **GJ**—General journal

| Account Titles | Transactions | Answers | | |
|---|---|---|---|---|
| | | Journal | Debit | Credit |
| A. Cash | 1-2-3. Sold merchandise on account to Tom Jenkins, plus sales tax. (p. 40) | 1. _____ | 2. _____ | 3. _____ |
| B. Accounts Receivable | | | | |
| C. Sales Tax Payable | 4-5-6. Granted credit to Tom Jenkins for returned merchandise. (p. 43) | 4. _____ | 5. _____ | 6. _____ |
| D. Sales | 7-8-9. Received cash on account from Hanna Nelson, less sales discount. (p. 48) | 7. _____ | 8. _____ | 9. _____ |
| E. Sales Discount | | | | |
| F. Sales Returns and Allowances | 10-11-12. Recorded cash and credit card sales, plus sales tax. (p. 49) | 10. _____ | 11. _____ | 12. _____ |
| G. Tom Jenkins | | | | |
| H. Hanna Nelson | | | | |

## 2-1 WORK TOGETHER, p. 46

**Journalizing and posting departmental sales on account and sales returns and allowances**

**1., 2.**

### SALES JOURNAL

PAGE _____

| | DATE | ACCOUNT DEBITED | SALE NO. | POST. REF. | 1 ACCOUNTS RECEIVABLE DEBIT | 2 SALES TAX PAYABLE CREDIT | 3 SALES CREDIT CHAIRS | 4 SALES CREDIT DESKS | |
|---|---|---|---|---|---|---|---|---|---|
| 1 | | | | | | | | | 1 |
| 2 | | | | | | | | | 2 |
| 3 | | | | | | | | | 3 |
| 4 | | | | | | | | | 4 |
| 5 | | | | | | | | | 5 |
| 6 | | | | | | | | | 6 |
| 7 | | | | | | | | | 7 |
| 8 | | | | | | | | | 8 |
| 9 | | | | | | | | | 9 |
| 10 | | | | | | | | | 10 |
| 11 | | | | | | | | | 11 |

### GENERAL JOURNAL

PAGE _____

| | DATE | ACCOUNT TITLE | DOC. NO. | POST. REF. | DEBIT | CREDIT | |
|---|---|---|---|---|---|---|---|
| 1 | | | | | | | 1 |
| 2 | | | | | | | 2 |
| 3 | | | | | | | 3 |
| 4 | | | | | | | 4 |
| 5 | | | | | | | 5 |
| 6 | | | | | | | 6 |
| 7 | | | | | | | 7 |
| 8 | | | | | | | 8 |
| 9 | | | | | | | 9 |
| 10 | | | | | | | 10 |
| 11 | | | | | | | 11 |
| 12 | | | | | | | 12 |
| 13 | | | | | | | 13 |
| 14 | | | | | | | 14 |

**1.**                                    **ACCOUNTS RECEIVABLE LEDGER**

CUSTOMER Davenport Corp.                                           CUSTOMER NO. 110

| DATE | ITEM | POST. REF. | DEBIT | CREDIT | DEBIT BALANCE |
|---|---|---|---|---|---|
| 20-- Sept. 1 | Balance | ✔ | | | 1 5 3 3 00 |
| | | | | | |
| | | | | | |

CUSTOMER Grasson, Inc.                                            CUSTOMER NO. 120

| DATE | ITEM | POST. REF. | DEBIT | CREDIT | DEBIT BALANCE |
|---|---|---|---|---|---|
| 20-- Sept. 1 | Balance | ✔ | | | 1 6 3 4 00 |
| | | | | | |
| | | | | | |
| | | | | | |

CUSTOMER LKL Products Co.                                          CUSTOMER NO. 130

| DATE | ITEM | POST. REF. | DEBIT | CREDIT | DEBIT BALANCE |
|---|---|---|---|---|---|
| 20-- Sept. 1 | Balance | ✔ | | | 5 2 5 00 |
| | | | | | |
| | | | | | |
| | | | | | |

CUSTOMER United Charities                                         CUSTOMER NO. 140

| DATE | ITEM | POST. REF. | DEBIT | CREDIT | DEBIT BALANCE |
|---|---|---|---|---|---|
| 20-- Sept. 1 | Balance | ✔ | | | 8 5 5 00 |
| | | | | | |
| | | | | | |

## 2-1 WORK TOGETHER (concluded)

**2.**                                                   **GENERAL LEDGER**

ACCOUNT **Accounts Receivable**                                ACCOUNT NO. 1205

| DATE | | ITEM | POST. REF. | DEBIT | CREDIT | BALANCE | |
|---|---|---|---|---|---|---|---|
| | | | | | | DEBIT | CREDIT |
| 20--<br>Sept. | 1 | Balance | ✔ | | | 16 762 50 | |
| | | | | | | | |
| | | | | | | | |
| | | | | | | | |

ACCOUNT **Sales Tax Payable**                                 ACCOUNT NO. 2110

| DATE | | ITEM | POST. REF. | DEBIT | CREDIT | BALANCE | |
|---|---|---|---|---|---|---|---|
| | | | | | | DEBIT | CREDIT |
| 20--<br>Sept. | 1 | Balance | ✔ | | | | 7 15 75 |
| | | | | | | | |
| | | | | | | | |
| | | | | | | | |

ACCOUNT **Sales—Chairs**                                      ACCOUNT NO. 4105

| DATE | | ITEM | POST. REF. | DEBIT | CREDIT | BALANCE | |
|---|---|---|---|---|---|---|---|
| | | | | | | DEBIT | CREDIT |
| 20--<br>Sept. | 1 | Balance | ✔ | | | | 54 367 95 |
| | | | | | | | |
| | | | | | | | |

ACCOUNT **Sales Returns and Allowances—Chairs**               ACCOUNT NO. 4115

| DATE | | ITEM | POST. REF. | DEBIT | CREDIT | BALANCE | |
|---|---|---|---|---|---|---|---|
| | | | | | | DEBIT | CREDIT |
| 20--<br>Sept. | 1 | Balance | ✔ | | | 1 955 76 | |
| | | | | | | | |
| | | | | | | | |

ACCOUNT **Sales—Desks**                                       ACCOUNT NO. 4205

| DATE | | ITEM | POST. REF. | DEBIT | CREDIT | BALANCE | |
|---|---|---|---|---|---|---|---|
| | | | | | | DEBIT | CREDIT |
| 20--<br>Sept. | 1 | Balance | ✔ | | | | 49 087 98 |
| | | | | | | | |
| | | | | | | | |

ACCOUNT **Sales Returns and Allowances—Desks**                ACCOUNT NO. 4215

| DATE | | ITEM | POST. REF. | DEBIT | CREDIT | BALANCE | |
|---|---|---|---|---|---|---|---|
| | | | | | | DEBIT | CREDIT |
| 20--<br>Sept. | 1 | Balance | ✔ | | | 2 421 67 | |
| | | | | | | | |

**Journalizing and posting departmental sales on account and sales returns and allowances**

**1., 2.**

SALES JOURNAL                                                                 PAGE

| | DATE | ACCOUNT DEBITED | SALE NO. | POST. REF. | ACCOUNTS RECEIVABLE DEBIT (1) | SALES TAX PAYABLE CREDIT (2) | SALES CREDIT EQUIPMENT (3) | SALES CREDIT ACCESSORIES (4) | |
|---|---|---|---|---|---|---|---|---|---|
| 1 | | | | | | | | | 1 |
| 2 | | | | | | | | | 2 |
| 3 | | | | | | | | | 3 |
| 4 | | | | | | | | | 4 |
| 5 | | | | | | | | | 5 |
| 6 | | | | | | | | | 6 |
| 7 | | | | | | | | | 7 |
| 8 | | | | | | | | | 8 |
| 9 | | | | | | | | | 9 |
| 10 | | | | | | | | | 10 |
| 11 | | | | | | | | | 11 |

GENERAL JOURNAL                                                               PAGE

| | DATE | ACCOUNT TITLE | DOC. NO. | POST. REF. | DEBIT | CREDIT | |
|---|---|---|---|---|---|---|---|
| 1 | | | | | | | 1 |
| 2 | | | | | | | 2 |
| 3 | | | | | | | 3 |
| 4 | | | | | | | 4 |
| 5 | | | | | | | 5 |
| 6 | | | | | | | 6 |
| 7 | | | | | | | 7 |
| 8 | | | | | | | 8 |
| 9 | | | | | | | 9 |
| 10 | | | | | | | 10 |
| 11 | | | | | | | 11 |
| 12 | | | | | | | 12 |
| 13 | | | | | | | 13 |
| 14 | | | | | | | 14 |

## 2-1 ON YOUR OWN (continued)

**1.**                          **ACCOUNTS RECEIVABLE LEDGER**

CUSTOMER Mason Dent                                                    CUSTOMER NO. 110

| DATE | | ITEM | POST. REF. | DEBIT | CREDIT | DEBIT BALANCE |
|---|---|---|---|---|---|---|
| 20--<br>Oct. | 1 | Balance | ✔ | | | 6 4 0 62 |
| | | | | | | |
| | | | | | | |
| | | | | | | |

CUSTOMER Mountain Pass High School                                     CUSTOMER NO. 120

| DATE | | ITEM | POST. REF. | DEBIT | CREDIT | DEBIT BALANCE |
|---|---|---|---|---|---|---|
| 20--<br>Oct. | 1 | Balance | ✔ | | | 1 7 2 6 00 |
| | | | | | | |
| | | | | | | |

CUSTOMER Davis Reese                                                   CUSTOMER NO. 130

| DATE | | ITEM | POST. REF. | DEBIT | CREDIT | DEBIT BALANCE |
|---|---|---|---|---|---|---|
| 20--<br>Oct. | 1 | Balance | ✔ | | | 1 6 4 34 |
| | | | | | | |
| | | | | | | |

CUSTOMER Sara Stennis                                                  CUSTOMER NO. 140

| DATE | | ITEM | POST. REF. | DEBIT | CREDIT | DEBIT BALANCE |
|---|---|---|---|---|---|---|
| 20--<br>Oct. | 1 | Balance | ✔ | | | 5 3 23 |
| | | | | | | |
| | | | | | | |
| | | | | | | |

2.                                    **GENERAL LEDGER**

ACCOUNT Accounts Receivable                                          ACCOUNT NO. 1205

| DATE | | ITEM | POST. REF. | DEBIT | CREDIT | BALANCE | |
|---|---|---|---|---|---|---|---|
| | | | | | | DEBIT | CREDIT |
| Oct. | 1 | Balance | ✔ | | | 10 9 8 3 64 | |
| | | | | | | | |
| | | | | | | | |
| | | | | | | | |

ACCOUNT Sales Tax Payable                                           ACCOUNT NO. 2110

| DATE | | ITEM | POST. REF. | DEBIT | CREDIT | BALANCE | |
|---|---|---|---|---|---|---|---|
| | | | | | | DEBIT | CREDIT |
| Oct. | 1 | Balance | ✔ | | | | 6 3 5 23 |
| | | | | | | | |
| | | | | | | | |
| | | | | | | | |

ACCOUNT Sales—Equipment                                            ACCOUNT NO. 4105

| DATE | | ITEM | POST. REF. | DEBIT | CREDIT | BALANCE | |
|---|---|---|---|---|---|---|---|
| | | | | | | DEBIT | CREDIT |
| Oct. | 1 | Balance | ✔ | | | | 87 6 2 7 23 |
| | | | | | | | |

ACCOUNT Sales Returns and Allowances—Equipment                     ACCOUNT NO. 4115

| DATE | | ITEM | POST. REF. | DEBIT | CREDIT | BALANCE | |
|---|---|---|---|---|---|---|---|
| | | | | | | DEBIT | CREDIT |
| Oct. | 1 | Balance | ✔ | | | 3 6 5 3 44 | |
| | | | | | | | |

ACCOUNT Sales—Accessories                                          ACCOUNT NO. 4205

| DATE | | ITEM | POST. REF. | DEBIT | CREDIT | BALANCE | |
|---|---|---|---|---|---|---|---|
| | | | | | | DEBIT | CREDIT |
| Oct. | 1 | Balance | ✔ | | | | 27 5 4 3 16 |
| | | | | | | | |

ACCOUNT Sales Returns and Allowances—Accessories                   ACCOUNT NO. 4215

| DATE | | ITEM | POST. REF. | DEBIT | CREDIT | BALANCE | |
|---|---|---|---|---|---|---|---|
| | | | | | | DEBIT | CREDIT |
| Oct. | 1 | Balance | ✔ | | | 2 6 4 7 97 | |
| | | | | | | | |

**2-2** **WORK TOGETHER, p. 54**

**Journalizing and posting departmental cash receipts**

**1., 2.**

**CASH RECEIPTS JOURNAL**

PAGE 9

| | DATE | ACCOUNT TITLE | DOC. NO. | POST. REF. | GENERAL DEBIT | GENERAL CREDIT | ACCOUNTS RECEIVABLE CREDIT | SALES TAX PAYABLE CREDIT | SALES CREDIT HARDWARE | SALES CREDIT LUMBER | SALES DISCOUNT DEBIT HARDWARE | SALES DISCOUNT DEBIT LUMBER | CASH DEBIT |
|---|---|---|---|---|---|---|---|---|---|---|---|---|---|
| | | | | | 1 | 2 | 3 | 4 | 5 | 6 | 7 | 8 | 9 |
| 1 | | | | | | | | | | | | | |
| 2 | | | | | | | | | | | | | |
| 3 | | | | | | | | | | | | | |
| 4 | | | | | | | | | | | | | |
| 5 | | | | | | | | | | | | | |
| 6 | | | | | | | | | | | | | |
| 7 | | | | | | | | | | | | | |
| 8 | | | | | | | | | | | | | |
| 9 | | | | | | | | | | | | | |
| 10 | | | | | | | | | | | | | |
| 11 | | | | | | | | | | | | | |
| 12 | | | | | | | | | | | | | |
| 13 | | | | | | | | | | | | | |
| 14 | | | | | | | | | | | | | |
| 15 | | | | | | | | | | | | | |
| 16 | | | | | | | | | | | | | |
| 17 | | | | | | | | | | | | | |
| 18 | | | | | | | | | | | | | |
| 19 | | | | | | | | | | | | | |
| 20 | | | | | | | | | | | | | |
| 21 | | | | | | | | | | | | | |

**1.** **ACCOUNTS RECEIVABLE LEDGER**

CUSTOMER  Andrews Homes                                          CUSTOMER NO. 110

| DATE | | ITEM | POST. REF. | DEBIT | CREDIT | DEBIT BALANCE |
|---|---|---|---|---|---|---|
| 20-- Mar. | 1 | Balance | ✔ | | | 14 8 1 4 97 |
| | | | | | | |
| | | | | | | |
| | | | | | | |

CUSTOMER  Estate Housing                                          CUSTOMER NO. 120

| DATE | | ITEM | POST. REF. | DEBIT | CREDIT | DEBIT BALANCE |
|---|---|---|---|---|---|---|
| 20-- Mar. | 1 | Balance | ✔ | | | 9 2 4 8 17 |
| | 3 | | G3 | | 8 3 3 02 | 8 4 1 5 15 |
| | | | | | | |
| | | | | | | |

CUSTOMER  Lisle Construction                                          CUSTOMER NO. 130

| DATE | | ITEM | POST. REF. | DEBIT | CREDIT | DEBIT BALANCE |
|---|---|---|---|---|---|---|
| 20-- Mar. | 12 | | S3 | 2 4 7 3 61 | | 2 4 7 3 61 |
| | 16 | | G3 | | 3 2 5 51 | 2 1 4 8 10 |
| | | | | | | |
| | | | | | | |
| | | | | | | |

**2-2** **WORK TOGETHER (continued)**

**2.** **GENERAL LEDGER**

ACCOUNT Cash                                                    ACCOUNT NO. 1105

| DATE | ITEM | POST. REF. | DEBIT | CREDIT | BALANCE DEBIT | BALANCE CREDIT |
|------|------|-----------|-------|--------|--------|--------|
| 20-- Mar. 1 | Balance | ✔ | | | 14 5 8 9 15 | |
| | | | | | | |
| | | | | | | |

ACCOUNT Accounts Receivable                                    ACCOUNT NO. 1205

| DATE | ITEM | POST. REF. | DEBIT | CREDIT | BALANCE DEBIT | BALANCE CREDIT |
|------|------|-----------|-------|--------|--------|--------|
| 20-- Mar. 1 | Balance | ✔ | | | 32 1 5 4 67 | |
| 3 | | G3 | | 8 3 3 02 | 31 3 2 1 65 | |
| 16 | | G3 | | 3 2 5 51 | 30 9 9 6 14 | |
| | | | | | | |
| | | | | | | |

ACCOUNT Sales Tax Payable                                      ACCOUNT NO. 2110

| DATE | ITEM | POST. REF. | DEBIT | CREDIT | BALANCE DEBIT | BALANCE CREDIT |
|------|------|-----------|-------|--------|--------|--------|
| 20-- Mar. 1 | Balance | ✔ | | | | 4 8 5 15 |
| 3 | | G3 | 5 8 12 | | | 4 2 7 03 |
| 16 | | G3 | 2 2 71 | | | 4 0 4 32 |
| | | | | | | |
| | | | | | | |

ACCOUNT Sales—Hardware                                         ACCOUNT NO. 4105

| DATE | ITEM | POST. REF. | DEBIT | CREDIT | BALANCE DEBIT | BALANCE CREDIT |
|------|------|-----------|-------|--------|--------|--------|
| 20-- Mar. 1 | Balance | ✔ | | | | 22 1 8 4 17 |
| | | | | | | |
| | | | | | | |

ACCOUNT Sales Discount—Hardware                                    ACCOUNT NO. 4110

| DATE | ITEM | POST. REF. | DEBIT | CREDIT | BALANCE DEBIT | BALANCE CREDIT |
|------|------|-----------|-------|--------|-------|--------|
| 20-- Mar. 1 | Balance | ✔ | | | 3 2 4 94 | |
| | | | | | | |
| | | | | | | |
| | | | | | | |

ACCOUNT Sales—Lumber                                              ACCOUNT NO. 4205

| DATE | ITEM | POST. REF. | DEBIT | CREDIT | BALANCE DEBIT | BALANCE CREDIT |
|------|------|-----------|-------|--------|-------|--------|
| 20-- Mar. 1 | Balance | ✔ | | | | 29 4 8 1 31 |
| | | | | | | |
| | | | | | | |
| | | | | | | |

ACCOUNT Sales Discount—Lumber                                     ACCOUNT NO. 4210

| DATE | ITEM | POST. REF. | DEBIT | CREDIT | BALANCE DEBIT | BALANCE CREDIT |
|------|------|-----------|-------|--------|-------|--------|
| 20-- Mar. 1 | Balance | ✔ | | | 6 1 4 19 | |
| | | | | | | |
| | | | | | | |
| | | | | | | |

**2-2**  ON YOUR OWN, p. 54

**Journalizing and posting departmental cash receipts**

**1., 2.**

## CASH RECEIPTS JOURNAL

PAGE ____

| | | | | 1 | 2 | 3 | 4 | 5 | 6 | 7 | 8 | 9 |
|---|---|---|---|---|---|---|---|---|---|---|---|---|
| | | | | GENERAL | | ACCOUNTS RECEIVABLE CREDIT | SALES TAX PAYABLE CREDIT | SALES CREDIT | | SALES DISCOUNT DEBIT | | CASH DEBIT |
| DATE | ACCOUNT TITLE | DOC. NO. | POST. REF. | DEBIT | CREDIT | | | FLOWERS | PLANTS | FLOWERS | PLANTS | |

**1.** **ACCOUNTS RECEIVABLE LEDGER**

CUSTOMER Bakersville Gardens                                   CUSTOMER NO. 110

| DATE | | ITEM | POST. REF. | DEBIT | CREDIT | DEBIT BALANCE |
|---|---|---|---|---|---|---|
| Apr. | 1 | Balance | ✔ | | | 1 1 4 7 05 |
| | | | | | | |
| | | | | | | |
| | | | | | | |

CUSTOMER Grendon Clinic                                        CUSTOMER NO. 120

| DATE | | ITEM | POST. REF. | DEBIT | CREDIT | DEBIT BALANCE |
|---|---|---|---|---|---|---|
| Apr. | 1 | Balance | ✔ | | | 4 1 4 19 |
| | 5 | | G3 | | 3 5 20 | 3 7 8 99 |
| | | | | | | |
| | | | | | | |

CUSTOMER Hillside Manor                                        CUSTOMER NO. 130

| DATE | | ITEM | POST. REF. | DEBIT | CREDIT | DEBIT BALANCE |
|---|---|---|---|---|---|---|
| Apr. | 1 | Balance | ✔ | | | 6 1 5 17 |
| | | | | | | |
| | | | | | | |
| | | | | | | |

CUSTOMER Platte Hotels                                         CUSTOMER NO. 140

| DATE | | ITEM | POST. REF. | DEBIT | CREDIT | DEBIT BALANCE |
|---|---|---|---|---|---|---|
| Apr. | 18 | | S4 | 8 4 1 95 | | 8 4 1 95 |
| | 22 | | G5 | | 2 9 4 33 | 5 4 7 62 |
| | | | | | | |
| | | | | | | |

**2-2** **ON YOUR OWN (continued)**

2.                                              **GENERAL LEDGER**

ACCOUNT  Cash                                                          ACCOUNT NO.  1105

| DATE | ITEM | POST. REF. | DEBIT | CREDIT | BALANCE DEBIT | BALANCE CREDIT |
|------|------|-----------|-------|--------|---------------|----------------|
| 20-- Apr. 1 | Balance | ✔ | | | 6 4 9 8 17 | |
| | | | | | | |

ACCOUNT  Accounts Receivable                                          ACCOUNT NO.  1205

| DATE | ITEM | POST. REF. | DEBIT | CREDIT | BALANCE DEBIT | BALANCE CREDIT |
|------|------|-----------|-------|--------|---------------|----------------|
| 20-- Apr. 1 | Balance | ✔ | | | 18 4 8 9 69 | |
| 5 | | G3 | | 3 5 20 | 18 4 5 4 49 | |
| 22 | | G3 | | 2 9 4 33 | 18 1 6 0 16 | |

ACCOUNT  Sales Tax Payable                                            ACCOUNT NO.  2110

| DATE | ITEM | POST. REF. | DEBIT | CREDIT | BALANCE DEBIT | BALANCE CREDIT |
|------|------|-----------|-------|--------|---------------|----------------|
| 20-- Apr. 1 | Balance | ✔ | | | | 8 9 5 21 |
| 5 | | G3 | 2 15 | | | 8 9 3 06 |
| 22 | | G3 | 1 7 96 | | | 8 7 5 10 |

ACCOUNT  Sales—Flowers                                                ACCOUNT NO.  4105

| DATE | ITEM | POST. REF. | DEBIT | CREDIT | BALANCE DEBIT | BALANCE CREDIT |
|------|------|-----------|-------|--------|---------------|----------------|
| 20-- Apr. 1 | Balance | ✔ | | | | 14 8 9 4 11 |
| | | | | | | |

ACCOUNT Sales Discount—Flowers                                        ACCOUNT NO. 4110

| DATE | | ITEM | POST. REF. | DEBIT | CREDIT | BALANCE DEBIT | BALANCE CREDIT |
|---|---|---|---|---|---|---|---|
| 20-- Apr. | 1 | Balance | ✔ | | | 6 9 49 | |
| | | | | | | | |
| | | | | | | | |
| | | | | | | | |

ACCOUNT Sales—Plants                                                  ACCOUNT NO. 4205

| DATE | | ITEM | POST. REF. | DEBIT | CREDIT | BALANCE DEBIT | BALANCE CREDIT |
|---|---|---|---|---|---|---|---|
| 20-- Apr. | 1 | Balance | ✔ | | | | 16 9 9 4 08 |
| | | | | | | | |
| | | | | | | | |
| | | | | | | | |

ACCOUNT Sales Discount—Plants                                        ACCOUNT NO. 4210

| DATE | | ITEM | POST. REF. | DEBIT | CREDIT | BALANCE DEBIT | BALANCE CREDIT |
|---|---|---|---|---|---|---|---|
| 20-- Apr. | 1 | Balance | ✔ | | | 1 0 4 15 | |
| | | | | | | | |
| | | | | | | | |
| | | | | | | | |

## 2-1 APPLICATION PROBLEM (LO2, 3), p. 58

**Journalizing and posting departmental sales on account and sales returns and allowances**

**1., 2.**

### SALES JOURNAL

PAGE

| | DATE | ACCOUNT DEBITED | SALE NO. | POST. REF. | ACCOUNTS RECEIVABLE DEBIT (1) | SALES TAX PAYABLE CREDIT (2) | SALES CREDIT | | |
|---|------|-----------------|----------|-----------|-------------------------------|------------------------------|--------------|---|---|
| | | | | | | | CHAIRS (3) | TABLES (4) | |
| 1 | | | | | | | | | 1 |
| 2 | | | | | | | | | 2 |
| 3 | | | | | | | | | 3 |
| 4 | | | | | | | | | 4 |
| 5 | | | | | | | | | 5 |
| 6 | | | | | | | | | 6 |
| 7 | | | | | | | | | 7 |
| 8 | | | | | | | | | 8 |
| 9 | | | | | | | | | 9 |
| 10 | | | | | | | | | 10 |
| 11 | | | | | | | | | 11 |

### GENERAL JOURNAL

PAGE

| | DATE | ACCOUNT TITLE | DOC. NO. | POST. REF. | DEBIT | CREDIT | |
|---|------|---------------|----------|-----------|-------|--------|---|
| 1 | | | | | | | 1 |
| 2 | | | | | | | 2 |
| 3 | | | | | | | 3 |
| 4 | | | | | | | 4 |
| 5 | | | | | | | 5 |
| 6 | | | | | | | 6 |
| 7 | | | | | | | 7 |
| 8 | | | | | | | 8 |
| 9 | | | | | | | 9 |
| 10 | | | | | | | 10 |
| 11 | | | | | | | 11 |
| 12 | | | | | | | 12 |
| 13 | | | | | | | 13 |
| 14 | | | | | | | 14 |

**1.** **ACCOUNTS RECEIVABLE LEDGER**

CUSTOMER Elrod Clinic                                                                      CUSTOMER NO. 110

| DATE | | ITEM | POST. REF. | DEBIT | CREDIT | DEBIT BALANCE |
|---|---|---|---|---|---|---|
| 20-- May | 1 | Balance | ✔ | | | 9 4 5 25 |
| | | | | | | |
| | | | | | | |

CUSTOMER Lincoln City Schools                                                             CUSTOMER NO. 120

| DATE | | ITEM | POST. REF. | DEBIT | CREDIT | DEBIT BALANCE |
|---|---|---|---|---|---|---|
| 20-- May | 1 | Balance | ✔ | | | 2 4 8 5 30 |
| | | | | | | |
| | | | | | | |

CUSTOMER Anna Patrick                                                                      CUSTOMER NO. 130

| DATE | | ITEM | POST. REF. | DEBIT | CREDIT | DEBIT BALANCE |
|---|---|---|---|---|---|---|
| | | | | | | |
| | | | | | | |
| | | | | | | |

CUSTOMER Keller Stendal                                                                    CUSTOMER NO. 140

| DATE | | ITEM | POST. REF. | DEBIT | CREDIT | DEBIT BALANCE |
|---|---|---|---|---|---|---|
| 20-- May | 1 | Balance | ✔ | | | 3 2 1 5 84 |
| | | | | | | |
| | | | | | | |

**2-1**   **APPLICATION PROBLEM (concluded)**

**2.**                                   **GENERAL LEDGER**

ACCOUNT **Accounts Receivable**                                ACCOUNT NO. **1205**

| DATE | ITEM | POST. REF. | DEBIT | CREDIT | BALANCE DEBIT | BALANCE CREDIT |
|------|------|-----------|-------|--------|-------|--------|
| 20-- May 1 | Balance | ✔ | | | 16 4 5 8 02 | |
| | | | | | | |
| | | | | | | |
| | | | | | | |

ACCOUNT **Sales Tax Payable**                                ACCOUNT NO. **2110**

| DATE | ITEM | POST. REF. | DEBIT | CREDIT | BALANCE DEBIT | BALANCE CREDIT |
|------|------|-----------|-------|--------|-------|--------|
| 20-- May 1 | Balance | ✔ | | | | 5 5 1 19 |
| | | | | | | |
| | | | | | | |

ACCOUNT **Sales—Chairs**                                ACCOUNT NO. **4105**

| DATE | ITEM | POST. REF. | DEBIT | CREDIT | BALANCE DEBIT | BALANCE CREDIT |
|------|------|-----------|-------|--------|-------|--------|
| 20-- May 1 | Balance | ✔ | | | | 151 1 9 4 92 |

ACCOUNT **Sales Returns and Allowances—Chairs**                                ACCOUNT NO. **4115**

| DATE | ITEM | POST. REF. | DEBIT | CREDIT | BALANCE DEBIT | BALANCE CREDIT |
|------|------|-----------|-------|--------|-------|--------|
| 20-- May 1 | Balance | ✔ | | | 4 1 4 8 61 | |

ACCOUNT **Sales—Tables**                                ACCOUNT NO. **4205**

| DATE | ITEM | POST. REF. | DEBIT | CREDIT | BALANCE DEBIT | BALANCE CREDIT |
|------|------|-----------|-------|--------|-------|--------|
| 20-- May 1 | Balance | ✔ | | | | 134 2 1 8 95 |

ACCOUNT **Sales Returns and Allowances—Tables**                                ACCOUNT NO. **4215**

| DATE | ITEM | POST. REF. | DEBIT | CREDIT | BALANCE DEBIT | BALANCE CREDIT |
|------|------|-----------|-------|--------|-------|--------|
| 20-- May 1 | Balance | ✔ | | | 3 4 9 5 18 | |

**2-2** **APPLICATION PROBLEM (LO4, 5), p. 58**

Journalizing and posting departmental cash receipts

**1., 2.**

CASH RECEIPTS JOURNAL

PAGE _____

| DATE | ACCOUNT TITLE | DOC. NO. | POST. REF. | GENERAL | | ACCOUNTS RECEIVABLE CREDIT | SALES TAX PAYABLE CREDIT | SALES CREDIT | | SALES DISCOUNT DEBIT | | CASH DEBIT |
|------|---------------|----------|------------|---------|---------|----------------------------|--------------------------|--------------|--------|----------------------|--------|------------|
| | | | | DEBIT | CREDIT | | | PARTS | TIRES | PARTS | TIRES | |
| | | | | 1 | 2 | 3 | 4 | 5 | 6 | 7 | 8 | 9 |
| 1 | | | | | | | | | | | | |
| 2 | | | | | | | | | | | | |
| 3 | | | | | | | | | | | | |
| 4 | | | | | | | | | | | | |
| 5 | | | | | | | | | | | | |
| 6 | | | | | | | | | | | | |
| 7 | | | | | | | | | | | | |
| 8 | | | | | | | | | | | | |
| 9 | | | | | | | | | | | | |
| 10 | | | | | | | | | | | | |
| 11 | | | | | | | | | | | | |
| 12 | | | | | | | | | | | | |
| 13 | | | | | | | | | | | | |
| 14 | | | | | | | | | | | | |
| 15 | | | | | | | | | | | | |
| 16 | | | | | | | | | | | | |
| 17 | | | | | | | | | | | | |
| 18 | | | | | | | | | | | | |
| 19 | | | | | | | | | | | | |
| 20 | | | | | | | | | | | | |
| 21 | | | | | | | | | | | | |

**2-2** **APPLICATION PROBLEM (continued)**

**1.** **ACCOUNTS RECEIVABLE LEDGER**

CUSTOMER Bob's Auto Repair                                   CUSTOMER NO. 110

| DATE | | ITEM | POST. REF. | DEBIT | CREDIT | DEBIT BALANCE |
|---|---|---|---|---|---|---|
| 20-- June | 1 | Balance | ✔ | | | 8 4 2 62 |
| | | | | | | |
| | | | | | | |
| | | | | | | |

CUSTOMER Delta Transportation                               CUSTOMER NO. 120

| DATE | | ITEM | POST. REF. | DEBIT | CREDIT | DEBIT BALANCE |
|---|---|---|---|---|---|---|
| 20-- June | 1 | Balance | ✔ | | | 3 2 2 1 94 |
| | 20 | | G9 | | 2 8 0 17 | 2 9 4 1 77 |
| | | | | | | |
| | | | | | | |

CUSTOMER Foreign Car Center                                 CUSTOMER NO. 130

| DATE | | ITEM | POST. REF. | DEBIT | CREDIT | DEBIT BALANCE |
|---|---|---|---|---|---|---|
| 20-- June | 1 | Balance | ✔ | | | 3 2 4 19 |
| | | | | | | |
| | | | | | | |
| | | | | | | |

CUSTOMER Sam's Service Station                              CUSTOMER NO. 140

| DATE | | ITEM | POST. REF. | DEBIT | CREDIT | DEBIT BALANCE |
|---|---|---|---|---|---|---|
| 20-- June | 1 | Balance | ✔ | | | 1 8 4 2 21 |
| | | | | | | |
| | | | | | | |
| | | | | | | |

2.                                            **GENERAL LEDGER**

ACCOUNT Cash                                                    ACCOUNT NO. 1105

| DATE | | ITEM | POST. REF. | DEBIT | CREDIT | BALANCE DEBIT | BALANCE CREDIT |
|---|---|---|---|---|---|---|---|
| June 1 | | Balance | ✔ | | | 4 2 1 8 94 | |
| | | | | | | | |
| | | | | | | | |

ACCOUNT Accounts Receivable                                    ACCOUNT NO. 1205

| DATE | | ITEM | POST. REF. | DEBIT | CREDIT | BALANCE DEBIT | BALANCE CREDIT |
|---|---|---|---|---|---|---|---|
| June 1 | | Balance | ✔ | | | 22 1 4 9 91 | |
| | 20 | | G9 | | 2 8 0 17 | 21 8 6 9 74 | |
| | | | | | | | |
| | | | | | | | |

ACCOUNT Sales Tax Payable                                      ACCOUNT NO. 2110

| DATE | | ITEM | POST. REF. | DEBIT | CREDIT | BALANCE DEBIT | BALANCE CREDIT |
|---|---|---|---|---|---|---|---|
| June 1 | | Balance | ✔ | | | | 2 2 4 8 31 |
| | 20 | | G9 | 1 7 10 | | | 2 2 3 1 21 |
| | | | | | | | |
| | | | | | | | |

ACCOUNT Sales—Parts                                            ACCOUNT NO. 4105

| DATE | | ITEM | POST. REF. | DEBIT | CREDIT | BALANCE DEBIT | BALANCE CREDIT |
|---|---|---|---|---|---|---|---|
| June 1 | | Balance | ✔ | | | | 54 9 1 8 71 |
| | | | | | | | |
| | | | | | | | |

**2-2** **APPLICATION PROBLEM (concluded)**

ACCOUNT Sales Discount—Parts                                                                ACCOUNT NO. 4110

| DATE | | ITEM | POST. REF. | DEBIT | CREDIT | BALANCE | |
|------|--|------|-----------|-------|--------|---------|--|
| | | | | | | DEBIT | CREDIT |
| June 20-- | 1 | Balance | ✔ | | | 3 4 5 14 | |
| | | | | | | | |
| | | | | | | | |

ACCOUNT Sales—Tires                                                                           ACCOUNT NO. 4205

| DATE | | ITEM | POST. REF. | DEBIT | CREDIT | BALANCE | |
|------|--|------|-----------|-------|--------|---------|--|
| | | | | | | DEBIT | CREDIT |
| June 20-- | 1 | Balance | ✔ | | | | 85 1 4 1 31 |
| | | | | | | | |
| | | | | | | | |

ACCOUNT Sales Discount—Tires                                                                  ACCOUNT NO. 4210

| DATE | | ITEM | POST. REF. | DEBIT | CREDIT | BALANCE | |
|------|--|------|-----------|-------|--------|---------|--|
| | | | | | | DEBIT | CREDIT |
| June 20-- | 1 | Balance | ✔ | | | 1 8 4 22 | |
| | | | | | | | |
| | | | | | | | |

**Journalizing departmental sales, sales returns and allowances, and cash receipts**

**1., 2.**

## SALES JOURNAL

PAGE

| | DATE | ACCOUNT DEBITED | SALE NO. | POST. REF. | ACCOUNTS RECEIVABLE DEBIT 1 | SALES TAX PAYABLE CREDIT 2 | SALES CREDIT | |
|---|---|---|---|---|---|---|---|---|
| | | | | | | | EQUIPMENT 3 | SUPPLIES 4 |
| 1 | | | | | | | | | 1 |
| 2 | | | | | | | | | 2 |
| 3 | | | | | | | | | 3 |
| 4 | | | | | | | | | 4 |
| 5 | | | | | | | | | 5 |
| 6 | | | | | | | | | 6 |
| 7 | | | | | | | | | 7 |
| 8 | | | | | | | | | 8 |
| 9 | | | | | | | | | 9 |
| 10 | | | | | | | | | 10 |
| 11 | | | | | | | | | 11 |

## GENERAL JOURNAL

PAGE

| | DATE | ACCOUNT TITLE | DOC. NO. | POST. REF. | DEBIT | CREDIT | |
|---|---|---|---|---|---|---|---|
| 1 | | | | | | | 1 |
| 2 | | | | | | | 2 |
| 3 | | | | | | | 3 |
| 4 | | | | | | | 4 |
| 5 | | | | | | | 5 |
| 6 | | | | | | | 6 |
| 7 | | | | | | | 7 |
| 8 | | | | | | | 8 |
| 9 | | | | | | | 9 |
| 10 | | | | | | | 10 |
| 11 | | | | | | | 11 |
| 12 | | | | | | | 12 |
| 13 | | | | | | | 13 |
| 14 | | | | | | | 14 |

## 2-M MASTERY PROBLEM (continued)

**1., 3.**

**CASH RECEIPTS JOURNAL**

| DATE | ACCOUNT TITLE | DOC. NO. | POST. REF. | GENERAL DEBIT | GENERAL CREDIT | ACCOUNTS RECEIVABLE CREDIT | SALES TAX PAYABLE CREDIT | SALES CREDIT EQUIPMENT | SALES CREDIT SUPPLIES | SALES DISCOUNT DEBIT EQUIPMENT | SALES DISCOUNT DEBIT SUPPLIES | CASH DEBIT |
|------|---------------|----------|-----------|---------------|----------------|----------------------------|--------------------------|------------------------|-----------------------|--------------------------------|-------------------------------|------------|
| | | | | | | | | | | | | |

**1.**

**ACCOUNTS RECEIVABLE LEDGER**

CUSTOMER  BLC Storage                                                                CUSTOMER NO. 110

| DATE | ITEM | POST. REF. | DEBIT | CREDIT | DEBIT BALANCE |
|------|------|-----------|-------|--------|---------------|
|      |      |           |       |        |               |
|      |      |           |       |        |               |
|      |      |           |       |        |               |

CUSTOMER  Eastern Realty                                                            CUSTOMER NO. 120

| DATE | ITEM | POST. REF. | DEBIT | CREDIT | DEBIT BALANCE |
|------|------|-----------|-------|--------|---------------|
|      |      |           |       |        |               |
|      |      |           |       |        |               |
|      |      |           |       |        |               |

CUSTOMER  Lakeland Church                                                           CUSTOMER NO. 130

| DATE | | ITEM | POST. REF. | DEBIT | CREDIT | DEBIT BALANCE |
|------|--|------|-----------|-------|--------|---------------|
| 20-- May | 1 | Balance | ✔ |  |  | 3 1 5 74 |
|  |  |  |  |  |  |  |
|  |  |  |  |  |  |  |
|  |  |  |  |  |  |  |
|  |  |  |  |  |  |  |

CUSTOMER  Natural Products                                                          CUSTOMER NO. 140

| DATE | | ITEM | POST. REF. | DEBIT | CREDIT | DEBIT BALANCE |
|------|--|------|-----------|-------|--------|---------------|
| 20-- May | 1 | Balance | ✔ |  |  | 1 8 2 0 94 |
|  |  |  |  |  |  |  |
|  |  |  |  |  |  |  |
|  |  |  |  |  |  |  |

## 2-M MASTERY PROBLEM (continued)

**2., 3.**                    GENERAL LEDGER

ACCOUNT Cash                                                    ACCOUNT NO. 1105

| DATE | | ITEM | POST. REF. | DEBIT | CREDIT | BALANCE DEBIT | BALANCE CREDIT |
|------|---|------|------------|-------|--------|---------------|----------------|
| 20-- May | 1 | Balance | ✔ | | | 6 1 8 4 19 | |
| | | | | | | | |
| | | | | | | | |

ACCOUNT Accounts Receivable                                    ACCOUNT NO. 1205

| DATE | | ITEM | POST. REF. | DEBIT | CREDIT | BALANCE DEBIT | BALANCE CREDIT |
|------|---|------|------------|-------|--------|---------------|----------------|
| 20-- May | 1 | Balance | ✔ | | | 28 1 4 9 61 | |
| | | | | | | | |
| | | | | | | | |
| | | | | | | | |
| | | | | | | | |
| | | | | | | | |

ACCOUNT Sales Tax Payable                                      ACCOUNT NO. 2110

| DATE | | ITEM | POST. REF. | DEBIT | CREDIT | BALANCE DEBIT | BALANCE CREDIT |
|------|---|------|------------|-------|--------|---------------|----------------|
| 20-- May | 1 | Balance | ✔ | | | | 9 3 2 54 |
| | | | | | | | |
| | | | | | | | |
| | | | | | | | |

ACCOUNT Sales—Equipment                                        ACCOUNT NO. 4105

| DATE | | ITEM | POST. REF. | DEBIT | CREDIT | BALANCE DEBIT | BALANCE CREDIT |
|------|---|------|------------|-------|--------|---------------|----------------|
| 20-- May | 1 | Balance | ✔ | | | | 61 2 1 4 09 |
| | | | | | | | |
| | | | | | | | |
| | | | | | | | |

ACCOUNT Sales Discount—Equipment      ACCOUNT NO. 4110

| DATE | | ITEM | POST. REF. | DEBIT | CREDIT | BALANCE | |
|------|--|------|-----------|-------|--------|---------|--|
| | | | | | | DEBIT | CREDIT |
| 20-- May | 1 | Balance | ✔ | | | 2 4 1 10 | |
| | | | | | | | |
| | | | | | | | |

ACCOUNT Sales Returns and Allowances—Equipment      ACCOUNT NO. 4115

| DATE | | ITEM | POST. REF. | DEBIT | CREDIT | BALANCE | |
|------|--|------|-----------|-------|--------|---------|--|
| | | | | | | DEBIT | CREDIT |
| 20-- May | 1 | Balance | ✔ | | | 1 4 1 5 99 | |
| | | | | | | | |
| | | | | | | | |

ACCOUNT Sales—Supplies      ACCOUNT NO. 4205

| DATE | | ITEM | POST. REF. | DEBIT | CREDIT | BALANCE | |
|------|--|------|-----------|-------|--------|---------|--|
| | | | | | | DEBIT | CREDIT |
| 20-- May | 1 | Balance | ✔ | | | | 38 4 1 0 07 |
| | | | | | | | |
| | | | | | | | |
| | | | | | | | |

ACCOUNT Sales Discount—Supplies      ACCOUNT NO. 4210

| DATE | | ITEM | POST. REF. | DEBIT | CREDIT | BALANCE | |
|------|--|------|-----------|-------|--------|---------|--|
| | | | | | | DEBIT | CREDIT |
| 20-- May | 1 | Balance | ✔ | | | 1 8 9 94 | |
| | | | | | | | |
| | | | | | | | |

ACCOUNT Sales Returns and Allowances—Supplies      ACCOUNT NO. 4215

| DATE | | ITEM | POST. REF. | DEBIT | CREDIT | BALANCE | |
|------|--|------|-----------|-------|--------|---------|--|
| | | | | | | DEBIT | CREDIT |
| 20-- May | 1 | Balance | ✔ | | | 1 0 9 4 61 | |
| | | | | | | | |
| | | | | | | | |

## 2-S  SOURCE DOCUMENTS PROBLEM (LO2, 4, 5), p. 59

**Journalizing departmental sales, sales returns and allowances, and cash receipts**

---

**Ozark AV SHACK**
5701 Madison Ave.
Fort Smith, AR 72903

INVOICE

SOLD TO:  Peter Simms
2345 S. Boston Street
Fort Smith, AR 72903

| | |
|---|---|
| DATE: | 11/6/-- |
| INV. NO.: | 541 |
| TERMS: | n/30 |
| CUST. NO.: | 178 |

| QUANTITY | PART NO. | DESCRIPTION | UNIT PRICE | TOTAL |
|---|---|---|---|---|
| 2 | 6345 | 54" Interactive HD television | $949.00 | **$1,898.00** |
| | | SUBTOTAL | | **$1,898.00** |
| | | TAX | | 142.35 |
| | | TOTAL | | **$2,040.35** |

*Look to Ozark AV Shack for all your audio/video needs*

---

**Ozark AV SHACK**
5701 Madison Ave.
Fort Smith, AR 72903

INVOICE

SOLD TO:  Janice Tillman
106 N. Plum Street
Hackett, AR 72937

| | |
|---|---|
| DATE: | 11/15/-- |
| INV. NO.: | 542 |
| TERMS: | n/30 |
| CUST. NO.: | 184 |

| QUANTITY | PART NO. | DESCRIPTION | UNIT PRICE | TOTAL |
|---|---|---|---|---|
| 1 | 948 | Home theater sound system | $899.00 | **$ 899.00** |
| 2 | 732 | 48" SOUND BAR | 149.95 | **299.90** |
| 3 | 733 | 54" SOUND BAR | 199.95 | **599.85** |
| | | SUBTOTAL | | **$1,798.75** |
| | | TAX | | **134.91** |
| | | TOTAL | | **$1,933.66** |

*Look to Ozark AV Shack for all your audio/video needs*

---

**Ozark AV SHACK**
5701 Madison Ave.
Fort Smith, AR 72903

INVOICE

SOLD TO: Stan O'Brien
1406 Parkview Drive
Van Buren, AR 72956

| DATE: | 11/22/-- |
| INV. NO.: | 543 |
| TERMS: | n/30 |
| CUST. NO.: | 164 |

| QUANTITY | PART NO. | DESCRIPTION | UNIT PRICE | TOTAL |
|---|---|---|---|---|
| 1 | 1949 | Premium in-wall surround system | $2,299.00 | **$2,299.00** |
| | | SUBTOTAL | | **$2,299.00** |
| | | TAX | | 172.43 |
| | | TOTAL | | **$2,471.43** |

*Look to Ozark AV Shack for all your audio/video needs*

**Ozark AV SHACK**
5701 Madison Ave.
Fort Smith, AR 72903

RECEIPT

FROM: *Daniel Campbell*

| DATE: | 11/6/-- |
| RECEIPT NO.: | 569 |

| PAYMENT METHOD | CHECK NO. | CUSTOMER ACCT. NO. | RECEIVED BY |
|---|---|---|---|
| *Check* | *1848* | *132* | *Sandi Blake* |

| DESCRIPTION | INVOICE | GROSS AMOUNT | DISCOUNT | CASH RECEIVED |
|---|---|---|---|---|
| *On account (invoice was for video equipment)* | *538* | *$1,112.31* | *$ 22.25* | *$1,090.06* |
| | | TOTAL DISCOUNT | *$ 22.25* | |
| | | | TOTAL | *$1,090.06* |

**2-S**  **SOURCE DOCUMENTS PROBLEM (continued)**

---

**Ozark AV SHACK**
5701 Madison Ave.
Fort Smith, AR 72903

RECEIPT

FROM: *Stan O'Brien*

DATE: *11/7/--*
RECEIPT NO.: 570

| PAYMENT METHOD | CHECK NO. | CUSTOMER ACCT. NO. | RECEIVED BY |
|---|---|---|---|
| *Check* | *944* | *164* | *Sandi Blake* |

| DESCRIPTION | INVOICE | GROSS AMOUNT | DISCOUNT | CASH RECEIVED |
|---|---|---|---|---|
| *On account (invoice was for video equipment)* | *540* | *$ 349.18* | *$ 6.98* | *$ 342.20* |
| | | TOTAL DISCOUNT | *$ 6.98* | |
| | | | TOTAL | *$ 342.20* |

---

**Ozark AV SHACK**
5701 Madison Ave.
Fort Smith, AR 72903

RECEIPT

FROM: *Peter Simms*

DATE: *11/15/--*
RECEIPT NO.: 571

| PAYMENT METHOD | CHECK NO. | CUSTOMER ACCT. NO. | RECEIVED BY |
|---|---|---|---|
| *Check* | *532* | *178* | *Sally Richards* |

| DESCRIPTION | INVOICE | GROSS AMOUNT | DISCOUNT | CASH RECEIVED |
|---|---|---|---|---|
| *On account* | *501* | *$1,243.09* | *$ —* | *$1,243.09* |
| *On account* | *541* | *$2,040.35* | *$ 40.81* | *$1,999.54* |
| | | TOTAL DISCOUNT | *$ 40.81* | |
| | | | TOTAL | *$3,242.63* |

---

---

**Ozark AV SHACK**
5701 Madison Ave.
Fort Smith, AR 72903

RECEIPT

FROM: _Janice Tillman_

DATE: 11/24/--

RECEIPT NO.: 572

| PAYMENT METHOD | CHECK NO. | CUSTOMER ACCT. NO. | RECEIVED BY |
|---|---|---|---|
| Check | 865 | 184 | Sally Richards |

| DESCRIPTION | INVOICE | GROSS AMOUNT | DISCOUNT | CASH RECEIVED |
|---|---|---|---|---|
| Partial payment on account | 542 | $1,020.41 | $ 20.41 | $1,000.00 |
| | | TOTAL DISCOUNT | $ 20.41 | |
| | | | TOTAL | $1,000.00 |

---

**Ozark AV SHACK**
5701 Madison Ave.
Fort Smith, AR 72903

Credit Memorandum

TO: Daniel Campbell
152 S. Durant Street
Muldrow, OK 74948

DATE: 11/3/--

CM. NO.: 25

CUST. ID: 132

| QUANTITY | ITEM NO. | DESCRIPTION | UNIT PRICE | TOTALS |
|---|---|---|---|---|
| 1 | 7438 | 48" HD television | $499.00 | **$499.00** |
| | | SUBTOTAL | | **$499.00** |
| | | SALES TAX | | 37.43 |
| | | TOTAL | | **$536.43** |

---

**Ozark AV SHACK**
5701 Madison Ave.
Fort Smith, AR 72903

Credit Memorandum

TO: Janice Tillman
106 N. Plum Street
Hackett, AR 72937

DATE: 11/18/--

CM. NO.: 26

CUST. ID: 184

| QUANTITY | ITEM NO. | DESCRIPTION | UNIT PRICE | TOTALS |
|---|---|---|---|---|
| 2 | 732 | 48" Sound bar | $149.95 | **$299.90** |
| | | SUBTOTAL | | **$299.90** |
| | | SALES TAX | | 22.49 |
| | | TOTAL | | **$322.39** |

---

**2-S** **SOURCE DOCUMENTS PROBLEM (continued)**

| TERMINAL SUMMARY | | |
| --- | --- | --- |
| Ozark AV Shack | | |
| **SUMMARY NO.:** | | 32 |
| **DATE:** | | 11/10/-- |
| **TIME:** | | 18:30 |
| **VISA** | 023 | |
| Sales | | 3,218.99 |
| Sales Tax | | 241.42 |
| Total | | 3,460.41 |
| **MasterCard** | 025 | |
| Sales | | 3,418.13 |
| Sales Tax | | 256.36 |
| Total | | 3,674.49 |
| **Debit Cards** | 057 | |
| Sales | | 6,419.36 |
| Sales Tax | | 481.45 |
| Total | | 6,900.81 |
| **Cash** | 121 | |
| Sales | | 3,198.11 |
| Sales Tax | | 239.86 |
| Total | | 3,437.97 |
| **Totals** | | |
| Audio | | 7,841.91 |
| Video | | 8,412.68 |
| Sales Tax | | 1,219.09 |
| Total | | 17,473.68 |

| TERMINAL SUMMARY | | |
| --- | --- | --- |
| Ozark AV Shack | | |
| **SUMMARY NO.:** | | 33 |
| **DATE:** | | 11/20/-- |
| **TIME:** | | 19:04 |
| **VISA** | 019 | |
| Sales | | 2,814.11 |
| Sales Tax | | 211.06 |
| Total | | 3,025.17 |
| **MasterCard** | 017 | |
| Sales | | 2,189.99 |
| Sales Tax | | 164.25 |
| Total | | 2,354.24 |
| **Debit Cards** | 062 | |
| Sales | | 7,019.64 |
| Sales Tax | | 526.47 |
| Total | | 7,546.11 |
| **Cash** | 098 | |
| Sales | | 2,991.61 |
| Sales Tax | | 224.37 |
| Total | | 3,215.98 |
| **Totals** | | |
| Audio | | 5,534.25 |
| Video | | 9,481.10 |
| Sales Tax | | 1,126.15 |
| Total | | 16,141.50 |

**1., 2.**

## SALES JOURNAL

PAGE

| | DATE | | ACCOUNT DEBITED | SALE NO. | POST. REF. | ACCOUNTS RECEIVABLE DEBIT (1) | SALES TAX PAYABLE CREDIT (2) | SALES CREDIT AUDIO (3) | SALES CREDIT VIDEO (4) | |
|---|---|---|---|---|---|---|---|---|---|---|
| 1 | | | | | | | | | | 1 |
| 2 | | | | | | | | | | 2 |
| 3 | | | | | | | | | | 3 |
| 4 | | | | | | | | | | 4 |
| 5 | | | | | | | | | | 5 |
| 6 | | | | | | | | | | 6 |
| 7 | | | | | | | | | | 7 |
| 8 | | | | | | | | | | 8 |
| 9 | | | | | | | | | | 9 |
| 10 | | | | | | | | | | 10 |
| 11 | | | | | | | | | | 11 |

**1.**

## GENERAL JOURNAL

PAGE

| | DATE | | ACCOUNT TITLE | DOC. NO. | POST. REF. | DEBIT | CREDIT | |
|---|---|---|---|---|---|---|---|---|
| 1 | | | | | | | | 1 |
| 2 | | | | | | | | 2 |
| 3 | | | | | | | | 3 |
| 4 | | | | | | | | 4 |
| 5 | | | | | | | | 5 |
| 6 | | | | | | | | 6 |
| 7 | | | | | | | | 7 |
| 8 | | | | | | | | 8 |
| 9 | | | | | | | | 9 |
| 10 | | | | | | | | 10 |
| 11 | | | | | | | | 11 |
| 12 | | | | | | | | 12 |
| 13 | | | | | | | | 13 |
| 14 | | | | | | | | 14 |

## 2-S SOURCE DOCUMENTS PROBLEM (continued)

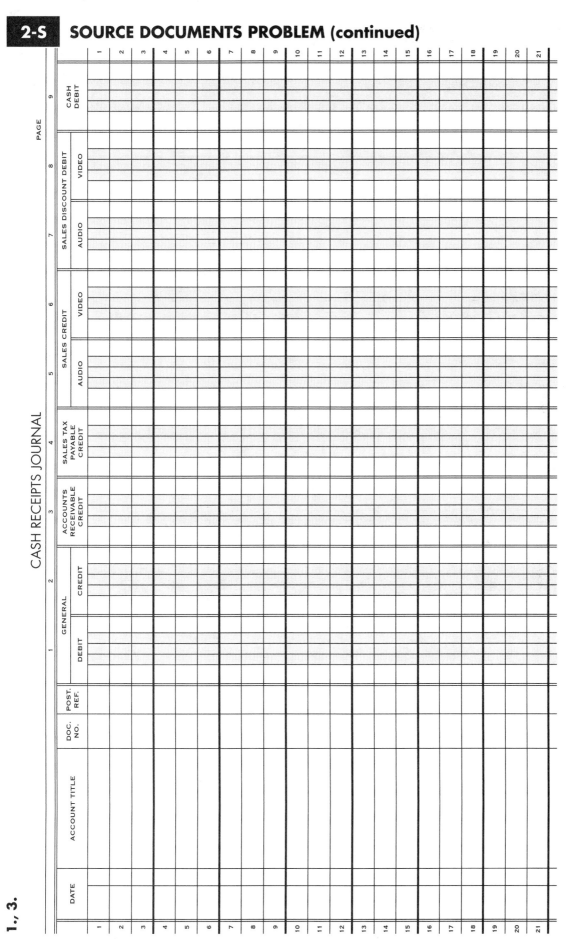

**1., 3.**

CASH RECEIPTS JOURNAL

PAGE

| | | | GENERAL | | ACCOUNTS RECEIVABLE CREDIT | SALES TAX PAYABLE CREDIT | SALES CREDIT | | SALES DISCOUNT DEBIT | | CASH DEBIT |
|---|---|---|---|---|---|---|---|---|---|---|---|
| DATE | ACCOUNT TITLE | DOC. NO. | POST. REF. | DEBIT | CREDIT | | | AUDIO | VIDEO | AUDIO | VIDEO | |

**1.**

**ACCOUNTS RECEIVABLE LEDGER**

CUSTOMER Daniel Campbell

CUSTOMER NO. 132

| DATE | ITEM | POST. REF. | DEBIT | CREDIT | DEBIT BALANCE |
|------|------|------------|-------|--------|---------------|
| 20-- Nov. 1 | Balance | ✔ | | | 1 6 4 8 74 |
| | | | | | |
| | | | | | |
| | | | | | |

CUSTOMER Stan O'Brien

CUSTOMER NO. 164

| DATE | ITEM | POST. REF. | DEBIT | CREDIT | DEBIT BALANCE |
|------|------|------------|-------|--------|---------------|
| 20-- Nov. 1 | Balance | ✔ | | | 3 4 9 18 |
| | | | | | |
| | | | | | |

CUSTOMER Peter Simms

CUSTOMER NO. 178

| DATE | ITEM | POST. REF. | DEBIT | CREDIT | DEBIT BALANCE |
|------|------|------------|-------|--------|---------------|
| 20-- Nov. 1 | Balance | ✔ | | | 1 2 4 3 09 |
| | | | | | |
| | | | | | |
| | | | | | |

CUSTOMER Janice Tillman

CUSTOMER NO. 184

| DATE | ITEM | POST. REF. | DEBIT | CREDIT | DEBIT BALANCE |
|------|------|------------|-------|--------|---------------|
| | | | | | |
| | | | | | |
| | | | | | |

## 2-S SOURCE DOCUMENTS PROBLEM (continued)

**2., 3.**                                    **GENERAL LEDGER**

ACCOUNT Cash                                                    ACCOUNT NO. 1105

| DATE | ITEM | POST. REF. | DEBIT | CREDIT | BALANCE DEBIT | BALANCE CREDIT |
|------|------|-----------|-------|--------|------|------|
| 20-- Nov. 1 | Balance | ✔ | | | 11 2 0 4 66 | |
| | | | | | | |
| | | | | | | |

ACCOUNT Accounts Receivable                                    ACCOUNT NO. 1205

| DATE | ITEM | POST. REF. | DEBIT | CREDIT | BALANCE DEBIT | BALANCE CREDIT |
|------|------|-----------|-------|--------|------|------|
| 20-- Nov. 1 | Balance | ✔ | | | 29 1 8 0 06 | |
| | | | | | | |
| | | | | | | |
| | | | | | | |
| | | | | | | |
| | | | | | | |

ACCOUNT Sales Tax Payable                                      ACCOUNT NO. 2110

| DATE | ITEM | POST. REF. | DEBIT | CREDIT | BALANCE DEBIT | BALANCE CREDIT |
|------|------|-----------|-------|--------|------|------|
| 20-- Nov. 1 | Balance | ✔ | | | | 2 2 1 9 94 |
| | | | | | | |
| | | | | | | |
| | | | | | | |
| | | | | | | |

ACCOUNT Sales—Audio                                            ACCOUNT NO. 4105

| DATE | ITEM | POST. REF. | DEBIT | CREDIT | BALANCE DEBIT | BALANCE CREDIT |
|------|------|-----------|-------|--------|------|------|
| 20-- Nov. 1 | Balance | ✔ | | | | 108 1 8 4 99 |
| | | | | | | |
| | | | | | | |

ACCOUNT Sales Discount—Audio ACCOUNT NO. 4110

| DATE | | ITEM | POST. REF. | DEBIT | CREDIT | BALANCE | |
|---|---|---|---|---|---|---|---|
| | | | | | | DEBIT | CREDIT |
| Nov. 20-- | 1 | Balance | ✔ | | | 5 9 4 19 | |
| | | | | | | | |
| | | | | | | | |

ACCOUNT Sales Returns and Allowances—Audio ACCOUNT NO. 4115

| DATE | | ITEM | POST. REF. | DEBIT | CREDIT | BALANCE | |
|---|---|---|---|---|---|---|---|
| | | | | | | DEBIT | CREDIT |
| Nov. 20-- | 1 | Balance | ✔ | | | 6 1 4 8 28 | |
| | | | | | | | |
| | | | | | | | |

ACCOUNT Sales—Video ACCOUNT NO. 4205

| DATE | | ITEM | POST. REF. | DEBIT | CREDIT | BALANCE | |
|---|---|---|---|---|---|---|---|
| | | | | | | DEBIT | CREDIT |
| Nov. 20-- | 1 | Balance | ✔ | | | | 154 8 1 9 10 |
| | | | | | | | |
| | | | | | | | |
| | | | | | | | |

ACCOUNT Sales Discount—Video ACCOUNT NO. 4210

| DATE | | ITEM | POST. REF. | DEBIT | CREDIT | BALANCE | |
|---|---|---|---|---|---|---|---|
| | | | | | | DEBIT | CREDIT |
| Nov. 20-- | 1 | Balance | ✔ | | | 7 1 4 19 | |
| | | | | | | | |
| | | | | | | | |

ACCOUNT Sales Returns and Allowances—Video ACCOUNT NO. 4215

| DATE | | ITEM | POST. REF. | DEBIT | CREDIT | BALANCE | |
|---|---|---|---|---|---|---|---|
| | | | | | | DEBIT | CREDIT |
| Nov. 20-- | 1 | Balance | ✔ | | | 9 1 4 8 31 | |
| | | | | | | | |
| | | | | | | | |

**2-C** **CHALLENGE PROBLEM (LO2, 4, 5), p. 60**

**Journalizing departmental sales, sales returns and allowances, and cash receipts**

**1.**

## CASH RECEIPTS JOURNAL

PAGE 9

| DATE | ACCOUNT TITLE | DOC. NO. | POST. REF. | GENERAL DEBIT | GENERAL CREDIT | ACCOUNTS RECEIVABLE CREDIT | SALES TAX PAYABLE CREDIT | SALES CREDIT PAINT | SALES CREDIT SUPPLIES | SALES DISCOUNT DEBIT PAINT | SALES DISCOUNT DEBIT SUPPLIES | CASH DEBIT |
|------|---------------|----------|------------|--------|--------|--------|--------|--------|--------|--------|--------|--------|
| | | | | 1 | 2 | 3 | 4 | 5 | 6 | 7 | 8 | 9 |
| 1 | | | | | | | | | | | | |
| 2 | | | | | | | | | | | | |
| 3 | | | | | | | | | | | | |
| 4 | | | | | | | | | | | | |
| 5 | | | | | | | | | | | | |
| 6 | | | | | | | | | | | | |
| 7 | | | | | | | | | | | | |
| 8 | | | | | | | | | | | | |
| 9 | | | | | | | | | | | | |
| 10 | | | | | | | | | | | | |
| 11 | | | | | | | | | | | | |
| 12 | | | | | | | | | | | | |
| 13 | | | | | | | | | | | | |

| Name | Perfect Score | Your Score |
|---|---|---|
| Analyzing Departmental Payroll Procedures | 25 Pts. | |
| Identifying Accounting Terms | 11 Pts. | |
| Analyzing Payroll Accounting | 10 Pts. | |
| **Total** | 46 Pts. | |

**Study Guide 3**

## Part One—Analyzing Departmental Payroll Procedures

**Directions:** Place a *T* for True or an *F* for False in the Answers column to show whether each of the following statements is true or false.

**Answers**

1. Laws require employers to keep records of the payroll information and other payments related to employee services. (p. 64)

    1. _____

2. Employers are required by law to withhold certain payroll taxes from employee salaries each pay period. (p. 64)

    2. _____

3. The yearly report of an employee's earnings and deductions that is provided to the employee is Form W-2. (p. 64)

    3. _____

4. Employers pay government agencies all payroll taxes withheld from employee salaries on an annual basis. (p. 64)

    4. _____

5. By January 31, businesses must report to employees the earnings and amounts withheld for the previous calendar year. (p. 64)

    5. _____

6. Payroll records must show an employee's earnings, amounts withheld, net amount paid, and the total amount of payroll taxes that a business must pay. (p. 64)

    6. _____

7. Income and Medicare taxes are the only two federal taxes deducted from earnings of each employee. (p. 65)

    7. _____

8. The amount of federal income tax to be withheld is determined solely by the number of withholding allowances. (p. 65)

    8. _____

9. The Internal Revenue Service sets the tax base and the tax rates for the social security tax. (p. 65)

    9. _____

10. Like social security, Medicare has a tax base. (p. 65)

    10. _____

11. Laws for handling state, city, and county taxes vary. (p. 65)

    11. _____

12. Other deductions from employee earnings include health insurance, life insurance, retirement plan contributions, and charitable contributions. (p. 65)

    12. _____

13. All time worked in excess of 40 hours in any one week is considered overtime. (p. 66)

    13. _____

14. Employees are paid two times the regular rate for overtime hours. (p. 66)

    14. _____

15. Commissions, cost-of-living adjustments, a share of profits, and a bonus are included in an employee's earnings. (p. 67)

    15. _____

16. In proving a payroll register's accuracy, the total of the Net Pay column is subtracted from the Total Deductions column. (p. 69)

    16. _____

17. An employee's total earnings and deductions for the quarter are summarized on one line of the employee earnings record. (p. 73)

    17. _____

18. After a biweekly payroll register has been completed, a check for the total earnings indicated on the payroll register is written for each employee. (p. 76)

    18. _____

19. Transferring payroll amounts electronically from the employer's account to the employee's bank account is known as electronic funds transfer (EFT). (p. 76)

19. _____

20. Unemployment taxes are used to pay qualified workers cash benefits for limited periods of unemployment. (p. 77)

20. _____

21. Both employers and employees are required to pay a federal unemployment tax. (p. 78)

21. _____

22. The frequency of payments for federal, state, and local government taxes is determined by the amount of tax paid each year. (p. 80)

22. _____

23. If a business is classified as a monthly schedule depositor, the business must pay the total amount due by the 15th day of the following month. (p. 80)

23. _____

24. Only employers having total payroll taxes due greater than $1 million are required to use the Electronic Federal Tax Payment System. (p. 80)

24. _____

25. A memorandum with an attached receipt is the source document for a payment made using the Electronic Federal Tax Payment System. (p. 81)

25. _____

## Part Two—Identifying Accounting Terms

**Directions:** Select the one term in Column I that best fits each definition in Column II. Print the letter identifying your choice in the Answers column.

| Column I | Column II | Answers |
|---|---|---|
| A. automatic check deposit | 1. The amount paid to an employee for every hour worked. (p. 64) | 1. _____ |
| B. electronic funds transfer (EFT) | 2. A fixed annual sum of money divided among equal pay periods. (p. 64) | 2. _____ |
| C. employee earnings record | 3. The number of days or weeks of work covered by an employee's paycheck. (p. 64) | 3. _____ |
| D. pay period | 4. The total amount earned by all employees for a pay period. (p. 64) | 4. _____ |
| E. payroll | 5. Taxes based on the payroll of a business. (p. 64) | 5. _____ |
| F. payroll register | 6. A deduction from total earnings for each person legally supported by a taxpayer, including the employee. (p. 65) | 6. _____ |
| G. payroll taxes | 7. The maximum amount of earnings on which a tax is calculated. (p. 65) | 7. _____ |
| H. salary | | |
| I. tax base | 8. An accounting form that summarizes the earnings, deductions, and net pay of all employees for one pay period. (p. 68) | 8. _____ |
| J. wage | | |
| K. withholding allowance | 9. A business form used to record details of an employee's earnings and deductions. (p. 73) | 9. _____ |
| | 10. Depositing payroll checks directly to an employee's checking or savings account. (p. 76) | 10. _____ |
| | 11. A computerized cash payments system that transfers funds without the use of checks, currency, or other paper documents. (p. 76) | 11. _____ |

## Part Three—Analyzing Payroll Accounting

**Directions:** For each item below, select the choice that best completes the sentence.
Print the letter identifying your choice in the Answers column.

**Answers**

1. The social security tax provides insurance for (A) old-age (B) survivors (C) disability (D) all of the above. (p. 65)

1. _____

2. In a biweekly payroll system employees are paid (A) once a week (B) twice a year (C) every two weeks (D) twice a month. (p. 66)

2. _____

3. When employees are paid a percentage of sales in addition to their regular salary, the earnings are often referred to as (A) salary (B) pensions (C) commissions (D) wages. (p. 67)

3. _____

4. The amount due an individual for a pay period, after deductions, is referred to as (A) regular earnings (B) overtime (C) total earnings (D) none of these. (p. 69)

4. _____

5. When all employees have cashed their payroll checks, the balance of the payroll bank account (A) equals zero (B) equals the net pay for the period (C) equals total earnings for the period (D) none of these. (p. 76)

5. _____

6. A payroll tax which the employer does not pay is (A) social security tax (B) Medicare tax (C) federal income tax (D) federal unemployment tax. (p. 78)

6. _____

7. Social security and Medicare taxes are paid by (A) the employees (B) the employer (C) both A and B (D) none of these. (p. 78)

7. _____

8. A tax which is not deducted from employees' pay is (A) Medicare tax (B) state income tax (C) federal unemployment tax (D) federal income tax. (p. 78)

8. _____

9. The frequency of employer payments of payroll taxes is determined by (A) the amount owed (B) the employer's geographic location (C) the type of business (D) none of these. (p. 80)

9. _____

10. If the quarterly federal unemployment tax for a business is $500.00 or more, the business must (A) make quarterly payments in the month following the end of the quarter (B) pay the tax in one payment by January 31 of the following year (C) make the payment at the end of each month (D) make the payment at the end of each quarter. (p. 81)

10. _____

**3-1**  **WORK TOGETHER, p. 74**

## Completing payroll records

**1.**

---

### COMMISSIONS RECORD

EMPLOYEE NO. _____  EMPLOYEE NAME _____

PAY PERIOD ENDED _____  REGULAR BIWEEKLY SALARY _____

DEPARTMENT _____  POSITION _____

---

|  | Carpet | Tile |
|---|---|---|
| Sales on Account ........................................................ | _____ | _____ |
| Cash and Credit Card Sales .................................... | _____ | _____ |
| *equals* Total Sales for the Month.............................. | _____ | _____ |
| *Less:* | | |
| Sales Discounts......................................................... | _____ | _____ |
| Sales Returns and Allowances ................................ | _____ | _____ |
| *equals* Total Reductions in Sales .............................. | _____ | _____ |
| *Equals:* | | |
| Net Sales.................................................................... | _____ | _____ |
| *times* Commission Rate.............................................. | _____ | _____ |
| *equals* Commission on Net Sales.............................. | _____ | _____ |

---

**4.**

## EARNINGS RECORD FOR QUARTER ENDED _____

EMPLOYEE NO. _____  NAME _____  MARITAL STATUS _____  WITHHOLDING ALLOWANCES _____

HOURLY WAGE _____  SALARY _____  DEPARTMENT _____  POSITION _____

| PAY PERIOD | | TOTAL EARNINGS | DEDUCTIONS | | | | | | TOTAL | NET PAY | ACCUMULATED EARNINGS |
| NO. | ENDED | | FEDERAL INCOME TAX | STATE INCOME TAX | SOC. SEC. TAX | MEDICARE TAX | HEALTH INSURANCE | RETIREMENT PLAN | | | |
|---|---|---|---|---|---|---|---|---|---|---|---|
| | | 1 | 2 | 3 | 4 | 5 | 6 | 7 | 8 | 9 | 10 |
| 1 | | | | | | | | | | | |
| 2 | | | | | | | | | | | |
| TOTALS | | | | | | | | | | | |

**2., 3.**

## PAYROLL REGISTER

SEMIMONTHLY PERIOD ENDED _____  DATE OF PAYMENT _____

| EMPL. NO. | EMPLOYEE'S NAME | MARITAL STATUS | NO. OF ALLOWANCES | EARNINGS | | | | DEPARTMENT | | | DEDUCTIONS | | | | | | TOTAL | NET PAY | CHECK NO. |
| | | | | REGULAR | OVERTIME | COMMISSION | TOTAL | CARPET | TILE | ADMINISTRATIVE | FEDERAL INCOME TAX | STATE INCOME TAX | SOCIAL SECURITY TAX | MEDICARE TAX | HEALTH INSURANCE | RETIREMENT PLAN | | | |
|---|---|---|---|---|---|---|---|---|---|---|---|---|---|---|---|---|---|---|---|
| | | | | 1 | 2 | 3 | 4 | 5 | 6 | 7 | 8 | 9 | 10 | 11 | 12 | 13 | 14 | 15 | |
| 22 | Belizean, Thomas C. | M | 4 | 80000 | | 62105 | 142105 | 38911 | 103194 | | 5100 | 7105 | 8811 | 2061 | 9000 | 6500 | 38577 | 103528 | 1 |
| 20 | Foxworth, Nevaeh A. | M | 1 | 112000 | 10500 | | 122500 | | 122500 | | 8000 | 6125 | 7595 | 1776 | 5000 | 2500 | 30996 | 91504 | 2 |
| 4 | Kirkwood, Nandi P. | S | 2 | 96000 | 3600 | | 99600 | 99600 | | | 7400 | 4980 | 6175 | 1444 | 6000 | 5000 | 30999 | 68601 | 3 |
| 9 | Marist, Brenda C. | M | 3 | 176000 | | | 176000 | | | 176000 | 11600 | 8800 | 10912 | 2552 | 8000 | 8000 | 49864 | 126136 | 4 |
| | | | | | | | | | | | | | | | | | | | 5 |
| | | | | | | | | | | | | | | | | | | | 6 |
| | | | | | | | | | | | | | | | | | | | 7 |
| | | | | | | | | | | | | | | | | | | | 8 |

**3-1** **ON YOUR OWN, p. 75**

## Completing payroll records

**1.**

---

### COMMISSIONS RECORD

EMPLOYEE NO. _____  EMPLOYEE NAME _____

PAY PERIOD ENDED _____  REGULAR BIWEEKLY SALARY _____

DEPARTMENT _____  POSITION _____

---

| | Audio | Video | |
|---|---|---|---|
| Sales on Account ........................................ | _____ | _____ | |
| Cash and Credit Card Sales ................................ | _____ | _____ | |
| *equals* Total Sales for the Month.......................... | _____ | _____ | |
| | | | |
| *Less:* | | | |
| Sales Discounts ........................................ | _____ | _____ | |
| Sales Returns and Allowances ............................ | _____ | _____ | |
| *equals* Total Reductions in Sales........................... | _____ | _____ | |
| | | | |
| *Equals:* | | | |
| Net Sales ........................................ | _____ | _____ | |
| *times* Commission Rate.......................... | _____ | _____ | _____ |
| *equals* Commission on Net Sales........................... | _____ | _____ | _____ |

---

**4.**

## EARNINGS RECORD FOR QUARTER ENDED

EMPLOYEE NO. _____  NAME _____  WITHHOLDING ALLOWANCES _____

HOURLY WAGE _____  SALARY _____  MARITAL STATUS _____  DEPARTMENT _____  POSITION _____

| PAY PERIOD | | TOTAL EARNINGS | DEDUCTIONS | | | | | | NET PAY | ACCUMULATED EARNINGS |
|---|---|---|---|---|---|---|---|---|---|---|
| NO. | ENDED | 1 | FEDERAL INCOME TAX 2 | STATE INCOME TAX 3 | SOC. SEC. TAX 4 | MEDICARE TAX 5 | HEALTH INSURANCE 6 | RETIREMENT PLAN 7 | TOTAL 8 | 9 | 10 |
| 1 | | | | | | | | | | | |
| 2 | | | | | | | | | | | |
| TOTALS | | | | | | | | | | | |

**2., 3.**

## PAYROLL REGISTER

SEMIMONTHLY PERIOD ENDED _____  DATE OF PAYMENT _____

| EMPL. NO. | EMPLOYEE'S NAME | MARITAL STATUS | NO. OF ALLOWANCES | EARNINGS | | | | DEPARTMENT | | | DEDUCTIONS | | | | | | | NET PAY | CHECK NO. |
|---|---|---|---|---|---|---|---|---|---|---|---|---|---|---|---|---|---|---|---|
| | | | | REGULAR 1 | OVERTIME 2 | COMMIS-SION 3 | TOTAL 4 | AUDIO 5 | VIDEO 6 | ADMINIS-TRATIVE 7 | FEDERAL INCOME TAX 8 | STATE INCOME TAX 9 | SOCIAL SECURITY TAX 10 | MEDICARE TAX 11 | HEALTH INSURANCE 12 | RETIRE-MENT PLAN 13 | TOTAL 14 | 15 | |
| 3 | Avilo, Alexi P. | S | 1 | 120000 | | 39851 | 159851 | | 159851 | | 18600 | 6394 | 9911 | 2318 | 6000 | 8000 | 51223 | 108628 | 1 |
| 10 | Becker, Xavier T. | M | 3 | 96000 | 5400 | | 101400 | | 101400 | | 2400 | 4056 | 6287 | 1470 | 10000 | 12000 | 36213 | 65187 | 2 |
| 4 | Johnson, Patrick T. | S | 2 | 162800 | | | 162800 | | | 162800 | 17000 | 6512 | 10094 | 2361 | 8000 | 10000 | 53967 | 108833 | 3 |
| 8 | Hu, Fang D. | M | 3 | 128000 | 14400 | | 142400 | 142400 | | | 6600 | 5696 | 8829 | 2065 | 10000 | 6500 | 39690 | 102710 | 4 |
| 5 | | | | | | | | | | | | | | | | | | | 5 |
| 6 | | | | | | | | | | | | | | | | | | | 6 |
| 7 | | | | | | | | | | | | | | | | | | | 7 |
| 8 | | | | | | | | | | | | | | | | | | | 8 |

**3-2** **WORK TOGETHER, p. 83**

## Journalizing and paying payroll and payroll taxes

**1.**

| Department | Social Security Earnings | Social Security 6.2% | Medicare 1.45% | FUTA Earnings | Federal Unemployment 0.6% | State Unemployment 5.4% | Total Payroll Taxes |
|---|---|---|---|---|---|---|---|
| Carpet | | | | | | | |
| Tile | | | | | | | |
| Administrative | | | | | | | |
| Total | | | | | | | |

**2.**

## CASH PAYMENTS JOURNAL

PAGE 6

| | | | | | GENERAL | | ACCOUNTS PAYABLE DEBIT | PURCH. DISCOUNT CR. | | CASH CREDIT |
|---|---|---|---|---|---|---|---|---|---|---|
| DATE | ACCOUNT TITLE | CK. NO. | POST. REF. | | DEBIT | CREDIT | | CARPET | TILE | |
| | | | | | 1 | 2 | 3 | 4 | 5 | 6 |
| | | | | 1 | | | | | | |
| | | | | 2 | | | | | | |
| | | | | 3 | | | | | | |
| | | | | 4 | | | | | | |
| | | | | 5 | | | | | | |
| | | | | 6 | | | | | | |
| | | | | 7 | | | | | | |
| | | | | 8 | | | | | | |
| | | | | 9 | | | | | | |
| | | | | 10 | | | | | | |
| | | | | 11 | | | | | | |
| | | | | 12 | | | | | | |
| | | | | 13 | | | | | | |
| | | | | 14 | | | | | | |
| | | | | 15 | | | | | | |

**2.**

GENERAL JOURNAL

PAGE

| | DATE | | ACCOUNT TITLE | DOC. NO. | POST. REF. | DEBIT | CREDIT | |
|---|---|---|---|---|---|---|---|---|
| 1 | | | | | | | | 1 |
| 2 | | | | | | | | 2 |
| 3 | | | | | | | | 3 |
| 4 | | | | | | | | 4 |
| 5 | | | | | | | | 5 |
| 6 | | | | | | | | 6 |
| 7 | | | | | | | | 7 |
| 8 | | | | | | | | 8 |
| 9 | | | | | | | | 9 |
| 10 | | | | | | | | 10 |
| 11 | | | | | | | | 11 |
| 12 | | | | | | | | 12 |
| 13 | | | | | | | | 13 |
| 14 | | | | | | | | 14 |
| 15 | | | | | | | | 15 |
| 16 | | | | | | | | 16 |
| 17 | | | | | | | | 17 |
| 18 | | | | | | | | 18 |
| 19 | | | | | | | | 19 |
| 20 | | | | | | | | 20 |
| 21 | | | | | | | | 21 |
| 22 | | | | | | | | 22 |
| 23 | | | | | | | | 23 |
| 24 | | | | | | | | 24 |
| 25 | | | | | | | | 25 |
| 26 | | | | | | | | 26 |
| 27 | | | | | | | | 27 |
| 28 | | | | | | | | 28 |
| 29 | | | | | | | | 29 |
| 30 | | | | | | | | 30 |
| 31 | | | | | | | | 31 |
| 32 | | | | | | | | 32 |

## 3-2 ON YOUR OWN, p. 83

**Journalizing and paying payroll and payroll taxes**

**1.**

| Department | Social Security Earnings | Social Security 6.2% | Medicare 1.45% | FUTA Earnings | Federal Unemployment 0.6% | State Unemployment 5.4% | Total Payroll Taxes |
|---|---|---|---|---|---|---|---|
| Audio | | | | | | | |
| Video | | | | | | | |
| Administrative | | | | | | | |
| Total | | | | | | | |

**2.**

CASH PAYMENTS JOURNAL

PAGE _____

| | DATE | ACCOUNT TITLE | CK. NO. | POST. REF. | GENERAL DEBIT | GENERAL CREDIT | ACCOUNTS PAYABLE DEBIT | PURCH. DISCOUNT CR. AUDIO | PURCH. DISCOUNT CR. VIDEO | CASH CREDIT |
|---|---|---|---|---|---|---|---|---|---|---|
| 1 | | | | | | | | | | |
| 2 | | | | | | | | | | |
| 3 | | | | | | | | | | |
| 4 | | | | | | | | | | |
| 5 | | | | | | | | | | |
| 6 | | | | | | | | | | |
| 7 | | | | | | | | | | |
| 8 | | | | | | | | | | |
| 9 | | | | | | | | | | |
| 10 | | | | | | | | | | |
| 11 | | | | | | | | | | |
| 12 | | | | | | | | | | |
| 13 | | | | | | | | | | |
| 14 | | | | | | | | | | |
| 15 | | | | | | | | | | |

Chapter 3 Calculating and Recording Departmental Payroll Data • **95**

**2.**

GENERAL JOURNAL                                          PAGE

| | DATE | ACCOUNT TITLE | DOC. NO. | POST. REF. | DEBIT | CREDIT | |
|---|---|---|---|---|---|---|---|
| 1 | | | | | | | 1 |
| 2 | | | | | | | 2 |
| 3 | | | | | | | 3 |
| 4 | | | | | | | 4 |
| 5 | | | | | | | 5 |
| 6 | | | | | | | 6 |
| 7 | | | | | | | 7 |
| 8 | | | | | | | 8 |
| 9 | | | | | | | 9 |
| 10 | | | | | | | 10 |
| 11 | | | | | | | 11 |
| 12 | | | | | | | 12 |
| 13 | | | | | | | 13 |
| 14 | | | | | | | 14 |
| 15 | | | | | | | 15 |
| 16 | | | | | | | 16 |
| 17 | | | | | | | 17 |
| 18 | | | | | | | 18 |
| 19 | | | | | | | 19 |
| 20 | | | | | | | 20 |
| 21 | | | | | | | 21 |
| 22 | | | | | | | 22 |
| 23 | | | | | | | 23 |
| 24 | | | | | | | 24 |
| 25 | | | | | | | 25 |
| 26 | | | | | | | 26 |
| 27 | | | | | | | 27 |
| 28 | | | | | | | 28 |
| 29 | | | | | | | 29 |
| 30 | | | | | | | 30 |
| 31 | | | | | | | 31 |
| 32 | | | | | | | 32 |

## 3-1 APPLICATION PROBLEM (LO1, 2, 3), p. 87

**Completing payroll records**

**1.**

---

### COMMISSIONS RECORD

EMPLOYEE NO. _____     EMPLOYEE NAME _____

PAY PERIOD ENDED _____     REGULAR BIWEEKLY SALARY _____

DEPARTMENT _____     POSITION _____

---

|  | Equipment | Parts |  |
|---|---|---|---|
| Sales on Account ........................................... | _____ | _____ | |
| Cash and Credit Card Sales ................................. | _____ | _____ | |
| *equals* Total Sales for the Month........................... | _____ | _____ | |
| | | | |
| *Less:* | | | |
| Sales Discounts............................................ | _____ | _____ | |
| Sales Returns and Allowances ............................. | _____ | _____ | |
| *equals* Total Reductions in Sales ........................... | _____ | _____ | |
| | | | |
| *Equals:* | | | |
| Net Sales................................................. | _____ | _____ | |
| *times* Commission Rate....................................... | _____ | _____ | _____ |
| *equals* Commission on Net Sales............................ | _____ | _____ | _____ |

## 4.

### EARNINGS RECORD FOR QUARTER ENDED

EMPLOYEE NO. _____  NAME _____

HOURLY WAGE _____  MARITAL STATUS _____  WITHHOLDING ALLOWANCES _____

SALARY _____  DEPARTMENT _____  POSITION _____

| PAY PERIOD | | TOTAL EARNINGS 1 | DEDUCTIONS | | | | | | NET PAY 9 | ACCUMULATED EARNINGS 10 |
| NO. | ENDED | | FEDERAL INCOME TAX 2 | STATE INCOME TAX 3 | SOC. SEC. TAX 4 | MEDICARE TAX 5 | HEALTH INSURANCE 6 | RETIREMENT PLAN 7 | TOTAL 8 | | |
| --- | --- | --- | --- | --- | --- | --- | --- | --- | --- | --- | --- |
| 1 | | | | | | | | | | | |
| 2 | | | | | | | | | | | |
| TOTALS | | | | | | | | | | | |

## 2., 3.

### PAYROLL REGISTER

SEMIMONTHLY PERIOD ENDED _____  DATE OF PAYMENT _____

| EMPL. NO. | EMPLOYEE'S NAME | MARITAL STATUS | NO. OF ALLOWANCES | EARNINGS | | | | DEPARTMENT | | | DEDUCTIONS | | | | | | | NET PAY | CHECK NO. |
| | | | | REGULAR 1 | OVERTIME 2 | COMMISSION 3 | TOTAL 4 | EQUIPMENT 5 | PARTS 6 | ADMINIS-TRATIVE 7 | FEDERAL INCOME TAX 8 | STATE INCOME TAX 9 | SOCIAL SECURITY TAX 10 | MEDICARE TAX 11 | HEALTH INSURANCE 12 | RETIRE-MENT PLAN 13 | TOTAL 14 | 15 | |
| --- | --- | --- | --- | --- | --- | --- | --- | --- | --- | --- | --- | --- | --- | --- | --- | --- | --- | --- | --- |
| 6 | Bui, Duong M | S | 1 | 148000 | | 411142 | 1889142 | | | 1889142 | 257700 | 94457 | 117727 | 27743 | 6000 | 6000 | 616627 | 1277515 | 1 |
| 21 | Collins, Daniel T. | M | 3 | 124800 | 7200 | | 132000 | | 132000 | | 5600 | 6600 | 8184 | 1914 | 10000 | 8000 | 40298 | 917702 | 2 |
| 3 | Porkony, Libena C. | M | 2 | 112000 | 4200 | | 1116200 | 1116200 | | | 5500 | 5810 | 7204 | 1685 | 8000 | 10000 | 38199 | 78001 | 3 |
| 4 | | | | | | | | | | | | | | | | | | | |
| 5 | | | | | | | | | | | | | | | | | | | |
| 6 | | | | | | | | | | | | | | | | | | | |
| 7 | | | | | | | | | | | | | | | | | | | |

**3-2** **APPLICATION PROBLEM (LO4, 5), p. 87**

## Journalizing and paying payroll and payroll taxes

**1.**

| Department | Social Security Earnings | Social Security 6.2% | Medicare 1.45% | FUTA Earnings | Federal Unemployment 0.6% | State Unemployment 5.4% | Total Payroll Taxes |
|---|---|---|---|---|---|---|---|
| Equipment | | | | | | | |
| Parts | | | | | | | |
| Administrative | | | | | | | |
| Total | | | | | | | |

**2.**

CASH PAYMENTS JOURNAL

PAGE

| | DATE | ACCOUNT TITLE | CK. NO. | POST. REF. | GENERAL DEBIT | GENERAL CREDIT | ACCOUNTS PAYABLE DEBIT | PURCH. DISCOUNT CR. EQUIPMENT | PURCH. DISCOUNT CR. PARTS | CASH CREDIT | |
|---|---|---|---|---|---|---|---|---|---|---|---|
| 1 | | | | | | | | | | | 1 |
| 2 | | | | | | | | | | | 2 |
| 3 | | | | | | | | | | | 3 |
| 4 | | | | | | | | | | | 4 |
| 5 | | | | | | | | | | | 5 |
| 6 | | | | | | | | | | | 6 |
| 7 | | | | | | | | | | | 7 |
| 8 | | | | | | | | | | | 8 |
| 9 | | | | | | | | | | | 9 |
| 10 | | | | | | | | | | | 10 |
| 11 | | | | | | | | | | | 11 |
| 12 | | | | | | | | | | | 12 |
| 13 | | | | | | | | | | | 13 |
| 14 | | | | | | | | | | | 14 |
| 15 | | | | | | | | | | | 15 |

**2.**

GENERAL JOURNAL                                                    PAGE

| | DATE | | ACCOUNT TITLE | DOC. NO. | POST. REF. | DEBIT | CREDIT | |
|---|---|---|---|---|---|---|---|---|
| 1 | | | | | | | | 1 |
| 2 | | | | | | | | 2 |
| 3 | | | | | | | | 3 |
| 4 | | | | | | | | 4 |
| 5 | | | | | | | | 5 |
| 6 | | | | | | | | 6 |
| 7 | | | | | | | | 7 |
| 8 | | | | | | | | 8 |
| 9 | | | | | | | | 9 |
| 10 | | | | | | | | 10 |
| 11 | | | | | | | | 11 |
| 12 | | | | | | | | 12 |
| 13 | | | | | | | | 13 |
| 14 | | | | | | | | 14 |
| 15 | | | | | | | | 15 |
| 16 | | | | | | | | 16 |
| 17 | | | | | | | | 17 |
| 18 | | | | | | | | 18 |
| 19 | | | | | | | | 19 |
| 20 | | | | | | | | 20 |
| 21 | | | | | | | | 21 |
| 22 | | | | | | | | 22 |
| 23 | | | | | | | | 23 |
| 24 | | | | | | | | 24 |
| 25 | | | | | | | | 25 |
| 26 | | | | | | | | 26 |
| 27 | | | | | | | | 27 |
| 28 | | | | | | | | 28 |
| 29 | | | | | | | | 29 |
| 30 | | | | | | | | 30 |
| 31 | | | | | | | | 31 |
| 32 | | | | | | | | 32 |

## 3-M MASTERY PROBLEM (LO2, 3, 4, 5), p. 88

**Completing payroll records, journalizing payment of a payroll, and journalizing payroll taxes**

**1.**

### COMMISSIONS RECORD

EMPLOYEE NO. _____     EMPLOYEE NAME _____

PAY PERIOD ENDED _____     REGULAR BIWEEKLY SALARY _____

DEPARTMENT _____     POSITION _____

|  | Carpet | Drapery |
|---|---|---|
| Sales on Account ................................................ | _____ | _____ |
| Cash and Credit Card Sales................................. | _____ | _____ |
| *equals* Total Sales for the Month........................... | _____ | _____ |
| | | |
| *Less:* | | |
| Sales Discounts.................................................. | _____ | _____ |
| Sales Returns and Allowances ............................ | _____ | _____ |
| *equals* Total Reductions in Sales ........................... | _____ | _____ |
| | | |
| *Equals:* | | |
| Net Sales ........................................................... | _____ | _____ |
| *times* Commission Rate.......................................... | _____ | _____ |
| *equals* Commission on Net Sales............................. | _____ | _____ |

## 4.

### EARNINGS RECORD FOR QUARTER ENDED

EMPLOYEE NO. _____  NAME _____

HOURLY WAGE _____  MARITAL STATUS _____  WITHHOLDING ALLOWANCES _____

SALARY _____  DEPARTMENT _____  POSITION _____

| PAY PERIOD | | TOTAL EARNINGS | DEDUCTIONS | | | | | | | NET PAY | ACCUMULATED EARNINGS |
| --- | --- | --- | --- | --- | --- | --- | --- | --- | --- | --- | --- |
| NO. | ENDED | 1 | FEDERAL INCOME TAX | STATE INCOME TAX | SOC. SEC. TAX | MEDICARE TAX | HEALTH INSURANCE | RETIREMENT PLAN | TOTAL | 9 | 10 |
| | | | 2 | 3 | 4 | 5 | 6 | 7 | 8 | | |
| 1 | | | | | | | | | | | |
| 2 | | | | | | | | | | | |
| TOTALS | | | | | | | | | | | |

## 2., 3.

### PAYROLL REGISTER

SEMIMONTHLY PERIOD ENDED _____  DATE OF PAYMENT _____

| EMPL. NO. | EMPLOYEE'S NAME | MARITAL STATUS | NO. OF ALLOWANCES | EARNINGS | | | | DEPARTMENT | | | DEDUCTIONS | | | | | | | NET PAY | CHECK NO. |
| --- | --- | --- | --- | --- | --- | --- | --- | --- | --- | --- | --- | --- | --- | --- | --- | --- | --- | --- | --- |
| | | | | REGULAR | OVERTIME | COMMISSION | TOTAL | CARPET | DRAPERY | ADMINISTRATIVE | FEDERAL INCOME TAX | STATE INCOME TAX | SOCIAL SECURITY TAX | MEDICARE TAX | HEALTH INSURANCE | RETIREMENT PLAN | TOTAL | | |
| | | | | 1 | 2 | 3 | 4 | 5 | 6 | 7 | 8 | 9 | 10 | 11 | 12 | 13 | 14 | 15 | |
| 1 | 16 Cannon, Ester A. | M | 4 | 1368 00 | | | 1368 00 | 1368 00 | | | 45 00 | 41 04 | 84 82 | 19 84 | 125 00 | 100 00 | 415 70 | 952 30 | 1 |
| 2 | 12 Guadalupe, Jorge P. | M | 3 | 1200 00 | | 612 15 | 1812 15 | 198 85 | 1613 30 | | 122 00 | 54 36 | 1112 35 | 26 28 | 100 00 | 50 00 | 464 99 | 1347 16 | 2 |
| 3 | 3 Miller, Tina S. | S | 2 | 1280 00 | 48 00 | | 1328 00 | | | 1328 00 | 125 00 | 39 84 | 82 34 | 19 26 | 75 00 | 125 00 | 466 44 | 861 56 | 3 |
| 4 | 18 Phung, Xuan T. | M | 3 | 952 00 | 21 00 | | 973 00 | 973 00 | | | 20 00 | 29 19 | 60 33 | 14 11 | 100 00 | 120 00 | 343 63 | 629 37 | 4 |
| 5 | | | | | | | | | | | | | | | | | | | 5 |
| 6 | | | | | | | | | | | | | | | | | | | 6 |
| 7 | | | | | | | | | | | | | | | | | | | 7 |
| 8 | | | | | | | | | | | | | | | | | | | 8 |

# 3-M  MASTERY PROBLEM (continued)

**5.**

| Department | Social Security Earnings | Social Security 6.2% | Medicare 1.45% | FUTA Earnings | Federal Unemployment 0.6% | State Unemployment 5.4% | Total Payroll Taxes |
|---|---|---|---|---|---|---|---|
| Carpet | | | | | | | |
| Drapery | | | | | | | |
| Administrative | | | | | | | |
| Total | | | | | | | |

## CASH PAYMENTS JOURNAL

PAGE

| | DATE | ACCOUNT TITLE | CK. NO. | POST. REF. | GENERAL DEBIT | GENERAL CREDIT | ACCOUNTS PAYABLE DEBIT | PURCH. DISCOUNT CR. CARPET | PURCH. DISCOUNT CR. TILE | CASH CREDIT | |
|---|---|---|---|---|---|---|---|---|---|---|---|
| 1 | | | | | | | | | | | 1 |
| 2 | | | | | | | | | | | 2 |
| 3 | | | | | | | | | | | 3 |
| 4 | | | | | | | | | | | 4 |
| 5 | | | | | | | | | | | 5 |
| 6 | | | | | | | | | | | 6 |
| 7 | | | | | | | | | | | 7 |
| 8 | | | | | | | | | | | 8 |
| 9 | | | | | | | | | | | 9 |
| 10 | | | | | | | | | | | 10 |
| 11 | | | | | | | | | | | 11 |
| 12 | | | | | | | | | | | 12 |
| 13 | | | | | | | | | | | 13 |
| 14 | | | | | | | | | | | 14 |
| 15 | | | | | | | | | | | 15 |

**6.**

GENERAL JOURNAL

PAGE

| | DATE | | ACCOUNT TITLE | DOC. NO. | POST. REF. | DEBIT | CREDIT | |
|---|---|---|---|---|---|---|---|---|
| 1 | | | | | | | | 1 |
| 2 | | | | | | | | 2 |
| 3 | | | | | | | | 3 |
| 4 | | | | | | | | 4 |
| 5 | | | | | | | | 5 |
| 6 | | | | | | | | 6 |
| 7 | | | | | | | | 7 |
| 8 | | | | | | | | 8 |
| 9 | | | | | | | | 9 |
| 10 | | | | | | | | 10 |
| 11 | | | | | | | | 11 |
| 12 | | | | | | | | 12 |
| 13 | | | | | | | | 13 |
| 14 | | | | | | | | 14 |
| 15 | | | | | | | | 15 |
| 16 | | | | | | | | 16 |
| 17 | | | | | | | | 17 |
| 18 | | | | | | | | 18 |
| 19 | | | | | | | | 19 |
| 20 | | | | | | | | 20 |
| 21 | | | | | | | | 21 |
| 22 | | | | | | | | 22 |
| 23 | | | | | | | | 23 |
| 24 | | | | | | | | 24 |
| 25 | | | | | | | | 25 |
| 26 | | | | | | | | 26 |
| 27 | | | | | | | | 27 |
| 28 | | | | | | | | 28 |
| 29 | | | | | | | | 29 |
| 30 | | | | | | | | 30 |
| 31 | | | | | | | | 31 |
| 32 | | | | | | | | 32 |

## 3-S SOURCE DOCUMENTS PROBLEM (LO1, 2, 3, 4, 5), p. 89

**Completing payroll records, journalizing payment of a payroll, and journalizing payroll taxes**

### Hourly Employee Time Summary

Pay Period: 6/25/20-- to 7/9/20--
Prepared on: 7/11/20--

| Name | Department | ID | Week Ended | Regular | Overtime | Totals |
|---|---|---|---|---|---|---|
| Dobbins, Clint A. | Windows | 3 | 6/25/20-- | 40 | 3 | 43 |
| | | | 7/9/20-- | 36 | | 36 |
| | | | | 76 | 3 | 79 |
| Godfrey, Betty S. | Doors | 2 | 6/25/20-- | 40 | | 40 |
| | | | 7/9/20-- | 40 | | 40 |
| | | | | 80 | | 80 |
| Rainwater, Chanta P. | Administrative | 12 | 6/25/20-- | 40 | 2 | 42 |
| | | | 7/9/20-- | 40 | 3 | 43 |
| | | | | 80 | 5 | 85 |

## COMMISSION SALES REPORT

Month: June

Prepared on: 7/11/20--

| Name | Account Title | Doors | Windows |
|------|---------------|-------|---------|
| Pizzo, Daniel C. | Sales on Account | 5,108.62 | 2,194.16 |
| | Cash and Credit Card Sales | 1,618.31 | 548.94 |
| | Sales Discounts | 99.08 | 33.37 |
| | Sales Returns and Allowances | 219.39 | 148.34 |
| | Commission Rate | 6% | 2% |
| Verdell, May E. | Sales on Account | 1,058.38 | 8,514.16 |
| | Cash and Credit Card Sales | 947.11 | 3,491.36 |
| | Sales Discounts | 19.25 | 124.15 |
| | Sales Returns and Allowances | 108.74 | 615.74 |
| | Commission Rate | 6% | 8% |

## Personnel Report

Prepared on: 7/11/20--

| ID | Name | Position | Marital Status | Number of Allowances | Hourly Wage Rate | Biweekly Salary | Retirement Contribution |
|----|------|----------|----------------|----------------------|------------------|-----------------|-------------------------|
| 3 | Dobbins, Clint A. | Windows Clerk | S | 1 | $ 16.00 | $ — | $ 60.00 |
| 2 | Godfrey, Betty S. | Doors Clerk | M | 1 | 18.00 | — | 80.00 |
| 8 | Pizzo, Daniel C. | Doors Manager | M | 2 | — | 1,200.00 | 200.00 |
| 12 | Rainwater, Chanta P. | Accountant | M | 4 | 22.00 | — | 90.00 |
| 10 | Verdell, May E. | Windows Manager | S | 3 | — | 900.00 | 150.00 |

**3-S    SOURCE DOCUMENTS PROBLEM (continued)**

NO. **905**          $ *5,260.02* _____

Date: *7/13* _____ 20 _-_

To: *First National Bank* _____

For: *July 9 payroll* _____

| | | |
|---|---|---|
| BALANCE BROUGHT FORWARD | 9,148 | 15 |
| AMOUNT DEPOSITED | | |
| SUBTOTAL          Date | 9,148 | 15 |
| OTHER: | | |
| _____ | | |
| _____ | | |
| SUBTOTAL | 9,148 | 15 |
| AMOUNT THIS CHECK | 5,260 | 02 |
| BALANCE CARRIED FORWARD | 3,888 | 13 |

NO. **916**          $ *335.61* _____

Date: *7/30* _____ 20 _-_

To: _____

For: *State unemployment taxes for second* _____
*quarter* _____

| | | |
|---|---|---|
| BALANCE BROUGHT FORWARD | 10,894 | 16 |
| AMOUNT DEPOSITED  7 29 -- | 1,511 | 15 |
| SUBTOTAL          Date | 12,405 | 31 |
| OTHER: | | |
| _____ | | |
| _____ | | |
| SUBTOTAL | 12,405 | 31 |
| AMOUNT THIS CHECK | 335 | 61 |
| BALANCE CARRIED FORWARD | 12,069 | 70 |

| No. 65 | **Exterior Design** |
|---|---|
| | **MEMORANDUM** |

*Employer payroll taxes for the July 9, 20-- pay period.*

*See attached analysis.*

| No. 66 | **Exterior Design** |
|---|---|
| | **MEMORANDUM** |

*Made deposit using the EFTPS for employee and employer payroll taxes for the June pay periods: employee federal income tax withholding, $1,098.00; social security tax, $2,119.75; and Medicare tax, $495.75.*

| No. 72 | **Exterior Design** |
|---|---|
| | **MEMORANDUM** |

*Made deposit using the EFTPS for federal unemployment taxes for January to June, $506.61.*

**3-S  SOURCE DOCUMENTS PROBLEM (continued)**

**1.**

---

### COMMISSIONS RECORD

EMPLOYEE NO. _____  EMPLOYEE NAME _____

PAY PERIOD ENDED _____  REGULAR BIWEEKLY SALARY _____

DEPARTMENT _____  POSITION _____

| | Doors | Windows |
|---|---|---|
| Sales on Account ......................................................... | _____ | _____ |
| Cash and Credit Card Sales ...................................... | _____ | _____ |
| *equals* Total Sales for the Month............................. | _____ | _____ |
| *Less:* | | |
| Sales Discounts.......................................................... | _____ | _____ |
| Sales Returns and Allowances ................................. | _____ | _____ |
| *equals* Total Reductions in Sales ............................. | _____ | _____ |
| *Equals:* | | |
| Net Sales .................................................................... | _____ | _____ |
| *times* Commission Rate............................................. | _____ | _____ |
| *equals* Commission on Net Sales............................. | _____ | _____ |

---

## COMMISSIONS RECORD

EMPLOYEE NO. _____     EMPLOYEE NAME _____

PAY PERIOD ENDED _____     REGULAR BIWEEKLY SALARY _____

DEPARTMENT _____     POSITION _____

| | Doors | Windows | |
|---|---|---|---|
| Sales on Account .......................................... | _____ | _____ | |
| Cash and Credit Card Sales .......................... | _____ | _____ | |
| *equals* Total Sales for the Month ................... | _____ | _____ | |
| | | | |
| *Less:* | | | |
| Sales Discounts ............................................ | _____ | _____ | |
| Sales Returns and Allowances ...................... | _____ | _____ | |
| *equals* Total Reductions in Sales .................. | _____ | _____ | |
| | | | |
| *Equals:* | | | |
| Net Sales ..................................................... | _____ | _____ | |
| *times* Commission Rate ............................... | _____ | _____ | _____ |
| *equals* Commission on Net Sales ................. | _____ | _____ | _____ |

## 3-S SOURCE DOCUMENTS PROBLEM (continued)

**2.**

PAYROLL REGISTER

SEMIMONTHLY PERIOD ENDED _____  DATE OF PAYMENT _____

| EMPL. NO. | EMPLOYEE'S NAME | MARITAL STATUS | NO. OF ALLOWANCES | EARNINGS 1 REGULAR | EARNINGS 2 OVERTIME | EARNINGS 3 COMMIS- SION | EARNINGS 4 TOTAL | DEPARTMENT 5 DOORS | DEPARTMENT 6 WINDOWS | 7 ADMINIS- TRATIVE | DEDUCTIONS 8 FEDERAL INCOME TAX | DEDUCTIONS 9 STATE INCOME TAX | DEDUCTIONS 10 SOCIAL SECURITY TAX | DEDUCTIONS 11 MEDICARE TAX | DEDUCTIONS 12 HEALTH INSURANCE | DEDUCTIONS 13 RETIRE- MENT PLAN | 14 TOTAL | 15 NET PAY | CHECK NO. |
|---|---|---|---|---|---|---|---|---|---|---|---|---|---|---|---|---|---|---|---|
| 3 | Dobbins, Clint A. | S | 1 | | | | | | | | | | | | | | | | 1 |
| 2 | Godfrey, Betty S. | M | 1 | | | | | | | | | | | | | | | | 2 |
| 8 | Pizzo, Daniel C. | M | 2 | | | | | | | | | | | | | | | | 3 |
| 12 | Rainwater, Chanta P. | M | 4 | | | | | | | | | | | | | | | | 4 |
| 10 | Verdell, May E. | S | 3 | | | | | | | | | | | | | | | | 5 |
| | | | | | | | | | | | | | | | | | | | 6 |
| | | | | | | | | | | | | | | | | | | | 7 |
| | | | | | | | | | | | | | | | | | | | 8 |
| | | | | | | | | | | | | | | | | | | | 9 |
| | | | | | | | | | | | | | | | | | | | 10 |
| | | | | | | | | | | | | | | | | | | | 11 |
| | | | | | | | | | | | | | | | | | | | 12 |
| | | | | | | | | | | | | | | | | | | | 13 |
| | | | | | | | | | | | | | | | | | | | 14 |
| | | | | | | | | | | | | | | | | | | | 15 |
| | | | | | | | | | | | | | | | | | | | 16 |
| | | | | | | | | | | | | | | | | | | | 17 |

**3.**

## EARNINGS RECORD FOR QUARTER ENDED — September 30, 20--

EMPLOYEE NO. 3    NAME Dobbins, Clint A.    MARITAL STATUS S    WITHHOLDING ALLOWANCES 1

HOURLY WAGE $16.00    DEPARTMENT Windows    POSITION Clerk

| PAY PERIOD | | | DEDUCTIONS | | | | | | | |
| NO. | ENDED | 1. TOTAL EARNINGS | 2. FEDERAL INCOME TAX | 3. STATE INCOME TAX | 4. SOC. SEC. TAX | 5. MEDICARE TAX | 6. HEALTH INSURANCE | 7. RETIREMENT PLAN | 8. TOTAL | 9. NET PAY | 10. ACCUMULATED EARNINGS |
|---|---|---|---|---|---|---|---|---|---|---|---|
| 1 | | | | | | | | | | | 2560 00 |
| 2 | | | | | | | | | | | |
| TOTALS | | | | | | | | | | | |

## EARNINGS RECORD FOR QUARTER ENDED — September 30, 20--

EMPLOYEE NO. 2    NAME Godfrey, Betty S.    MARITAL STATUS M    WITHHOLDING ALLOWANCES 1

HOURLY WAGE $18.00    DEPARTMENT Doors    POSITION Clerk

| PAY PERIOD | | | DEDUCTIONS | | | | | | | |
| NO. | ENDED | 1. TOTAL EARNINGS | 2. FEDERAL INCOME TAX | 3. STATE INCOME TAX | 4. SOC. SEC. TAX | 5. MEDICARE TAX | 6. HEALTH INSURANCE | 7. RETIREMENT PLAN | 8. TOTAL | 9. NET PAY | 10. ACCUMULATED EARNINGS |
|---|---|---|---|---|---|---|---|---|---|---|---|
| 1 | | | | | | | | | | | 16081 00 |
| 2 | | | | | | | | | | | |
| TOTALS | | | | | | | | | | | |

## EARNINGS RECORD FOR QUARTER ENDED — September 30, 20--

EMPLOYEE NO. 8    NAME Pizzo, Daniel C.    MARITAL STATUS M    WITHHOLDING ALLOWANCES 2

HOURLY WAGE    SALARY $1,200.00    DEPARTMENT Doors    POSITION Manager

| PAY PERIOD | | | DEDUCTIONS | | | | | | | |
| NO. | ENDED | 1. TOTAL EARNINGS | 2. FEDERAL INCOME TAX | 3. STATE INCOME TAX | 4. SOC. SEC. TAX | 5. MEDICARE TAX | 6. HEALTH INSURANCE | 7. RETIREMENT PLAN | 8. TOTAL | 9. NET PAY | 10. ACCUMULATED EARNINGS |
|---|---|---|---|---|---|---|---|---|---|---|---|
| 1 | | | | | | | | | | | 19628 88 |
| 2 | | | | | | | | | | | |
| TOTALS | | | | | | | | | | | |

**3-S  SOURCE DOCUMENTS PROBLEM (continued)**

## EARNINGS RECORD FOR QUARTER ENDED _____

EMPLOYEE NO. _____  NAME _____  MARITAL STATUS _____  WITHHOLDING ALLOWANCES _____

HOURLY WAGE _____  SALARY _____  DEPARTMENT _____  POSITION _____

| PAY PERIOD | | 1 TOTAL EARNINGS | 2 FEDERAL INCOME TAX | 3 STATE INCOME TAX | 4 SOC. SEC. TAX | 5 MEDICARE TAX | 6 HEALTH INSURANCE | 7 RETIREMENT PLAN | 8 TOTAL | 9 NET PAY | 10 ACCUMULATED EARNINGS |
|---|---|---|---|---|---|---|---|---|---|---|---|
| NO. | ENDED | | | | | | | | | | |
| 1 | | | | | | | | | | | 1 2 0 0 00 |
| 2 | | | | | | | | | | | |
| TOTALS | | | | | | | | | | | |

## EARNINGS RECORD FOR QUARTER ENDED _____

EMPLOYEE NO. _____  NAME _____  MARITAL STATUS _____  WITHHOLDING ALLOWANCES _____

HOURLY WAGE _____  SALARY _____  DEPARTMENT _____  POSITION _____

| PAY PERIOD | | 1 TOTAL EARNINGS | 2 FEDERAL INCOME TAX | 3 STATE INCOME TAX | 4 SOC. SEC. TAX | 5 MEDICARE TAX | 6 HEALTH INSURANCE | 7 RETIREMENT PLAN | 8 TOTAL | 9 NET PAY | 10 ACCUMULATED EARNINGS |
|---|---|---|---|---|---|---|---|---|---|---|---|
| NO. | ENDED | | | | | | | | | | |
| 1 | | | | | | | | | | | 20 1 4 3 50 |
| 2 | | | | | | | | | | | |
| TOTALS | | | | | | | | | | | |

**4.**

| Department | Social Security Earnings | Social Security 6.2% | Medicare 1.45% | FUTA Earnings | Federal Unemployment 0.6% | State Unemployment 5.4% | Total Payroll Taxes |
|---|---|---|---|---|---|---|---|
| Doors | | | | | | | |
| Windows | | | | | | | |
| Administrative | | | | | | | |
| Total | | | | | | | |

**5.**

CASH PAYMENTS JOURNAL

PAGE 12

| | | | | | 1 | 2 | 3 | 4 | 5 | 6 | |
|---|---|---|---|---|---|---|---|---|---|---|---|
| | | | | | GENERAL | GENERAL | ACCOUNTS PAYABLE DEBIT | PURCH. DISCOUNT CR. | PURCH. DISCOUNT CR. | CASH CREDIT | |
| DATE | ACCOUNT TITLE | CK. NO. | POST. REF. | | DEBIT | CREDIT | | WINDOWS | DOORS | | |
| | | | | 1 | | | | | | | 1 |
| | | | | 2 | | | | | | | 2 |
| | | | | 3 | | | | | | | 3 |
| | | | | 4 | | | | | | | 4 |
| | | | | 5 | | | | | | | 5 |
| | | | | 6 | | | | | | | 6 |
| | | | | 7 | | | | | | | 7 |
| | | | | 8 | | | | | | | 8 |
| | | | | 9 | | | | | | | 9 |
| | | | | 10 | | | | | | | 10 |
| | | | | 11 | | | | | | | 11 |
| | | | | 12 | | | | | | | 12 |
| | | | | 13 | | | | | | | 13 |
| | | | | 14 | | | | | | | 14 |
| | | | | 15 | | | | | | | 15 |

## 3-S SOURCE DOCUMENTS PROBLEM (concluded)

**5.**

GENERAL JOURNAL

| | DATE | ACCOUNT TITLE | DOC. NO. | POST. REF. | DEBIT | CREDIT | |
|---|---|---|---|---|---|---|---|
| 1 | | | | | | | 1 |
| 2 | | | | | | | 2 |
| 3 | | | | | | | 3 |
| 4 | | | | | | | 4 |
| 5 | | | | | | | 5 |
| 6 | | | | | | | 6 |
| 7 | | | | | | | 7 |
| 8 | | | | | | | 8 |
| 9 | | | | | | | 9 |
| 10 | | | | | | | 10 |
| 11 | | | | | | | 11 |
| 12 | | | | | | | 12 |
| 13 | | | | | | | 13 |
| 14 | | | | | | | 14 |
| 15 | | | | | | | 15 |
| 16 | | | | | | | 16 |
| 17 | | | | | | | 17 |
| 18 | | | | | | | 18 |
| 19 | | | | | | | 19 |
| 20 | | | | | | | 20 |
| 21 | | | | | | | 21 |
| 22 | | | | | | | 22 |
| 23 | | | | | | | 23 |
| 24 | | | | | | | 24 |
| 25 | | | | | | | 25 |
| 26 | | | | | | | 26 |
| 27 | | | | | | | 27 |
| 28 | | | | | | | 28 |
| 29 | | | | | | | 29 |
| 30 | | | | | | | 30 |
| 31 | | | | | | | 31 |
| 32 | | | | | | | 32 |

**Calculating federal income tax withholdings using the percentage method**

| Employee | Earnings | Marital Status | Number of Allowances | Withholding Allowance | Earnings Subject to Withholding | Minimum Tax | Additional Tax | Total Tax |
|---|---|---|---|---|---|---|---|---|
| Atkinson | $4,000.00 | M | 3 | $450.00 | $3,550.00 | $384.00 | $110.50 | $494.50 |
| Cooper | 4,041.00 | M | 5 | | | ___ | ___ | ___ |
| Futral | 4,306.00 | S | 1 | | | ___ | ___ | ___ |
| Lowery | 3,492.00 | M | 3 | | | ___ | ___ | ___ |
| Pettit | 3,383.00 | S | 2 | | | ___ | ___ | ___ |
| Saenz | 4,851.00 | M | 2 | | | | | |

| Name | Perfect Score | Your Score |
|---|---|---|
| Identifying Accounting Terms | 36 Pts. | |
| Analyzing Departmental Adjusting and Closing Entries | 22 Pts. | |
| Analyzing Financial Reporting Procedures for a Departmentalized Business | 10 Pts. | |
| **Total** | 68 Pts. | |

## Part One—Identifying Accounting Terms

**Directions:** Select the one term in Column I that best fits each definition in Column II. Print the letter identifying your choice in the Answers column.

*Contains accounting terms for Lesson 4-1.*

| Column I | Column II | Answers |
|---|---|---|
| A. adjusted trial balance | **1.** The length of time for which a business summarizes its financial information and reports its financial performance. (p. 96) | 1._____ |
| B. adjusting entries | **2.** A fiscal period consisting of 12 consecutive months. (p. 96) | 2._____ |
| C. depreciation expense | **3.** A listing of customer accounts, account balances, and total amount due from all customers. (p. 97) | 3._____ |
| D. fiscal period | **4.** A listing of vendor accounts, account balances, and the total amount due all vendors. (p. 97) | 4._____ |
| E. fiscal year | **5.** A proof of the equality of debits and credits in a general ledger. (p. 98) | 5._____ |
| F. marginal tax rate | **6.** Journal entries recorded to update general ledger accounts at the end of a fiscal period. (p. 98) | 6._____ |
| G. plant assets | **7.** A trial balance prepared before adjusting entries are posted. (p. 98) | 7._____ |
| H. schedule of accounts payable | **8.** Physical assets that will be used for a number of years in the operation of a business. (p. 102) | 8._____ |
| I. schedule of accounts receivable | **9.** The portion of a plant asset's cost that is transferred to an expense account in each fiscal period during that asset's useful life. (p. 102) | 9._____ |
| J. tax bracket | **10.** A trial balance prepared after adjusting entries are posted. (p. 103) | 10._____ |
| K. trial balance | **11.** Each tax rate and taxable income amount on one line of a tax table. (p. 104) | 11._____ |
| L. unadjusted trial balance | **12.** The tax rate associated with a tax bracket. (p. 104) | 12._____ |
| M. work sheet | **13.** A columnar accounting form used to summarize the general ledger information needed to prepare financial statements. (p. 106) | 13._____ |

*Accounting terms for Lessons 4-2 through 4-4 are presented on the following page.*

**Directions:** Select the one term in Column I that best fits each definition in Column II.
Print the letter identifying your choice in the Answers column.

*Contains accounting terms for Lessons 4-2 through 4-4.*

| Column I | Column II | Answers |
|---|---|---|
| A. accounting cycle | 1. Assigning control of revenues, costs, and expenses to a specific manager. (p. 108) | 1._____ |
| B. balance sheet | 2. An operating expense identifiable with and chargeable to the operation of a specific department. (p. 108) | 2._____ |
| C. capital stock | 3. An operating expense chargeable to overall business operations and not identifiable with a specific department. (p. 108) | 3._____ |
| D. cash flow | 4. Financial statements reporting revenue, costs, and direct expenses under a specific department's control. (p. 109) | 4._____ |
| E. closing entries | 5. The revenue earned by a department less its cost of merchandise sold and less its direct expenses. (p. 109) | 5._____ |
| F. departmental margin | 6. A statement that reports departmental margin for a specific department. (p. 109) | 6._____ |
| G. departmental margin statement | 7. The operating revenue remaining after cost of merchandise sold has been deducted. (p. 109) | 7._____ |
| H. direct expense | 8. A comparison between two components of financial information. (p. 110) | 8._____ |
| I. dividends | 9. Reporting an amount on a financial statement as a percentage of another item on the same financial statement. (p. 110) | 9._____ |
| J. financial ratio | 10. A financial statement showing the revenue and expenses for a fiscal period. (p. 112) | 10._____ |
| K. financing activities | 11. A financial statement that shows changes in a corporation's ownership for a fiscal period. (p. 113) | 11._____ |
| L. gross profit | 12. Total shares of ownership in a corporation. (p. 113) | 12._____ |
| M. income statement | 13. An amount earned by a corporation and not yet distributed to stockholders. (p. 113) | 13._____ |
| N. indirect expense | 14. Earnings distributed to stockholders. (p. 113) | 14._____ |
| O. investing activities | 15. A financial statement that reports assets, liabilities, and owners' equity on a specific date. (p. 114) | 15._____ |
| P. operating activities | 16. The cash receipts and cash payments of a company. (p. 115) | 16._____ |
| Q. post-closing trial balance | 17. A financial statement that summarizes cash receipts and cash payments resulting from business activities during a fiscal period. (p. 115) | 17._____ |
| R. responsibility accounting | 18. The cash receipts and payments necessary to operate a business on a day-to-day basis. (p. 115) | 18._____ |
| S. responsibility statements | 19. Cash receipts and cash payments involving the sale or purchase of assets used to earn revenue over a period of time. (p. 115) | 19._____ |
| T. retained earnings | 20. Cash receipts and payments involving debt or equity transactions. (p. 115) | 20._____ |
| U. statement of cash flows | 21. Journal entries used to prepare temporary accounts for a new fiscal period. (p. 117) | 21._____ |
| V. statement of stockholders'equity | 22. A trial balance prepared after the closing entries are posted. (p. 120) | 22._____ |
| W. vertical analysis | 23. The series of accounting activities included in recording financial information for a fiscal period. (p. 121) | 23._____ |

## Part Two—Analyzing Departmental Adjusting and Closing Entries

**Directions:** For each transaction below, print in the proper Answers column the identifying letters of the accounts or descriptions of those accounts to be debited and credited.

| Account Titles | Transactions | Answers Debit | Credit |
|---|---|---|---|

**Account Titles**

A. Accum. Depr.—Equipment

B. Allow. for Uncoll. Accounts

C. departmental contra cost accounts

D. departmental contra revenue accounts

E. departmental cost accounts

F. departmental income summary

G. departmental merchandise inventory accounts

H. departmental sales accounts

I. Depr. Expense—Equipment

J. Dividends

K. expense accounts

L. Federal Income Tax Expense

M. Federal Income Tax Payable

N. Income Summary—General

O. Insurance Expense

P. Prepaid Insurance

Q. Retained Earnings

R. Supplies

S. Supplies Expense

T. Uncollectible Accounts Expense

**Transactions** — **Answers: Debit / Credit**

1. Adjust Allowance for Uncollectible Accounts. (p. 99) — 1._____ 2._____

2. Adjust ending merchandise inventory (increase). (p. 100) — 3._____ 4._____

3. Adjust ending merchandise inventory (decrease). (p. 100) — 5._____ 6._____

4. Adjust Supplies. (p. 101) — 7._____ 8._____

5. Adjust Prepaid Insurance. (p. 101) — 9._____ 10._____

6. Adjust Depr. Expense—Equipment. (p. 102) — 11._____ 12._____

7. Adjust Federal Income Tax Payable. (p. 104) — 13._____ 14._____

8. Close departmental income statement accounts (credit balances), sales, and contra cost accounts. (p. 117) — 15._____ 16._____

9. Close departmental income statement accounts (debit balances), contra revenue, cost, and expense accounts. (p. 118) — 17._____ 18._____

10. Close Income Summary—General account (assume a net income). (p. 119) — 19._____ 20._____

11. Close Dividends. (p. 120) — 21._____ 22._____

## Part Three—Analyzing Financial Reporting Procedures for a Departmentalized Business

**Directions:** Place a *T* for True or an *F* for False in the Answers column to show whether each of the following statements is true or false.

1. A common length of time for a fiscal period is one year. (p. 96)      1. _____

2. Adjusting entries are posted to the general ledger before an adjusted trial balance is prepared. (p. 103)      2. _____

3. The cost of supplies used by a specific department is an example of a direct expense. (p. 108)      3. _____

4. The cost of electricity used by a business's overall operations is an example of a direct expense. (p. 108)      4. _____

5. A departmental statement of gross profit provides a manager with information about revenue and costs for each department. (p. 109)      5. _____

6. Vertical analysis ratios in a departmentalized business are used to analyze the financial results for each department. (p. 110)      6. _____

7. Purchasing merchandise is an example of an operating activity as reported on a statement of cash flows. (p. 115)      7. _____

8. Cash receipts and payments involving debt and equity transactions are examples of investing activities as reported on a statement of cash flows. (p. 115)      8. _____

9. After the second closing entry, the Income Summary—General account balance should be equal to the net income (or net loss) for the fiscal period. (p. 119)      9. _____

10. A departmentalized business does not need to prepare a post-closing trial balance. (p. 120)      10. _____

**4-1** **WORK TOGETHER, p. 107**

**Preparing an adjusted trial balance**

**1., 2., 4.**

### GENERAL JOURNAL

PAGE _____

| | DATE | ACCOUNT TITLE | DOC. NO. | POST. REF. | DEBIT | CREDIT | |
|----|------|---------------|----------|-----------|-------|--------|----|
| 1 | | | | | | | 1 |
| 2 | | | | | | | 2 |
| 3 | | | | | | | 3 |
| 4 | | | | | | | 4 |
| 5 | | | | | | | 5 |
| 6 | | | | | | | 6 |
| 7 | | | | | | | 7 |
| 8 | | | | | | | 8 |
| 9 | | | | | | | 9 |
| 10 | | | | | | | 10 |
| 11 | | | | | | | 11 |
| 12 | | | | | | | 12 |
| 13 | | | | | | | 13 |
| 14 | | | | | | | 14 |
| 15 | | | | | | | 15 |
| 16 | | | | | | | 16 |
| 17 | | | | | | | 17 |
| 18 | | | | | | | 18 |

**4.**

| Net Income before Federal Income Taxes | − | Tax Bracket Minimum Taxable Income | = | Net Income Subject to Marginal Tax Rate |
|---|---|---|---|---|
| $ | − | $ | = | $ |

| Net Income Subject to Marginal Tax Rate | × | Marginal Tax Rate | = | Marginal Income Tax |
|---|---|---|---|---|
| $ | × | | = | $ |

| Bracket Minimum Income Tax | + | Marginal Income Tax | = | Federal Income Tax |
|---|---|---|---|---|
| $ | + | $ | = | $ |

**2., 4.** **GENERAL LEDGER**

ACCOUNT Allowance for Uncollectible Accounts ACCOUNT NO. 1210

| DATE | | ITEM | POST. REF. | DEBIT | CREDIT | BALANCE | |
|------|---|------|------------|-------|--------|---------|---|
| | | | | | | DEBIT | CREDIT |
| 20-- Dec. | 31 | Balance | ✔ | | | | 7 7 38 |
| | | | | | | | |
| | | | | | | | |

ACCOUNT Merchandise Inventory—Kitchen ACCOUNT NO. 1305

| DATE | | ITEM | POST. REF. | DEBIT | CREDIT | BALANCE | |
|------|---|------|------------|-------|--------|---------|---|
| | | | | | | DEBIT | CREDIT |
| 20-- Dec. | 31 | Balance | ✔ | | | 140 8 9 0 00 | |
| | | | | | | | |
| | | | | | | | |

ACCOUNT Merchandise Inventory—Bath ACCOUNT NO. 1310

| DATE | | ITEM | POST. REF. | DEBIT | CREDIT | BALANCE | |
|------|---|------|------------|-------|--------|---------|---|
| | | | | | | DEBIT | CREDIT |
| 20-- Dec. | 31 | Balance | ✔ | | | 98 6 2 0 00 | |
| | | | | | | | |
| | | | | | | | |

ACCOUNT Supplies ACCOUNT NO. 1405

| DATE | | ITEM | POST. REF. | DEBIT | CREDIT | BALANCE | |
|------|---|------|------------|-------|--------|---------|---|
| | | | | | | DEBIT | CREDIT |
| 20-- Dec. | 31 | Balance | ✔ | | | 6 0 9 7 89 | |
| | | | | | | | |
| | | | | | | | |

ACCOUNT Prepaid Insurance ACCOUNT NO. 1410

| DATE | | ITEM | POST. REF. | DEBIT | CREDIT | BALANCE | |
|------|---|------|------------|-------|--------|---------|---|
| | | | | | | DEBIT | CREDIT |
| 20-- Dec. | 31 | Balance | ✔ | | | 18 0 0 0 00 | |
| | | | | | | | |
| | | | | | | | |

ACCOUNT Accumulated Depreciation—Office Equipment                    ACCOUNT NO. 1510

| DATE | ITEM | POST. REF. | DEBIT | CREDIT | BALANCE DEBIT | BALANCE CREDIT |
|------|------|-----------|-------|--------|-------|--------|
| 20-- Dec. 31 | Balance | ✔ | | | | 11 4 2 4 00 |
| | | | | | | |
| | | | | | | |

ACCOUNT Accumulated Depreciation—Store Equipment                    ACCOUNT NO. 1520

| DATE | ITEM | POST. REF. | DEBIT | CREDIT | BALANCE DEBIT | BALANCE CREDIT |
|------|------|-----------|-------|--------|-------|--------|
| 20-- Dec. 31 | Balance | ✔ | | | | 27 7 6 5 00 |
| | | | | | | |
| | | | | | | |

ACCOUNT Federal Income Tax Payable                    ACCOUNT NO. 2305

| DATE | ITEM | POST. REF. | DEBIT | CREDIT | BALANCE DEBIT | BALANCE CREDIT |
|------|------|-----------|-------|--------|-------|--------|
| | | | | | | |
| | | | | | | |
| | | | | | | |

ACCOUNT Income Summary—Kitchen                    ACCOUNT NO. 3210

| DATE | ITEM | POST. REF. | DEBIT | CREDIT | BALANCE DEBIT | BALANCE CREDIT |
|------|------|-----------|-------|--------|-------|--------|
| | | | | | | |
| | | | | | | |

ACCOUNT Income Summary—Bath                    ACCOUNT NO. 3215

| DATE | ITEM | POST. REF. | DEBIT | CREDIT | BALANCE DEBIT | BALANCE CREDIT |
|------|------|-----------|-------|--------|-------|--------|
| | | | | | | |
| | | | | | | |

ACCOUNT Depreciation Expense—Office Equipment                    ACCOUNT NO. 7110

| DATE | ITEM | POST. REF. | DEBIT | CREDIT | BALANCE | |
|------|------|-----------|-------|--------|---------|---|
| | | | | | DEBIT | CREDIT |
| | | | | | | |
| | | | | | | |

ACCOUNT Depreciation Expense—Store Equipment                    ACCOUNT NO. 7115

| DATE | ITEM | POST. REF. | DEBIT | CREDIT | BALANCE | |
|------|------|-----------|-------|--------|---------|---|
| | | | | | DEBIT | CREDIT |
| | | | | | | |
| | | | | | | |

ACCOUNT Insurance Expense                    ACCOUNT NO. 7120

| DATE | ITEM | POST. REF. | DEBIT | CREDIT | BALANCE | |
|------|------|-----------|-------|--------|---------|---|
| | | | | | DEBIT | CREDIT |
| | | | | | | |
| | | | | | | |

ACCOUNT Supplies Expense                    ACCOUNT NO. 7150

| DATE | ITEM | POST. REF. | DEBIT | CREDIT | BALANCE | |
|------|------|-----------|-------|--------|---------|---|
| | | | | | DEBIT | CREDIT |
| | | | | | | |
| | | | | | | |

ACCOUNT Uncollectible Accounts Expense                    ACCOUNT NO. 7155

| DATE | ITEM | POST. REF. | DEBIT | CREDIT | BALANCE | |
|------|------|-----------|-------|--------|---------|---|
| | | | | | DEBIT | CREDIT |
| | | | | | | |
| | | | | | | |

ACCOUNT Federal Income Tax Expense                    ACCOUNT NO. 8105

| DATE | ITEM | POST. REF. | DEBIT | CREDIT | BALANCE | |
|------|------|-----------|-------|--------|---------|---|
| | | | | | DEBIT | CREDIT |
| 20-- Dec. 31 | Balance | ✔ | | | 12 0 0 0 00 | |
| | | | | | | |
| | | | | | | |

## 4-1 WORK TOGETHER (continued)

**3., 5.**

Foley's Interiors

Adjusted Trial Balance

December 31, 20--

| ACCOUNT TITLE | DEBIT | CREDIT |
|---|---|---|
| Cash | 36 4 6 0 79 | |
| Petty Cash | 3 0 0 00 | |
| Accounts Receivable | 23 0 1 8 95 | |
| Allowance for Uncollectible Accounts | | |
| Merchandise Inventory—Kitchen | | |
| Merchandise Inventory—Bath | | |
| Supplies | | |
| Prepaid Insurance | | |
| Office Equipment | 26 0 1 5 89 | |
| Accumulated Depreciation—Office Equipment | | |
| Store Equipment | 51 8 5 2 82 | |
| Accumulated Depreciation—Store Equipment | | |
| Accounts Payable | | 24 1 1 6 31 |
| Sales Tax Payable | | 4 9 2 5 59 |
| Employee Income Tax Payable—Federal | | 1 3 3 5 44 |
| Employee Income Tax Payable—State | | 9 5 6 99 |
| Social Security Tax Payable | | 2 3 7 6 90 |
| Medicare Tax Payable | | 5 5 3 24 |
| Medical Insurance Payable | | 8 4 6 42 |
| Retirement Plan Payable | | 5 7 1 94 |
| Unemployment Tax Payable—Federal | | 1 6 72 |
| Unemployment Tax Payable—State | | 1 1 2 08 |
| Federal Income Tax Payable | | |
| Dividends Payable | | 4 0 0 0 00 |
| Capital Stock | | 75 0 0 0 00 |
| Retained Earnings | | 165 0 7 3 83 |
| Dividends | 16 0 0 0 00 | |
| Income Summary—General | | |
| Income Summary—Kitchen | | |
| Income Summary—Bath | | |

*(Note: Trial balance is continued on the next page.)*

Foley's Interiors

Adjusted Trial Balance (Concluded)

December 31, 20--

| ACCOUNT TITLE | DEBIT | CREDIT |
|---|---:|---:|
| Sales—Kitchen | | 417 953 07 |
| Sales Discount—Kitchen | 6 655 27 | |
| Sales Returns and Allowances—Kitchen | 7 634 77 | |
| Sales—Bath | | 316 014 76 |
| Sales Discount—Bath | 4 220 29 | |
| Sales Returns and Allowances—Bath | 11 070 52 | |
| Purchases—Kitchen | 204 164 91 | |
| Purchases Discount—Kitchen | | 2 505 71 |
| Purchases Returns and Allowances—Kitchen | | 4 925 52 |
| Purchases—Bath | 128 451 62 | |
| Purchases Discount—Bath | | 2 157 01 |
| Purchases Returns and Allowances—Bath | | 6 495 71 |
| Advertising Expense—Kitchen | 11 900 00 | |
| Payroll Taxes Expense—Kitchen | 5 193 25 | |
| Salary Expense—Kitchen | 59 121 95 | |
| Advertising Expense—Bath | 4 500 00 | |
| Payroll Taxes Expense—Bath | 7 028 66 | |
| Salary Expense—Bath | 81 103 91 | |
| Credit Card Fee Expense | 4 502 93 | |
| Depreciation Expense—Office Equipment | | |
| Depreciation Expense—Store Equipment | | |
| Insurance Expense | | |
| Miscellaneous Expense | 2 813 28 | |
| Payroll Taxes Expense—Administrative | 6 149 34 | |
| Rent Expense | 18 000 00 | |
| Salary Expense—Administrative | 71 001 51 | |
| Supplies Expense | | |
| Uncollectible Accounts Expense | | |
| Utilities Expense | 6 435 07 | |

## 4-1 ON YOUR OWN, p. 107

**Preparing an adjusted trial balance**

**1., 2., 4.**

GENERAL JOURNAL                                          PAGE ____

| | DATE | ACCOUNT TITLE | DOC. NO. | POST. REF. | DEBIT | CREDIT | |
|---|---|---|---|---|---|---|---|
| 1 | | | | | | | 1 |
| 2 | | | | | | | 2 |
| 3 | | | | | | | 3 |
| 4 | | | | | | | 4 |
| 5 | | | | | | | 5 |
| 6 | | | | | | | 6 |
| 7 | | | | | | | 7 |
| 8 | | | | | | | 8 |
| 9 | | | | | | | 9 |
| 10 | | | | | | | 10 |
| 11 | | | | | | | 11 |
| 12 | | | | | | | 12 |
| 13 | | | | | | | 13 |
| 14 | | | | | | | 14 |
| 15 | | | | | | | 15 |
| 16 | | | | | | | 16 |
| 17 | | | | | | | 17 |
| 18 | | | | | | | 18 |

**4.**

| Net Income before Federal Income Taxes | − | Tax Bracket Minimum Taxable Income | = | Net Income Subject to Marginal Tax Rate |
|---|---|---|---|---|
| $ | − | $ | = | $ |

| Net Income Subject to Marginal Tax Rate | × | Marginal Tax Rate | = | Marginal Income Tax |
|---|---|---|---|---|
| $ | × | | = | $ |

| Bracket Minimum Income Tax | + | Marginal Income Tax | = | Federal Income Tax |
|---|---|---|---|---|
| $ | + | $ | = | $ |

**2., 4.**             **GENERAL LEDGER**

ACCOUNT Allowance for Uncollectible Accounts      ACCOUNT NO. 1210

| DATE | ITEM | POST. REF. | DEBIT | CREDIT | BALANCE DEBIT | BALANCE CREDIT |
|------|------|-----------|-------|--------|-------|--------|
| Dec. 31 | Balance | ✔ | | | 1 4 8 36 | |

ACCOUNT Merchandise Inventory—Parts      ACCOUNT NO. 1305

| DATE | ITEM | POST. REF. | DEBIT | CREDIT | BALANCE DEBIT | BALANCE CREDIT |
|------|------|-----------|-------|--------|-------|--------|
| Dec. 31 | Balance | ✔ | | | 256 4 7 0 00 | |

ACCOUNT Merchandise Inventory—Accessories      ACCOUNT NO. 1310

| DATE | ITEM | POST. REF. | DEBIT | CREDIT | BALANCE DEBIT | BALANCE CREDIT |
|------|------|-----------|-------|--------|-------|--------|
| Dec. 31 | Balance | ✔ | | | 112 7 4 0 00 | |

ACCOUNT Supplies      ACCOUNT NO. 1405

| DATE | ITEM | POST. REF. | DEBIT | CREDIT | BALANCE DEBIT | BALANCE CREDIT |
|------|------|-----------|-------|--------|-------|--------|
| Dec. 31 | Balance | ✔ | | | 4 9 3 5 98 | |

ACCOUNT Prepaid Insurance      ACCOUNT NO. 1410

| DATE | ITEM | POST. REF. | DEBIT | CREDIT | BALANCE DEBIT | BALANCE CREDIT |
|------|------|-----------|-------|--------|-------|--------|
| Dec. 31 | Balance | ✔ | | | 15 0 0 0 00 | |

## 4-1 ON YOUR OWN (continued)

ACCOUNT Accumulated Depreciation—Office Equipment     ACCOUNT NO. 1510

| DATE | ITEM | POST. REF. | DEBIT | CREDIT | BALANCE DEBIT | BALANCE CREDIT |
|------|------|-----------|-------|--------|---------------|----------------|
| Dec. 31 | Balance | ✔ | | | | 9 1 4 5 86 |
| | | | | | | |
| | | | | | | |

ACCOUNT Accumulated Depreciation—Store Equipment     ACCOUNT NO. 1520

| DATE | ITEM | POST. REF. | DEBIT | CREDIT | BALANCE DEBIT | BALANCE CREDIT |
|------|------|-----------|-------|--------|---------------|----------------|
| Dec. 31 | Balance | ✔ | | | | 22 2 9 8 99 |
| | | | | | | |
| | | | | | | |

ACCOUNT Federal Income Tax Payable     ACCOUNT NO. 2305

| DATE | ITEM | POST. REF. | DEBIT | CREDIT | BALANCE DEBIT | BALANCE CREDIT |
|------|------|-----------|-------|--------|---------------|----------------|
| | | | | | | |
| | | | | | | |
| | | | | | | |
| | | | | | | |

ACCOUNT Income Summary—Parts     ACCOUNT NO. 3210

| DATE | ITEM | POST. REF. | DEBIT | CREDIT | BALANCE DEBIT | BALANCE CREDIT |
|------|------|-----------|-------|--------|---------------|----------------|
| | | | | | | |
| | | | | | | |
| | | | | | | |

ACCOUNT Income Summary—Accessories     ACCOUNT NO. 3215

| DATE | ITEM | POST. REF. | DEBIT | CREDIT | BALANCE DEBIT | BALANCE CREDIT |
|------|------|-----------|-------|--------|---------------|----------------|
| | | | | | | |
| | | | | | | |

ACCOUNT Depreciation Expense—Office Equipment        ACCOUNT NO. 7110

| DATE | ITEM | POST. REF. | DEBIT | CREDIT | BALANCE DEBIT | BALANCE CREDIT |
|------|------|------------|-------|--------|---------------|----------------|
|      |      |            |       |        |               |                |
|      |      |            |       |        |               |                |

ACCOUNT Depreciation Expense—Store Equipment        ACCOUNT NO. 7115

| DATE | ITEM | POST. REF. | DEBIT | CREDIT | BALANCE DEBIT | BALANCE CREDIT |
|------|------|------------|-------|--------|---------------|----------------|
|      |      |            |       |        |               |                |
|      |      |            |       |        |               |                |

ACCOUNT Insurance Expense        ACCOUNT NO. 7120

| DATE | ITEM | POST. REF. | DEBIT | CREDIT | BALANCE DEBIT | BALANCE CREDIT |
|------|------|------------|-------|--------|---------------|----------------|
|      |      |            |       |        |               |                |
|      |      |            |       |        |               |                |

ACCOUNT Supplies Expense        ACCOUNT NO. 7150

| DATE | ITEM | POST. REF. | DEBIT | CREDIT | BALANCE DEBIT | BALANCE CREDIT |
|------|------|------------|-------|--------|---------------|----------------|
|      |      |            |       |        |               |                |
|      |      |            |       |        |               |                |

ACCOUNT Uncollectible Accounts Expense        ACCOUNT NO. 7155

| DATE | ITEM | POST. REF. | DEBIT | CREDIT | BALANCE DEBIT | BALANCE CREDIT |
|------|------|------------|-------|--------|---------------|----------------|
|      |      |            |       |        |               |                |
|      |      |            |       |        |               |                |

ACCOUNT Federal Income Tax Expense        ACCOUNT NO. 8105

| DATE | ITEM | POST. REF. | DEBIT | CREDIT | BALANCE DEBIT | BALANCE CREDIT |
|------|------|------------|-------|--------|---------------|----------------|
| 20-- Dec. 31 | Balance | ✔ |  |  | 10 0 0 0 00 |  |
|      |      |            |       |        |               |                |

Name _____ Date _____ Class _____

**3., 5.**

Mixon Auto Supplies

Adjusted Trial Balance

December 31, 20--

| ACCOUNT TITLE | DEBIT | CREDIT |
|---|---|---|
| Cash | 61 3 5 4 03 | |
| Petty Cash | 2 4 1 66 | |
| Accounts Receivable | 18 5 3 3 67 | |
| Allowance for Uncollectible Accounts | | |
| Merchandise Inventory—Parts | | |
| Merchandise Inventory—Accessories | | |
| Supplies | | |
| Prepaid Insurance | | |
| Office Equipment | 20 8 2 7 76 | |
| Accumulated Depreciation—Office Equipment | | |
| Store Equipment | 41 5 3 1 75 | |
| Accumulated Depreciation—Store Equipment | | |
| Accounts Payable | | 19 3 0 1 35 |
| Sales Tax Payable | | 3 9 7 6 77 |
| Employee Income Tax Payable—Federal | | 1 0 8 0 01 |
| Employee Income Tax Payable—State | | 7 6 9 94 |
| Social Security Tax Payable | | 1 9 1 8 06 |
| Medicare Tax Payable | | 4 4 3 15 |
| Medical Plan Payable | | 6 8 2 54 |
| Retirement Plan Payable | | 4 5 8 39 |
| Unemployment Tax Payable—Federal | | 1 3 52 |
| Unemployment Tax Payable—State | | 9 0 64 |
| Federal Income Tax Payable | | |
| Dividends Payable | | 10 0 0 0 00 |
| Capital Stock | | 200 0 0 0 00 |
| Retained Earnings | | 204 2 6 5 75 |
| Dividends | 37 0 0 0 00 | |
| Income Summary—General | | |
| Income Summary—Parts | | |
| Income Summary—Accessories | | |

*(Note: Trial balance is continued on the next page.)*

Mixon Auto Supplies

Adjusted Trial Balance (Concluded)

December 31, 20--

| ACCOUNT TITLE | DEBIT | CREDIT |
|---|---:|---:|
| Sales—Parts | | 442 2 0 8 00 |
| Sales Discount—Parts | 5 3 4 6 15 | |
| Sales Returns and Allowances—Parts | 6 1 7 1 57 | |
| Sales—Accessories | | 255 3 8 0 00 |
| Sales Discount—Accessories | 3 3 7 8 04 | |
| Sales Returns and Allowances—Accessories | 8 9 1 7 49 | |
| Purchases—Parts | 201 7 6 5 00 | |
| Purchases Discount—Parts | | 2 0 1 9 21 |
| Purchases Returns and Allowances—Parts | | 3 9 6 0 33 |
| Purchases—Accessories | 140 4 8 1 19 | |
| Purchases Discount—Accessories | | 1 7 2 6 79 |
| Purchases Returns and Allowances—Accessories | | 6 2 1 6 27 |
| Advertising Expense—Parts | 6 2 0 0 00 | |
| Payroll Taxes Expense—Parts | 4 1 9 2 36 | |
| Salary Expense—Parts | 47 6 4 5 19 | |
| Advertising Expense—Accessories | 3 8 0 0 00 | |
| Payroll Taxes Expense—Accessories | 7 0 7 0 97 | |
| Salary Expense—Accessories | 81 5 5 4 20 | |
| Credit Card Fee Expense | 4 4 3 0 92 | |
| Depreciation Expense—Office Equipment | | |
| Depreciation Expense—Store Equipment | | |
| Insurance Expense | | |
| Miscellaneous Expense | 2 2 5 7 64 | |
| Payroll Taxes Expense—Administrative | 4 9 4 5 34 | |
| Rent Expense | 16 5 0 0 00 | |
| Salary Expense—Administrative | 57 0 5 7 83 | |
| Supplies Expense | | |
| Uncollectible Accounts Expense | | |
| Utilities Expense | 5 4 5 8 47 | |
| | | |
| | | |
| | | |

## 4-2 WORK TOGETHER, p. 111

**Preparing a departmental margin statement**

**1., 2.**

Foley's Interiors

Departmental Margin Statement—Kitchen

For Year Ended December 31, 20--

| | | % OF NET SALES* |
|---|---|---|
| Operating Revenue: | | |
|   Sales | | |
|   Less: Sales Discount | | |
|       Sales Returns and Allowances | | |
|   Net Sales | | |
| Cost of Merchandise Sold: | | |
|   Merchandise Inventory, Jan. 1, 20-- | | |
|   Purchases | | |
|   Less: Purchases Discount | | |
|       Purchases Returns and Allowances | | |
|   Net Purchases | | |
|   Total Cost of Merchandise Available for Sale | | |
|   Less Merchandise Inventory, Dec. 31, 20-- | | |
|   Cost of Merchandise Sold | | |
| Gross Profit | | |
| Direct Expenses: | | |
|   Advertising Expense | | |
|   Payroll Taxes Expense | | |
|   Salary Expense | | |
|   Total Direct Expenses | | |
| Departmental Margin | | |
| | | |
| *Rounded to the nearest 0.1%. | | |

Foley's Interiors

Departmental Margin Statement—Bath

For Year Ended December 31, 20--

| | | | | | % OF NET SALES* |
|---|---|---|---|---|---|
| Operating Revenue: | | | | | |
| Sales | | | | | |
| Less: Sales Discount | | | | | |
| Sales Returns and Allowances | | | | | |
| Net Sales | | | | | |
| Cost of Merchandise Sold: | | | | | |
| Merchandise Inventory, Jan. 1, 20-- | | | | | |
| Purchases | | | | | |
| Less: Purchases Discount | | | | | |
| Purchases Returns and Allowances | | | | | |
| Net Purchases | | | | | |
| Total Cost of Merchandise Available for Sale | | | | | |
| Less Merchandise Inventory, Dec. 31, 20-- | | | | | |
| Cost of Merchandise Sold | | | | | |
| Gross Profit | | | | | |
| Direct Expenses: | | | | | |
| Advertising Expense | | | | | |
| Payroll Taxes Expense | | | | | |
| Salary Expense | | | | | |
| Total Direct Expenses | | | | | |
| Departmental Margin | | | | | |
| | | | | | |
| *Rounded to the nearest 0.1%. | | | | | |

## 4-2 ON YOUR OWN, p. 111

**Preparing a departmental margin statement**

**1., 2.**

Mixon Auto Supplies

Departmental Margin Statement—Parts

For Year Ended December 31, 20--

| | | % OF NET SALES* |
|---|---|---|
| Operating Revenue: | | |
|   Sales | | |
|   Less: Sales Discount | | |
|       Sales Returns and Allowances | | |
|   Net Sales | | |
| Cost of Merchandise Sold: | | |
|   Merchandise Inventory, Jan. 1, 20-- | | |
|   Purchases | | |
|   Less: Purchases Discount | | |
|       Purchases Returns and Allowances | | |
|   Net Purchases | | |
|   Total Cost of Merchandise Available for Sale | | |
|   Less Merchandise Inventory, Dec. 31, 20-- | | |
|   Cost of Merchandise Sold | | |
| Gross Profit | | |
| Direct Expenses: | | |
|   Advertising Expense | | |
|   Payroll Taxes Expense | | |
|   Salary Expense | | |
|   Total Direct Expenses | | |
| Departmental Margin | | |
| | | |
| *Rounded to the nearest 0.1%. | | |

Mixon Auto Supplies

Departmental Margin Statement—Accessories

For Year Ended December 31, 20--

| | | | | | | % OF NET SALES* |
|---|---|---|---|---|---|---|
| Operating Revenue: | | | | | | |
| Sales | | | | | | |
| Less: Sales Discount | | | | | | |
| Sales Returns and Allowances | | | | | | |
| Net Sales | | | | | | |
| Cost of Merchandise Sold: | | | | | | |
| Merchandise Inventory, Jan. 1, 20-- | | | | | | |
| Purchases | | | | | | |
| Less: Purchases Discount | | | | | | |
| Purchases Returns and Allowances | | | | | | |
| Net Purchases | | | | | | |
| Total Cost of Merchandise Available for Sale | | | | | | |
| Less Merchandise Inventory, Dec. 31, 20-- | | | | | | |
| Cost of Merchandise Sold | | | | | | |
| Gross Profit | | | | | | |
| Direct Expenses: | | | | | | |
| Advertising Expense | | | | | | |
| Payroll Taxes Expense | | | | | | |
| Salary Expense | | | | | | |
| Total Direct Expenses | | | | | | |
| Departmental Margin | | | | | | |
| | | | | | | |
| *Rounded to the nearest 0.1%. | | | | | | |

## 4-3 WORK TOGETHER, p. 116

**Preparing financial statements**

**1.**

Foley's Interiors

Income Statement

For Year Ended December 31, 20--

| | DEPARTMENTAL | | COMPANY | % OF NET SALES* |
| | KITCHEN | BATH | | |
|---|---|---|---|---|
| Net Sales | | | | |
| Cost of Merchandise Sold | | | | |
| Gross Profit | | | | |
| Direct Expenses | | | | |
| Departmental Margin | | | | |
| Indirect Expenses: | | | | |
|   Credit Card Fee Expense | | | | |
|   Depreciation Expense—Office Equipment | | | | |
|   Depreciation Expense—Store Equipment | | | | |
|   Insurance Expense | | | | |
|   Miscellaneous Expense | | | | |
|   Payroll Taxes Expense | | | | |
|   Rent Expense | | | | |
|   Salary Expense—Administrative | | | | |
|   Supplies Expense | | | | |
|   Uncollectible Accounts Expense | | | | |
|   Utilities Expense | | | | |
|   Total Indirect Expenses | | | | |
| Income before Income Tax | | | | |
| Less Federal Income Tax Expense | | | | |
| Net Income | | | | |
| | | | | |
| *Rounded to the nearest 0.1%. | | | | |

**2.**

Foley's Interiors

Statement of Stockholders' Equity

For Year Ended December 31, 20--

| | | | | | | |
|---|---|---|---|---|---|---|
| Capital Stock: | | | | | | |
| | | | | | | |
| | | | | | | |
| | | | | | | |
| | | | | | | |
| Retained Earnings: | | | | | | |
|     Balance, January 1, 20-- | | | | | | |
|     Net Income for 20-- | | | | | | |
|     Less Dividends Declared during 20-- | | | | | | |
|     Net Increase during 20-- | | | | | | |
|     Balance, December 31, 20-- | | | | | | |
| Total Stockholders' Equity, December 31, 20-- | | | | | | |

**3.**

Foley's Interiors

Balance Sheet

December 31, 20--

| | | | | | | | % OF ASSETS* |
|---|---|---|---|---|---|---|---|
| Assets | | | | | | | |
| Current Assets: | | | | | | | |
|   Cash | | | | | | | |
|   Petty Cash | | | | | | | |
|   Accounts Receivable | | | | | | | |
|     Less Allowance for Uncollectible Accounts | | | | | | | |
|   Merchandise Inventory—Kitchen | | | | | | | |
|   Merchandise Inventory—Bath | | | | | | | |
|   Supplies | | | | | | | |
|   Prepaid Insurance | | | | | | | |
|   Total Current Assets | | | | | | | |
| Plant Assets: | | | | | | | |
|   Office Equipment | | | | | | | |
|     Less Accumulated Depreciation—Office Equipment | | | | | | | |
|   Store Equipment | | | | | | | |
|     Less Accumulated Depreciation—Store Equipment | | | | | | | |
|   Total Plant Assets | | | | | | | |
| Total Assets | | | | | | | |
| Liabilities | | | | | | | |
| Current Liabilities: | | | | | | | |
|   Accounts Payable | | | | | | | |
|   Sales Tax Payable | | | | | | | |
|   Employee Income Tax Payable—Federal | | | | | | | |
|   Employee Income Tax Payable—State | | | | | | | |
|   Social Security Tax Payable | | | | | | | |
|   Medicare Tax Payable | | | | | | | |
|   Medical Insurance Payable | | | | | | | |
|   Retirement Plan Payable | | | | | | | |
|   Unemployment Tax Payable—Federal | | | | | | | |
|   Unemployment Tax Payable—State | | | | | | | |
|   Federal Income Tax Payable | | | | | | | |
|   Dividends Payable | | | | | | | |
| Total Liabilities | | | | | | | |
| Stockholders' Equity | | | | | | | |
| Capital Stock | | | | | | | |
| Retained Earnings | | | | | | | |
| Total Stockholders' Equity | | | | | | | |
| Total Liabilities and Stockholders' Equity | | | | | | | |
| | | | | | | | |
| *Rounded to the nearest 0.1%. | | | | | | | |

**4.**

Foley's Interiors

Statement of Cash Flows

For Year Ended December 31, 20--

| | | | | | | |
|---|---|---|---|---|---|---|
| Cash flows from operating activities: | | | | | | |
| Cash receipts from customers | | | | | | |
| Cash payments for: | | | | | | |
| | | | | | | |
| | | | | | | |
| | | | | | | |
| | | | | | | |
| | | | | | | |
| Total cash payments | | | | | | |
| Net cash provided (used) by operating activities | | | | | | |
| Cash flows from investing activities: | | | | | | |
| | | | | | | |
| | | | | | | |
| Net cash provided (used) by investing activities | | | | | | |
| Cash flows from financing activities: | | | | | | |
| | | | | | | |
| | | | | | | |
| Net cash provided (used) by financing activities | | | | | | |
| Net change in cash | | | | | | |
| Cash balance, January 1, 20-- | | | | | | |
| Cash balance, December 31, 20-- | | | | | | |

# 4-3 ON YOUR OWN, p. 116

**Preparing financial statements**

**1.**

Mixon Auto Supplies

Income Statement

For Year Ended December 31, 20--

| | DEPARTMENTAL | | COMPANY | % OF NET SALES* |
| --- | --- | --- | --- | --- |
| | PARTS | ACCESSORIES | | |
| Net Sales | | | | |
| Cost of Merchandise Sold | | | | |
| Gross Profit | | | | |
| Direct Expenses | | | | |
| Departmental Margin | | | | |
| Indirect Expenses: | | | | |
|   Credit Card Fee Expense | | | | |
|   Depreciation Expense—Office Equipment | | | | |
|   Depreciation Expense—Store Equipment | | | | |
|   Insurance Expense | | | | |
|   Miscellaneous Expense | | | | |
|   Payroll Taxes Expense | | | | |
|   Rent Expense | | | | |
|   Salary Expense—Administrative | | | | |
|   Supplies Expense | | | | |
|   Uncollectible Accounts Expense | | | | |
|   Utilities Expense | | | | |
|   Total Indirect Expenses | | | | |
| Income before Income Tax | | | | |
| Less Federal Income Tax Expense | | | | |
| Net Income | | | | |
| | | | | |
| *Rounded to the nearest 0.1%. | | | | |

**2.**

Mixon Auto Supplies

Statement of Stockholders' Equity

For Year Ended December 31, 20--

| Capital Stock: | | | | |
|---|---|---|---|---|
| | | | | |
| | | | | |
| | | | | |
| | | | | |
| Retained Earnings: | | | | |
|    Balance, January 1, 20-- | | | | |
|    Net Income for 20-- | | | | |
|    Less Dividends Declared during 20-- | | | | |
|    Net Increase during 20-- | | | | |
|    Balance, December 31, 20-- | | | | |
| Total Stockholders' Equity, December 31, 20-- | | | | |
| | | | | |

**4-3** **ON YOUR OWN (continued)**

**3.**

Mixon Auto Supplies

Balance Sheet

December 31, 20--

| | | | % OF ASSETS* |
|---|---|---|---|
| Assets | | | |
| Current Assets: | | | |
| Cash | | | |
| Petty Cash | | | |
| Accounts Receivable | | | |
| Less Allowance for Uncollectible Accounts | | | |
| Merchandise Inventory—Parts | | | |
| Merchandise Inventory—Accessories | | | |
| Supplies | | | |
| Prepaid Insurance | | | |
| Total Current Assets | | | |
| Plant Assets: | | | |
| Office Equipment | | | |
| Less Accumulated Depreciation—Office Equipment | | | |
| Store Equipment | | | |
| Less Accumulated Depreciation—Store Equipment | | | |
| Total Plant Assets | | | |
| Total Assets | | | |
| Liabilities | | | |
| Current Liabilities: | | | |
| Accounts Payable | | | |
| Sales Tax Payable | | | |
| Employee Income Tax Payable—Federal | | | |
| Employee Income Tax Payable—State | | | |
| Social Security Tax Payable | | | |
| Medicare Tax Payable | | | |
| Medical Plan Payable | | | |
| Retirement Plan Payable | | | |
| Unemployment Tax Payable—Federal | | | |
| Unemployment Tax Payable—State | | | |
| Federal Income Tax Payable | | | |
| Dividends Payable | | | |
| Total Liabilities | | | |
| Stockholders' Equity | | | |
| Capital Stock | | | |
| Retained Earnings | | | |
| Total Stockholders' Equity | | | |
| Total Liabilities and Stockholders' Equity | | | |

*Rounded to the nearest 0.1%.

**4.**

| Mixon Auto Supplies | | | | | | | | | | |
|---|---|---|---|---|---|---|---|---|---|---|
| Statement of Cash Flows | | | | | | | | | | |
| For Year Ended December 31, 20-- | | | | | | | | | | |
| Cash flows from operating activities: | | | | | | | | | | |
| Cash receipts from customers | | | | | | | | | | |
| Cash payments for: | | | | | | | | | | |
| | | | | | | | | | | |
| | | | | | | | | | | |
| | | | | | | | | | | |
| | | | | | | | | | | |
| Total cash payments | | | | | | | | | | |
| Net cash provided (used) by operating activities | | | | | | | | | | |
| Cash flows from investing activities: | | | | | | | | | | |
| | | | | | | | | | | |
| Net cash provided (used) by investing activities | | | | | | | | | | |
| Cash flows from financing activities: | | | | | | | | | | |
| | | | | | | | | | | |
| Net cash provided (used) by financing activities | | | | | | | | | | |
| Net change in cash | | | | | | | | | | |
| Cash balance, January 1, 20-- | | | | | | | | | | |
| Cash balance, December 31, 20-- | | | | | | | | | | |

# 4-4 WORK TOGETHER, p. 122

**Journalizing closing entries**

## GENERAL JOURNAL

PAGE _____

| | DATE | ACCOUNT TITLE | DOC. NO. | POST. REF. | DEBIT | CREDIT | |
|---|---|---|---|---|---|---|---|
| 1 | | | | | | | 1 |
| 2 | | | | | | | 2 |
| 3 | | | | | | | 3 |
| 4 | | | | | | | 4 |
| 5 | | | | | | | 5 |
| 6 | | | | | | | 6 |
| 7 | | | | | | | 7 |
| 8 | | | | | | | 8 |
| 9 | | | | | | | 9 |
| 10 | | | | | | | 10 |
| 11 | | | | | | | 11 |
| 12 | | | | | | | 12 |
| 13 | | | | | | | 13 |
| 14 | | | | | | | 14 |
| 15 | | | | | | | 15 |
| 16 | | | | | | | 16 |
| 17 | | | | | | | 17 |
| 18 | | | | | | | 18 |
| 19 | | | | | | | 19 |
| 20 | | | | | | | 20 |
| 21 | | | | | | | 21 |
| 22 | | | | | | | 22 |
| 23 | | | | | | | 23 |
| 24 | | | | | | | 24 |
| 25 | | | | | | | 25 |
| 26 | | | | | | | 26 |
| 27 | | | | | | | 27 |
| 28 | | | | | | | 28 |
| 29 | | | | | | | 29 |
| 30 | | | | | | | 30 |
| 31 | | | | | | | 31 |
| 32 | | | | | | | 32 |
| 33 | | | | | | | 33 |
| 34 | | | | | | | 34 |
| 35 | | | | | | | 35 |
| 36 | | | | | | | 36 |
| 37 | | | | | | | 37 |
| 38 | | | | | | | 38 |
| 39 | | | | | | | 39 |
| 40 | | | | | | | 40 |
| 41 | | | | | | | 41 |
| 42 | | | | | | | 42 |

**Journalizing closing entries**

## GENERAL JOURNAL

PAGE

| | DATE | ACCOUNT TITLE | DOC. NO. | POST. REF. | DEBIT | CREDIT | |
|---|---|---|---|---|---|---|---|
| 1 | | | | | | | 1 |
| 2 | | | | | | | 2 |
| 3 | | | | | | | 3 |
| 4 | | | | | | | 4 |
| 5 | | | | | | | 5 |
| 6 | | | | | | | 6 |
| 7 | | | | | | | 7 |
| 8 | | | | | | | 8 |
| 9 | | | | | | | 9 |
| 10 | | | | | | | 10 |
| 11 | | | | | | | 11 |
| 12 | | | | | | | 12 |
| 13 | | | | | | | 13 |
| 14 | | | | | | | 14 |
| 15 | | | | | | | 15 |
| 16 | | | | | | | 16 |
| 17 | | | | | | | 17 |
| 18 | | | | | | | 18 |
| 19 | | | | | | | 19 |
| 20 | | | | | | | 20 |
| 21 | | | | | | | 21 |
| 22 | | | | | | | 22 |
| 23 | | | | | | | 23 |
| 24 | | | | | | | 24 |
| 25 | | | | | | | 25 |
| 26 | | | | | | | 26 |
| 27 | | | | | | | 27 |
| 28 | | | | | | | 28 |
| 29 | | | | | | | 29 |
| 30 | | | | | | | 30 |
| 31 | | | | | | | 31 |
| 32 | | | | | | | 32 |
| 33 | | | | | | | 33 |
| 34 | | | | | | | 34 |
| 35 | | | | | | | 35 |
| 36 | | | | | | | 36 |
| 37 | | | | | | | 37 |
| 38 | | | | | | | 38 |
| 39 | | | | | | | 39 |
| 40 | | | | | | | 40 |
| 41 | | | | | | | 41 |
| 42 | | | | | | | 42 |

## 4-1 APPLICATION PROBLEM (LO2, 3, 4), p. 127

**Preparing an adjusted trial balance**

**1., 2., 4.**

### GENERAL JOURNAL

PAGE

| | DATE | ACCOUNT TITLE | DOC. NO. | POST. REF. | DEBIT | CREDIT | |
|---|---|---|---|---|---|---|---|
| 1 | | | | | | | 1 |
| 2 | | | | | | | 2 |
| 3 | | | | | | | 3 |
| 4 | | | | | | | 4 |
| 5 | | | | | | | 5 |
| 6 | | | | | | | 6 |
| 7 | | | | | | | 7 |
| 8 | | | | | | | 8 |
| 9 | | | | | | | 9 |
| 10 | | | | | | | 10 |
| 11 | | | | | | | 11 |
| 12 | | | | | | | 12 |
| 13 | | | | | | | 13 |
| 14 | | | | | | | 14 |
| 15 | | | | | | | 15 |
| 16 | | | | | | | 16 |
| 17 | | | | | | | 17 |
| 18 | | | | | | | 18 |

**4.**

| Net Income before Federal Income Taxes | − | Tax Bracket Minimum Taxable Income | = | Net Income Subject to Marginal Tax Rate |
|---|---|---|---|---|
| $ | − | $ | = | $ |

| Net Income Subject to Marginal Tax Rate | × | Marginal Tax Rate | = | Marginal Income Tax |
|---|---|---|---|---|
| $ | × | | = | $ |

| Bracket Minimum Income Tax | + | Marginal Income Tax | = | Federal Income Tax |
|---|---|---|---|---|
| $ | + | $ | = | $ |

**2., 3.** **GENERAL LEDGER**

ACCOUNT Allowance for Uncollectible Accounts      ACCOUNT NO. 1210

| DATE | ITEM | POST. REF. | DEBIT | CREDIT | BALANCE DEBIT | BALANCE CREDIT |
|---|---|---|---|---|---|---|
| 20--<br>Dec. 31 | Balance | ✔ | | | | 5 1 6 36 |
| | | | | | | |
| | | | | | | |

ACCOUNT Merchandise Inventory—Golf      ACCOUNT NO. 1305

| DATE | ITEM | POST. REF. | DEBIT | CREDIT | BALANCE DEBIT | BALANCE CREDIT |
|---|---|---|---|---|---|---|
| 20--<br>Dec. 31 | Balance | ✔ | | | 62 8 4 9 00 | |
| | | | | | | |
| | | | | | | |
| | | | | | | |

ACCOUNT Merchandise Inventory—Tennis      ACCOUNT NO. 1310

| DATE | ITEM | POST. REF. | DEBIT | CREDIT | BALANCE DEBIT | BALANCE CREDIT |
|---|---|---|---|---|---|---|
| 20--<br>Dec. 31 | Balance | ✔ | | | 49 1 8 3 00 | |
| | | | | | | |
| | | | | | | |
| | | | | | | |

ACCOUNT Supplies      ACCOUNT NO. 1405

| DATE | ITEM | POST. REF. | DEBIT | CREDIT | BALANCE DEBIT | BALANCE CREDIT |
|---|---|---|---|---|---|---|
| 20--<br>Dec. 31 | Balance | ✔ | | | 3 1 0 5 04 | |
| | | | | | | |
| | | | | | | |

ACCOUNT Prepaid Insurance      ACCOUNT NO. 1410

| DATE | ITEM | POST. REF. | DEBIT | CREDIT | BALANCE DEBIT | BALANCE CREDIT |
|---|---|---|---|---|---|---|
| 20--<br>Dec. 31 | Balance | ✔ | | | 13 0 0 0 00 | |
| | | | | | | |
| | | | | | | |

## 4-1    APPLICATION PROBLEM (continued)

ACCOUNT  Accumulated Depreciation—Office Equipment                ACCOUNT NO. 1510

| DATE | | ITEM | POST. REF. | DEBIT | CREDIT | BALANCE | |
|---|---|---|---|---|---|---|---|
| | | | | | | DEBIT | CREDIT |
| 20--<br>Dec. | 31 | Balance | ✓ | | | | 9 1 9 5 00 |
| | | | | | | | |
| | | | | | | | |

ACCOUNT  Accumulated Depreciation—Store Equipment                ACCOUNT NO. 1520

| DATE | | ITEM | POST. REF. | DEBIT | CREDIT | BALANCE | |
|---|---|---|---|---|---|---|---|
| | | | | | | DEBIT | CREDIT |
| 20--<br>Dec. | 31 | Balance | ✓ | | | | 22 3 9 0 00 |
| | | | | | | | |
| | | | | | | | |

ACCOUNT  Federal Income Tax Payable                ACCOUNT NO. 2305

| DATE | ITEM | POST. REF. | DEBIT | CREDIT | BALANCE | |
|---|---|---|---|---|---|---|
| | | | | | DEBIT | CREDIT |
| | | | | | | |
| | | | | | | |
| | | | | | | |

ACCOUNT  Income Summary—Golf                ACCOUNT NO. 3210

| DATE | ITEM | POST. REF. | DEBIT | CREDIT | BALANCE | |
|---|---|---|---|---|---|---|
| | | | | | DEBIT | CREDIT |
| | | | | | | |
| | | | | | | |

ACCOUNT  Income Summary—Tennis                ACCOUNT NO. 3215

| DATE | ITEM | POST. REF. | DEBIT | CREDIT | BALANCE | |
|---|---|---|---|---|---|---|
| | | | | | DEBIT | CREDIT |
| | | | | | | |
| | | | | | | |
| | | | | | | |

ACCOUNT Depreciation Expense—Office Equipment      ACCOUNT NO. 7110

| DATE | ITEM | POST. REF. | DEBIT | CREDIT | BALANCE DEBIT | BALANCE CREDIT |
|------|------|-----------|-------|--------|--------|--------|
|      |      |           |       |        |        |        |
|      |      |           |       |        |        |        |
|      |      |           |       |        |        |        |

ACCOUNT Depreciation Expense—Store Equipment      ACCOUNT NO. 7115

| DATE | ITEM | POST. REF. | DEBIT | CREDIT | BALANCE DEBIT | BALANCE CREDIT |
|------|------|-----------|-------|--------|--------|--------|
|      |      |           |       |        |        |        |
|      |      |           |       |        |        |        |
|      |      |           |       |        |        |        |

ACCOUNT Insurance Expense      ACCOUNT NO. 7120

| DATE | ITEM | POST. REF. | DEBIT | CREDIT | BALANCE DEBIT | BALANCE CREDIT |
|------|------|-----------|-------|--------|--------|--------|
|      |      |           |       |        |        |        |
|      |      |           |       |        |        |        |
|      |      |           |       |        |        |        |

ACCOUNT Supplies Expense      ACCOUNT NO. 7150

| DATE | ITEM | POST. REF. | DEBIT | CREDIT | BALANCE DEBIT | BALANCE CREDIT |
|------|------|-----------|-------|--------|--------|--------|
|      |      |           |       |        |        |        |
|      |      |           |       |        |        |        |
|      |      |           |       |        |        |        |

ACCOUNT Uncollectible Accounts Expense      ACCOUNT NO. 7155

| DATE | ITEM | POST. REF. | DEBIT | CREDIT | BALANCE DEBIT | BALANCE CREDIT |
|------|------|-----------|-------|--------|--------|--------|
|      |      |           |       |        |        |        |
|      |      |           |       |        |        |        |
|      |      |           |       |        |        |        |

ACCOUNT Federal Income Tax Expense      ACCOUNT NO. 8105

| DATE | ITEM | POST. REF. | DEBIT | CREDIT | BALANCE DEBIT | BALANCE CREDIT |
|------|------|-----------|-------|--------|--------|--------|
| Dec. 31 | Balance | ✔ |  |  | 10 0 0 0 00 |  |
|      |      |           |       |        |        |        |
|      |      |           |       |        |        |        |

**4-1**  **APPLICATION PROBLEM (continued)**

**3., 4., 5.**

Sunset Sports, Inc.

Adjusted Trial Balance

December 31, 20--

| ACCOUNT TITLE | DEBIT | CREDIT |
|---|---|---|
| Cash | 53 3 1 4 47 | |
| Petty Cash | 1 5 0 15 | |
| Accounts Receivable | 11 6 7 7 03 | |
| Allowance for Uncollectible Accounts | | |
| Merchandise Inventory—Golf | | |
| Merchandise Inventory—Tennis | | |
| Supplies | | |
| Prepaid Insurance | | |
| Office Equipment | 13 1 2 2 52 | |
| Accumulated Depreciation—Office Equipment | | |
| Store Equipment | 41 7 1 4 34 | |
| Accumulated Depreciation—Store Equipment | | |
| Accounts Payable | | 22 4 5 7 79 |
| Sales Tax Payable | | 2 9 5 9 35 |
| Employee Income Tax Payable—Federal | | 1 0 7 8 32 |
| Employee Income Tax Payable—State | | 7 6 8 39 |
| Social Security Tax Payable | | 1 9 0 5 07 |
| Medicare Tax Payable | | 4 4 3 83 |
| Medical Plan Payable | | 6 8 5 15 |
| Retirement Plan Payable | | 4 5 9 36 |
| Unemployment Tax Payable—Federal | | 1 3 53 |
| Unemployment Tax Payable—State | | 9 0 24 |
| Federal Income Tax Payable | | |
| Dividends Payable | | 5 0 0 0 00 |
| Capital Stock | | 60 0 0 0 00 |
| Retained Earnings | | 66 7 6 8 35 |
| Dividends | 23 4 0 0 00 | |
| Income Summary—General | | |
| Income Summary—Golf | | |
| Income Summary—Tennis | | |

*(Note: Trial balance is continued on the next page.)*

Sunset Sports, Inc.

Adjusted Trial Balance (Concluded)

December 31, 20--

| ACCOUNT TITLE | DEBIT | CREDIT |
|---|---:|---:|
| Sales—Golf | | 362 4 8 3 36 |
| Sales Discount—Golf | 5 3 8 5 63 | |
| Sales Returns and Allowances—Golf | 6 1 2 6 18 | |
| Sales—Tennis | | 230 4 9 5 71 |
| Sales Discount—Tennis | 3 4 1 6 57 | |
| Sales Returns and Allowances—Tennis | 8 8 8 2 27 | |
| Purchases—Golf | 154 6 9 4 05 | |
| Purchases Discount—Golf | | 2 0 2 0 23 |
| Purchases Returns and Allowances—Golf | | 3 9 6 8 96 |
| Purchases—Tennis | 117 4 6 5 31 | |
| Purchases Discount—Tennis | | 1 7 3 4 91 |
| Purchases Returns and Allowances—Tennis | | 5 2 3 4 63 |
| Advertising Expense—Golf | 4 5 2 0 00 | |
| Payroll Taxes Expense—Golf | 4 2 0 2 27 | |
| Salary Expense—Golf | 47 6 1 7 46 | |
| Advertising Expense—Tennis | 3 8 2 5 00 | |
| Payroll Taxes Expense—Tennis | 5 6 8 1 90 | |
| Salary Expense—Tennis | 65 5 8 9 31 | |
| Credit Card Fee Expense | 3 4 1 5 18 | |
| Depreciation Expense—Office Equipment | | |
| Depreciation Expense—Store Equipment | | |
| Insurance Expense | | |
| Miscellaneous Expense | 6 2 1 0 16 | |
| Payroll Taxes Expense—Administrative | 4 9 3 2 43 | |
| Rent Expense | 14 5 0 0 00 | |
| Salary Expense—Administrative | 57 4 6 9 05 | |
| Supplies Expense | | |
| Uncollectible Accounts Expense | | |
| Utilities Expense | 5 2 2 0 22 | |
| | | |
| | | |

## 4-2 APPLICATION PROBLEM (LO6, 7), p. 127

**Preparing a departmental margin statement**

**1., 2.**

Sunset Sports, Inc.

Departmental Margin Statement—Golf

For Year Ended December 31, 20--

| | | | | | % OF NET SALES* |
|---|---|---|---|---|---|
| Operating Revenue: | | | | | |
| Sales | | | | | |
| Less: Sales Discount | | | | | |
| Sales Returns and Allowances | | | | | |
| Net Sales | | | | | |
| Cost of Merchandise Sold: | | | | | |
| Merchandise Inventory, Jan. 1, 20-- | | | | | |
| Purchases | | | | | |
| Less: Purchases Discount | | | | | |
| Purchases Returns and Allowances | | | | | |
| Net Purchases | | | | | |
| Total Cost of Merchandise Available for Sale | | | | | |
| Less Merchandise Inventory, Dec. 31, 20-- | | | | | |
| Cost of Merchandise Sold | | | | | |
| Gross Profit | | | | | |
| Direct Expenses: | | | | | |
| Advertising Expense | | | | | |
| Payroll Taxes Expense | | | | | |
| Salary Expense | | | | | |
| Total Direct Expenses | | | | | |
| Departmental Margin | | | | | |
| | | | | | |
| *Rounded to the nearest 0.1%. | | | | | |

Sunset Sports, Inc.

Departmental Margin Statement—Tennis

For Year Ended December 31, 20--

| | | | | | % OF NET SALES* |
|---|---|---|---|---|---|
| Operating Revenue: | | | | | |
| Sales | | | | | |
| Less: Sales Discount | | | | | |
| Sales Returns and Allowances | | | | | |
| Net Sales | | | | | |
| Cost of Merchandise Sold: | | | | | |
| Merchandise Inventory, Jan. 1, 20-- | | | | | |
| Purchases | | | | | |
| Less: Purchases Discount | | | | | |
| Purchases Returns and Allowances | | | | | |
| Net Purchases | | | | | |
| Total Cost of Merchandise Available for Sale | | | | | |
| Less Merchandise Inventory, Dec. 31, 20-- | | | | | |
| Cost of Merchandise Sold | | | | | |
| Gross Profit | | | | | |
| Direct Expenses: | | | | | |
| Advertising Expense | | | | | |
| Payroll Taxes Expense | | | | | |
| Salary Expense | | | | | |
| Total Direct Expenses | | | | | |
| Departmental Margin | | | | | |
| | | | | | |
| *Rounded to the nearest 0.1%. | | | | | |

## 4-3   APPLICATION PROBLEM (LO8), p. 127

**Preparing financial statements**

**1.**

Sunset Sports, Inc.

Income Statement

For Year Ended December 31, 20--

| | DEPARTMENTAL | | COMPANY | % OF NET SALES* |
|---|---|---|---|---|
| | GOLF | TENNIS | | |
| Net Sales | | | | |
| Cost of Merchandise Sold | | | | |
| Gross Profit | | | | |
| Direct Expenses | | | | |
| Departmental Margin | | | | |
| Indirect Expenses: | | | | |
|   Credit Card Fee Expense | | | | |
|   Depreciation Expense—Office Equipment | | | | |
|   Depreciation Expense—Store Equipment | | | | |
|   Insurance Expense | | | | |
|   Miscellaneous Expense | | | | |
|   Payroll Taxes Expense | | | | |
|   Rent Expense | | | | |
|   Salary Expense—Administrative | | | | |
|   Supplies Expense | | | | |
|   Uncollectible Accounts Expense | | | | |
|   Utilities Expense | | | | |
|   Total Indirect Expenses | | | | |
| Income before Income Tax | | | | |
| Less Federal Income Tax Expense | | | | |
| Net Income | | | | |
| | | | | |
| *Rounded to the nearest 0.1%. | | | | |

**2.**

Sunset Sports, Inc.

Statement of Stockholders' Equity

For Year Ended December 31, 20--

| | | | | |
|---|---|---|---|---|
| Capital Stock: | | | | |
| | | | | |
| | | | | |
| | | | | |
| | | | | |
| Retained Earnings: | | | | |
|     Balance, January 1, 20-- | | | | |
|     Net Income for 20-- | | | | |
|     Less Dividends Declared during 20-- | | | | |
|     Net Increase during 20-- | | | | |
|     Balance, December 31, 20-- | | | | |
| Total Stockholders' Equity, December 31, 20-- | | | | |

## 4-3 APPLICATION PROBLEM (continued)

**3.**

Sunset Sports, Inc.

Balance Sheet

December 31, 20--

| | | | | | % OF ASSETS* |
|---|---|---|---|---|---|
| **Assets** | | | | | |
| Current Assets: | | | | | |
| Cash | | | | | |
| Petty Cash | | | | | |
| Accounts Receivable | | | | | |
| Less Allowance for Uncollectible Accounts | | | | | |
| Merchandise Inventory—Golf | | | | | |
| Merchandise Inventory—Tennis | | | | | |
| Supplies | | | | | |
| Prepaid Insurance | | | | | |
| Total Current Assets | | | | | |
| Plant Assets: | | | | | |
| Office Equipment | | | | | |
| Less Accumulated Depreciation—Office Equipment | | | | | |
| Store Equipment | | | | | |
| Less Accumulated Depreciation—Store Equipment | | | | | |
| Total Plant Assets | | | | | |
| Total Assets | | | | | |
| **Liabilities** | | | | | |
| Current Liabilities: | | | | | |
| Accounts Payable | | | | | |
| Sales Tax Payable | | | | | |
| Employee Income Tax Payable—Federal | | | | | |
| Employee Income Tax Payable—State | | | | | |
| Social Security Tax Payable | | | | | |
| Medicare Tax Payable | | | | | |
| Medical Plan Payable | | | | | |
| Retirement Plan Payable | | | | | |
| Unemployment Tax Payable—Federal | | | | | |
| Unemployment Tax Payable—State | | | | | |
| Federal Income Tax Payable | | | | | |
| Dividends Payable | | | | | |
| Total Liabilities | | | | | |
| **Stockholders' Equity** | | | | | |
| Capital Stock | | | | | |
| Retained Earnings | | | | | |
| Total Stockholders' Equity | | | | | |
| Total Liabilities and Stockholders' Equity | | | | | |

*Rounded to the nearest 0.1%.

**4.**

Sunset Sports, Inc.

Statement of Cash Flows

For Year Ended December 31, 20--

| | | | | | |
|---|---|---|---|---|---|
| Cash flows from operating activities: | | | | | |
| Cash receipts from customers | | | | | |
| Cash payments for: | | | | | |
| | | | | | |
| | | | | | |
| | | | | | |
| | | | | | |
| | | | | | |
| Total cash payments | | | | | |
| Net cash provided (used) by operating activities | | | | | |
| Cash flows from investing activities: | | | | | |
| | | | | | |
| | | | | | |
| Net cash provided (used) by investing activities | | | | | |
| Cash flows from financing activities: | | | | | |
| | | | | | |
| | | | | | |
| Net cash provided (used) by financing activities | | | | | |
| Net change in cash | | | | | |
| Cash balance, January 1, 20-- | | | | | |
| Cash balance, December 31, 20-- | | | | | |

## 4-4 APPLICATION PROBLEM (LO9), p. 128

**Journalizing closing entries**

### GENERAL JOURNAL

PAGE _____

| | DATE | ACCOUNT TITLE | DOC. NO. | POST. REF. | DEBIT | CREDIT | |
|---|---|---|---|---|---|---|---|
| 1 | | | | | | | 1 |
| 2 | | | | | | | 2 |
| 3 | | | | | | | 3 |
| 4 | | | | | | | 4 |
| 5 | | | | | | | 5 |
| 6 | | | | | | | 6 |
| 7 | | | | | | | 7 |
| 8 | | | | | | | 8 |
| 9 | | | | | | | 9 |
| 10 | | | | | | | 10 |
| 11 | | | | | | | 11 |
| 12 | | | | | | | 12 |
| 13 | | | | | | | 13 |
| 14 | | | | | | | 14 |
| 15 | | | | | | | 15 |
| 16 | | | | | | | 16 |
| 17 | | | | | | | 17 |
| 18 | | | | | | | 18 |
| 19 | | | | | | | 19 |
| 20 | | | | | | | 20 |
| 21 | | | | | | | 21 |
| 22 | | | | | | | 22 |
| 23 | | | | | | | 23 |
| 24 | | | | | | | 24 |
| 25 | | | | | | | 25 |
| 26 | | | | | | | 26 |
| 27 | | | | | | | 27 |
| 28 | | | | | | | 28 |
| 29 | | | | | | | 29 |
| 30 | | | | | | | 30 |
| 31 | | | | | | | 31 |
| 32 | | | | | | | 32 |
| 33 | | | | | | | 33 |
| 34 | | | | | | | 34 |
| 35 | | | | | | | 35 |
| 36 | | | | | | | 36 |
| 37 | | | | | | | 37 |
| 38 | | | | | | | 38 |
| 39 | | | | | | | 39 |
| 40 | | | | | | | 40 |
| 41 | | | | | | | 41 |
| 42 | | | | | | | 42 |

**Completing end-of-fiscal-period work for a departmentalized merchandising business**

**1., 2., 4.**

GENERAL JOURNAL                                         PAGE

| | DATE | | ACCOUNT TITLE | DOC. NO. | POST. REF. | DEBIT | CREDIT | |
|---|---|---|---|---|---|---|---|---|
| 1 | | | | | | | | 1 |
| 2 | | | | | | | | 2 |
| 3 | | | | | | | | 3 |
| 4 | | | | | | | | 4 |
| 5 | | | | | | | | 5 |
| 6 | | | | | | | | 6 |
| 7 | | | | | | | | 7 |
| 8 | | | | | | | | 8 |
| 9 | | | | | | | | 9 |
| 10 | | | | | | | | 10 |
| 11 | | | | | | | | 11 |
| 12 | | | | | | | | 12 |
| 13 | | | | | | | | 13 |
| 14 | | | | | | | | 14 |
| 15 | | | | | | | | 15 |
| 16 | | | | | | | | 16 |
| 17 | | | | | | | | 17 |
| 18 | | | | | | | | 18 |

**4.**

| Net Income before Federal Income Taxes | – | Tax Bracket Minimum Taxable Income | = | Net Income Subject to Marginal Tax Rate |
|---|---|---|---|---|
| $ | – | $ | = | $ |

| Net Income Subject to Marginal Tax Rate | × | Marginal Tax Rate | = | Marginal Income Tax |
|---|---|---|---|---|
| $ | × | | = | $ |

| Bracket Minimum Income Tax | + | Marginal Income Tax | = | Federal Income Tax |
|---|---|---|---|---|
| $ | + | $ | = | $ |

**4-M** **MASTERY PROBLEM (continued)**

**2., 4.** **GENERAL LEDGER**

ACCOUNT Allowance for Uncollectible Accounts     ACCOUNT NO. 1210

| DATE | ITEM | POST. REF. | DEBIT | CREDIT | BALANCE DEBIT | BALANCE CREDIT |
|---|---|---|---|---|---|---|
| Dec. 31 | Balance | ✔ | | | 2 4 8 3 55 | |
| | | | | | | |
| | | | | | | |

ACCOUNT Merchandise Inventory—Antiques     ACCOUNT NO. 1305

| DATE | ITEM | POST. REF. | DEBIT | CREDIT | BALANCE DEBIT | BALANCE CREDIT |
|---|---|---|---|---|---|---|
| Dec. 31 | Balance | ✔ | | | 246 1 2 9 27 | |
| | | | | | | |
| | | | | | | |

ACCOUNT Merchandise Inventory—Modern     ACCOUNT NO. 1310

| DATE | ITEM | POST. REF. | DEBIT | CREDIT | BALANCE DEBIT | BALANCE CREDIT |
|---|---|---|---|---|---|---|
| Dec. 31 | Balance | ✔ | | | 223 0 5 4 45 | |
| | | | | | | |
| | | | | | | |

ACCOUNT Supplies     ACCOUNT NO. 1405

| DATE | ITEM | POST. REF. | DEBIT | CREDIT | BALANCE DEBIT | BALANCE CREDIT |
|---|---|---|---|---|---|---|
| Dec. 31 | Balance | ✔ | | | 6 7 2 5 58 | |
| | | | | | | |
| | | | | | | |

ACCOUNT Prepaid Insurance     ACCOUNT NO. 1410

| DATE | ITEM | POST. REF. | DEBIT | CREDIT | BALANCE DEBIT | BALANCE CREDIT |
|---|---|---|---|---|---|---|
| Dec. 31 | Balance | ✔ | | | 16 0 0 0 00 | |
| | | | | | | |
| | | | | | | |

ACCOUNT Accumulated Depreciation—Office Equipment          ACCOUNT NO. 1510

| DATE | ITEM | POST. REF. | DEBIT | CREDIT | BALANCE DEBIT | BALANCE CREDIT |
|------|------|-----------|-------|--------|-------|--------|
| Dec. 31 | Balance | ✔ | | | | 10 9 8 8 99 |
| | | | | | | |

ACCOUNT Accumulated Depreciation—Store Equipment          ACCOUNT NO. 1520

| DATE | ITEM | POST. REF. | DEBIT | CREDIT | BALANCE DEBIT | BALANCE CREDIT |
|------|------|-----------|-------|--------|-------|--------|
| Dec. 31 | Balance | ✔ | | | | 14 0 9 0 41 |
| | | | | | | |

ACCOUNT Federal Income Tax Payable          ACCOUNT NO. 2305

| DATE | ITEM | POST. REF. | DEBIT | CREDIT | BALANCE DEBIT | BALANCE CREDIT |
|------|------|-----------|-------|--------|-------|--------|
| | | | | | | |
| | | | | | | |
| | | | | | | |

ACCOUNT Income Summary—General          ACCOUNT NO. 3205

| DATE | ITEM | POST. REF. | DEBIT | CREDIT | BALANCE DEBIT | BALANCE CREDIT |
|------|------|-----------|-------|--------|-------|--------|
| | | | | | | |
| | | | | | | |

ACCOUNT Income Summary—Antiques          ACCOUNT NO. 3210

| DATE | ITEM | POST. REF. | DEBIT | CREDIT | BALANCE DEBIT | BALANCE CREDIT |
|------|------|-----------|-------|--------|-------|--------|
| | | | | | | |
| | | | | | | |

ACCOUNT Income Summary—Modern          ACCOUNT NO. 3215

| DATE | ITEM | POST. REF. | DEBIT | CREDIT | BALANCE DEBIT | BALANCE CREDIT |
|------|------|-----------|-------|--------|-------|--------|
| | | | | | | |
| | | | | | | |

## 4-M  MASTERY PROBLEM (continued)

ACCOUNT Depreciation Expense—Office Equipment          ACCOUNT NO. 7110

| DATE | ITEM | POST. REF. | DEBIT | CREDIT | BALANCE DEBIT | BALANCE CREDIT |
|------|------|-----------|-------|--------|---------------|----------------|
|      |      |           |       |        |               |                |
|      |      |           |       |        |               |                |

ACCOUNT Depreciation Expense—Store Equipment          ACCOUNT NO. 7115

| DATE | ITEM | POST. REF. | DEBIT | CREDIT | BALANCE DEBIT | BALANCE CREDIT |
|------|------|-----------|-------|--------|---------------|----------------|
|      |      |           |       |        |               |                |
|      |      |           |       |        |               |                |

ACCOUNT Insurance Expense          ACCOUNT NO. 7120

| DATE | ITEM | POST. REF. | DEBIT | CREDIT | BALANCE DEBIT | BALANCE CREDIT |
|------|------|-----------|-------|--------|---------------|----------------|
|      |      |           |       |        |               |                |
|      |      |           |       |        |               |                |

ACCOUNT Supplies Expense          ACCOUNT NO. 7150

| DATE | ITEM | POST. REF. | DEBIT | CREDIT | BALANCE DEBIT | BALANCE CREDIT |
|------|------|-----------|-------|--------|---------------|----------------|
|      |      |           |       |        |               |                |
|      |      |           |       |        |               |                |

ACCOUNT Uncollectible Accounts Expense          ACCOUNT NO. 7155

| DATE | ITEM | POST. REF. | DEBIT | CREDIT | BALANCE DEBIT | BALANCE CREDIT |
|------|------|-----------|-------|--------|---------------|----------------|
|      |      |           |       |        |               |                |
|      |      |           |       |        |               |                |

ACCOUNT Federal Income Tax Expense          ACCOUNT NO. 8105

| DATE | ITEM | POST. REF. | DEBIT | CREDIT | BALANCE DEBIT | BALANCE CREDIT |
|------|------|-----------|-------|--------|---------------|----------------|
| Dec. 31 | Balance | ✔ |       |        | 48 0 0 0 00 |                |
|      |      |           |       |        |               |                |

**3., 5.**

Forde Furniture Gallery

Adjusted Trial Balance

December 31, 20--

| ACCOUNT TITLE | DEBIT | CREDIT |
|---|---:|---:|
| Cash | 62 048 36 | |
| Petty Cash | 478 24 | |
| Accounts Receivable | 36 638 89 | |
| Allowance for Uncollectible Accounts | | |
| Merchandise Inventory—Antiques | | |
| Merchandise Inventory—Modern | | |
| Supplies | | |
| Prepaid Insurance | | |
| Office Equipment | 51 309 14 | |
| Accumulated Depreciation—Office Equipment | | |
| Store Equipment | 62 263 88 | |
| Accumulated Depreciation—Store Equipment | | |
| Accounts Payable | | 38 216 85 |
| Sales Tax Payable | | 7 825 99 |
| Employee Income Tax Payable—Federal | | 2 126 15 |
| Employee Income Tax Payable—State | | 1 519 03 |
| Social Security Tax Payable | | 3 775 91 |
| Medicare Tax Payable | | 879 96 |
| Medical Insurance Payable | | 1 351 24 |
| Retirement Plan Payable | | 905 60 |
| Unemployment Tax Payable—Federal | | 26 75 |
| Unemployment Tax Payable—State | | 179 56 |
| Federal Income Tax Payable | | |
| Dividends Payable | | 15 000 00 |
| Capital Stock | | 300 000 00 |
| Retained Earnings | | 214 211 56 |
| Dividends | 60 000 00 | |
| Income Summary—General | | |
| Income Summary—Antiques | | |
| Income Summary—Modern | | |

*(Note: Trial balance is continued on the next page.)*

## 4-M  MASTERY PROBLEM (continued)

Forde Furniture Gallery

Adjusted Trial Balance (Concluded)

December 31, 20--

| ACCOUNT TITLE | DEBIT | CREDIT |
|---|---|---|
| Sales—Antiques | | 870 0 5 2 67 |
| Sales Discount—Antiques | 10 5 8 7 38 | |
| Sales Returns and Allowances—Antiques | 12 2 0 1 54 | |
| Sales—Modern | | 505 6 3 3 93 |
| Sales Discount—Modern | 6 6 9 3 73 | |
| Sales Returns and Allowances—Modern | 17 6 6 6 89 | |
| Purchases—Antiques | 399 4 7 2 04 | |
| Purchases Discount—Antiques | | 3 9 8 3 45 |
| Purchases Returns and Allowances—Antiques | | 7 8 5 6 02 |
| Purchases—Modern | 275 9 6 8 46 | |
| Purchases Discount—Modern | | 3 4 2 4 51 |
| Purchases Returns and Allowances—Modern | | 12 2 8 1 20 |
| Advertising Expense—Antiques | 16 2 0 0 00 | |
| Payroll Taxes Expense—Antiques | 8 3 0 2 37 | |
| Salary Expense—Antiques | 94 0 2 3 44 | |
| Advertising Expense—Modern | 12 6 0 0 00 | |
| Payroll Taxes Expense—Modern | 13 9 9 5 63 | |
| Salary Expense—Modern | 161 1 0 6 96 | |
| Credit Card Fee Expense | 8 7 4 6 70 | |
| Depreciation Expense—Office Equipment | | |
| Depreciation Expense—Store Equipment | | |
| Insurance Expense | | |
| Miscellaneous Expense | 4 4 4 7 60 | |
| Payroll Taxes Expense—Administrative | 9 7 3 8 93 | |
| Rent Expense | 24 0 0 0 00 | |
| Salary Expense—Administrative | 112 7 2 8 83 | |
| Supplies Expense | | |
| Uncollectible Accounts Expense | | |
| Utilities Expense | 10 7 1 7 92 | |
| | | |
| | | |
| | | |

Total of income statement credit accounts ..................... $ _____

*Less* total of income statement debit accounts

excluding federal income tax expense ........................ _____

*Equals* net income before federal income tax expense ..... $ _____

6.

Forde Furniture Gallery

Departmental Margin Statement—Antiques

For Year Ended December 31, 20--

| | | | | % OF NET SALES* |
|---|---|---|---|---|
| | | | | |
| | | | | |
| | | | | |
| | | | | |
| | | | | |
| | | | | |
| | | | | |
| | | | | |
| | | | | |
| | | | | |
| | | | | |
| | | | | |
| | | | | |
| | | | | |
| | | | | |
| | | | | |
| | | | | |
| | | | | |
| | | | | |
| | | | | |
| | | | | |
| *Rounded to the nearest 0.1%. | | | | |
| | | | | |
| | | | | |

Forde Furniture Gallery

Departmental Margin Statement—Modern

For Year Ended December 31, 20--

| | | | | | % OF NET SALES* |
|---|---|---|---|---|---|
| | | | | | |
| | | | | | |
| | | | | | |
| | | | | | |
| | | | | | |
| | | | | | |
| | | | | | |
| | | | | | |
| | | | | | |
| | | | | | |
| | | | | | |
| | | | | | |
| | | | | | |
| | | | | | |
| | | | | | |
| | | | | | |
| | | | | | |
| | | | | | |
| | | | | | |
| | | | | | |
| | | | | | |
| | | | | | |
| *Rounded to the nearest 0.1%. | | | | | |
| | | | | | |
| | | | | | |

**7.**

<table>
<tr><td colspan="9" align="center">Forde Furniture Gallery</td></tr>
<tr><td colspan="9" align="center">Income Statement</td></tr>
<tr><td colspan="9" align="center">For Year Ended December 31, 20--</td></tr>
<tr>
<td></td>
<td colspan="2" align="center">DEPARTMENTAL</td>
<td colspan="4" align="center">COMPANY</td>
<td align="center">% OF NET<br>SALES*</td>
</tr>
<tr>
<td></td>
<td align="center">ANTIQUES</td>
<td align="center">MODERN</td>
<td></td>
<td></td>
<td></td>
<td></td>
<td></td>
</tr>
<tr><td></td><td></td><td></td><td></td><td></td><td></td><td></td><td></td></tr>
<tr><td></td><td></td><td></td><td></td><td></td><td></td><td></td><td></td></tr>
<tr><td></td><td></td><td></td><td></td><td></td><td></td><td></td><td></td></tr>
<tr><td></td><td></td><td></td><td></td><td></td><td></td><td></td><td></td></tr>
<tr><td></td><td></td><td></td><td></td><td></td><td></td><td></td><td></td></tr>
<tr><td></td><td></td><td></td><td></td><td></td><td></td><td></td><td></td></tr>
<tr><td></td><td></td><td></td><td></td><td></td><td></td><td></td><td></td></tr>
<tr><td></td><td></td><td></td><td></td><td></td><td></td><td></td><td></td></tr>
<tr><td></td><td></td><td></td><td></td><td></td><td></td><td></td><td></td></tr>
<tr><td></td><td></td><td></td><td></td><td></td><td></td><td></td><td></td></tr>
<tr><td></td><td></td><td></td><td></td><td></td><td></td><td></td><td></td></tr>
<tr><td></td><td></td><td></td><td></td><td></td><td></td><td></td><td></td></tr>
<tr><td>*Rounded to the nearest 0.1%.</td><td></td><td></td><td></td><td></td><td></td><td></td><td></td></tr>
<tr><td></td><td></td><td></td><td></td><td></td><td></td><td></td><td></td></tr>
<tr><td></td><td></td><td></td><td></td><td></td><td></td><td></td><td></td></tr>
</table>

**4-M** **MASTERY PROBLEM (continued)**

**7.**

Forde Furniture Gallery

Statement of Stockholders' Equity

For Year Ended December 31, 20--

| | | | | | | | |
|---|---|---|---|---|---|---|---|
| | | | | | | | |
| | | | | | | | |
| | | | | | | | |
| | | | | | | | |
| | | | | | | | |
| | | | | | | | |
| | | | | | | | |
| | | | | | | | |
| | | | | | | | |
| | | | | | | | |
| | | | | | | | |
| | | | | | | | |
| | | | | | | | |
| | | | | | | | |
| | | | | | | | |
| | | | | | | | |
| | | | | | | | |
| | | | | | | | |
| | | | | | | | |
| | | | | | | | |
| | | | | | | | |
| | | | | | | | |
| | | | | | | | |
| | | | | | | | |
| | | | | | | | |

**7.**

Forde Furniture Gallery

Balance Sheet

December 31, 20--

| | | | | | % OF ASSETS* |
|---|---|---|---|---|---|
| | | | | | |

*Rounded to the nearest 0.1%.

**4-M** **MASTERY PROBLEM (continued)**

8.

Forde Furniture Gallery

Statement of Cash Flows

For Year Ended December 31, 20--

**9.**

GENERAL JOURNAL

PAGE

| | DATE | ACCOUNT TITLE | DOC. NO. | POST. REF. | DEBIT | CREDIT | |
|---|---|---|---|---|---|---|---|
| 1 | | | | | | | 1 |
| 2 | | | | | | | 2 |
| 3 | | | | | | | 3 |
| 4 | | | | | | | 4 |
| 5 | | | | | | | 5 |
| 6 | | | | | | | 6 |
| 7 | | | | | | | 7 |
| 8 | | | | | | | 8 |
| 9 | | | | | | | 9 |
| 10 | | | | | | | 10 |
| 11 | | | | | | | 11 |
| 12 | | | | | | | 12 |
| 13 | | | | | | | 13 |
| 14 | | | | | | | 14 |
| 15 | | | | | | | 15 |
| 16 | | | | | | | 16 |
| 17 | | | | | | | 17 |
| 18 | | | | | | | 18 |
| 19 | | | | | | | 19 |
| 20 | | | | | | | 20 |
| 21 | | | | | | | 21 |
| 22 | | | | | | | 22 |
| 23 | | | | | | | 23 |
| 24 | | | | | | | 24 |
| 25 | | | | | | | 25 |
| 26 | | | | | | | 26 |
| 27 | | | | | | | 27 |
| 28 | | | | | | | 28 |
| 29 | | | | | | | 29 |
| 30 | | | | | | | 30 |
| 31 | | | | | | | 31 |
| 32 | | | | | | | 32 |
| 33 | | | | | | | 33 |
| 34 | | | | | | | 34 |
| 35 | | | | | | | 35 |
| 36 | | | | | | | 36 |
| 37 | | | | | | | 37 |
| 38 | | | | | | | 38 |
| 39 | | | | | | | 39 |
| 40 | | | | | | | 40 |
| 41 | | | | | | | 41 |
| 42 | | | | | | | 42 |

## 4-C CHALLENGE PROBLEM (LO2, 3), p. 129

**Analyzing a departmental margin statement**

**1.**

Crystal Pools

Departmental Margin Statement—Chemicals Department

For Years Ended December 31, 20X7 and 20X6

| | 20X7 AMOUNTS | 20X7 % OF NET SALES | 20X6 AMOUNTS | 20X6 % OF NET SALES |
|---|---|---|---|---|
| Operating Revenue: | | | | |
| Net Sales | 514 85 1 36 | | 480 1 6 4 68 | 100.0 |
| Cost of Merchandise Sold: | | | | |
| Merchandise Inventory, Jan. 1, 20-- | 61 8 4 8 08 | | 58 1 4 8 61 | |
| Purchases | 302 1 8 4 61 | | 274 0 1 8 61 | |
| Total Cost of Merchandise Available for Sale | 364 0 3 2 69 | | 332 1 6 7 22 | |
| Less Merchandise Inventory, Dec. 31, 20-- | 65 1 0 8 47 | | 61 8 4 8 08 | |
| Cost of Merchandise Sold | 298 9 2 4 22 | | 270 3 1 9 14 | 56.3 |
| Gross Profit | 215 9 2 7 14 | | 209 8 4 5 54 | 43.7 |
| Direct Expenses: | | | | |
| Advertising Expense | 16 5 0 0 00 | | 16 1 0 0 00 | 3.4 |
| Delivery Expense | 8 1 4 8 36 | | 8 1 6 8 15 | 1.7 |
| Depreciation Expense—Store Equipment | 6 2 5 0 00 | | 5 9 5 0 00 | 1.2 |
| Payroll Taxes Expense | 5 2 6 5 30 | | 5 1 0 2 79 | 1.1 |
| Salary Expense | 50 2 4 3 70 | | 48 6 8 6 15 | 10.1 |
| Supplies Expense | 4 9 1 6 68 | | 3 8 3 1 14 | 0.8 |
| Total Direct Expenses | 91 3 2 4 04 | | 87 8 3 8 23 | 18.3 |
| Departmental Margin | 124 6 0 3 10 | | 122 0 0 7 31 | 25.4 |

**2.**

| Change in % of Net Sales | |
|---|---|
| a. Cost of Merchandise Sold | |
| b. Gross Profit | |
| c. Total Direct Expenses | |
| d. Departmental Margin | |

**3.**

**a.**

_____

_____

_____

_____

_____

_____

**b.**

_____

_____

_____

_____

_____

_____

**c.**

_____

_____

_____

_____

_____

# APPENDIX PROBLEM 4-1, p. 135

**Preparing a work sheet**

**1., 2., 3.**

Foley's Interiors

Adjusted Trial Balance

December 31, 20--

| | | | TRIAL BALANCE | | ADJUSTMENTS | |
| --- | --- | --- | --- | --- | --- | --- |
| | ACCOUNT TITLE | DEBIT | CREDIT | DEBIT | CREDIT |
| 1 | Cash | 36 4 6 0 79 | | | |
| 2 | Petty Cash | 3 0 0 00 | | | |
| 3 | Accounts Receivable | 23 0 1 8 95 | | | |
| 4 | Allowance for Uncollectible Accounts | | 7 7 38 | | |
| 5 | Merchandise Inventory—Kitchen | 140 8 9 0 00 | | | |
| 6 | Merchandise Inventory—Bath | 98 6 2 0 00 | | | |
| 7 | Supplies | 6 0 9 7 89 | | | |
| 8 | Prepaid Insurance | 18 0 0 0 00 | | | |
| 9 | Office Equipment | 26 0 1 5 89 | | | |
| 10 | Accumulated Depreciation—Office Equipment | | 11 4 2 4 00 | | |
| 11 | Store Equipment | 51 8 5 2 82 | | | |
| 12 | Accumulated Depreciation—Store Equipment | | 27 7 6 5 00 | | |
| 13 | Accounts Payable | | 24 1 1 6 31 | | |
| 14 | Sales Tax Payable | | 4 9 2 5 59 | | |
| 15 | Employee Income Tax Payable—Federal | | 1 3 3 5 44 | | |
| 16 | Employee Income Tax Payable—State | | 9 5 6 99 | | |
| 17 | Social Security Tax Payable | | 2 3 7 6 90 | | |
| 18 | Medicare Tax Payable | | 5 5 3 24 | | |
| 19 | Medical Insurance Payable | | 8 4 6 42 | | |
| 20 | Retirement Plan Payable | | 5 7 1 94 | | |
| 21 | Unemployment Tax Payable—Federal | | 1 6 72 | | |
| 22 | Unemployment Tax Payable—State | | 1 1 2 08 | | |
| 23 | Federal Income Tax Payable | | | | |
| 24 | Dividends Payable | | 4 0 0 0 00 | | |
| 25 | Capital Stock | | 75 0 0 0 00 | | |
| 26 | Retained Earnings | | 165 0 7 3 83 | | |
| 27 | Dividends | 16 0 0 0 00 | | | |
| 28 | Income Summary—Kitchen | | | | |
| 29 | Income Summary—Bath | | | | |
| 30 | Sales—Kitchen | | 417 9 5 3 07 | | |
| 31 | Sales Discount—Kitchen | 6 6 5 5 27 | | | |
| 32 | Sales Returns and Allowances—Kitchen | 7 6 3 4 77 | | | |
| 33 | Sales—Bath | | 316 0 1 4 76 | | |
| 34 | Sales Discount—Bath | 4 2 2 0 29 | | | |

*(Note: Work Sheet continues on p. 177.)*

# APPENDIX PROBLEM 4-1 (continued)

| | 5 | 6 | 7 | 8 | 9 | 10 | 11 | 12 | |
|---|---|---|---|---|---|---|---|---|---|
| | DEPARTMENTAL STATEMENTS | | | | INCOME STATEMENT | | BALANCE SHEET | | |
| | KITCHEN | | BATH | | | | | | |
| | DEBIT | CREDIT | DEBIT | CREDIT | DEBIT | CREDIT | DEBIT | CREDIT | |
| | | | | | | | | | 1 |
| | | | | | | | | | 2 |
| | | | | | | | | | 3 |
| | | | | | | | | | 4 |
| | | | | | | | | | 5 |
| | | | | | | | | | 6 |
| | | | | | | | | | 7 |
| | | | | | | | | | 8 |
| | | | | | | | | | 9 |
| | | | | | | | | | 10 |
| | | | | | | | | | 11 |
| | | | | | | | | | 12 |
| | | | | | | | | | 13 |
| | | | | | | | | | 14 |
| | | | | | | | | | 15 |
| | | | | | | | | | 16 |
| | | | | | | | | | 17 |
| | | | | | | | | | 18 |
| | | | | | | | | | 19 |
| | | | | | | | | | 20 |
| | | | | | | | | | 21 |
| | | | | | | | | | 22 |
| | | | | | | | | | 23 |
| | | | | | | | | | 24 |
| | | | | | | | | | 25 |
| | | | | | | | | | 26 |
| | | | | | | | | | 27 |
| | | | | | | | | | 28 |
| | | | | | | | | | 29 |
| | | | | | | | | | 30 |
| | | | | | | | | | 31 |
| | | | | | | | | | 32 |
| | | | | | | | | | 33 |
| | | | | | | | | | 34 |

(Note: Work Sheet continues on p. 178.)

|  | ACCOUNT TITLE | TRIAL BALANCE | | ADJUSTMENTS | |
|---|---|---|---|---|---|
|  |  | DEBIT | CREDIT | DEBIT | CREDIT |
| 35 | Sales Returns and Allowances—Bath | 11 0 7 0 52 | | | |
| 36 | Purchases—Kitchen | 204 1 6 4 91 | | | |
| 37 | Purchases Discount—Kitchen | | 2 5 0 5 71 | | |
| 38 | Purchases Returns and Allowances—Kitchen | | 4 9 2 5 52 | | |
| 39 | Purchases—Bath | 128 4 5 1 62 | | | |
| 40 | Purchases Discount—Bath | | 2 1 5 7 01 | | |
| 41 | Purchases Returns and Allowances—Bath | | 6 4 9 5 71 | | |
| 42 | Advertising Expense—Kitchen | 11 9 0 0 00 | | | |
| 43 | Payroll Taxes Expense—Kitchen | 5 1 9 3 25 | | | |
| 44 | Salary Expense—Kitchen | 59 1 2 1 95 | | | |
| 45 | Advertising Expense—Bath | 4 5 0 0 00 | | | |
| 46 | Payroll Taxes Expense—Bath | 7 0 2 8 66 | | | |
| 47 | Salary Expense—Bath | 81 1 0 3 91 | | | |
| 48 | Credit Card Fee Expense | 4 5 0 2 93 | | | |
| 49 | Depreciation Expense—Office Equipment | | | | |
| 50 | Depreciation Expense—Store Equipment | | | | |
| 51 | Insurance Expense | | | | |
| 52 | Miscellaneous Expense | 2 8 1 3 28 | | | |
| 53 | Payroll Taxes Expense—Administrative | 6 1 4 9 34 | | | |
| 54 | Rent Expense | 18 0 0 0 00 | | | |
| 55 | Salary Expense—Administrative | 71 0 0 1 51 | | | |
| 56 | Supplies Expense | | | | |
| 57 | Uncollectible Accounts Expense | | | | |
| 58 | Utilities Expense | 6 4 3 5 07 | | | |
| 59 | | | | | |
| 60 | Department Margin—Kitchen | | | | |
| 61 | Department Margin—Bath | | | | |
| 62 | | | | | |
| 63 | Federal Income Tax Expense | 12 0 0 0 00 | | | |
| 64 | | 1069 2 0 3 62 | 1069 2 0 3 62 | | |
| 65 | Net Income | | | | |
| 66 | | | | | |
| 67 | | | | | |
| 68 | | | | | |

# APPENDIX PROBLEM 4-1 (concluded)

| | 5 | | 6 | | 7 | | 8 | | 9 | | 10 | | 11 | | 12 | | |
|---|---|---|---|---|---|---|---|---|---|---|---|---|---|---|---|---|---|
| | DEPARTMENTAL STATEMENTS | | | | | | | | INCOME STATEMENT | | | | BALANCE SHEET | | | | |
| | KITCHEN | | | | BATH | | | | | | | | | | | | |
| | DEBIT | | CREDIT | | DEBIT | | CREDIT | | DEBIT | | CREDIT | | DEBIT | | CREDIT | | |
| | | | | | | | | | | | | | | | | | 35 |
| | | | | | | | | | | | | | | | | | 36 |
| | | | | | | | | | | | | | | | | | 37 |
| | | | | | | | | | | | | | | | | | 38 |
| | | | | | | | | | | | | | | | | | 39 |
| | | | | | | | | | | | | | | | | | 40 |
| | | | | | | | | | | | | | | | | | 41 |
| | | | | | | | | | | | | | | | | | 42 |
| | | | | | | | | | | | | | | | | | 43 |
| | | | | | | | | | | | | | | | | | 44 |
| | | | | | | | | | | | | | | | | | 45 |
| | | | | | | | | | | | | | | | | | 46 |
| | | | | | | | | | | | | | | | | | 47 |
| | | | | | | | | | | | | | | | | | 48 |
| | | | | | | | | | | | | | | | | | 49 |
| | | | | | | | | | | | | | | | | | 50 |
| | | | | | | | | | | | | | | | | | 51 |
| | | | | | | | | | | | | | | | | | 52 |
| | | | | | | | | | | | | | | | | | 53 |
| | | | | | | | | | | | | | | | | | 54 |
| | | | | | | | | | | | | | | | | | 55 |
| | | | | | | | | | | | | | | | | | 56 |
| | | | | | | | | | | | | | | | | | 57 |
| | | | | | | | | | | | | | | | | | 58 |
| | | | | | | | | | | | | | | | | | 59 |
| | | | | | | | | | | | | | | | | | 60 |
| | | | | | | | | | | | | | | | | | 61 |
| | | | | | | | | | | | | | | | | | 62 |
| | | | | | | | | | | | | | | | | | 63 |
| | | | | | | | | | | | | | | | | | 64 |
| | | | | | | | | | | | | | | | | | 65 |
| | | | | | | | | | | | | | | | | | 66 |
| | | | | | | | | | | | | | | | | | 67 |
| | | | | | | | | | | | | | | | | | 68 |

# APPENDIX PROBLEM 4-2, p. 135

**Preparing a work sheet**

**1., 2., 3.**

Mixon Auto Supplies

Adjusted Trial Balance

December 31, 20--

| | | TRIAL BALANCE | | ADJUSTMENTS | |
| --- | --- | --- | --- | --- | --- |
| ACCOUNT TITLE | DEBIT | CREDIT | DEBIT | CREDIT |
| 1 Cash | 61 3 5 4 03 | | | |
| 2 Petty Cash | 2 4 1 66 | | | |
| 3 Accounts Receivable | 18 5 3 3 67 | | | |
| 4 Allowance for Uncollectible Accounts | | 1 4 8 36 | | |
| 5 Merchandise Inventory—Parts | 256 4 7 0 00 | | | |
| 6 Merchandise Inventory—Accessories | 112 7 4 0 00 | | | |
| 7 Supplies | 4 9 3 5 98 | | | |
| 8 Prepaid Insurance | 15 0 0 0 00 | | | |
| 9 Office Equipment | 20 8 2 7 76 | | | |
| 10 Accumulated Depreciation—Office Equipment | | 9 1 4 5 86 | | |
| 11 Store Equipment | 41 5 3 1 75 | | | |
| 12 Accumulated Depreciation—Store Equipment | | 22 2 9 8 99 | | |
| 13 Accounts Payable | | 19 3 0 1 35 | | |
| 14 Sales Tax Payable | | 3 9 7 6 77 | | |
| 15 Employee Income Tax Payable—Federal | | 1 0 8 0 01 | | |
| 16 Employee Income Tax Payable—State | | 7 6 9 94 | | |
| 17 Social Security Tax Payable | | 1 9 1 8 06 | | |
| 18 Medicare Tax Payable | | 4 4 3 15 | | |
| 19 Medical Plan Payable | | 6 8 2 54 | | |
| 20 Retirement Plan Payable | | 4 5 8 39 | | |
| 21 Unemployment Tax Payable—Federal | | 1 3 52 | | |
| 22 Unemployment Tax Payable—State | | 9 0 64 | | |
| 23 Federal Income Tax Payable | | | | |
| 24 Dividends Payable | | 10 0 0 0 00 | | |
| 25 Capital Stock | | 200 0 0 0 00 | | |
| 26 Retained Earnings | | 204 2 6 5 75 | | |
| 27 Dividends | 37 0 0 0 00 | | | |
| 28 Income Summary—General | | | | |
| 29 Income Summary—Parts | | | | |
| 30 Income Summary—Accessories | | | | |
| 31 Sales—Parts | | 442 2 0 8 00 | | |
| 32 Sales Discount—Parts | 5 3 4 6 15 | | | |
| 33 Sales Returns and Allowances—Parts | 6 1 7 1 57 | | | |
| 34 Sales—Accessories | | 255 3 8 0 00 | | |

*(Note: Work Sheet continues on p. 181.)*

| | 5 | 6 | 7 | 8 | 9 | 10 | 11 | 12 |
|---|---|---|---|---|---|---|---|---|
| | DEPARTMENTAL STATEMENTS | | | | INCOME STATEMENT | | BALANCE SHEET | |
| | PARTS | | ACCESSORIES | | | | | |
| | DEBIT | CREDIT | DEBIT | CREDIT | DEBIT | CREDIT | DEBIT | CREDIT |
| 1 | | | | | | | | |
| 2 | | | | | | | | |
| 3 | | | | | | | | |
| 4 | | | | | | | | |
| 5 | | | | | | | | |
| 6 | | | | | | | | |
| 7 | | | | | | | | |
| 8 | | | | | | | | |
| 9 | | | | | | | | |
| 10 | | | | | | | | |
| 11 | | | | | | | | |
| 12 | | | | | | | | |
| 13 | | | | | | | | |
| 14 | | | | | | | | |
| 15 | | | | | | | | |
| 16 | | | | | | | | |
| 17 | | | | | | | | |
| 18 | | | | | | | | |
| 19 | | | | | | | | |
| 20 | | | | | | | | |
| 21 | | | | | | | | |
| 22 | | | | | | | | |
| 23 | | | | | | | | |
| 24 | | | | | | | | |
| 25 | | | | | | | | |
| 26 | | | | | | | | |
| 27 | | | | | | | | |
| 28 | | | | | | | | |
| 29 | | | | | | | | |
| 30 | | | | | | | | |
| 31 | | | | | | | | |
| 32 | | | | | | | | |
| 33 | | | | | | | | |
| 34 | | | | | | | | |

*(Note: Work Sheet continues on p. 182.)*

| | | | 1 | | 2 | | 3 | | 4 | |
|---|---|---|---|---|---|---|---|---|---|---|
| | ACCOUNT TITLE | | TRIAL BALANCE | | | | ADJUSTMENTS | | | |
| | | | DEBIT | | CREDIT | | DEBIT | | CREDIT | |
| 35 | Sales Discount—Accessories | | 3 3 7 8 04 | | | | | | | |
| 36 | Sales Returns and Allowances—Accessories | | 8 9 1 7 49 | | | | | | | |
| 37 | Purchases—Parts | | 201 7 6 5 00 | | | | | | | |
| 38 | Purchases Discount—Parts | | | | 2 0 1 9 21 | | | | | |
| 39 | Purchases Returns and Allowances—Parts | | | | 3 9 6 0 33 | | | | | |
| 40 | Purchases—Accessories | | 140 4 8 1 19 | | | | | | | |
| 41 | Purchases Discount—Accessories | | | | 1 7 2 6 79 | | | | | |
| 42 | Purchases Returns and Allowances—Accessories | | | | 6 2 1 6 27 | | | | | |
| 43 | Advertising Expense—Parts | | 6 2 0 0 00 | | | | | | | |
| 44 | Payroll Taxes Expense—Parts | | 4 1 9 2 36 | | | | | | | |
| 45 | Salary Expense—Parts | | 47 6 4 5 19 | | | | | | | |
| 46 | Advertising Expense—Accessories | | 3 8 0 0 00 | | | | | | | |
| 47 | Payroll Taxes Expense—Accessories | | 7 0 7 0 97 | | | | | | | |
| 48 | Salary Expense—Accessories | | 81 5 5 4 20 | | | | | | | |
| 49 | Credit Card Fee Expense | | 4 4 3 0 92 | | | | | | | |
| 50 | Depreciation Expense—Office Equipment | | | | | | | | | |
| 51 | Depreciation Expense—Store Equipment | | | | | | | | | |
| 52 | Insurance Expense | | | | | | | | | |
| 53 | Miscellaneous Expense | | 2 2 5 7 64 | | | | | | | |
| 54 | Payroll Taxes Expense—Administrative | | 4 9 4 5 34 | | | | | | | |
| 55 | Rent Expense | | 16 5 0 0 00 | | | | | | | |
| 56 | Salary Expense—Administrative | | 57 0 5 7 83 | | | | | | | |
| 57 | Supplies Expense | | | | | | | | | |
| 58 | Uncollectible Accounts Expense | | | | | | | | | |
| 59 | Utilities Expense | | 5 4 5 8 47 | | | | | | | |
| 60 | | | | | | | | | | |
| 61 | Department Margin—Parts | | | | | | | | | |
| 62 | Department Margin—Accessories | | | | | | | | | |
| 63 | | | | | | | | | | |
| 64 | Federal Income Tax Expense | | 10 0 0 0 00 | | | | | | | |
| 65 | Totals | | 1185 9 5 5 57 | | 1185 9 5 5 57 | | | | | |
| 66 | | | | | | | | | | |
| 67 | | | | | | | | | | |
| 68 | | | | | | | | | | |

# APPENDIX PROBLEM 4-2 (concluded)

| | 5 | 6 | 7 | 8 | 9 | 10 | 11 | 12 | |
|---|---|---|---|---|---|---|---|---|---|
| | DEPARTMENTAL STATEMENTS | | | | INCOME STATEMENT | | BALANCE SHEET | | |
| | PARTS | | ACCESSORIES | | | | | | |
| | DEBIT | CREDIT | DEBIT | CREDIT | DEBIT | CREDIT | DEBIT | CREDIT | |
| | | | | | | | | | 35 |
| | | | | | | | | | 36 |
| | | | | | | | | | 37 |
| | | | | | | | | | 38 |
| | | | | | | | | | 39 |
| | | | | | | | | | 40 |
| | | | | | | | | | 41 |
| | | | | | | | | | 42 |
| | | | | | | | | | 43 |
| | | | | | | | | | 44 |
| | | | | | | | | | 45 |
| | | | | | | | | | 46 |
| | | | | | | | | | 47 |
| | | | | | | | | | 48 |
| | | | | | | | | | 49 |
| | | | | | | | | | 50 |
| | | | | | | | | | 51 |
| | | | | | | | | | 52 |
| | | | | | | | | | 53 |
| | | | | | | | | | 54 |
| | | | | | | | | | 55 |
| | | | | | | | | | 56 |
| | | | | | | | | | 57 |
| | | | | | | | | | 58 |
| | | | | | | | | | 59 |
| | | | | | | | | | 60 |
| | | | | | | | | | 61 |
| | | | | | | | | | 62 |
| | | | | | | | | | 63 |
| | | | | | | | | | 64 |
| | | | | | | | | | 65 |
| | | | | | | | | | 66 |
| | | | | | | | | | 67 |
| | | | | | | | | | 68 |

Name _____ Date _____ Class _____

# APPENDIX PROBLEM 4-3, p. 135

**Preparing a work sheet**

**1., 2., 3.**

Sunset Sports, Inc.

Work Sheet

December 31, 20--

| | ACCOUNT TITLE | TRIAL BALANCE | | ADJUSTMENTS | |
|---|---|---|---|---|---|
| | | DEBIT | CREDIT | DEBIT | CREDIT |
| 1 | Cash | 53 3 1 4 47 | | | |
| 2 | Petty Cash | 1 5 0 15 | | | |
| 3 | Accounts Receivable | 11 6 7 7 03 | | | |
| 4 | Allowance for Uncollectible Accounts | | 5 1 6 36 | | |
| 5 | Merchandise Inventory—Golf | 62 8 4 9 00 | | | |
| 6 | Merchandise Inventory—Tennis | 49 1 8 3 00 | | | |
| 7 | Supplies | 3 1 0 5 04 | | | |
| 8 | Prepaid Insurance | 13 0 0 0 00 | | | |
| 9 | Office Equipment | 13 1 2 2 52 | | | |
| 10 | Accumulated Depreciation—Office Equipment | | 9 1 9 5 00 | | |
| 11 | Store Equipment | 41 7 1 4 34 | | | |
| 12 | Accumulated Depreciation—Store Equipment | | 22 3 9 0 00 | | |
| 13 | Accounts Payable | | 22 4 5 7 79 | | |
| 14 | Sales Tax Payable | | 2 9 5 9 35 | | |
| 15 | Employee Income Tax Payable—Federal | | 1 0 7 8 32 | | |
| 16 | Employee Income Tax Payable—State | | 7 6 8 39 | | |
| 17 | Social Security Tax Payable | | 1 9 0 5 07 | | |
| 18 | Medicare Tax Payable | | 4 4 3 83 | | |
| 19 | Medical Plan Payable | | 6 8 5 15 | | |
| 20 | Retirement Plan Payable | | 4 5 9 36 | | |
| 21 | Unemployment Tax Payable—Federal | | 1 3 53 | | |
| 22 | Unemployment Tax Payable—State | | 9 0 24 | | |
| 23 | Federal Income Tax Payable | | | | |
| 24 | Dividends Payable | | 5 0 0 0 00 | | |
| 25 | Capital Stock | | 60 0 0 0 00 | | |
| 26 | Retained Earnings | | 66 7 6 8 35 | | |
| 27 | Dividends | 23 4 0 0 00 | | | |
| 28 | Income Summary—General | | | | |
| 29 | Income Summary—Golf | | | | |
| 30 | Income Summary—Tennis | | | | |
| 31 | Sales—Golf | | 362 4 8 3 36 | | |
| 32 | Sales Discount—Golf | 5 3 8 5 63 | | | |
| 33 | Sales Returns and Allowances—Golf | 6 1 2 6 18 | | | |
| 34 | Sales—Tennis | | 230 4 9 5 71 | | |

*(Note: Work Sheet continues on p. 185.)*

# APPENDIX PROBLEM 4-3 (continued)

| | 5 | 6 | 7 | 8 | 9 | 10 | 11 | 12 | |
|---|---|---|---|---|---|---|---|---|---|
| | DEPARTMENTAL STATEMENTS | | | | INCOME STATEMENT | | BALANCE SHEET | | |
| | GOLF | | TENNIS | | | | | | |
| | DEBIT | CREDIT | DEBIT | CREDIT | DEBIT | CREDIT | DEBIT | CREDIT | |
| | | | | | | | | | 1 |
| | | | | | | | | | 2 |
| | | | | | | | | | 3 |
| | | | | | | | | | 4 |
| | | | | | | | | | 5 |
| | | | | | | | | | 6 |
| | | | | | | | | | 7 |
| | | | | | | | | | 8 |
| | | | | | | | | | 9 |
| | | | | | | | | | 10 |
| | | | | | | | | | 11 |
| | | | | | | | | | 12 |
| | | | | | | | | | 13 |
| | | | | | | | | | 14 |
| | | | | | | | | | 15 |
| | | | | | | | | | 16 |
| | | | | | | | | | 17 |
| | | | | | | | | | 18 |
| | | | | | | | | | 19 |
| | | | | | | | | | 20 |
| | | | | | | | | | 21 |
| | | | | | | | | | 22 |
| | | | | | | | | | 23 |
| | | | | | | | | | 24 |
| | | | | | | | | | 25 |
| | | | | | | | | | 26 |
| | | | | | | | | | 27 |
| | | | | | | | | | 28 |
| | | | | | | | | | 29 |
| | | | | | | | | | 30 |
| | | | | | | | | | 31 |
| | | | | | | | | | 32 |
| | | | | | | | | | 33 |
| | | | | | | | | | 34 |

(Note: Work Sheet continues on p. 186.)

**184** • Working Papers

## APPENDIX PROBLEM 4-3 (continued)

| | ACCOUNT TITLE | TRIAL BALANCE DEBIT | TRIAL BALANCE CREDIT | ADJUSTMENTS DEBIT | ADJUSTMENTS CREDIT |
|---|---|---|---|---|---|
| 35 | Sales Discount—Tennis | 3 4 1 6 57 | | | |
| 36 | Sales Returns and Allowances—Tennis | 8 8 8 2 27 | | | |
| 37 | Purchases—Golf | 154 6 9 4 05 | | | |
| 38 | Purchases Discount—Golf | | 2 0 2 0 23 | | |
| 39 | Purchases Returns and Allowances—Golf | | 3 9 6 8 96 | | |
| 40 | Purchases—Tennis | 117 4 6 5 31 | | | |
| 41 | Purchases Discount—Tennis | | 1 7 3 4 91 | | |
| 42 | Purchases Returns and Allowances—Tennis | | 5 2 3 4 63 | | |
| 43 | Advertising Expense—Golf | 4 5 2 0 00 | | | |
| 44 | Payroll Taxes Expense—Golf | 4 2 0 2 27 | | | |
| 45 | Salary Expense—Golf | 47 6 1 7 46 | | | |
| 46 | Advertising Expense—Tennis | 3 8 2 5 00 | | | |
| 47 | Payroll Taxes Expense—Tennis | 5 6 8 1 90 | | | |
| 48 | Salary Expense—Tennis | 65 5 8 9 31 | | | |
| 49 | Credit Card Fee Expense | 3 4 1 5 18 | | | |
| 50 | Depreciation Expense—Office Equipment | | | | |
| 51 | Depreciation Expense—Store Equipment | | | | |
| 52 | Insurance Expense | | | | |
| 53 | Miscellaneous Expense | 6 2 1 0 16 | | | |
| 54 | Payroll Taxes Expense—Administrative | 4 9 3 2 43 | | | |
| 55 | Rent Expense | 14 5 0 0 00 | | | |
| 56 | Salary Expense—Administrative | 57 4 6 9 05 | | | |
| 57 | Supplies Expense | | | | |
| 58 | Uncollectible Accounts Expense | | | | |
| 59 | Utilities Expense | 5 2 2 0 22 | | | |
| 60 | | | | | |
| 61 | Department Margin—Golf | | | | |
| 62 | Department Margin—Tennis | | | | |
| 63 | | | | | |
| 64 | Federal Income Tax Expense | 10 0 0 0 00 | | | |
| 65 | Totals | 800 6 6 8 54 | 800 6 6 8 54 | | |
| 66 | | | | | |
| 67 | | | | | |
| 68 | | | | | |

# APPENDIX PROBLEM 4-3 (concluded)

| | 5 | 6 | 7 | 8 | 9 | 10 | 11 | 12 | |
|---|---|---|---|---|---|---|---|---|---|
| | DEPARTMENTAL STATEMENTS | | | | INCOME STATEMENT | | BALANCE SHEET | | |
| | GOLF | | TENNIS | | | | | | |
| | DEBIT | CREDIT | DEBIT | CREDIT | DEBIT | CREDIT | DEBIT | CREDIT | |
| | | | | | | | | | 35 |
| | | | | | | | | | 36 |
| | | | | | | | | | 37 |
| | | | | | | | | | 38 |
| | | | | | | | | | 39 |
| | | | | | | | | | 40 |
| | | | | | | | | | 41 |
| | | | | | | | | | 42 |
| | | | | | | | | | 43 |
| | | | | | | | | | 44 |
| | | | | | | | | | 45 |
| | | | | | | | | | 46 |
| | | | | | | | | | 47 |
| | | | | | | | | | 48 |
| | | | | | | | | | 49 |
| | | | | | | | | | 50 |
| | | | | | | | | | 51 |
| | | | | | | | | | 52 |
| | | | | | | | | | 53 |
| | | | | | | | | | 54 |
| | | | | | | | | | 55 |
| | | | | | | | | | 56 |
| | | | | | | | | | 57 |
| | | | | | | | | | 58 |
| | | | | | | | | | 59 |
| | | | | | | | | | 60 |
| | | | | | | | | | 61 |
| | | | | | | | | | 62 |
| | | | | | | | | | 63 |
| | | | | | | | | | 64 |
| | | | | | | | | | 65 |
| | | | | | | | | | 66 |
| | | | | | | | | | 67 |
| | | | | | | | | | 68 |

# REINFORCEMENT ACTIVITY 1, p. 136

## Processing and Reporting Departmentalized Accounting Data

## 1., 2., 4., 5., 8., 9., 12., 14., 21.

### GENERAL LEDGER

ACCOUNT Cash                                                                          ACCOUNT NO. 1105

| DATE | | ITEM | POST. REF. | DEBIT | CREDIT | BALANCE DEBIT | BALANCE CREDIT |
|------|---|------|-----------|-------|--------|---------------|----------------|
| 20-- Dec. | 1 | Balance | ✔ | | | 38 1 4 2 62 | |
| | | | | | | | |
| | | | | | | | |
| | | | | | | | |
| | | | | | | | |

ACCOUNT Petty Cash                                                                   ACCOUNT NO. 1110

| DATE | | ITEM | POST. REF. | DEBIT | CREDIT | BALANCE DEBIT | BALANCE CREDIT |
|------|---|------|-----------|-------|--------|---------------|----------------|
| 20-- Dec. | 1 | Balance | ✔ | | | 5 0 0 00 | |
| | | | | | | | |

ACCOUNT Accounts Receivable                                                          ACCOUNT NO. 1205

| DATE | | ITEM | POST. REF. | DEBIT | CREDIT | BALANCE DEBIT | BALANCE CREDIT |
|------|---|------|-----------|-------|--------|---------------|----------------|
| 20-- Dec. | 1 | Balance | ✔ | | | 12 3 5 6 74 | |
| | | | | | | | |
| | | | | | | | |

ACCOUNT Allowance for Uncollectible Accounts                                         ACCOUNT NO. 1210

| DATE | | ITEM | POST. REF. | DEBIT | CREDIT | BALANCE DEBIT | BALANCE CREDIT |
|------|---|------|-----------|-------|--------|---------------|----------------|
| 20-- Dec. | 1 | Balance | ✔ | | | | 5 1 7 43 |
| | | | | | | | |

ACCOUNT Merchandise Inventory—Equipment                                              ACCOUNT NO. 1305

| DATE | | ITEM | POST. REF. | DEBIT | CREDIT | BALANCE DEBIT | BALANCE CREDIT |
|------|---|------|-----------|-------|--------|---------------|----------------|
| 20-- Dec. | 1 | Balance | ✔ | | | 81 4 8 3 61 | |
| | | | | | | | |

Reinforcement Activity 1 • **187**

ACCOUNT Merchandise Inventory—Accessories     ACCOUNT NO. 1310

| DATE | | ITEM | POST. REF. | DEBIT | CREDIT | BALANCE DEBIT | BALANCE CREDIT |
|------|---|------|-----------|-------|--------|---------------|----------------|
| 20-- Dec. | 1 | Balance | ✔ | | | 157 4 1 4 10 | |
| | | | | | | | |
| | | | | | | | |

ACCOUNT Supplies     ACCOUNT NO. 1405

| DATE | | ITEM | POST. REF. | DEBIT | CREDIT | BALANCE DEBIT | BALANCE CREDIT |
|------|---|------|-----------|-------|--------|---------------|----------------|
| 20-- Dec. | 1 | Balance | ✔ | | | 8 1 4 3 04 | |
| | | | | | | | |
| | | | | | | | |
| | | | | | | | |

ACCOUNT Prepaid Insurance     ACCOUNT NO. 1410

| DATE | | ITEM | POST. REF. | DEBIT | CREDIT | BALANCE DEBIT | BALANCE CREDIT |
|------|---|------|-----------|-------|--------|---------------|----------------|
| 20-- Dec. | 1 | Balance | ✔ | | | 16 2 0 0 00 | |
| | | | | | | | |
| | | | | | | | |

ACCOUNT Office Equipment     ACCOUNT NO. 1505

| DATE | | ITEM | POST. REF. | DEBIT | CREDIT | BALANCE DEBIT | BALANCE CREDIT |
|------|---|------|-----------|-------|--------|---------------|----------------|
| 20-- Dec. | 1 | Balance | ✔ | | | 29 1 4 0 61 | |
| | | | | | | | |
| | | | | | | | |

ACCOUNT Accumulated Depreciation—Office Equipment     ACCOUNT NO. 1510

| DATE | | ITEM | POST. REF. | DEBIT | CREDIT | BALANCE DEBIT | BALANCE CREDIT |
|------|---|------|-----------|-------|--------|---------------|----------------|
| 20-- Dec. | 1 | Balance | ✔ | | | | 13 0 5 0 00 |
| | | | | | | | |
| | | | | | | | |

## REINFORCEMENT ACTIVITY 1 (continued)

ACCOUNT Store Equipment      ACCOUNT NO. 1515

| DATE | | ITEM | POST. REF. | DEBIT | CREDIT | BALANCE DEBIT | BALANCE CREDIT |
|---|---|---|---|---|---|---|---|
| 20-- Dec. | 1 | Balance | ✔ | | | 38 1 6 7 51 | |
| | | | | | | | |
| | | | | | | | |

ACCOUNT Accumulated Depreciation—Store Equipment      ACCOUNT NO. 1520

| DATE | | ITEM | POST. REF. | DEBIT | CREDIT | BALANCE DEBIT | BALANCE CREDIT |
|---|---|---|---|---|---|---|---|
| 20-- Dec. | 1 | Balance | ✔ | | | | 15 3 6 0 00 |
| | | | | | | | |
| | | | | | | | |

ACCOUNT Accounts Payable      ACCOUNT NO. 2105

| DATE | | ITEM | POST. REF. | DEBIT | CREDIT | BALANCE DEBIT | BALANCE CREDIT |
|---|---|---|---|---|---|---|---|
| 20-- Dec. | 1 | Balance | ✔ | | | | 20 3 7 6 63 |
| | | | | | | | |
| | | | | | | | |
| | | | | | | | |
| | | | | | | | |

ACCOUNT Sales Tax Payable      ACCOUNT NO. 2110

| DATE | | ITEM | POST. REF. | DEBIT | CREDIT | BALANCE DEBIT | BALANCE CREDIT |
|---|---|---|---|---|---|---|---|
| 20-- Dec. | 1 | Balance | ✔ | | | | 2 6 4 1 62 |
| | | | | | | | |
| | | | | | | | |
| | | | | | | | |

ACCOUNT Employee Income Tax Payable—Federal      ACCOUNT NO. 2115

| DATE | | ITEM | POST. REF. | DEBIT | CREDIT | BALANCE DEBIT | BALANCE CREDIT |
|---|---|---|---|---|---|---|---|
| 20-- Dec. | 1 | Balance | ✔ | | | | 5 2 4 00 |
| | | | | | | | |
| | | | | | | | |

# REINFORCEMENT ACTIVITY 1 (continued)

ACCOUNT Employee Income Tax Payable—State     ACCOUNT NO. 2120

| DATE | ITEM | POST. REF. | DEBIT | CREDIT | BALANCE DEBIT | BALANCE CREDIT |
|------|------|------------|-------|--------|---------------|----------------|
| Dec. 1 | Balance | ✔ | | | | 4 2 9 00 |
| | | | | | | |
| | | | | | | |

ACCOUNT Social Security Tax Payable     ACCOUNT NO. 2125

| DATE | ITEM | POST. REF. | DEBIT | CREDIT | BALANCE DEBIT | BALANCE CREDIT |
|------|------|------------|-------|--------|---------------|----------------|
| Dec. 1 | Balance | ✔ | | | | 9 6 1 85 |
| | | | | | | |
| | | | | | | |
| | | | | | | |
| | | | | | | |

ACCOUNT Medicare Tax Payable     ACCOUNT NO. 2130

| DATE | ITEM | POST. REF. | DEBIT | CREDIT | BALANCE DEBIT | BALANCE CREDIT |
|------|------|------------|-------|--------|---------------|----------------|
| Dec. 1 | Balance | ✔ | | | | 2 2 4 95 |
| | | | | | | |
| | | | | | | |
| | | | | | | |

ACCOUNT Medical Insurance Payable     ACCOUNT NO. 2135

| DATE | ITEM | POST. REF. | DEBIT | CREDIT | BALANCE DEBIT | BALANCE CREDIT |
|------|------|------------|-------|--------|---------------|----------------|
| Dec. 1 | Balance | ✔ | | | | 4 5 0 00 |
| | | | | | | |
| | | | | | | |

ACCOUNT Retirement Plan Payable     ACCOUNT NO. 2140

| DATE | ITEM | POST. REF. | DEBIT | CREDIT | BALANCE DEBIT | BALANCE CREDIT |
|------|------|------------|-------|--------|---------------|----------------|
| Dec. 1 | Balance | ✔ | | | | 5 2 0 00 |
| | | | | | | |
| | | | | | | |

# REINFORCEMENT ACTIVITY 1 (continued)

ACCOUNT **Unemployment Tax Payable—Federal**          ACCOUNT NO. 2145

| DATE | | ITEM | POST. REF. | DEBIT | CREDIT | BALANCE DEBIT | BALANCE CREDIT |
|---|---|---|---|---|---|---|---|
| Dec. | 1 | Balance | ✔ | | | | 2 1 0 60 |
| | | | | | | | |
| | | | | | | | |

ACCOUNT **Unemployment Tax Payable—State**          ACCOUNT NO. 2150

| DATE | | ITEM | POST. REF. | DEBIT | CREDIT | BALANCE DEBIT | BALANCE CREDIT |
|---|---|---|---|---|---|---|---|
| Dec. | 1 | Balance | ✔ | | | | 4 2 4 62 |
| | | | | | | | |
| | | | | | | | |

ACCOUNT **Federal Income Tax Payable**          ACCOUNT NO. 2155

| DATE | | ITEM | POST. REF. | DEBIT | CREDIT | BALANCE DEBIT | BALANCE CREDIT |
|---|---|---|---|---|---|---|---|
| | | | | | | | |
| | | | | | | | |
| | | | | | | | |
| | | | | | | | |
| | | | | | | | |

ACCOUNT **Dividends Payable**          ACCOUNT NO. 2160

| DATE | | ITEM | POST. REF. | DEBIT | CREDIT | BALANCE DEBIT | BALANCE CREDIT |
|---|---|---|---|---|---|---|---|
| | | | | | | | |
| | | | | | | | |
| | | | | | | | |
| | | | | | | | |
| | | | | | | | |

ACCOUNT **Capital Stock**          ACCOUNT NO. 3105

| DATE | | ITEM | POST. REF. | DEBIT | CREDIT | BALANCE DEBIT | BALANCE CREDIT |
|---|---|---|---|---|---|---|---|
| Dec. | 1 | Balance | ✔ | | | | 150 0 0 0 00 |
| | | | | | | | |
| | | | | | | | |

ACCOUNT Retained Earnings                                    ACCOUNT NO. 3110

| DATE | | ITEM | POST. REF. | DEBIT | CREDIT | BALANCE DEBIT | BALANCE CREDIT |
|------|---|------|-----------|-------|--------|-------|--------|
| Dec. | 1 | Balance | ✔ | | | | 114 8 0 3 91 |
| | | | | | | | |
| | | | | | | | |

ACCOUNT Dividends                                            ACCOUNT NO. 3115

| DATE | | ITEM | POST. REF. | DEBIT | CREDIT | BALANCE DEBIT | BALANCE CREDIT |
|------|---|------|-----------|-------|--------|-------|--------|
| Dec. | 1 | Balance | ✔ | | | 21 5 0 0 00 | |
| | | | | | | | |
| | | | | | | | |
| | | | | | | | |

ACCOUNT Income Summary—General                              ACCOUNT NO. 3205

| DATE | ITEM | POST. REF. | DEBIT | CREDIT | BALANCE DEBIT | BALANCE CREDIT |
|------|------|-----------|-------|--------|-------|--------|
| | | | | | | |
| | | | | | | |
| | | | | | | |
| | | | | | | |
| | | | | | | |

ACCOUNT Income Summary—Equipment                           ACCOUNT NO. 3210

| DATE | ITEM | POST. REF. | DEBIT | CREDIT | BALANCE DEBIT | BALANCE CREDIT |
|------|------|-----------|-------|--------|-------|--------|
| | | | | | | |
| | | | | | | |
| | | | | | | |

ACCOUNT Income Summary—Accessories                         ACCOUNT NO. 3215

| DATE | ITEM | POST. REF. | DEBIT | CREDIT | BALANCE DEBIT | BALANCE CREDIT |
|------|------|-----------|-------|--------|-------|--------|
| | | | | | | |
| | | | | | | |
| | | | | | | |

## REINFORCEMENT ACTIVITY 1 (continued)

ACCOUNT Sales—Equipment                                    ACCOUNT NO. 4105

| DATE | | ITEM | POST. REF. | DEBIT | CREDIT | BALANCE | |
|---|---|---|---|---|---|---|---|
| | | | | | | DEBIT | CREDIT |
| 20-- Dec. | 1 | Balance | ✔ | | | | 203 01 8 62 |
| | | | | | | | |
| | | | | | | | |

ACCOUNT Sales Discount—Equipment                           ACCOUNT NO. 4110

| DATE | | ITEM | POST. REF. | DEBIT | CREDIT | BALANCE | |
|---|---|---|---|---|---|---|---|
| | | | | | | DEBIT | CREDIT |
| 20-- Dec. | 1 | Balance | ✔ | | | 2 1 4 62 | |
| | | | | | | | |
| | | | | | | | |

ACCOUNT Sales Returns and Allowances—Equipment             ACCOUNT NO. 4115

| DATE | | ITEM | POST. REF. | DEBIT | CREDIT | BALANCE | |
|---|---|---|---|---|---|---|---|
| | | | | | | DEBIT | CREDIT |
| 20-- Dec. | 1 | Balance | ✔ | | | 2 4 8 6 68 | |
| | | | | | | | |

ACCOUNT Sales—Accessories                                  ACCOUNT NO. 4205

| DATE | | ITEM | POST. REF. | DEBIT | CREDIT | BALANCE | |
|---|---|---|---|---|---|---|---|
| | | | | | | DEBIT | CREDIT |
| 20-- Dec. | 1 | Balance | ✔ | | | | 394 5 4 8 62 |
| | | | | | | | |
| | | | | | | | |

ACCOUNT Sales Discount—Accessories                         ACCOUNT NO. 4210

| DATE | | ITEM | POST. REF. | DEBIT | CREDIT | BALANCE | |
|---|---|---|---|---|---|---|---|
| | | | | | | DEBIT | CREDIT |
| 20-- Dec. | 1 | Balance | ✔ | | | 2 8 4 6 62 | |

ACCOUNT Sales Returns and Allowances—Accessories ACCOUNT NO. 4215

| DATE | | ITEM | POST. REF. | DEBIT | CREDIT | BALANCE | |
|---|---|---|---|---|---|---|---|
| | | | | | | DEBIT | CREDIT |
| Dec. 20-- | 1 | Balance | ✔ | | | 6 1 1 4 15 | |

ACCOUNT Purchases—Equipment ACCOUNT NO. 5105

| DATE | | ITEM | POST. REF. | DEBIT | CREDIT | BALANCE | |
|---|---|---|---|---|---|---|---|
| | | | | | | DEBIT | CREDIT |
| Dec. 20-- | 1 | Balance | ✔ | | | 102 4 8 3 31 | |

ACCOUNT Purchases Discount—Equipment ACCOUNT NO. 5110

| DATE | | ITEM | POST. REF. | DEBIT | CREDIT | BALANCE | |
|---|---|---|---|---|---|---|---|
| | | | | | | DEBIT | CREDIT |
| Dec. 20-- | 1 | Balance | ✔ | | | | 1 1 8 4 14 |

ACCOUNT Purchases Returns and Allowances—Equipment ACCOUNT NO. 5115

| DATE | | ITEM | POST. REF. | DEBIT | CREDIT | BALANCE | |
|---|---|---|---|---|---|---|---|
| | | | | | | DEBIT | CREDIT |
| Dec. 20-- | 1 | Balance | ✔ | | | | 4 1 1 7 61 |

ACCOUNT Purchases—Accessories ACCOUNT NO. 5205

| DATE | | ITEM | POST. REF. | DEBIT | CREDIT | BALANCE | |
|---|---|---|---|---|---|---|---|
| | | | | | | DEBIT | CREDIT |
| Dec. 20-- | 1 | Balance | ✔ | | | 221 4 9 3 61 | |

## REINFORCEMENT ACTIVITY 1 (continued)

ACCOUNT Purchases Discount—Accessories      ACCOUNT NO. 5210

| DATE | ITEM | POST. REF. | DEBIT | CREDIT | BALANCE DEBIT | BALANCE CREDIT |
|------|------|-----------|-------|--------|-------|--------|
| Dec. 1 | Balance | ✔ | | | | 4 1 6 2 04 |
| | | | | | | |
| | | | | | | |

ACCOUNT Purchases Returns and Allowances—Accessories      ACCOUNT NO. 5215

| DATE | ITEM | POST. REF. | DEBIT | CREDIT | BALANCE DEBIT | BALANCE CREDIT |
|------|------|-----------|-------|--------|-------|--------|
| Dec. 1 | Balance | ✔ | | | | 12 9 1 4 62 |
| | | | | | | |
| | | | | | | |

ACCOUNT Advertising Expense—Equipment      ACCOUNT NO. 6105

| DATE | ITEM | POST. REF. | DEBIT | CREDIT | BALANCE DEBIT | BALANCE CREDIT |
|------|------|-----------|-------|--------|-------|--------|
| Dec. 1 | Balance | ✔ | | | 16 2 0 0 00 | |
| | | | | | | |
| | | | | | | |

ACCOUNT Payroll Taxes Expense—Equipment      ACCOUNT NO. 6110

| DATE | ITEM | POST. REF. | DEBIT | CREDIT | BALANCE DEBIT | BALANCE CREDIT |
|------|------|-----------|-------|--------|-------|--------|
| Dec. 1 | Balance | ✔ | | | 3 6 5 4 08 | |
| | | | | | | |
| | | | | | | |

ACCOUNT Salary Expense—Equipment      ACCOUNT NO. 6115

| DATE | ITEM | POST. REF. | DEBIT | CREDIT | BALANCE DEBIT | BALANCE CREDIT |
|------|------|-----------|-------|--------|-------|--------|
| Dec. 1 | Balance | ✔ | | | 36 4 1 9 57 | |
| | | | | | | |
| | | | | | | |

ACCOUNT Advertising Expense—Accessories    ACCOUNT NO. 6205

| DATE | | ITEM | POST. REF. | DEBIT | CREDIT | BALANCE | |
|---|---|---|---|---|---|---|---|
| | | | | | | DEBIT | CREDIT |
| Dec. | 1 | Balance | ✔ | | | 6 3 5 0 00 | |
| | | | | | | | |
| | | | | | | | |

ACCOUNT Payroll Taxes Expense—Accessories    ACCOUNT NO. 6210

| DATE | | ITEM | POST. REF. | DEBIT | CREDIT | BALANCE | |
|---|---|---|---|---|---|---|---|
| | | | | | | DEBIT | CREDIT |
| Dec. | 1 | Balance | ✔ | | | 3 8 8 3 11 | |
| | | | | | | | |
| | | | | | | | |

ACCOUNT Salary Expense—Accessories    ACCOUNT NO. 6215

| DATE | | ITEM | POST. REF. | DEBIT | CREDIT | BALANCE | |
|---|---|---|---|---|---|---|---|
| | | | | | | DEBIT | CREDIT |
| Dec. | 1 | Balance | ✔ | | | 39 4 1 3 25 | |
| | | | | | | | |
| | | | | | | | |

ACCOUNT Credit Card Fee Expense    ACCOUNT NO. 7105

| DATE | | ITEM | POST. REF. | DEBIT | CREDIT | BALANCE | |
|---|---|---|---|---|---|---|---|
| | | | | | | DEBIT | CREDIT |
| Dec. | 1 | Balance | ✔ | | | 5 1 2 1 64 | |
| | | | | | | | |
| | | | | | | | |

ACCOUNT Depreciation Expense—Office Equipment    ACCOUNT NO. 7110

| DATE | | ITEM | POST. REF. | DEBIT | CREDIT | BALANCE | |
|---|---|---|---|---|---|---|---|
| | | | | | | DEBIT | CREDIT |
| Dec. | 1 | Balance | ✔ | | | 10 4 8 0 00 | |
| | | | | | | | |
| | | | | | | | |

# REINFORCEMENT ACTIVITY 1 (continued)

ACCOUNT Depreciation Expense—Store Equipment    ACCOUNT NO. 7115

| DATE | | ITEM | POST. REF. | DEBIT | CREDIT | BALANCE DEBIT | BALANCE CREDIT |
|---|---|---|---|---|---|---|---|
| 20-- Dec. | 1 | Balance | ✔ | | | 16 1 8 0 00 | |
| | | | | | | | |
| | | | | | | | |

ACCOUNT Insurance Expense    ACCOUNT NO. 7120

| DATE | | ITEM | POST. REF. | DEBIT | CREDIT | BALANCE DEBIT | BALANCE CREDIT |
|---|---|---|---|---|---|---|---|
| | | | | | | | |
| | | | | | | | |
| | | | | | | | |

ACCOUNT Miscellaneous Expense    ACCOUNT NO. 7125

| DATE | | ITEM | POST. REF. | DEBIT | CREDIT | BALANCE DEBIT | BALANCE CREDIT |
|---|---|---|---|---|---|---|---|
| 20-- Dec. | 1 | Balance | ✔ | | | 6 4 1 8 22 | |
| | | | | | | | |
| | | | | | | | |

ACCOUNT Payroll Taxes Expense—Administrative    ACCOUNT NO. 7130

| DATE | | ITEM | POST. REF. | DEBIT | CREDIT | BALANCE DEBIT | BALANCE CREDIT |
|---|---|---|---|---|---|---|---|
| 20-- Dec. | 1 | Balance | ✔ | | | 2 0 4 9 28 | |
| | | | | | | | |
| | | | | | | | |

ACCOUNT Rent Expense    ACCOUNT NO. 7135

| DATE | | ITEM | POST. REF. | DEBIT | CREDIT | BALANCE DEBIT | BALANCE CREDIT |
|---|---|---|---|---|---|---|---|
| 20-- Dec. | 1 | Balance | ✔ | | | 25 3 0 0 00 | |
| | | | | | | | |
| | | | | | | | |

# REINFORCEMENT ACTIVITY 1 (continued)

ACCOUNT Salary Expense—Administrative                                                ACCOUNT NO. 7140

| DATE | | ITEM | POST. REF. | DEBIT | CREDIT | BALANCE | |
|---|---|---|---|---|---|---|---|
| | | | | | | DEBIT | CREDIT |
| Dec. | 1 | Balance | ✔ | | | 15 4 4 1 63 | |
| | | | | | | | |
| | | | | | | | |

ACCOUNT Supplies Expense                                                             ACCOUNT NO. 7145

| DATE | | ITEM | POST. REF. | DEBIT | CREDIT | BALANCE | |
|---|---|---|---|---|---|---|---|
| | | | | | | DEBIT | CREDIT |
| | | | | | | | |
| | | | | | | | |
| | | | | | | | |

ACCOUNT Uncollectible Accounts Expense                                               ACCOUNT NO. 7150

| DATE | | ITEM | POST. REF. | DEBIT | CREDIT | BALANCE | |
|---|---|---|---|---|---|---|---|
| | | | | | | DEBIT | CREDIT |
| | | | | | | | |
| | | | | | | | |
| | | | | | | | |

ACCOUNT Utilities Expense                                                            ACCOUNT NO. 7155

| DATE | | ITEM | POST. REF. | DEBIT | CREDIT | BALANCE | |
|---|---|---|---|---|---|---|---|
| | | | | | | DEBIT | CREDIT |
| Dec. | 1 | Balance | ✔ | | | 6 8 4 2 26 | |
| | | | | | | | |
| | | | | | | | |

ACCOUNT Federal Income Tax Expense                                                   ACCOUNT NO. 8105

| DATE | | ITEM | POST. REF. | DEBIT | CREDIT | BALANCE | |
|---|---|---|---|---|---|---|---|
| | | | | | | DEBIT | CREDIT |
| Dec. | 1 | Balance | ✔ | | | 8 0 0 0 00 | |
| | | | | | | | |
| | | | | | | | |

# REINFORCEMENT ACTIVITY 1 (continued)

## 1., 5.

PURCHASES JOURNAL     PAGE 12

| | DATE | | ACCOUNT CREDITED | PURCH. NO. | POST. REF. | ACCOUNTS PAYABLE CREDIT (1) | PURCHASES DEBIT EQUIPMENT (2) | PURCHASES DEBIT ACCESSORIES (3) | |
|---|---|---|---|---|---|---|---|---|---|
| 1 | | | | | | | | | 1 |
| 2 | | | | | | | | | 2 |
| 3 | | | | | | | | | 3 |
| 4 | | | | | | | | | 4 |
| 5 | | | | | | | | | 5 |
| 6 | | | | | | | | | 6 |
| 7 | | | | | | | | | 7 |
| 8 | | | | | | | | | 8 |
| 9 | | | | | | | | | 9 |
| 10 | | | | | | | | | 10 |
| 11 | | | | | | | | | 11 |
| 12 | | | | | | | | | 12 |
| 13 | | | | | | | | | 13 |
| 14 | | | | | | | | | 14 |
| 15 | | | | | | | | | 15 |
| 16 | | | | | | | | | 16 |
| 17 | | | | | | | | | 17 |
| 18 | | | | | | | | | 18 |
| 19 | | | | | | | | | 19 |
| 20 | | | | | | | | | 20 |
| 21 | | | | | | | | | 21 |
| 22 | | | | | | | | | 22 |
| 23 | | | | | | | | | 23 |
| 24 | | | | | | | | | 24 |
| 25 | | | | | | | | | 25 |
| 26 | | | | | | | | | 26 |
| 27 | | | | | | | | | 27 |
| 28 | | | | | | | | | 28 |
| 29 | | | | | | | | | 29 |
| 30 | | | | | | | | | 30 |
| 31 | | | | | | | | | 31 |

**1., 2.**

CASH PAYMENTS JOURNAL

| | DATE | ACCOUNT TITLE | CK. NO. | POST. REF. | GENERAL DEBIT 1 | GENERAL CREDIT 2 | ACCOUNTS PAYABLE DEBIT 3 | PURCH. DISCOUNT CR. EQUIPMENT 4 | PURCH. DISCOUNT CR. ACCESSORIES 5 | CASH CREDIT 6 | |
|---|---|---|---|---|---|---|---|---|---|---|---|
| 1 | | | | | | | | | | | 1 |
| 2 | | | | | | | | | | | 2 |
| 3 | | | | | | | | | | | 3 |
| 4 | | | | | | | | | | | 4 |
| 5 | | | | | | | | | | | 5 |
| 6 | | | | | | | | | | | 6 |
| 7 | | | | | | | | | | | 7 |
| 8 | | | | | | | | | | | 8 |
| 9 | | | | | | | | | | | 9 |
| 10 | | | | | | | | | | | 10 |
| 11 | | | | | | | | | | | 11 |
| 12 | | | | | | | | | | | 12 |
| 13 | | | | | | | | | | | 13 |
| 14 | | | | | | | | | | | 14 |
| 15 | | | | | | | | | | | 15 |
| 16 | | | | | | | | | | | 16 |
| 17 | | | | | | | | | | | 17 |
| 18 | | | | | | | | | | | 18 |
| 19 | | | | | | | | | | | 19 |
| 20 | | | | | | | | | | | 20 |
| 21 | | | | | | | | | | | 21 |
| 22 | | | | | | | | | | | 22 |
| 23 | | | | | | | | | | | 23 |
| 24 | | | | | | | | | | | 24 |
| 25 | | | | | | | | | | | 25 |
| 26 | | | | | | | | | | | 26 |
| 27 | | | | | | | | | | | 27 |

**3., 6., 9.**

CASH PAYMENTS JOURNAL

PAGE 16

| DATE | ACCOUNT TITLE | CK. NO. | POST. REF. | GENERAL DEBIT (1) | GENERAL CREDIT (2) | ACCOUNTS PAYABLE DEBIT (3) | PURCH. DISCOUNT CR. EQUIPMENT (4) | PURCH. DISCOUNT CR. ACCESSORIES (5) | CASH CREDIT (6) |
|------|---------------|---------|------------|-------------------|--------------------|-----------------------------|------------------------------------|-------------------------------------|-----------------|
| | | | | | | | | | |
| | | | | | | | | | |
| | | | | | | | | | |
| | | | | | | | | | |
| | | | | | | | | | |
| | | | | | | | | | |
| | | | | | | | | | |
| | | | | | | | | | |
| | | | | | | | | | |
| | | | | | | | | | |
| | | | | | | | | | |
| | | | | | | | | | |
| | | | | | | | | | |
| | | | | | | | | | |
| | | | | | | | | | |
| | | | | | | | | | |
| | | | | | | | | | |
| | | | | | | | | | |
| | | | | | | | | | |
| | | | | | | | | | |
| | | | | | | | | | |
| | | | | | | | | | |
| | | | | | | | | | |
| | | | | | | | | | |
| | | | | | | | | | |
| | | | | | | | | | |
| | | | | | | | | | |

**1., 4.**

SALES JOURNAL

| | DATE | | ACCOUNT DEBITED | SALE. NO. | POST. REF. | ACCOUNTS RECEIVABLE DEBIT (1) | SALES TAX PAYABLE CREDIT (2) | SALES CREDIT | | |
|---|---|---|---|---|---|---|---|---|---|---|
| | | | | | | | | EQUIPMENT (3) | ACCESSORIES (4) | |
| 1 | | | | | | | | | | 1 |
| 2 | | | | | | | | | | 2 |
| 3 | | | | | | | | | | 3 |
| 4 | | | | | | | | | | 4 |
| 5 | | | | | | | | | | 5 |
| 6 | | | | | | | | | | 6 |
| 7 | | | | | | | | | | 7 |
| 8 | | | | | | | | | | 8 |
| 9 | | | | | | | | | | 9 |
| 10 | | | | | | | | | | 10 |
| 11 | | | | | | | | | | 11 |
| 12 | | | | | | | | | | 12 |
| 13 | | | | | | | | | | 13 |
| 14 | | | | | | | | | | 14 |
| 15 | | | | | | | | | | 15 |
| 16 | | | | | | | | | | 16 |
| 17 | | | | | | | | | | 17 |
| 18 | | | | | | | | | | 18 |
| 19 | | | | | | | | | | 19 |
| 20 | | | | | | | | | | 20 |
| 21 | | | | | | | | | | 21 |
| 22 | | | | | | | | | | 22 |
| 23 | | | | | | | | | | 23 |
| 24 | | | | | | | | | | 24 |
| 25 | | | | | | | | | | 25 |
| 26 | | | | | | | | | | 26 |
| 27 | | | | | | | | | | 27 |
| 28 | | | | | | | | | | 28 |
| 29 | | | | | | | | | | 29 |
| 30 | | | | | | | | | | 30 |
| 31 | | | | | | | | | | 31 |

# REINFORCEMENT ACTIVITY 1 (continued)

**1., 6.**

CASH RECEIPTS JOURNAL

PAGE 12

| | DATE | ACCOUNT TITLE | DOC. NO. | POST. REF. | GENERAL DEBIT | GENERAL CREDIT | ACCOUNTS RECEIVABLE CREDIT | SALES TAX PAYABLE CREDIT | SALES CREDIT EQUIPMENT | SALES CREDIT ACCESSORIES | SALES DISCOUNT DEBIT EQUIPMENT | SALES DISCOUNT DEBIT ACCESSORIES | CASH DEBIT |
|---|---|---|---|---|---|---|---|---|---|---|---|---|---|
| 1 | | | | | | | | | | | | | |
| 2 | | | | | | | | | | | | | |
| 3 | | | | | | | | | | | | | |
| 4 | | | | | | | | | | | | | |
| 5 | | | | | | | | | | | | | |
| 6 | | | | | | | | | | | | | |
| 7 | | | | | | | | | | | | | |
| 8 | | | | | | | | | | | | | |
| 9 | | | | | | | | | | | | | |
| 10 | | | | | | | | | | | | | |
| 11 | | | | | | | | | | | | | |
| 12 | | | | | | | | | | | | | |
| 13 | | | | | | | | | | | | | |

*Prove Cash:*

Cash on hand at the beginning of the month.............. $ _____

*Plus* total cash received during the month _____

*Equals* total............................................ $ _____

*Less* total cash paid during the month.................. _____

*Equals* total cash on hand at the end of the month....... $ _____

# REINFORCEMENT ACTIVITY 1 (continued)

**1.**

## GENERAL JOURNAL

| | DATE | ACCOUNT TITLE | DOC. NO. | POST. REF. | DEBIT | CREDIT | |
|---|---|---|---|---|---|---|---|
| 1 | | | | | | | 1 |
| 2 | | | | | | | 2 |
| 3 | | | | | | | 3 |
| 4 | | | | | | | 4 |
| 5 | | | | | | | 5 |
| 6 | | | | | | | 6 |
| 7 | | | | | | | 7 |
| 8 | | | | | | | 8 |
| 9 | | | | | | | 9 |
| 10 | | | | | | | 10 |
| 11 | | | | | | | 11 |
| 12 | | | | | | | 12 |
| 13 | | | | | | | 13 |
| 14 | | | | | | | 14 |
| 15 | | | | | | | 15 |
| 16 | | | | | | | 16 |
| 17 | | | | | | | 17 |
| 18 | | | | | | | 18 |

| Net Income before Federal Income Taxes | − | Tax Bracket Minimum Taxable Amount | = | Net Income Subject to Marginal Tax Rate |
|---|---|---|---|---|
| $ | − | $ | = | $ |

| Net Income Subject to Marginal Tax Rate | × | Marginal Tax Rate | = | Marginal Income Tax |
|---|---|---|---|---|
| $ | × | | = | $ |

| Bracket Minimum Income Tax | + | Marginal Income Tax | = | Federal Income Tax |
|---|---|---|---|---|
| $ | + | $ | = | $ |

## REINFORCEMENT ACTIVITY 1 (continued)

**1.**                    **ACCOUNTS PAYABLE LEDGER**

VENDOR  Burkes Industries                                           VENDOR NO. 210

| DATE | ITEM | POST. REF. | DEBIT | CREDIT | CREDIT BALANCE |
|------|------|-----------|-------|--------|----------------|
|      |      |           |       |        |                |
|      |      |           |       |        |                |
|      |      |           |       |        |                |

VENDOR  Central Kitchen Supply                                      VENDOR NO. 220

| DATE | ITEM | POST. REF. | DEBIT | CREDIT | CREDIT BALANCE |
|------|------|-----------|-------|--------|----------------|
|      |      |           |       |        |                |
|      |      |           |       |        |                |
|      |      |           |       |        |                |
|      |      |           |       |        |                |

VENDOR  Fulgham Pottery                                             VENDOR NO. 230

| DATE | ITEM | POST. REF. | DEBIT | CREDIT | CREDIT BALANCE |
|------|------|-----------|-------|--------|----------------|
| Dec. 1 | Balance | ✔ |  |  | 3 1 4 8 04 |
|      |      |           |       |        |                |
|      |      |           |       |        |                |

VENDOR  Hunley Equipment Co.                                        VENDOR NO. 240

| DATE | ITEM | POST. REF. | DEBIT | CREDIT | CREDIT BALANCE |
|------|------|-----------|-------|--------|----------------|
| Dec. 1 | Balance | ✔ |  |  | 5 9 5 8 94 |
|      |      |           |       |        |                |
|      |      |           |       |        |                |

VENDOR  Kitchen Concepts                                            VENDOR NO. 250

| DATE | ITEM | POST. REF. | DEBIT | CREDIT | CREDIT BALANCE |
|------|------|-----------|-------|--------|----------------|
| Dec. 1 | Balance | ✔ |  |  | 5 1 4 8 57 |
|      |      |           |       |        |                |
|      |      |           |       |        |                |

VENDOR Specialty Supply      VENDOR NO. 260

| DATE | ITEM | POST. REF. | DEBIT | CREDIT | CREDIT BALANCE |
|------|------|------------|-------|--------|----------------|
| Dec. 1 | Balance | ✔ | | | 6 1 2 1 08 |
| | | | | | |
| | | | | | |
| | | | | | |

VENDOR Triangle Manufacturing      VENDOR NO. 270

| DATE | ITEM | POST. REF. | DEBIT | CREDIT | CREDIT BALANCE |
|------|------|------------|-------|--------|----------------|
| | | | | | |
| | | | | | |
| | | | | | |

**10.**

Jewel's Kitchen, Inc.

Schedule of Accounts Payable

December 31, 20--

| | |
|---|---|
| | |
| | |
| | |
| | |
| | |
| | |
| | |
| | |
| | |
| | |
| | |
| | |
| | |
| | |

## REINFORCEMENT ACTIVITY 1 (continued)

**1.**                                 **ACCOUNTS RECEIVABLE LEDGER**

CUSTOMER  Virgie Berger                                               CUSTOMER NO. 110

| DATE | ITEM | POST. REF. | DEBIT | CREDIT | DEBIT BALANCE |
|---|---|---|---|---|---|
| | | | | | |
| | | | | | |
| | | | | | |

CUSTOMER  Carlisle Steakhouse                                         CUSTOMER NO. 120

| DATE | ITEM | POST. REF. | DEBIT | CREDIT | DEBIT BALANCE |
|---|---|---|---|---|---|
| | | | | | |
| | | | | | |
| | | | | | |

CUSTOMER  Denton Seafood                                             CUSTOMER NO. 130

| DATE | ITEM | POST. REF. | DEBIT | CREDIT | DEBIT BALANCE |
|---|---|---|---|---|---|
| 20-- Dec. 1 | Balance | ✔ | | | 4 1 0 8 62 |
| | | | | | |
| | | | | | |

CUSTOMER  Hamilton Group                                            CUSTOMER NO. 140

| DATE | ITEM | POST. REF. | DEBIT | CREDIT | DEBIT BALANCE |
|---|---|---|---|---|---|
| 20-- Dec. 1 | Balance | ✔ | | | 3 6 1 8 29 |
| | | | | | |
| | | | | | |

CUSTOMER  LaFlore Café                                              CUSTOMER NO. 150

| DATE | ITEM | POST. REF. | DEBIT | CREDIT | DEBIT BALANCE |
|---|---|---|---|---|---|
| | | | | | |
| | | | | | |
| | | | | | |

CUSTOMER Mary McCrory     CUSTOMER NO. 160

| DATE | | ITEM | POST. REF. | DEBIT | CREDIT | DEBIT BALANCE |
|---|---|---|---|---|---|---|
| | | | | | | |
| | | | | | | |
| | | | | | | |

CUSTOMER Polk County Schools     CUSTOMER NO. 170

| DATE | | ITEM | POST. REF. | DEBIT | CREDIT | DEBIT BALANCE |
|---|---|---|---|---|---|---|
| 20--<br>Dec. | 1 | Balance | ✔ | | | 2 4 8 1 14 |
| | | | | | | |
| | | | | | | |

CUSTOMER Waukawy Country Club     CUSTOMER NO. 180

| DATE | | ITEM | POST. REF. | DEBIT | CREDIT | DEBIT BALANCE |
|---|---|---|---|---|---|---|
| 20--<br>Dec. | 1 | Balance | ✔ | | | 2 1 4 8 69 |
| | | | | | | |
| | | | | | | |

**10.**

Jewel's Kitchen, Inc.

Schedule of Accounts Receivable

December 31, 20--

| | |
|---|---|
| | |
| | |
| | |
| | |
| | |
| | |
| | |
| | |
| | |
| | |
| | |
| | |

# REINFORCEMENT ACTIVITY 1 (continued)

**11., 12., 14.**

GENERAL JOURNAL

| | DATE | ACCOUNT TITLE | DOC. NO. | POST. REF. | DEBIT | CREDIT | |
|---|---|---|---|---|---|---|---|
| 1 | | | | | | | 1 |
| 2 | | | | | | | 2 |
| 3 | | | | | | | 3 |
| 4 | | | | | | | 4 |
| 5 | | | | | | | 5 |
| 6 | | | | | | | 6 |
| 7 | | | | | | | 7 |
| 8 | | | | | | | 8 |
| 9 | | | | | | | 9 |
| 10 | | | | | | | 10 |
| 11 | | | | | | | 11 |
| 12 | | | | | | | 12 |
| 13 | | | | | | | 13 |
| 14 | | | | | | | 14 |
| 15 | | | | | | | 15 |
| 16 | | | | | | | 16 |
| 17 | | | | | | | 17 |
| 18 | | | | | | | 18 |
| 19 | | | | | | | 19 |
| 20 | | | | | | | 20 |
| 21 | | | | | | | 21 |
| 22 | | | | | | | 22 |
| 23 | | | | | | | 23 |
| 24 | | | | | | | 24 |
| 25 | | | | | | | 25 |
| 26 | | | | | | | 26 |
| 27 | | | | | | | 27 |
| 28 | | | | | | | 28 |
| 29 | | | | | | | 29 |
| 30 | | | | | | | 30 |
| 31 | | | | | | | 31 |

# REINFORCEMENT ACTIVITY 1 (continued)

## 13., 15.

Jewel's Kitchen, Inc.

Adjusted Trial Balance

December 31, 20--

| ACCOUNT TITLE | DEBIT | CREDIT |
|---|---|---|
| Cash | | |
| Petty Cash | | |
| Accounts Receivable | | |
| Allowance for Uncollectible Accounts | | |
| Merchandise Inventory—Equipment | | |
| Merchandise Inventory—Accessories | | |
| Supplies | | |
| Prepaid Insurance | | |
| Office Equipment | | |
| Accumulated Depreciation—Office Equipment | | |
| Store Equipment | | |
| Accumulated Depreciation—Store Equipment | | |
| Accounts Payable | | |
| Sales Tax Payable | | |
| Employee Income Tax Payable—Federal | | |
| Employee Income Tax Payable—State | | |
| Social Security Tax Payable | | |
| Medicare Tax Payable | | |
| Medical Insurance Payable | | |
| Retirement Plan Payable | | |
| Unemployment Tax Payable—Federal | | |
| Unemployment Tax Payable—State | | |
| Federal Income Tax Payable | | |
| Dividends Payable | | |
| Capital Stock | | |
| Retained Earnings | | |
| Dividends | | |
| Income Summary—General | | |
| Income Summary—Equipment | | |
| Income Summary—Accessories | | |

*(Note: Trial balance is continued on the next page.)*

**210** • Working Papers

## REINFORCEMENT ACTIVITY 1 (continued)

Jewel's Kitchen, Inc.

Adjusted Trial Balance (Concluded)

December 31, 20--

| ACCOUNT TITLE | DEBIT | CREDIT |
|---|---|---|
| Sales—Equipment | | |
| Sales Discount—Equipment | | |
| Sales Returns and Allowances—Equipment | | |
| Sales—Accessories | | |
| Sales Discount—Accessories | | |
| Sales Returns and Allowances—Accessories | | |
| Purchases—Equipment | | |
| Purchases Discount—Equipment | | |
| Purchases Returns and Allowances—Equipment | | |
| Purchases—Accessories | | |
| Purchases Discount—Accessories | | |
| Purchases Returns and Allowances—Accessories | | |
| Advertising Expense—Equipment | | |
| Payroll Taxes Expense—Equipment | | |
| Salary Expense—Equipment | | |
| Advertising Expense—Accessories | | |
| Payroll Taxes Expense—Accessories | | |
| Salary Expense—Accessories | | |
| Credit Card Fee Expense | | |
| Depreciation Expense—Office Equipment | | |
| Depreciation Expense—Store Equipment | | |
| Insurance Expense | | |
| Miscellaneous Expense | | |
| Payroll Taxes Expense—Administrative | | |
| Rent Expense | | |
| Salary Expense—Administrative | | |
| Supplies Expense | | |
| Uncollectible Accounts Expense | | |
| Utilities Expense | | |
| | | |
| | | |
| | | |

**16.**

| Jewel's Kitchen, Inc. | | | | | | | | % OF NET SALES* |
|---|---|---|---|---|---|---|---|---|
| Departmental Margin Statement—Equipment | | | | | | | | |
| For Year Ended December 31, 20-- | | | | | | | | |
| | | | | | | | | |
| | | | | | | | | |
| | | | | | | | | |
| | | | | | | | | |
| | | | | | | | | |
| | | | | | | | | |
| | | | | | | | | |
| | | | | | | | | |
| | | | | | | | | |
| | | | | | | | | |
| | | | | | | | | |
| | | | | | | | | |
| | | | | | | | | |
| | | | | | | | | |
| | | | | | | | | |
| | | | | | | | | |
| | | | | | | | | |
| | | | | | | | | |
| | | | | | | | | |
| | | | | | | | | |
| | | | | | | | | |
| | | | | | | | | |
| *Rounded to the nearest 0.1%. | | | | | | | | |

**REINFORCEMENT ACTIVITY 1 (continued)**

Jewel's Kitchen, Inc.

Departmental Margin Statement—Accessories

For Year Ended December 31, 20--

| | | | | | % OF NET SALES* |
|---|---|---|---|---|---|
| | | | | | |

*Rounded to the nearest 0.1%.

**17.**

Jewel's Kitchen, Inc.

Income Statement

For Year Ended December 31, 20--

| | DEPARTMENTAL | | COMPANY | % OF NET SALES* |
| --- | --- | --- | --- | --- |
| | EQUIPMENT | ACCESSORIES | | |
| | | | | |
| | | | | |
| | | | | |
| | | | | |
| | | | | |
| | | | | |
| | | | | |
| | | | | |
| | | | | |
| | | | | |
| | | | | |
| | | | | |
| | | | | |
| | | | | |
| | | | | |
| | | | | |
| | | | | |
| | | | | |
| | | | | |
| | | | | |
| | | | | |
| | | | | |
| | | | | |
| | | | | |
| *Rounded to the nearest 0.1%. | | | | |
| | | | | |
| | | | | |

# REINFORCEMENT ACTIVITY 1 (continued)

**18.**

|  | | | | | | | |
| --- | --- | --- | --- | --- | --- | --- | --- |
| Jewel's Kitchen, Inc. | | | | | | | |
| Statement of Stockholders' Equity | | | | | | | |
| For Year Ended December 31, 20-- | | | | | | | |
|  | | | | | | | |
|  | | | | | | | |
|  | | | | | | | |
|  | | | | | | | |
|  | | | | | | | |
|  | | | | | | | |
|  | | | | | | | |
|  | | | | | | | |
|  | | | | | | | |
|  | | | | | | | |
|  | | | | | | | |
|  | | | | | | | |
|  | | | | | | | |
|  | | | | | | | |
|  | | | | | | | |
|  | | | | | | | |

**19.**

| | | | % OF ASSETS* |
|---|---|---|---|
| Jewel's Kitchen, Inc. | | | |
| Balance Sheet | | | |
| December 31, 20-- | | | |

*Rounded to the nearest 0.1%.

**REINFORCEMENT ACTIVITY 1 (continued)**

**20.**

Jewel's Kitchen, Inc.

Statement of Cash Flows

For Year Ended December 31, 20--

**21.**

## GENERAL JOURNAL

PAGE

| | DATE | ACCOUNT TITLE | DOC. NO. | POST. REF. | DEBIT | CREDIT | |
|---|---|---|---|---|---|---|---|
| 1 | | | | | | | 1 |
| 2 | | | | | | | 2 |
| 3 | | | | | | | 3 |
| 4 | | | | | | | 4 |
| 5 | | | | | | | 5 |
| 6 | | | | | | | 6 |
| 7 | | | | | | | 7 |
| 8 | | | | | | | 8 |
| 9 | | | | | | | 9 |
| 10 | | | | | | | 10 |
| 11 | | | | | | | 11 |
| 12 | | | | | | | 12 |
| 13 | | | | | | | 13 |
| 14 | | | | | | | 14 |
| 15 | | | | | | | 15 |
| 16 | | | | | | | 16 |
| 17 | | | | | | | 17 |
| 18 | | | | | | | 18 |
| 19 | | | | | | | 19 |
| 20 | | | | | | | 20 |
| 21 | | | | | | | 21 |
| 22 | | | | | | | 22 |
| 23 | | | | | | | 23 |
| 24 | | | | | | | 24 |
| 25 | | | | | | | 25 |
| 26 | | | | | | | 26 |
| 27 | | | | | | | 27 |
| 28 | | | | | | | 28 |
| 29 | | | | | | | 29 |
| 30 | | | | | | | 30 |
| 31 | | | | | | | 31 |
| 32 | | | | | | | 32 |
| 33 | | | | | | | 33 |
| 34 | | | | | | | 34 |
| 35 | | | | | | | 35 |
| 36 | | | | | | | 36 |
| 37 | | | | | | | 37 |
| 38 | | | | | | | 38 |
| 39 | | | | | | | 39 |
| 40 | | | | | | | 40 |
| 41 | | | | | | | 41 |
| 42 | | | | | | | 42 |

## REINFORCEMENT ACTIVITY 1 (concluded)

**22.**

Jewel's Kitchen, Inc.

Post-Closing Trial Balance

December 31, 20--

| ACCOUNT TITLE | DEBIT | CREDIT |
|---|---|---|
| | | |
| | | |
| | | |
| | | |
| | | |
| | | |
| | | |
| | | |
| | | |
| | | |
| | | |
| | | |
| | | |
| | | |
| | | |
| | | |
| | | |
| | | |
| | | |
| | | |
| | | |
| | | |
| | | |
| | | |
| | | |
| | | |
| | | |
| | | |
| | | |
| | | |

# Study Guide 5

## Part One—Identifying Accounting Terms

**Directions:** Select the one term in Column I that best fits each definition in Column II. Print the letter identifying your choice in the Answers column.

| Column I | Column II | Answers |
|---|---|---|
| **A.** consignee | **1.** Goods that are given to a business to sell but for which title remains with the vendor. (p. 146) | **1.** _____ |
| **B.** consignment | **2.** The person or business that receives goods on consignment. (p. 146) | **2.** _____ |
| **C.** consignor | **3.** The person or business that gives goods on consignment. (p. 146) | **3.** _____ |
| **D.** days' sales in inventory | | |
| **E.** deflation | **4.** A form used to show the type of merchandise, quantity received, quantity sold, and balance on hand. (p. 147) | **4.** _____ |
| **F.** first-in, first-out inventory costing method | **5.** A file of stock records for all merchandise on hand. (p. 147) | **5.** _____ |
| **G.** generally accepted accounting principles | **6.** A form used during a physical inventory to record information about each item of merchandise on hand. (p. 148) | **6.** _____ |
| **H.** gross profit method of estimating inventory | **7.** The standards and rules that accountants follow while recording and reporting financial activities. (p. 151) | **7.** _____ |
| **I.** inflation | **8.** Using the price of merchandise purchased first to calculate the cost of merchandise sold first. (p. 151) | **8.** _____ |
| **J.** international financial reporting standards | **9.** Using the price of merchandise purchased last to calculate the cost of merchandise sold first. (p. 152) | **9.** _____ |
| **K.** inventory record | **10.** Using the average cost of the beginning inventory plus merchandise purchased during a fiscal period to calculate the cost of merchandise sold. (p. 153) | **10.** _____ |
| **L.** inventory turnover ratio | | |
| **M.** last-in, first-out inventory costing method | **11.** The rate at which the price for goods and services increases over time. (p. 154) | **11.** _____ |
| **N.** lower of cost or market inventory costing method | **12.** The rate at which the price for goods and services decreases over time. (p. 155) | **12.** _____ |
| **O.** retail method of estimating inventory | **13.** A set of accounting standards being adopted across the world. (p. 156) | **13.** _____ |
| **P.** stock ledger | **14.** Using the lower of cost or market price to calculate the cost of the ending merchandise inventory. (p. 157) | **14.** _____ |
| **Q.** stock record | **15.** Estimating inventory by using the previous year's percentage of gross profit on operations. (p. 159) | **15.** _____ |
| **R.** weighted-average inventory costing method | **16.** Estimating inventory by using a percentage based on both cost and retail prices. (p. 160) | **16.** _____ |
| | **17.** The number of times the average amount of merchandise inventory is sold during a specific period of time. (p. 161) | **17.** _____ |
| | **18.** The time needed to sell an average amount of merchandise inventory. (p. 161) | **18.** _____ |

## Part Two—Analyzing Concepts and Practices Related to Inventory Control

**Directions:** Place a *T* for True or an *F* for False in the Answers column to show whether each of the following statements is true or false.

**Answers**

1. The cost of merchandise available for sale consists of the cost of the beginning inventory and the purchases added to inventory during the fiscal period. (p. 145)

    1. _____

2. Calculating an accurate merchandise inventory cost in order to adequately report a business's financial progress and condition is an application of the accounting concept Adequate Disclosure. (p. 145)

    2. _____

3. If the cost of the ending merchandise inventory is overstated, the net income will be understated. (p. 145)

    3. _____

4. If the cost of the ending merchandise inventory is understated, the total stockholders' equity will be overstated. (p. 145)

    4. _____

5. When the terms of sale for goods in transit are FOB shipping point, the title to the goods passes to the buyer when the goods are received by the buyer. (p. 146)

    5. _____

6. When goods are sent to a business on consignment, title to the goods passes to the business accepting the consignment when the consignor delivers the goods to a transportation business. (p. 146)

    6. _____

7. A continuous record of merchandise inventory increases and decreases and the balance on hand is known as a *perpetual inventory.* (p. 147)

    7. _____

8. A periodic inventory provides day-to-day records about the quantity of merchandise on hand. (p. 147)

    8. _____

9. An inventory determined periodically by counting, weighing, or measuring items of merchandise on hand is known as a physical inventory. (p. 148)

    9. _____

10. Because of the expense, many businesses take a physical inventory only once a year. (p. 148)

    10. _____

11. Businesses using a perpetual inventory method never need to take a physical inventory. (p. 148)

    11. _____

12. The weighted-average inventory costing method is based on the assumption that each item in the ending inventory has a cost equal to the average price paid for similar items. (p. 153)

    12. _____

13. During a period of increasing prices, the weighted-average inventory costing method usually will give the lowest total inventory cost. (p. 154)

    13. _____

14. During a period of decreasing prices, the FIFO inventory costing method usually will give the lowest total inventory cost. (p. 154)

    14. _____

15. A business that uses the LIFO method for tax reporting must also using the LIFO method for financial reporting. (p. 154)

    15. _____

16. International financial reporting standards only allow the LIFO and weighted-average methods. (p. 156)

    16. _____

17. Taking a physical inventory once a month for interim monthly financial statements is usually too expensive to be worthwhile. (p. 159)

    17. _____

18. Using the retail method of estimating inventory is more expensive than the gross profit method because more records must be kept. (p. 160)

    18. _____

19. An inventory turnover ratio expresses a relationship between an average inventory and the cost of merchandise sold. (p. 161)

    19. _____

20. An inventory turnover ratio of 4.5 means that, on average, each item of inventory is sold 81 days after it is purchased. (p. 161)

    20. _____

**222** • Working Papers

**5-1** WORK TOGETHER, p. 150

**5-1** ON YOUR OWN, p. 150

**Completing a stock record for a perpetual inventory system**

**1., 2.**

# STOCK RECORD

Description _____  Stock No. _____

Reorder _____  Minimum _____  Location _____

| 1 | 2 | 3 | 4 | 5 | 6 | 7 |
|---|---|---|---|---|---|---|
| INCREASES | | | DECREASES | | | BALANCE |
| DATE | PURCHASE INVOICE NO. | QUANTITY | DATE | SALES INVOICE NO. | QUANTITY | QUANTITY |
|  |  |  |  |  |  |  |
|  |  |  |  |  |  |  |
|  |  |  |  |  |  |  |
|  |  |  |  |  |  |  |
|  |  |  |  |  |  |  |
|  |  |  |  |  |  |  |
|  |  |  |  |  |  |  |
|  |  |  |  |  |  |  |
|  |  |  |  |  |  |  |
|  |  |  |  |  |  |  |
|  |  |  |  |  |  |  |
|  |  |  |  |  |  |  |
|  |  |  |  |  |  |  |
|  |  |  |  |  |  |  |

**2.**

# INVENTORY RECORD

DATE  October 31, 20--          ITEM  Security Cameras

| 1 | 2 | 3 | 4 | 5 |
|---|---|---|---|---|
| STOCK NUMBER | DESCRIPTIONS | NO. OF UNITS ON HAND | UNIT PRICE | TOTAL COST |
| C-0264 | Monitoring station | 16 | 231.25 | 3,700.00 |
| D-3543 | Ceiling mount stationary camera | 52 | 30 @ 89.25 | 4,630.00 |
|  |  |  | 22 @ 88.75 |  |
| D-3643 | Ceiling mount 360-degree camera | 33 | 94.69 | 3,124.77 |
| C-2755 | Wireless Internet video camera | 25 | 214.75 | 5,368.75 |
| C-4264 | Wireless monitoring camera | 88 | 69.95 | 6,155.60 |
| C-7543 | Outdoor stationary camera | 62 | 89.25 | 5,533.50 |
| C-6275 | Outdoor night camera | 25 | 94.45 | 2,361.25 |
| A-253 | Mounting bracket | 124 | 21.58 | 2,675.92 |
| C-7542 | Rotating ceiling mount camera | 49 | 251.63 | 12,329.87 |
| C-7245 | Color wireless monitoring camera | 68 | 215.66 | 14,664.88 |
|  | Total |  |  | 60,544.54 |
|  |  |  |  |  |

## 5-2   WORK TOGETHER, p. 158

**Costing ending inventory using FIFO, LIFO, and weighted-average**

| FIFO Inventory Costing Method | | | | | |
|---|---|---|---|---|---|
| Purchase Dates | Units Purchased | Unit Price | Total Cost | FIFO Units on Hand | FIFO Cost |
| Beginning inventory | | | | | |
| February | | | | | |
| May | | | | | |
| August | | | | | |
| November | | | | | |
| Totals | | | | | |

| LIFO Inventory Costing Method | | | | | |
|---|---|---|---|---|---|
| Purchase Dates | Units Purchased | Unit Price | Total Cost | LIFO Units on Hand | LIFO Cost |
| Beginning inventory | | | | | |
| February | | | | | |
| May | | | | | |
| August | | | | | |
| November | | | | | |
| Totals | | | | | |

| Weighted-Average Inventory Costing Method | | | |
|---|---|---|---|
| Purchase Dates | Units Purchased | Unit Price | Total Cost |
| Beginning inventory | | | |
| February | | | |
| May | | | |
| August | | | |
| November | | | |
| Totals | | | |

**Costing ending inventory using FIFO, LIFO, and weighted-average**

| FIFO Inventory Costing Method | | | | | |
|---|---|---|---|---|---|
| Purchase Dates | Units Purchased | Unit Price | Total Cost | FIFO Units on Hand | FIFO Cost |
| Beginning inventory | | | | | |
| February | | | | | |
| May | | | | | |
| August | | | | | |
| November | | | | | |
| Totals | | | | | |

| LIFO Inventory Costing Method | | | | | |
|---|---|---|---|---|---|
| Purchase Dates | Units Purchased | Unit Price | Total Cost | LIFO Units on Hand | LIFO Cost |
| Beginning inventory | | | | | |
| February | | | | | |
| May | | | | | |
| August | | | | | |
| November | | | | | |
| Totals | | | | | |

| Weighted-Average Inventory Costing Method | | | |
|---|---|---|---|
| Purchase Dates | Units Purchased | Unit Price | Total Cost |
| Beginning inventory | | | |
| February | | | |
| May | | | |
| August | | | |
| November | | | |
| Totals | | | |

**5-3**  **WORK TOGETHER, p. 162**

**Estimating inventory using the gross profit and retail methods; financial anlysis of merchandise inventory**

**1.**

### ESTIMATED MERCHANDISE INVENTORY SHEET
### Gross Profit Method

DEPARTMENT _____  DATE _____

| | | | |
|---|---|---|---|
| 1 | Beginning inventory.......................................................... | | $ _____ |
| 2 | Net purchases to date....................................................... | | _____ |
| 3 | Merchandise available for sale ......................................... | | $ _____ |
| 4 | Net sales to date............................................................... | $ _____ | |
| 5 | Less estimated gross profit............................................... | _____ | |
| | (Net sales × Estimated gross profit percentage ____ %) | | |
| 6 | Estimated cost of merchandise sold................................... | | _____ |
| 7 | Estimated ending inventory .............................................. | | $ _____ |

**2.**

### ESTIMATED MERCHANDISE INVENTORY SHEET
### Retail Method

COMPANY _____  DATE _____

| | | Cost | Retail |
|---|---|---|---|
| 1 | Beginning inventory.......................................................... | $ _____ | $ _____ |
| 2 | Net purchases to date....................................................... | _____ | _____ |
| 3 | Merchandise available for sale ......................................... | $ _____ | $ _____ |
| 4 | Net sales to date............................................................... | | _____ |
| 5 | Estimated ending inventory at retail ................................. | | $ _____ |
| 6 | Estimated ending inventory .............................................. | $ _____ | |
| | (Inventory at retail × Percentage ____ %) | | |

**3.**

$$
\left(
\begin{array}{c}
\text{January 1} \\
\text{Merchandise} \\
\text{Inventory}
\end{array}
\quad + \quad
\begin{array}{c}
\text{December 31} \\
\text{Merchandise} \\
\text{Inventory}
\end{array}
\right)
\quad \div \quad 2 \quad = \quad
\begin{array}{c}
\text{Average} \\
\text{Merchandise} \\
\text{Inventory}
\end{array}
$$

$$
+ \qquad\qquad \div \quad 2 \quad =
$$

$$
\begin{array}{c}
\text{Cost of} \\
\text{Merchandise} \\
\text{Sold}
\end{array}
\quad \div \quad
\begin{array}{c}
\text{Average} \\
\text{Merchandise} \\
\text{Inventory}
\end{array}
\quad = \quad
\begin{array}{c}
\text{Inventory} \\
\text{Turnover} \\
\text{Ratio}
\end{array}
$$

$$
\div \qquad\qquad =
$$

$$
\text{Days in Year} \quad \div \quad
\begin{array}{c}
\text{Inventory Turnover} \\
\text{Ratio}
\end{array}
\quad = \quad
\begin{array}{c}
\text{Days' Sales in} \\
\text{Inventory}
\end{array}
$$

$$
\div \qquad\qquad =
$$

## 5-3 ON YOUR OWN, p. 162

**Estimating inventory using the gross profit and retail methods; financial analysis of merchandise inventory**

**1.**

### ESTIMATED MERCHANDISE INVENTORY SHEET
#### Gross Profit Method

DEPARTMENT _____  DATE _____

| | | | |
|---|---|---|---|
| 1 | Beginning inventory.................................................. | | $ _____ |
| 2 | Net purchases to date............................................... | | _____ |
| 3 | Merchandise available for sale ................................. | | $ _____ |
| 4 | Net sales to date....................................................... | $ _____ | |
| 5 | Less estimated gross profit....................................... | _____ | |
| | (Net sales × Estimated gross profit percentage ____ %) | | |
| 6 | Estimated cost of merchandise sold.......................... | | _____ |
| 7 | Estimated ending inventory ..................................... | | $ _____ |

**2.**

### ESTIMATED MERCHANDISE INVENTORY SHEET
#### Retail Method

COMPANY _____  DATE _____

| | | Cost | Retail |
|---|---|---|---|
| 1 | Beginning inventory.................................................. | $ _____ | $ _____ |
| 2 | Net purchases to date............................................... | _____ | _____ |
| 3 | Merchandise available for sale ................................. | $ _____ | $ _____ |
| 4 | Net sales to date....................................................... | | _____ |
| 5 | Estimated ending inventory at retail ........................ | | $ _____ |
| 6 | Estimated ending inventory ..................................... | $ _____ | |
| | (Inventory at retail × Percentage ____ %) | | |

**3.**

$$\left( \begin{array}{c} \text{January 1} \\ \text{Merchandise} \\ \text{Inventory} \end{array} \quad + \quad \begin{array}{c} \text{December 31} \\ \text{Merchandise} \\ \text{Inventory} \end{array} \right) \quad \div \quad 2 \quad = \quad \begin{array}{c} \text{Average} \\ \text{Merchandise} \\ \text{Inventory} \end{array}$$

$$+ \qquad \qquad \div \quad 2 \quad =$$

$$\begin{array}{c} \text{Cost of} \\ \text{Merchandise} \\ \text{Sold} \end{array} \quad \div \quad \begin{array}{c} \text{Average} \\ \text{Merchandise} \\ \text{Inventory} \end{array} \quad = \quad \begin{array}{c} \text{Inventory} \\ \text{Turnover} \\ \text{Ratio} \end{array}$$

$$\div \qquad \qquad =$$

$$\text{Days in Year} \quad \div \quad \begin{array}{c} \text{Inventory Turnover} \\ \text{Ratio} \end{array} \quad = \quad \begin{array}{c} \text{Days' Sales in} \\ \text{Inventory} \end{array}$$

$$\div \qquad \qquad =$$

**5-1**   **APPLICATION PROBLEM (LO2), p. 167**

**Keeping perpetual inventory records**

**1., 2.**

# STOCK RECORD

Description _____    Stock No. _____

Reorder _____ Minimum _____ Location _____

| 1 | 2 | 3 | 4 | 5 | 6 | 7 |
|---|---|---|---|---|---|---|
| INCREASES | | | DECREASES | | | BALANCE |
| DATE | PURCHASE INVOICE NO. | QUANTITY | DATE | SALES INVOICE NO. | QUANTITY | QUANTITY |
| | | | | | | |
| | | | | | | |
| | | | | | | |
| | | | | | | |
| | | | | | | |
| | | | | | | |
| | | | | | | |
| | | | | | | |
| | | | | | | |
| | | | | | | |
| | | | | | | |
| | | | | | | |
| | | | | | | |
| | | | | | | |

**Determining inventory cost using FIFO, LIFO, weighted-average, and lower of cost or market**

**1.**

**Stock Item: B26**

| Date | Units Purchased | Unit Price | Total Cost | FIFO Method Units | FIFO Method Cost | LIFO Method Units | LIFO Method Cost | Weighted-Average Method |
|------|-----------------|------------|------------|-------|------|-------|------|-------------------------|
| Beginning inventory | 6 | $6.50 | | | | | | |
| January | 15 | 6.60 | | | | | | |
| March | 18 | 6.60 | | | | | | |
| July | 15 | 6.80 | | | | | | |
| October | 20 | 6.80 | | | | | | |
| Totals | | | | | | | | |
| | | | | | | | | |
| Prices are _____ | | | | | | | | |
| Ending inventory | | | | | | | | |
| Cost of merchandise sold | | | | | | | | |
| Reported net income | | | | | | | | |

**Stock Item: C45**

| Date | Units Purchased | Unit Price | Total Cost | FIFO Method Units | FIFO Method Cost | LIFO Method Units | LIFO Method Cost | Weighted-Average Method |
|------|-----------------|------------|------------|-------|------|-------|------|-------------------------|
| Beginning inventory | 72 | $8.50 | | | | | | |
| March | 90 | 8.60 | | | | | | |
| June | 80 | 8.62 | | | | | | |
| August | 90 | 8.68 | | | | | | |
| December | 90 | 8.72 | | | | | | |
| Totals | | | | | | | | |
| | | | | | | | | |
| Prices are _____ | | | | | | | | |
| Ending inventory | | | | | | | | |
| Cost of merchandise sold | | | | | | | | |
| Reported net income | | | | | | | | |

**5-2**  **APPLICATION PROBLEM (concluded)**

| Stock Item: D55 | | | | | | | | | |
|---|---|---|---|---|---|---|---|---|---|
| Purchases | | | | | FIFO Method | | LIFO Method | | Weighted-Average Method |
| Date | Units Purchased | Unit Price | Total Cost | | Units | Cost | Units | Cost | |
| Beginning inventory | 3 | $12.62 | | | | | | | |
| February | 9 | 12.60 | | | | | | | |
| May | 12 | 12.60 | | | | | | | |
| September | 9 | 12.50 | | | | | | | |
| November | 15 | 11.95 | | | | | | | |
| Totals | | | | | | | | | |
| | | | | | | | | | |
| Prices are _____ | | | | | | | | | |
| Ending inventory | | | | | | | | | |
| Cost of merchandise sold | | | | | | | | | |
| Reported net income | | | | | | | | | |

**2.**

| Stock Item | Quantity of Units on Hand | Market Price | Total Market Price | FIFO Cost | Lower of Cost of Market |
|---|---|---|---|---|---|
| B26 | 24 | $ 6.90 | | | |
| C45 | 80 | 8.80 | | | |
| D55 | 18 | 11.75 | | | |
| | | | Reported cost of merchandise inventory | | |

Estimating cost of merchandise inventory; financial analysis of merchandise inventory

**1.**

## ESTIMATED MERCHANDISE INVENTORY SHEET
### Gross Profit Method

DEPARTMENT _____     DATE _____

| | | |
|---|---|---|
| 1 | Beginning inventory.................................................. | $ _____ |
| 2 | Net purchases to date............................................... | _____ |
| 3 | Merchandise available for sale ................................. | $ _____ |
| 4 | Net sales to date................................................ $ _____ | |
| 5 | Less estimated gross profit................................ _____ | |
| | (Net sales × Estimated gross profit percentage ____ %) | |
| 6 | Estimated cost of merchandise sold.......................... | _____ |
| 7 | Estimated ending inventory ....................................... | $ _____ |

**2.**

## ESTIMATED MERCHANDISE INVENTORY SHEET
### Retail Method

COMPANY _____     DATE _____

| | | Cost | Retail |
|---|---|---|---|
| 1 | Beginning inventory................................................. | $ _____ | $ _____ |
| 2 | Net purchases to date.............................................. | _____ | _____ |
| 3 | Merchandise available for sale ................................. | $ _____ | $ _____ |
| 4 | Net sales to date...................................................... | | _____ |
| 5 | Estimated ending inventory at retail ......................... | | $ _____ |
| 6 | Estimated ending inventory ....................................... | $ _____ | |
| | (Inventory at retail × Percentage ____ %) | | |

**5-3** **APPLICATION PROBLEM (concluded)**

**3.**

$$\left(\begin{array}{c}\text{January 1} \\ \text{Merchandise} \\ \text{Inventory}\end{array}\quad + \quad \begin{array}{c}\text{December 31} \\ \text{Merchandise} \\ \text{Inventory}\end{array}\right) \quad \div \quad 2 \quad = \quad \begin{array}{c}\text{Average} \\ \text{Merchandise} \\ \text{Inventory}\end{array}$$

+                      ÷   2   =

| Cost of Merchandise Sold | ÷ | Average Merchandise Inventory | = | Inventory Turnover Ratio |
|---|---|---|---|---|
| | ÷ | | = | |

| Days in Year | ÷ | Inventory Turnover Ratio | = | Days' Sales in Inventory |
|---|---|---|---|---|
| | ÷ | | = | |

**Costing and financial analysis of merchandise inventory**

**1.**

| Stock Item: 1548-C | | | | | | | | |
|---|---|---|---|---|---|---|---|---|
| Purchases | | | | FIFO Method | | LIFO Method | | Weighted-Average Method |
| Date | Units Purchased | Unit Price | Total Cost | Units | Cost | Units | Cost | |
| Beginning inventory | 12 | $9.40 | | | | | | |
| February | 20 | 9.82 | | | | | | |
| May | 25 | 9.75 | | | | | | |
| July | 20 | 9.80 | | | | | | |
| August | 15 | 9.85 | | | | | | |
| December | 16 | 9.95 | | | | | | |
| Totals | | | | | | | | |

| Stock Item: 5324-B | | | | | | | | |
|---|---|---|---|---|---|---|---|---|
| Purchases | | | | FIFO Method | | LIFO Method | | Weighted-Average Method |
| Date | Units Purchased | Unit Price | Total Cost | Units | Cost | Units | Cost | |
| Beginning inventory | 56 | $8.90 | | | | | | |
| May | 50 | 6.80 | | | | | | |
| August | 45 | 6.85 | | | | | | |
| October | 50 | 6.85 | | | | | | |
| Totals | | | | | | | | |

| Stock Item: 0234-H | | | | | | | | |
|---|---|---|---|---|---|---|---|---|
| Purchases | | | | FIFO Method | | LIFO Method | | Weighted-Average Method |
| Date | Units Purchased | Unit Price | Total Cost | Units | Cost | Units | Cost | |
| Beginning inventory | 3 | $6.45 | | | | | | |
| January | 9 | 8.40 | | | | | | |
| March | 12 | 8.42 | | | | | | |
| June | 12 | 8.45 | | | | | | |
| August | 9 | 8.45 | | | | | | |
| October | 10 | 8.50 | | | | | | |
| Totals | | | | | | | | |

**2.**

| Stock Item | Quantity of Units on Hand | Market Price | Total Market Price | LIFO Cost | Lower of Cost of Market |
|---|---|---|---|---|---|
| 1548-C | | | | | |
| 5324-B | | | | | |
| 0234-H | | | | | |
| | | | Reported cost of merchandise inventory | | |

**5-M** **MASTERY PROBLEM (continued)**

**3.**

### ESTIMATED MERCHANDISE INVENTORY SHEET
#### Gross Profit Method

DEPARTMENT _____ DATE _____

| | | |
|---|---|---|
| 1 | Beginning inventory................................................ | $ _____ |
| 2 | Net purchases to date............................................... | _____ |
| 3 | Merchandise available for sale ................................ | $ _____ |
| 4 | Net sales to date....................................................... $ _____ | |
| 5 | Less estimated gross profit...................................... _____ | |
| | (Net sales × Estimated gross profit percentage ____ %) | |
| 6 | Estimated cost of merchandise sold........................ | _____ |
| 7 | Estimated ending inventory ..................................... | $ _____ |

**4.**

### ESTIMATED MERCHANDISE INVENTORY SHEET
#### Retail Method

COMPANY _____ DATE _____

| | | Cost | Retail |
|---|---|---|---|
| 1 | Beginning inventory................................................ | $ _____ | $ _____ |
| 2 | Net purchases to date............................................... | _____ | _____ |
| 3 | Merchandise available for sale ................................ | $ _____ | $ _____ |
| 4 | Net sales to date....................................................... | | _____ |
| 5 | Estimated ending inventory at retail ...................... | | $ _____ |
| 6 | Estimated ending inventory ..................................... | $ _____ | |
| | (Inventory at retail × Percentage ____ %) | | |

**5., 6.**

$$\left(\begin{array}{c}\text{January 1} \\ \text{Merchandise} \\ \text{Inventory}\end{array} \quad + \quad \begin{array}{c}\text{December 31} \\ \text{Merchandise} \\ \text{Inventory}\end{array}\right) \quad \div \quad 2 \quad = \quad \begin{array}{c}\text{Average} \\ \text{Merchandise} \\ \text{Inventory}\end{array}$$

$$+ \qquad\qquad \div \quad 2 \quad =$$

$$\begin{array}{c}\text{Cost of} \\ \text{Merchandise} \\ \text{Sold}\end{array} \quad \div \quad \begin{array}{c}\text{Average} \\ \text{Merchandise} \\ \text{Inventory}\end{array} \quad = \quad \begin{array}{c}\text{Inventory} \\ \text{Turnover} \\ \text{Ratio}\end{array}$$

$$\div \qquad\qquad =$$

$$\text{Days in Year} \quad \div \quad \begin{array}{c}\text{Inventory Turnover} \\ \text{Ratio}\end{array} \quad = \quad \begin{array}{c}\text{Days' Sales in} \\ \text{Inventory}\end{array}$$

$$\div \qquad\qquad =$$

## 5-C CHALLENGE PROBLEM (LO6), p. 169

**Financial analysis of merchandise inventory**

**1.**

Corporation A
_____

$$\left(\begin{array}{c}\text{January 1}\\\text{Merchandise}\\\text{Inventory}\end{array} + \begin{array}{c}\text{December 31}\\\text{Merchandise}\\\text{Inventory}\end{array}\right) \div\ 2\ = \begin{array}{c}\text{Average}\\\text{Merchandise}\\\text{Inventory}\end{array}$$

$$+ \qquad\qquad \div\ 2\ =$$

$$\begin{array}{c}\text{Cost of}\\\text{Merchandise}\\\text{Sold}\end{array} \div \begin{array}{c}\text{Average}\\\text{Merchandise}\\\text{Inventory}\end{array} = \begin{array}{c}\text{Inventory}\\\text{Turnover}\\\text{Ratio}\end{array}$$

$$\div \qquad\qquad =$$

Corporation B
_____

$$\left(\begin{array}{c}\text{January 1}\\\text{Merchandise}\\\text{Inventory}\end{array} + \begin{array}{c}\text{December 31}\\\text{Merchandise}\\\text{Inventory}\end{array}\right) \div\ 2\ = \begin{array}{c}\text{Average}\\\text{Merchandise}\\\text{Inventory}\end{array}$$

$$+ \qquad\qquad \div\ 2\ =$$

$$\begin{array}{c}\text{Cost of}\\\text{Merchandise}\\\text{Sold}\end{array} \div \begin{array}{c}\text{Average}\\\text{Merchandise}\\\text{Inventory}\end{array} = \begin{array}{c}\text{Inventory}\\\text{Turnover}\\\text{Ratio}\end{array}$$

$$\div \qquad\qquad =$$

Corporation C
_____

$$\left(\begin{array}{c}\text{January 1}\\\text{Merchandise}\\\text{Inventory}\end{array} + \begin{array}{c}\text{December 31}\\\text{Merchandise}\\\text{Inventory}\end{array}\right) \div\ 2\ = \begin{array}{c}\text{Average}\\\text{Merchandise}\\\text{Inventory}\end{array}$$

$$+ \qquad\qquad \div\ 2\ =$$

$$\begin{array}{c}\text{Cost of}\\\text{Merchandise}\\\text{Sold}\end{array} \div \begin{array}{c}\text{Average}\\\text{Merchandise}\\\text{Inventory}\end{array} = \begin{array}{c}\text{Inventory}\\\text{Turnover}\\\text{Ratio}\end{array}$$

$$\div \qquad\qquad =$$

**2.**

Corporation A

| Days in Year | ÷ | Inventory Turnover Ratio | = | Days' Sales in Inventory |
|---|---|---|---|---|
| | ÷ | | = | |

Corporation B

| Days in Year | ÷ | Inventory Turnover Ratio | = | Days' Sales in Inventory |
|---|---|---|---|---|
| | ÷ | | = | |

Corporation C

| Days in Year | ÷ | Inventory Turnover Ratio | = | Days' Sales in Inventory |
|---|---|---|---|---|
| | ÷ | | = | |

Corporation A     _____

Corporation B     _____

Corporation C     _____

| Name | | Perfect Score | Your Score |
|---|---|---|---|
| | Identifying Accounting Terms | 8 Pts. | |
| | Analyzing Entries for Uncollectible Accounts Expense | 16 Pts. | |
| | Analyzing Practices Involved in Journalizing Uncollectible Accounts Expense | 20 Pts. | |
| | **Total** | 44 Pts. | |

## Part One—Identifying Accounting Terms

**Directions:** Select the one term in Column I that best fits each definition in Column II. Print the letter identifying your choice in the Answers column.

| Column I | Column II | Answers |
|---|---|---|
| **A.** accounts receivable turnover ratio | **1.** Accounts receivable that cannot be collected. (p. 174) | 1. _____ |
| **B.** aging accounts receivable | **2.** Canceling the balance of a customer account because the customer is not expected to pay. (p. 174) | 2. _____ |
| **C.** allowance method | **3.** Recording uncollectible accounts expense only when an amount is actually known to be uncollectible. (p. 175) | 3. _____ |
| **D.** book value | **4.** Crediting the estimated value of uncollectible accounts to a contra account. (p. 178) | 4. _____ |
| **E.** days' sales in accounts receivable | **5.** The difference between an asset's account balance and its related contra account balance. (p. 178) | 5. _____ |
| **F.** direct write-off method | **6.** Analyzing accounts receivable according to when they are due. (p. 180) | 6. _____ |
| **G.** uncollectible accounts | **7.** The number of times the average amount of accounts receivable is collected during a specified period. (p. 186) | 7. _____ |
| **H.** writing off an account | **8.** The average period of time to collect an account receivable. (p. 186) | 8. _____ |

# Part Two—Analyzing Transactions Recorded in Special Journals

**Directions:** For each entry below, print in the proper Answers column the letters identifying which accounts are to be debited and credited.

| Account Titles | Transactions | Answers Debit | Credit |
|---|---|---|---|
| **A.** Accounts Receivable | *(a) Direct write-off method:* | | |
| **B.** Allowance for Uncollectible Accounts | **1.** Wrote off customer's account as uncollectible. (p. 175) | 1._____ | _____ |
| **C.** Cash | **2.** Reopened customer account previously written off as uncollectible. (p. 176) | 2._____ | _____ |
| **D.** Uncollectible Accounts Expense | **3.** Received cash in full payment of customer account, described in question 2. (p. 176) | 3._____ | _____ |
| | *(b) Allowance method:* | | |
| | **4.** Recorded adjustment for uncollectible accounts expense. (p. 179) | 4._____ | _____ |
| | **5.** Recorded adjustment for uncollectible accounts expense when using aging accounts receivable method to calculate the amount. (pp. 179, 180) | 5._____ | _____ |
| | **6.** Recorded adjustment for uncollectible accounts expense when using the percentage of accounts receivable account balance to calculate the amount. (pp. 179, 181) | 6._____ | _____ |
| | **7.** Wrote off customer account as uncollectible. (p. 182) | 7._____ | _____ |
| | **8.** Reopened customer account previously written off as uncollectible. (p. 183) | 8._____ | _____ |

# Part Three—Analyzing Practices Involved in Journalizing Uncollectible Accounts Expense

**Directions:** Place a *T* for True or an *F* for False in the Answers column to show whether each of the following statements is true or false.

**Answers**

1. Uncollectible accounts are sometimes referred to as bad debts. (p. 174)  
   **1.** _____

2. Until a specific amount is actually known to be uncollectible, the amount remains recorded in Accounts Receivable. (p. 174)  
   **2.** _____

3. When a customer account is known to be uncollectible, the account becomes a liability. (p. 175)  
   **3.** _____

4. Using the direct write-off method, collecting a previously written off account results in a credit to an expense account. (p. 176)  
   **4.** _____

5. The direct write-off method is more difficult to apply than the allowance method. (p. 178)  
   **5.** _____

6. A business can use the direct write-off method if accounts receivable are reported on the balance sheet at net realizable value. (p. 178)  
   **6.** _____

7. A disadvantage of the direct write-off method of recording uncollectible accounts expense is that the expense may not be recorded in the same fiscal period as the revenue for the sale. (p. 178)  
   **7.** _____

8. Recording uncollectible accounts expense in the same fiscal period in which the original sale on account was made is an application of the Matching Expenses with Revenue accounting concept. (p. 178)  
   **8.** _____

9. Because there is no way of knowing for sure which customer accounts will become uncollectible, the allowance method uses an estimate based on past history to determine uncollectible accounts expense. (p. 178)  
   **9.** _____

10. The book value of accounts receivable represents the total amount owed to the business from sales on account. (p. 178)  
    **10.** _____

11. The book value of accounts receivable is often referred to as the net realizable value. (p. 178)  
    **11.** _____

12. The formula for calculating the amount of uncollectible accounts expense based on a percentage of net sales is: Net sales *times* percentage *equals* estimated uncollectible accounts expense. (p. 179)  
    **12.** _____

13. A company that estimates its uncollectible accounts receivable are $5,000.00 and a $200.00 credit balance in Allowances for Uncollectible Accounts will increase the allowance account by $5,200.00. (p. 179)  
    **13.** _____

14. An aging of accounts receivable analyzes accounts receivable by age categories according to when payments are due. (p. 180)  
    **14.** _____

15. The journal entry used to write off an uncollectible account is the same, regardless of the method used to calculate the estimate of Allowance for Uncollectible Accounts. (p. 182)  
    **15.** _____

16. A company may continue its attempts to collect an account even after the account has been written off. (p. 182)  
    **16.** _____

17. Using the allowance method, writing off an uncollectible accounts receivable reduces the net realizable value of accounts receivable. (p. 182)  
    **17.** _____

18. Using the allowance method, writing off an account increases Uncollectible Accounts Expense. (p. 182)  
    **18.** _____

19. The accounts receivable turnover ratio is calculated by dividing net sales by the average book value of accounts receivable. (p. 186)  
    **19.** _____

20. A company whose accounts receivable turnover ratio declines from 9.3 to 8.7 is doing a better job in collecting its accounts receivable. (p. 187)  
    **20.** _____

## 6-1 WORK TOGETHER, p. 177

**Journalizing entries to write off uncollectible accounts—direct write-off method**

### GENERAL JOURNAL

| | DATE | ACCOUNT TITLE | DOC. NO. | POST. REF. | DEBIT | CREDIT | |
|---|---|---|---|---|---|---|---|
| 1 | | | | | | | 1 |
| 2 | | | | | | | 2 |
| 3 | | | | | | | 3 |
| 4 | | | | | | | 4 |
| 5 | | | | | | | 5 |
| 6 | | | | | | | 6 |
| 7 | | | | | | | 7 |
| 8 | | | | | | | 8 |
| 9 | | | | | | | 9 |
| 10 | | | | | | | 10 |
| 11 | | | | | | | 11 |
| 12 | | | | | | | 12 |
| 13 | | | | | | | 13 |
| 14 | | | | | | | 14 |
| 15 | | | | | | | 15 |
| 16 | | | | | | | 16 |
| 17 | | | | | | | 17 |
| 18 | | | | | | | 18 |
| 19 | | | | | | | 19 |
| 20 | | | | | | | 20 |
| 21 | | | | | | | 21 |
| 22 | | | | | | | 22 |
| 23 | | | | | | | 23 |
| 24 | | | | | | | 24 |
| 25 | | | | | | | 25 |
| 26 | | | | | | | 26 |
| 27 | | | | | | | 27 |
| 28 | | | | | | | 28 |
| 29 | | | | | | | 29 |

CASH RECEIPTS JOURNAL

| DATE | ACCOUNT TITLE | DOC. NO. | POST. REF. | GENERAL DEBIT | GENERAL CREDIT | ACCOUNTS RECEIVABLE CREDIT | SALES CREDIT | SALES TAX PAYABLE CREDIT | SALES DISCOUNT DEBIT | CASH DEBIT |
|---|---|---|---|---|---|---|---|---|---|---|
| | | | | | | | | | | |
| | | | | | | | | | | |
| | | | | | | | | | | |
| | | | | | | | | | | |
| | | | | | | | | | | |
| | | | | | | | | | | |
| | | | | | | | | | | |
| | | | | | | | | | | |
| | | | | | | | | | | |
| | | | | | | | | | | |
| | | | | | | | | | | |
| | | | | | | | | | | |
| | | | | | | | | | | |
| | | | | | | | | | | |
| | | | | | | | | | | |
| | | | | | | | | | | |
| | | | | | | | | | | |
| | | | | | | | | | | |
| | | | | | | | | | | |
| | | | | | | | | | | |
| | | | | | | | | | | |
| | | | | | | | | | | |

## 6-1 ON YOUR OWN, p. 177

**Journalizing entries to write off uncollectible accounts—direct write-off method**

### GENERAL JOURNAL

PAGE _____

| | DATE | ACCOUNT TITLE | DOC. NO. | POST. REF. | DEBIT | CREDIT | |
|---|---|---|---|---|---|---|---|
| 1 | | | | | | | 1 |
| 2 | | | | | | | 2 |
| 3 | | | | | | | 3 |
| 4 | | | | | | | 4 |
| 5 | | | | | | | 5 |
| 6 | | | | | | | 6 |
| 7 | | | | | | | 7 |
| 8 | | | | | | | 8 |
| 9 | | | | | | | 9 |
| 10 | | | | | | | 10 |
| 11 | | | | | | | 11 |
| 12 | | | | | | | 12 |
| 13 | | | | | | | 13 |
| 14 | | | | | | | 14 |
| 15 | | | | | | | 15 |
| 16 | | | | | | | 16 |
| 17 | | | | | | | 17 |
| 18 | | | | | | | 18 |
| 19 | | | | | | | 19 |
| 20 | | | | | | | 20 |
| 21 | | | | | | | 21 |
| 22 | | | | | | | 22 |
| 23 | | | | | | | 23 |
| 24 | | | | | | | 24 |
| 25 | | | | | | | 25 |
| 26 | | | | | | | 26 |
| 27 | | | | | | | 27 |
| 28 | | | | | | | 28 |
| 29 | | | | | | | 29 |

CASH RECEIPTS JOURNAL

| DATE | ACCOUNT TITLE | DOC. NO. | POST. REF. | GENERAL DEBIT 1 | GENERAL CREDIT 2 | ACCOUNTS RECEIVABLE CREDIT 3 | SALES CREDIT 4 | SALES TAX PAYABLE CREDIT 5 | SALES DISCOUNT DEBIT 6 | CASH DEBIT 7 |
|------|--------------|----------|-----------|---------|---------|---------|---------|---------|---------|---------|
| | | | | | | | | | | |
| | | | | | | | | | | |
| | | | | | | | | | | |
| | | | | | | | | | | |
| | | | | | | | | | | |
| | | | | | | | | | | |
| | | | | | | | | | | |
| | | | | | | | | | | |
| | | | | | | | | | | |
| | | | | | | | | | | |
| | | | | | | | | | | |
| | | | | | | | | | | |
| | | | | | | | | | | |
| | | | | | | | | | | |
| | | | | | | | | | | |
| | | | | | | | | | | |
| | | | | | | | | | | |
| | | | | | | | | | | |
| | | | | | | | | | | |
| | | | | | | | | | | |
| | | | | | | | | | | |
| | | | | | | | | | | |

Name _____ Date _____ Class _____

**Estimating amount of uncollectible accounts expense; journalizing the adjusting entry**

**1.**

### GENERAL JOURNAL

PAGE ____

| | DATE | ACCOUNT TITLE | DOC. NO. | POST. REF. | DEBIT | CREDIT | |
|---|------|---------------|----------|------------|-------|--------|---|
| 1 | | | | | | | 1 |
| 2 | | | | | | | 2 |
| 3 | | | | | | | 3 |
| 4 | | | | | | | 4 |

**2.**

| Age Group | Amount | Percentage | Uncollectible |
|-----------|--------|------------|---------------|
| Current | $32,154.62 | 3.0% | |
| 1–30 | 14,178.96 | 6.0% | |
| 31–60 | 5,148.61 | 10.0% | |
| 61–90 | 3,215.11 | 20.0% | |
| Over 90 | 1,842.05 | 50.0% | |
| | $56,539.35 | | |
| Current Balance of Allowance for Uncollectible Accounts | | | |
| Estimated Addition to Allowance for Uncollectible Accounts | | | |

### GENERAL JOURNAL

PAGE ____

| | DATE | ACCOUNT TITLE | DOC. NO. | POST. REF. | DEBIT | CREDIT | |
|---|------|---------------|----------|------------|-------|--------|---|
| 1 | | | | | | | 1 |
| 2 | | | | | | | 2 |
| 3 | | | | | | | 3 |
| 4 | | | | | | | 4 |

### GENERAL JOURNAL

PAGE ____

| | DATE | ACCOUNT TITLE | DOC. NO. | POST. REF. | DEBIT | CREDIT | |
|---|------|---------------|----------|------------|-------|--------|---|
| 1 | | | | | | | 1 |
| 2 | | | | | | | 2 |
| 3 | | | | | | | 3 |
| 4 | | | | | | | 4 |
| 5 | | | | | | | 5 |

CASH RECEIPTS JOURNAL

| DATE | ACCOUNT TITLE | DOC. NO. | POST. REF. | GENERAL DEBIT | GENERAL CREDIT | ACCOUNTS RECEIVABLE CREDIT | SALES CREDIT | SALES TAX PAYABLE CREDIT | SALES DISCOUNT DEBIT | CASH DEBIT |
|---|---|---|---|---|---|---|---|---|---|---|
| | | | | | | | | | | |
| | | | | | | | | | | |
| | | | | | | | | | | |
| | | | | | | | | | | |
| | | | | | | | | | | |
| | | | | | | | | | | |
| | | | | | | | | | | |
| | | | | | | | | | | |
| | | | | | | | | | | |
| | | | | | | | | | | |
| | | | | | | | | | | |
| | | | | | | | | | | |
| | | | | | | | | | | |
| | | | | | | | | | | |
| | | | | | | | | | | |
| | | | | | | | | | | |
| | | | | | | | | | | |
| | | | | | | | | | | |
| | | | | | | | | | | |
| | | | | | | | | | | |
| | | | | | | | | | | |
| | | | | | | | | | | |

**6-2** **ON YOUR OWN, p. 185**

**Estimating amount of uncollectible accounts expense; journalizing the adjusting entry**

**1.**

GENERAL JOURNAL                                                                PAGE

| | DATE | ACCOUNT TITLE | DOC. NO. | POST. REF. | DEBIT | CREDIT | |
|---|---|---|---|---|---|---|---|
| 1 | | | | | | | 1 |
| 2 | | | | | | | 2 |
| 3 | | | | | | | 3 |
| 4 | | | | | | | 4 |

**2.**

| Age Group | Amount | Percentage | Uncollectible |
|---|---|---|---|
| Current | $28,106.64 | 2.0% | |
| 1–30 | 10,418.65 | 5.0% | |
| 31–60 | 6,109.46 | 12.0% | |
| 61–90 | 4,118.30 | 25.0% | |
| Over 90 | 2,219.36 | 60.0% | |
| | $50,972.41 | | |
| Current Balance of Allowance for Uncollectible Accounts | | | |
| Estimated Addition to Allowance for Uncollectible Accounts | | | |

GENERAL JOURNAL                                                                PAGE

| | DATE | ACCOUNT TITLE | DOC. NO. | POST. REF. | DEBIT | CREDIT | |
|---|---|---|---|---|---|---|---|
| 1 | | | | | | | 1 |
| 2 | | | | | | | 2 |
| 3 | | | | | | | 3 |
| 4 | | | | | | | 4 |

GENERAL JOURNAL                                                                PAGE

| | DATE | ACCOUNT TITLE | DOC. NO. | POST. REF. | DEBIT | CREDIT | |
|---|---|---|---|---|---|---|---|
| 1 | | | | | | | 1 |
| 2 | | | | | | | 2 |
| 3 | | | | | | | 3 |
| 4 | | | | | | | 4 |
| 5 | | | | | | | 5 |

CASH RECEIPTS JOURNAL

PAGE

| DATE | ACCOUNT TITLE | DOC. NO. | POST. REF. | GENERAL | | ACCOUNTS RECEIVABLE CREDIT | SALES CREDIT | SALES TAX PAYABLE CREDIT | SALES DISCOUNT DEBIT | CASH DEBIT |
|---|---|---|---|---|---|---|---|---|---|---|
| | | | | DEBIT | CREDIT | | | | | |
| | | | | 1 | 2 | 3 | 4 | 5 | 6 | 7 |

## 6-3 WORK TOGETHER, p. 188

**Financial analysis of accounts receivable**

**1. Accounts receivable turnover ratio:**

**2. Days' sales in accounts receivable:**

**3.**

_____

_____

_____

_____

_____

_____

_____

**Financial analysis of accounts receivable**

**1. Accounts receivable turnover ratio:**

**2. Days' sales in accounts receivable:**

**3.**

_____
_____
_____
_____
_____
_____
_____

## 6-1 APPLICATION PROBLEM (LO1), p. 192

**Journalizing entries to write off uncollectible accounts—direct write-off method**

GENERAL JOURNAL                                                                PAGE _____

| | DATE | ACCOUNT TITLE | DOC. NO. | POST. REF. | DEBIT | CREDIT | |
|---|---|---|---|---|---|---|---|
| 1 | | | | | | | 1 |
| 2 | | | | | | | 2 |
| 3 | | | | | | | 3 |
| 4 | | | | | | | 4 |
| 5 | | | | | | | 5 |
| 6 | | | | | | | 6 |
| 7 | | | | | | | 7 |
| 8 | | | | | | | 8 |
| 9 | | | | | | | 9 |
| 10 | | | | | | | 10 |
| 11 | | | | | | | 11 |
| 12 | | | | | | | 12 |
| 13 | | | | | | | 13 |
| 14 | | | | | | | 14 |
| 15 | | | | | | | 15 |
| 16 | | | | | | | 16 |
| 17 | | | | | | | 17 |
| 18 | | | | | | | 18 |
| 19 | | | | | | | 19 |
| 20 | | | | | | | 20 |
| 21 | | | | | | | 21 |
| 22 | | | | | | | 22 |
| 23 | | | | | | | 23 |
| 24 | | | | | | | 24 |
| 25 | | | | | | | 25 |
| 26 | | | | | | | 26 |
| 27 | | | | | | | 27 |
| 28 | | | | | | | 28 |
| 29 | | | | | | | 29 |

CASH RECEIPTS JOURNAL

PAGE

| | DATE | ACCOUNT TITLE | DOC. NO. | POST. REF. | GENERAL DEBIT | GENERAL CREDIT | ACCOUNTS RECEIVABLE CREDIT | SALES CREDIT | SALES TAX PAYABLE CREDIT | SALES DISCOUNT DEBIT | CASH DEBIT | |
|---|---|---|---|---|---|---|---|---|---|---|---|---|
| | | | | | 1 | 2 | 3 | 4 | 5 | 6 | 7 | |
| 1 | | | | | | | | | | | | 1 |
| 2 | | | | | | | | | | | | 2 |
| 3 | | | | | | | | | | | | 3 |
| 4 | | | | | | | | | | | | 4 |
| 5 | | | | | | | | | | | | 5 |
| 6 | | | | | | | | | | | | 6 |
| 7 | | | | | | | | | | | | 7 |
| 8 | | | | | | | | | | | | 8 |
| 9 | | | | | | | | | | | | 9 |
| 10 | | | | | | | | | | | | 10 |
| 11 | | | | | | | | | | | | 11 |
| 12 | | | | | | | | | | | | 12 |
| 13 | | | | | | | | | | | | 13 |
| 14 | | | | | | | | | | | | 14 |
| 15 | | | | | | | | | | | | 15 |
| 16 | | | | | | | | | | | | 16 |
| 17 | | | | | | | | | | | | 17 |
| 18 | | | | | | | | | | | | 18 |
| 19 | | | | | | | | | | | | 19 |
| 20 | | | | | | | | | | | | 20 |
| 21 | | | | | | | | | | | | 21 |
| 22 | | | | | | | | | | | | 22 |

**6-2** APPLICATION PROBLEM (LO2, 3, 4), p. 192

**Estimating amount of uncollectible accounts expense; journalizing the adjusting entry**

**1.**

GENERAL JOURNAL                                      PAGE ___

| | DATE | ACCOUNT TITLE | DOC. NO. | POST. REF. | DEBIT | CREDIT | |
|---|---|---|---|---|---|---|---|
| 1 | | | | | | | 1 |
| 2 | | | | | | | 2 |
| 3 | | | | | | | 3 |
| 4 | | | | | | | 4 |

**2.**

| Age Group | Amount | Percentage | Uncollectible |
|---|---|---|---|
| Current | $22,108.95 | 2.0% | |
| 1–30 | 13,048.62 | 5.0% | |
| 31–60 | 3,108.14 | 12.0% | |
| 61–90 | 4,094.46 | 30.0% | |
| Over 90 | 2,795.60 | 80.0% | |
| | $45,155.77 | | |
| Current Balance of Allowance for Uncollectible Accounts | | | |
| Estimated Addition to Allowance for Uncollectible Accounts | | | |

GENERAL JOURNAL                                      PAGE ___

| | DATE | ACCOUNT TITLE | DOC. NO. | POST. REF. | DEBIT | CREDIT | |
|---|---|---|---|---|---|---|---|
| 1 | | | | | | | 1 |
| 2 | | | | | | | 2 |
| 3 | | | | | | | 3 |
| 4 | | | | | | | 4 |
| 5 | | | | | | | 5 |
| 6 | | | | | | | 6 |
| 7 | | | | | | | 7 |
| 8 | | | | | | | 8 |
| 9 | | | | | | | 9 |
| 10 | | | | | | | 10 |
| 11 | | | | | | | 11 |

**3.**

## GENERAL JOURNAL

PAGE

| | DATE | ACCOUNT TITLE | DOC. NO. | POST. REF. | DEBIT | CREDIT | |
|---|---|---|---|---|---|---|---|
| 1 | | | | | | | 1 |
| 2 | | | | | | | 2 |
| 3 | | | | | | | 3 |
| 4 | | | | | | | 4 |
| 5 | | | | | | | 5 |
| 6 | | | | | | | 6 |
| 7 | | | | | | | 7 |
| 8 | | | | | | | 8 |
| 9 | | | | | | | 9 |
| 10 | | | | | | | 10 |
| 11 | | | | | | | 11 |
| 12 | | | | | | | 12 |
| 13 | | | | | | | 13 |
| 14 | | | | | | | 14 |
| 15 | | | | | | | 15 |
| 16 | | | | | | | 16 |
| 17 | | | | | | | 17 |
| 18 | | | | | | | 18 |
| 19 | | | | | | | 19 |
| 20 | | | | | | | 20 |
| 21 | | | | | | | 21 |
| 22 | | | | | | | 22 |
| 23 | | | | | | | 23 |
| 24 | | | | | | | 24 |
| 25 | | | | | | | 25 |
| 26 | | | | | | | 26 |
| 27 | | | | | | | 27 |
| 28 | | | | | | | 28 |
| 29 | | | | | | | 29 |
| 30 | | | | | | | 30 |

# 6-2 APPLICATION PROBLEM (concluded)

CASH RECEIPTS JOURNAL

| | | | | | | GENERAL | | ACCOUNTS RECEIVABLE CREDIT | SALES CREDIT | SALES TAX PAYABLE CREDIT | SALES DISCOUNT DEBIT | CASH DEBIT |
|---|---|---|---|---|---|---|---|---|---|---|---|---|
| | DATE | ACCOUNT TITLE | DOC. NO. | POST. REF. | DEBIT | CREDIT | | | | | | |
| 1 | | | | | | | | | | | | |
| 2 | | | | | | | | | | | | |
| 3 | | | | | | | | | | | | |
| 4 | | | | | | | | | | | | |
| 5 | | | | | | | | | | | | |
| 6 | | | | | | | | | | | | |
| 7 | | | | | | | | | | | | |
| 8 | | | | | | | | | | | | |
| 9 | | | | | | | | | | | | |
| 10 | | | | | | | | | | | | |
| 11 | | | | | | | | | | | | |
| 12 | | | | | | | | | | | | |
| 13 | | | | | | | | | | | | |
| 14 | | | | | | | | | | | | |
| 15 | | | | | | | | | | | | |
| 16 | | | | | | | | | | | | |
| 17 | | | | | | | | | | | | |
| 18 | | | | | | | | | | | | |
| 19 | | | | | | | | | | | | |
| 20 | | | | | | | | | | | | |
| 21 | | | | | | | | | | | | |
| 22 | | | | | | | | | | | | |

PAGE ___

**Financial analysis of accounts receivable**

**1. Accounts receivable turnover ratio:**

**2. Days' sales in accounts receivable:**

**3.**

_____
_____
_____
_____
_____
_____
_____

## 6-M MASTERY PROBLEM (LO2, 3, 4, 5), p. 193

**Journalizing entries for uncollectible accounts—allowance method; calculating and journalizing the adjusting entry for uncollectible accounts expense**

### 1., 2.

GENERAL JOURNAL                                      PAGE

| | DATE | | ACCOUNT TITLE | DOC. NO. | POST. REF. | DEBIT | CREDIT | |
|---|---|---|---|---|---|---|---|---|
| 1 | 01 | 1 | Accounts Receivable | | | 65 1 84 26 | | 1 |
| 2 | | | Allowance of Doubtful Accounts | | | | 3 48 62 | 2 |
| 3 | | | | | | | | 3 |
| 4 | | | | | | | | 4 |
| 5 | | | | | | | | 5 |
| 6 | | | | | | | | 6 |
| 7 | | | | | | | | 7 |
| 8 | | | | | | | | 8 |
| 9 | | | | | | | | 9 |
| 10 | | | | | | | | 10 |
| 11 | | | | | | | | 11 |
| 12 | | | | | | | | 12 |
| 13 | | | | | | | | 13 |
| 14 | | | | | | | | 14 |
| 15 | | | | | | | | 15 |
| 16 | | | | | | | | 16 |
| 17 | | | | | | | | 17 |
| 18 | | | | | | | | 18 |
| 19 | | | | | | | | 19 |
| 20 | | | | | | | | 20 |
| 21 | | | | | | | | 21 |
| 22 | | | | | | | | 22 |
| 23 | | | | | | | | 23 |
| 24 | | | | | | | | 24 |
| 25 | | | | | | | | 25 |
| 26 | | | | | | | | 26 |
| 27 | | | | | | | | 27 |
| 28 | | | | | | | | 28 |
| 29 | | | | | | | | 29 |

CASH RECEIPTS JOURNAL

PAGE

| | | | | DEBIT | CREDIT | | | | |
|---|---|---|---|---|---|---|---|---|---|
| DATE | ACCOUNT TITLE | DOC. NO. | POST. REF. | GENERAL 1 | GENERAL 2 | ACCOUNTS RECEIVABLE CREDIT 3 | SALES CREDIT 4 | SALES TAX PAYABLE CREDIT 5 | SALES DISCOUNT DEBIT 6 | CASH DEBIT 7 |

1.

# 6-M   MASTERY PROBLEM (concluded)

**3. Accounts receivable turnover ratio:**

**Days' sales in accounts receivable:**

**CHALLENGE PROBLEM (LO2), p. 194**

**Estimating amount of uncollectible accounts expense; journalizing the adjusting entry**

**1.**

| Customer | Account Balance | Not Yet Due | Days Account Balance Past Due | | | |
|---|---|---|---|---|---|---|
| | | | 1–30 | 31–60 | 61–90 | Over 90 |
| Ballard Corporation | $ 2,383.70 | | | | | |
| Colister Company | 3,874.80 | | | | | |
| Eads & Godfrey | 1,260.30 | | | | | |
| Garrett, Inc. | 2,031.00 | | | | | |
| Jeffries Distributors | 1,406.50 | | | | | |
| McEwen Industries | 2,722.10 | | | | | |
| Perryman Company | 2,047.20 | | | | | |
| Ruffin Associates | 3,615.20 | | | | | |
| Turnage Supply | 5,664.80 | | | | | |
| Totals | $25,005.60 | | | | | |

**2.**

| Age Group | Amount | Percentage | Uncollectible |
|---|---|---|---|
| Current 1–30 31–60 61–90 Over 90 | | | |
| | | | |
| Current Balance of Allowance for Uncollectible Accounts | | | |
| Estimated Addition to Allowance for Uncollectible Accounts | | | |

**3.**

GENERAL JOURNAL                                                           PAGE

| | DATE | ACCOUNT TITLE | DOC. NO. | POST. REF. | DEBIT | CREDIT | |
|---|---|---|---|---|---|---|---|
| 1 | | | | | | | 1 |
| 2 | | | | | | | 2 |
| 3 | | | | | | | 3 |
| 4 | | | | | | | 4 |

**Study Guide 7**

# Part One—Analyzing Concepts and Practices Related to Depreciation and Plant Assets

**Directions:** Place a *T* for True or an *F* for False in the Answers column to show whether each of the following statements is true or false.

**Answers**

1. Plant assets are sometimes referred to as fixed assets. (p. 198)

   1. _____

2. A company purchases a building and land for $400,000. The building is appraised for $300,000 and the land for $150,000. The cost assigned to the land should be $150,000. (p. 201)

   2. _____

3. International financial reporting standards require that significant components of a plant asset be recorded individually in different plant asset accounts. (p. 202)

   3. _____

4. An accounting form on which a business records information about each plant asset is called a plant asset record. (p. 203)

   4. _____

5. The value of an asset determined by tax authorities for the purpose of calculating taxes is called the millage rate. (p. 203)

   5. _____

6. Salvage value is also referred to as residual value, scrap value, or trade-in value. (p. 205)

   6. _____

7. Because of land's permanent nature, it is not subject to depreciation. (p. 205)

   7. _____

8. Original cost, estimated useful life, and miles driven in a year are the three factors considered when calculating annual depreciation expense. (p. 205)

   8. _____

9. The formula for calculating a plant asset's annual straight-line depreciation expense is: Original cost minus estimated salvage value divided by years of estimated useful life equals annual depreciation expense. (p. 206)

   9. _____

10. Whatever method a business selects to calculate depreciation expense for a portion of a year, that method should be used consistently from year to year. (p. 207)

    10. _____

11. The cost of replacing the roof of a warehouse should be added to the cost of the plant asset. (p. 209)

    11. _____

12. Three common ways of disposing of plant assets are discarding, selling, and trading. (p. 211)

    12. _____

13. When a plant asset is discarded, no notation needs to be made on the plant asset record. (p. 211)

    13. _____

14. If a plant asset is disposed of during a fiscal year, depreciation expense for part of a year is recorded. (p. 212)

    14. _____

15. A gain or loss on plant assets is not recorded when one plant asset is traded for a similar plant asset. (p. 214)

    15. _____

16. The double declining-balance rate of depreciation for a plant asset with a 4-year useful life is 25%. (p. 218)

    16. _____

17. Calculating the estimated annual depreciation expense based on the amount of production expected from a plant asset is called the units-of-production method of depreciation. (p. 219)

17. _____

18. The two most commonly-used MACRS classes, for plant assets other than real estate, are the three- and five-year property classes. (p. 220)

18. _____

19. MACRS depreciation is an acceptable depreciation method for financial reporting. (pp. 220–221)

19. _____

20. MACRS depreciation rates are based on the straight-line method using the modified half-year convention. (pp. 220–221)

20. _____

## Part Two—Identifying Accounting Terms

**Directions:** Select the one term in Column I that best fits each definition in Column II. Print the letter identifying your choice in the Answers column.

| **Column I** | **Column II** | **Answers** |
|---|---|---|
| A. book value of a plant asset | 1. Cash and other assets expected to be exchanged for cash or consumed within a year. (p. 198) | 1. _____ |
| B. current assets | 2. Land and anything attached to it. (p. 203) | 2. _____ |
| C. declining-balance method of depreciation | 3. All property not classified as real property. (p. 203) | 3. _____ |
| | 4. The amount that will be received for an asset at the time of its disposal. (p. 205) | 4. _____ |
| D. depletion | | |
| E. half-year convention | 5. Recording an equal amount of depreciation expense for a plant asset in each year of its useful life. (p. 206) | 5. _____ |
| F. modified half-year convention | 6. The original cost of a plant asset minus accumulated depreciation. (p. 206) | 6. _____ |
| G. personal property | 7. A method that recognizes one half of a year's depreciation in the year of acquisition. (p. 207) | 7. _____ |
| H. real property | 8. A method that recognizes a full year's depreciation if the asset is acquired in the first half of the year. (p. 207) | 8. _____ |
| I. salvage value | | |
| J. straight-line method of depreciation | 9. A type of accelerated depreciation that multiplies the book value of an asset by a constant depreciation rate to determine annual depreciation. (p. 218) | 9. _____ |
| | 10. The decrease in the value of a plant asset because of the removal of a natural resource. (p. 222) | 10. _____ |

# Part Three—Analyzing Plant Asset Transactions

**Directions:** For each transaction below, print in the proper Answers columns the identifying letter of the accounts to be debited and credited.

| Account Titles | Transactions | Answers Debit | Credit |
|---|---|---|---|
| **A.** Accum. Depr.—Equip. | **1-2.** Paid cash for new equipment. (p. 199) | **1.** _____ | **2.** _____ |
| **B.** Cash | **3-4.** Recorded annual depreciation on equipment. (p. 209) | **3.** _____ | **4.** _____ |
| **C.** Depr. Exp.—Equip. | | | |
| **D.** Gain on Plant Assets | **5-6.** Discarded equipment with no book value. (p. 211) | **5.** _____ | **6.** _____ |
| **E.** Equipment | **7-8.** Recorded depreciation for part of year. (p. 212) | **7.** _____ | **8.** _____ |
| **F.** Loss on Plant Assets | | | |
| | **9-10.** Discarded equipment with a book value, all depreciation recorded. (p. 212) | **9.** _____ | **10.** _____ |
| | **11-12.** Sold equipment for less than book value, all depreciation recorded. (p. 213) | **11.** _____ | **12.** _____ |
| | **13-14.** Sold equipment for more than book value, all depreciation recorded. (p. 213) | **13.** _____ | **14.** _____ |
| | **15-16.** Paid cash plus old equipment for new equipment with a list price of $4,500.00; original cost of old equipment, $3,500.00; total accumulated depreciation recorded to date of trade, $500.00. (p. 214) | **15.** _____ | **16.** _____ |

**7-1**  **WORK TOGETHER, p. 204**

**Journalizing asset purchase transactions**

**1.**

CASH PAYMENTS JOURNAL                                                                                                    PAGE 1

| DATE | ACCOUNT TITLE | CK. NO. | POST. REF. | GENERAL DEBIT | GENERAL CREDIT | ACCOUNTS PAYABLE DEBIT | PURCHASES DISCOUNT CREDIT | CASH CREDIT |
|------|---------------|---------|------------|---------------|----------------|------------------------|---------------------------|-------------|
| | | | | | | | | |
| | | | | | | | | |
| | | | | | | | | |
| | | | | | | | | |
| | | | | | | | | |
| | | | | | | | | |
| | | | | | | | | |
| | | | | | | | | |
| | | | | | | | | |

**1.**

GENERAL JOURNAL                                                                    PAGE 4

| DATE | ACCOUNT TITLE | DOC. NO. | POST. REF. | DEBIT | CREDIT |
|------|---------------|----------|------------|-------|--------|
| | | | | | |
| | | | | | |
| | | | | | |
| | | | | | |
| | | | | | |
| | | | | | |
| | | | | | |
| | | | | | |
| | | | | | |

**2.**

PLANT ASSET RECORD No. _____      General Ledger Account No. _____

Description _____    General Ledger Account _____

Date Bought _____   Serial Number _____   Original Cost _____

Estimated Useful Life _____   Estimated Salvage Value _____   Depreciation Method _____

Disposed of:    Discarded _____   Sold _____   Traded _____

Date _____      Disposal Amount _____

| Year | Annual Depreciation Expense | Accumulated Depreciation | Ending Book Value |
|------|------------------------------|---------------------------|-------------------|
|      |                              |                           |                   |
|      |                              |                           |                   |
|      |                              |                           |                   |
|      |                              |                           |                   |
|      |                              |                           |                   |
|      |                              |                           |                   |

PLANT ASSET RECORD No. _____      General Ledger Account No. _____

Description _____    General Ledger Account _____

Date Bought _____   Serial Number _____   Original Cost _____

Estimated Useful Life _____   Estimated Salvage Value _____   Depreciation Method _____

Disposed of:    Discarded _____   Sold _____   Traded _____

Date _____      Disposal Amount _____

| Year | Annual Depreciation Expense | Accumulated Depreciation | Ending Book Value |
|------|------------------------------|---------------------------|-------------------|
|      |                              |                           |                   |
|      |                              |                           |                   |
|      |                              |                           |                   |
|      |                              |                           |                   |
|      |                              |                           |                   |
|      |                              |                           |                   |

## 7-1  WORK TOGETHER (continued)

PLANT ASSET RECORD No. _____          General Ledger Account No. _____

Description _____          General Ledger Account _____

Date                          Serial
Bought _____            Number _____          Original Cost _____

                              Estimated
Estimated                     Salvage                      Depreciation
Useful Life _____       Value _____            Method _____

Disposed of:          Discarded _____    Sold _____    Traded _____
Date _____                   Disposal Amount _____

| Year | Annual Depreciation Expense | Accumulated Depreciation | Ending Book Value |
|------|------------------------------|--------------------------|-------------------|
|      |                              |                          |                   |
|      |                              |                          |                   |
|      |                              |                          |                   |
|      |                              |                          |                   |
|      |                              |                          |                   |
|      |                              |                          |                   |
|      |                              |                          |                   |
|      |                              |                          |                   |
|      |                              |                          |                   |

PLANT ASSET RECORD No. _____          General Ledger Account No. _____

Description _____          General Ledger Account _____

Date                    Serial
Bought _____    Number _____    Original Cost _____

                        Estimated
Estimated               Salvage                 Depreciation
Useful Life _____   Value _____          Method _____

Disposed of:           Discarded _____    Sold _____    Traded _____
Date _____                 Disposal Amount _____

| Year | Annual Depreciation Expense | Accumulated Depreciation | Ending Book Value |
|------|------------------------------|---------------------------|--------------------|
|      |                              |                           |                    |
|      |                              |                           |                    |
|      |                              |                           |                    |
|      |                              |                           |                    |
|      |                              |                           |                    |
|      |                              |                           |                    |

|                | Appraised Value | Percentage of Total Appraised Value | Assigned Cost |
|----------------|-----------------|--------------------------------------|---------------|
| Building........................... |                 |                                      |               |
| Land................................ | _____       |                                      | _____     |
| Total............................... | _____       |                                      | _____     |

**7-1**    **ON YOUR OWN, p. 204**

**Journalizing asset purchase transactions**

**1.**

CASH PAYMENTS JOURNAL      PAGE 2

| DATE | ACCOUNT TITLE | CK. NO. | POST. REF. | GENERAL DEBIT | GENERAL CREDIT | ACCOUNTS PAYABLE DEBIT | PURCHASES DISCOUNT CREDIT | CASH CREDIT |
|---|---|---|---|---|---|---|---|---|
| | | | | | | | | 1 |
| | | | | | | | | 2 |
| | | | | | | | | 3 |
| | | | | | | | | 4 |
| | | | | | | | | 5 |
| | | | | | | | | 6 |
| | | | | | | | | 7 |
| | | | | | | | | 8 |
| | | | | | | | | 9 |

**1.**

GENERAL JOURNAL      PAGE 1

| DATE | ACCOUNT TITLE | DOC. NO. | POST. REF. | DEBIT | CREDIT |
|---|---|---|---|---|---|
| | | | | | 1 |
| | | | | | 2 |
| | | | | | 3 |
| | | | | | 4 |
| | | | | | 5 |
| | | | | | 6 |
| | | | | | 7 |
| | | | | | 8 |
| | | | | | 9 |

**2.**

PLANT ASSET RECORD No. _____      General Ledger Account No. _____

Description _____    General Ledger Account _____

Date
Bought  _____   Serial
Number  _____   Original Cost  _____

Estimated
Useful Life _____   Estimated
Salvage
Value  _____   Depreciation
Method  _____

Disposed of:      Discarded _____   Sold _____   Traded _____

Date _____      Disposal Amount _____

| Year | Annual Depreciation Expense | Accumulated Depreciation | Ending Book Value |
|---|---|---|---|
| | | | |
| | | | |
| | | | |
| | | | |
| | | | |
| | | | |

PLANT ASSET RECORD No. _____      General Ledger Account No. _____

Description _____    General Ledger Account _____

Date
Bought  _____   Serial
Number  _____   Original Cost  _____

Estimated
Useful Life _____   Estimated
Salvage
Value  _____   Depreciation
Method  _____

Disposed of:      Discarded _____   Sold _____   Traded _____

Date _____      Disposal Amount _____

| Year | Annual Depreciation Expense | Accumulated Depreciation | Ending Book Value |
|---|---|---|---|
| | | | |
| | | | |
| | | | |
| | | | |
| | | | |
| | | | |

## 7-1 ON YOUR OWN (continued)

PLANT ASSET RECORD No. _____          General Ledger Account No. _____

Description _____          General Ledger Account _____

Date
Bought _____          Serial
                               Number _____ Original Cost _____

Estimated                      Estimated
Useful Life _____          Salvage          Depreciation
                               Value _____ Method _____

Disposed of:          Discarded _____ Sold _____ Traded _____
Date _____          Disposal Amount _____

| Year | Annual Depreciation Expense | Accumulated Depreciation | Ending Book Value |
|------|------------------------------|--------------------------|-------------------|
|      |                              |                          |                   |
|      |                              |                          |                   |
|      |                              |                          |                   |
|      |                              |                          |                   |
|      |                              |                          |                   |
|      |                              |                          |                   |
|      |                              |                          |                   |
|      |                              |                          |                   |

PLANT ASSET RECORD No. _____          General Ledger Account No. _____

Description _____          General Ledger Account _____

Date                          Serial
Bought _____          Number _____ Original Cost _____

Estimated                          Estimated
Estimated                          Salvage                          Depreciation
Useful Life _____          Value _____ Method _____

Disposed of:          Discarded _____  Sold _____ Traded _____
Date _____          Disposal Amount _____

| Year | Annual Depreciation Expense | Accumulated Depreciation | Ending Book Value |
|------|------------------------------|--------------------------|-------------------|
|      |                              |                          |                   |
|      |                              |                          |                   |
|      |                              |                          |                   |
|      |                              |                          |                   |
|      |                              |                          |                   |
|      |                              |                          |                   |

| | Appraised Value | Percentage of Total Appraised Value | Assigned Cost |
|---|---|---|---|
| Building.............................. | | | |
| Land.................................... | _____ | | _____ |
| Total................................... | _____ | | _____ |

## 7-2 WORK TOGETHER, p. 210

**Calculating and journalizing depreciation**

**1.**

| Plant asset: | Printer | Original cost: | $840.00 |
|---|---|---|---|
| Depreciation method: | Straight-line | Estimated salvage value: | $0.00 |
| | | Estimated useful life: | 3 years |

| Year | Beginning Book Value | Annual Depreciation | Accumulated Depreciation | Ending Book Value |
|---|---|---|---|---|
| | | | | |
| | | | | |
| | | | | |
| | | | | |
| | | | | |
| | | | | |

| Plant asset: | Conveyor table | Original cost: | $1,800.00 |
|---|---|---|---|
| Depreciation method: | Straight-line | Estimated salvage value: | $200.00 |
| | | Estimated useful life: | 5 years |

| Year | Beginning Book Value | Annual Depreciation | Accumulated Depreciation | Ending Book Value |
|---|---|---|---|---|
| | | | | |
| | | | | |
| | | | | |
| | | | | |
| | | | | |
| | | | | |

| Plant asset: | Warehouse | Original cost: | |
|---|---|---|---|
| Depreciation method: | Straight-line | Estimated salvage value: | $25,000.00 |
| | | Estimated useful life: | 25 years |

| Year | Beginning Book Value | Annual Depreciation | Accumulated Depreciation | Ending Book Value |
|---|---|---|---|---|
| | | | | |
| | | | | |
| | | | | |
| | | | | |
| | | | | |
| | | | | |

**3.**

GENERAL JOURNAL

| | DATE | | ACCOUNT TITLE | DOC. NO. | POST. REF. | DEBIT | CREDIT | |
|---|---|---|---|---|---|---|---|---|
| 1 | | | | | | | | 1 |
| 2 | | | | | | | | 2 |
| 3 | | | | | | | | 3 |
| 4 | | | | | | | | 4 |
| 5 | | | | | | | | 5 |
| 6 | | | | | | | | 6 |
| 7 | | | | | | | | 7 |
| 8 | | | | | | | | 8 |
| 9 | | | | | | | | 9 |
| 10 | | | | | | | | 10 |
| 11 | | | | | | | | 11 |
| 12 | | | | | | | | 12 |
| 13 | | | | | | | | 13 |
| 14 | | | | | | | | 14 |
| 15 | | | | | | | | 15 |
| 16 | | | | | | | | 16 |
| 17 | | | | | | | | 17 |
| 18 | | | | | | | | 18 |
| 19 | | | | | | | | 19 |
| 20 | | | | | | | | 20 |
| 21 | | | | | | | | 21 |
| 22 | | | | | | | | 22 |
| 23 | | | | | | | | 23 |
| 24 | | | | | | | | 24 |
| 25 | | | | | | | | 25 |
| 26 | | | | | | | | 26 |
| 27 | | | | | | | | 27 |
| 28 | | | | | | | | 28 |
| 29 | | | | | | | | 29 |
| 30 | | | | | | | | 30 |
| 31 | | | | | | | | 31 |
| 32 | | | | | | | | 32 |

## 7-2 ON YOUR OWN, p. 210

**Calculating and journalizing depreciation**

**1.**

| Plant asset: | Tablet computer | Original cost: | $650.00 |
|---|---|---|---|
| Depreciation method: | Straight-line | Estimated salvage value: | $0.00 |
| | | Estimated useful life: | 5 years |

| Year | Beginning Book Value | Annual Depreciation | Accumulated Depreciation | Ending Book Value |
|---|---|---|---|---|
| | | | | |
| | | | | |
| | | | | |
| | | | | |
| | | | | |
| | | | | |

| Plant asset: | Point-of-sale system | Original cost: | $2,500.00 |
|---|---|---|---|
| Depreciation method: | Straight-line | Estimated salvage value: | $500.00 |
| | | Estimated useful life: | 5 years |

| Year | Beginning Book Value | Annual Depreciation | Accumulated Depreciation | Ending Book Value |
|---|---|---|---|---|
| | | | | |
| | | | | |
| | | | | |
| | | | | |
| | | | | |
| | | | | |

| Plant asset: | Store | Original cost: | |
|---|---|---|---|
| Depreciation method: | Straight-line | Estimated salvage value: | $20,000.00 |
| | | Estimated useful life: | 25 years |

| Year | Beginning Book Value | Annual Depreciation | Accumulated Depreciation | Ending Book Value |
|---|---|---|---|---|
| | | | | |
| | | | | |
| | | | | |
| | | | | |
| | | | | |
| | | | | |

**3.**

GENERAL JOURNAL

| | DATE | ACCOUNT TITLE | DOC. NO. | POST. REF. | DEBIT | CREDIT | |
|---|---|---|---|---|---|---|---|
| 1 | | | | | | | 1 |
| 2 | | | | | | | 2 |
| 3 | | | | | | | 3 |
| 4 | | | | | | | 4 |
| 5 | | | | | | | 5 |
| 6 | | | | | | | 6 |
| 7 | | | | | | | 7 |
| 8 | | | | | | | 8 |
| 9 | | | | | | | 9 |
| 10 | | | | | | | 10 |
| 11 | | | | | | | 11 |
| 12 | | | | | | | 12 |
| 13 | | | | | | | 13 |
| 14 | | | | | | | 14 |
| 15 | | | | | | | 15 |
| 16 | | | | | | | 16 |
| 17 | | | | | | | 17 |
| 18 | | | | | | | 18 |
| 19 | | | | | | | 19 |
| 20 | | | | | | | 20 |
| 21 | | | | | | | 21 |
| 22 | | | | | | | 22 |
| 23 | | | | | | | 23 |
| 24 | | | | | | | 24 |
| 25 | | | | | | | 25 |
| 26 | | | | | | | 26 |
| 27 | | | | | | | 27 |
| 28 | | | | | | | 28 |
| 29 | | | | | | | 29 |
| 30 | | | | | | | 30 |
| 31 | | | | | | | 31 |
| 32 | | | | | | | 32 |

**7-3** **WORK TOGETHER, p. 217**

**Recording the disposal of plant assets**

**1.**

## CASH RECEIPTS JOURNAL

PAGE 1

| DATE | ACCOUNT TITLE | DOC. NO. | POST. REF. | GENERAL DEBIT 1 | GENERAL CREDIT 2 | ACCOUNTS RECEIVABLE CREDIT 3 | SALES CREDIT 4 | SALES TAX PAYABLE CREDIT 5 | SALES DISCOUNT DEBIT 6 | CASH DEBIT 7 |
|------|---------------|----------|-----------|------|-------|------|------|------|------|------|
| 1 | | | | | | | | | | |
| 2 | | | | | | | | | | |
| 3 | | | | | | | | | | |
| 4 | | | | | | | | | | |
| 5 | | | | | | | | | | |
| 6 | | | | | | | | | | |
| 7 | | | | | | | | | | |
| 8 | | | | | | | | | | |
| 9 | | | | | | | | | | |
| 10 | | | | | | | | | | |
| 11 | | | | | | | | | | |
| 12 | | | | | | | | | | |
| 13 | | | | | | | | | | |
| 14 | | | | | | | | | | |

## CASH PAYMENTS JOURNAL

PAGE 18

**1.**

| DATE | ACCOUNT TITLE | CK. NO. | POST. REF. | GENERAL DEBIT 1 | GENERAL CREDIT 2 | ACCOUNTS PAYABLE DEBIT 3 | PURCHASES DISCOUNT CREDIT 4 | CASH CREDIT 5 |
|------|---------------|---------|-----------|------|-------|------|------|------|
| 1 | | | | | | | | |
| 2 | | | | | | | | |
| 3 | | | | | | | | |
| 4 | | | | | | | | |

**1.**

GENERAL JOURNAL PAGE 1

| | DATE | ACCOUNT TITLE | DOC. NO. | POST. REF. | DEBIT | CREDIT | |
|---|---|---|---|---|---|---|---|
| 1 | | | | | | | 1 |
| 2 | | | | | | | 2 |
| 3 | | | | | | | 3 |
| 4 | | | | | | | 4 |
| 5 | | | | | | | 5 |
| 6 | | | | | | | 6 |
| 7 | | | | | | | 7 |
| 8 | | | | | | | 8 |
| 9 | | | | | | | 9 |
| 10 | | | | | | | 10 |
| 11 | | | | | | | 11 |
| 12 | | | | | | | 12 |
| 13 | | | | | | | 13 |
| 14 | | | | | | | 14 |
| 15 | | | | | | | 15 |
| 16 | | | | | | | 16 |
| 17 | | | | | | | 17 |
| 18 | | | | | | | 18 |
| 19 | | | | | | | 19 |
| 20 | | | | | | | 20 |
| 21 | | | | | | | 21 |
| 22 | | | | | | | 22 |
| 23 | | | | | | | 23 |
| 24 | | | | | | | 24 |
| 25 | | | | | | | 25 |
| 26 | | | | | | | 26 |
| 27 | | | | | | | 27 |
| 28 | | | | | | | 28 |
| 29 | | | | | | | 29 |
| 30 | | | | | | | 30 |
| 31 | | | | | | | 31 |
| 32 | | | | | | | 32 |

**7-3** **WORK TOGETHER (concluded)**

**2.**

---

PLANT ASSET RECORD No. __289__     General Ledger Account No. __1230__

Description __Desk__     General Ledger Account __Office Equipment__

Date Bought __January 14, 20X0__  Serial Number __6-33264-36__  Original Cost __$1,500.00__

Estimated Useful Life __7 years__  Estimated Salvage Value __$100.00__  Depreciation Method __Straight-line__

Disposed of:     Discarded _____  Sold _____  Traded _____
Date _____     Disposal Amount _____

| Year | Annual Depreciation Expense | Accumulated Depreciation | Ending Book Value |
|------|------|------|------|
| 20X0 | $200.00 | $ 200.00 | $1,300.00 |
| 20X1 | 200.00 | 400.00 | 1,100.00 |
| 20X2 | 200.00 | 600.00 | 900.00 |
| 20X3 | 200.00 | 800.00 | 700.00 |
| 20X4 | 200.00 | 1,000.00 | 500.00 |
| | | | |

---

PLANT ASSET RECORD No. __332__     General Ledger Account No. __1240__

Description __Truck__     General Ledger Account __Warehouse Equipment__

Date Bought __July 8, 20X2__  Serial Number __02-63232-6432__  Original Cost __$32,000.00__

Estimated Useful Life __5 years__  Estimated Salvage Value __$5,000.00__  Depreciation Method __Straight-line__

Disposed of:     Discarded _____  Sold _____  Traded _____
Date _____     Disposal Amount _____

| Year | Annual Depreciation Expense | Accumulated Depreciation | Ending Book Value |
|------|------|------|------|
| 20X2 | $2,700.00 | $ 2,700.00 | $29,300.00 |
| 20X3 | 5,400.00 | 8,100.00 | 23,900.00 |
| 20X4 | 5,400.00 | 13,500.00 | 18,500.00 |
| | | | |
| | | | |
| | | | |

---

**Recording the disposal of plant assets**

**1.**

## CASH RECEIPTS JOURNAL

PAGE 3

| | DATE | ACCOUNT TITLE | DOC. NO. | POST. REF. | GENERAL DEBIT (1) | GENERAL CREDIT (2) | ACCOUNTS RECEIVABLE CREDIT (3) | SALES CREDIT (4) | SALES TAX PAYABLE CREDIT (5) | SALES DISCOUNT DEBIT (6) | CASH DEBIT (7) | |
|---|---|---|---|---|---|---|---|---|---|---|---|---|
| 1 | | | | | | | | | | | | 1 |
| 2 | | | | | | | | | | | | 2 |
| 3 | | | | | | | | | | | | 3 |
| 4 | | | | | | | | | | | | 4 |
| 5 | | | | | | | | | | | | 5 |
| 6 | | | | | | | | | | | | 6 |
| 7 | | | | | | | | | | | | 7 |
| 8 | | | | | | | | | | | | 8 |
| 9 | | | | | | | | | | | | 9 |
| 10 | | | | | | | | | | | | 10 |
| 11 | | | | | | | | | | | | 11 |
| 12 | | | | | | | | | | | | 12 |
| 13 | | | | | | | | | | | | 13 |
| 14 | | | | | | | | | | | | 14 |

## CASH PAYMENTS JOURNAL

PAGE 18

**1.**

| | DATE | ACCOUNT TITLE | CK. NO. | POST. REF. | GENERAL DEBIT (1) | GENERAL CREDIT (2) | ACCOUNTS PAYABLE DEBIT (3) | PURCHASES DISCOUNT CREDIT (4) | CASH CREDIT (5) | |
|---|---|---|---|---|---|---|---|---|---|---|
| 1 | | | | | | | | | | 1 |
| 2 | | | | | | | | | | 2 |
| 3 | | | | | | | | | | 3 |
| 4 | | | | | | | | | | 4 |

**7-3**  **ON YOUR OWN (continued)**

**1.**

GENERAL JOURNAL                                              PAGE 3

| | DATE | ACCOUNT TITLE | DOC. NO. | POST. REF. | DEBIT | CREDIT | |
|---|---|---|---|---|---|---|---|
| 1 | | | | | | | 1 |
| 2 | | | | | | | 2 |
| 3 | | | | | | | 3 |
| 4 | | | | | | | 4 |
| 5 | | | | | | | 5 |
| 6 | | | | | | | 6 |
| 7 | | | | | | | 7 |
| 8 | | | | | | | 8 |
| 9 | | | | | | | 9 |
| 10 | | | | | | | 10 |
| 11 | | | | | | | 11 |
| 12 | | | | | | | 12 |
| 13 | | | | | | | 13 |
| 14 | | | | | | | 14 |
| 15 | | | | | | | 15 |
| 16 | | | | | | | 16 |
| 17 | | | | | | | 17 |
| 18 | | | | | | | 18 |
| 19 | | | | | | | 19 |
| 20 | | | | | | | 20 |
| 21 | | | | | | | 21 |
| 22 | | | | | | | 22 |
| 23 | | | | | | | 23 |
| 24 | | | | | | | 24 |
| 25 | | | | | | | 25 |
| 26 | | | | | | | 26 |
| 27 | | | | | | | 27 |
| 28 | | | | | | | 28 |
| 29 | | | | | | | 29 |
| 30 | | | | | | | 30 |
| 31 | | | | | | | 31 |
| 32 | | | | | | | 32 |

**2.**

PLANT ASSET RECORD No. __233__       General Ledger Account No. __1240__

Description __Display case__       General Ledger Account __Store Equipment__

Date Bought __March 20, 20X0__    Serial Number __9198-9CG__    Original Cost __$6,750.00__

Estimated Useful Life __7 years__    Estimated Salvage Value __$1,500.00__    Depreciation Method __Straight-line__

Disposed of:    Discarded _____    Sold _____    Traded _____

Date _____      Disposal Amount _____

| Year | Annual Depreciation Expense | Accumulated Depreciation | Ending Book Value |
|---|---|---|---|
| 20X0 | $562.50 | $ 562.50 | $6,187.50 |
| 20X1 | 750.00 | 1,312.50 | 5,437.50 |
| 20X2 | 750.00 | 2,062.50 | 4,687.50 |
| 20X3 | 750.00 | 2,812.50 | 3,937.50 |
| 20X4 | 750.00 | 3,562.50 | 3,187.50 |
| | | | |

PLANT ASSET RECORD No. __460__       General Ledger Account No. __1230__

Description __Chair__       General Ledger Account __Office Eqiupment__

Date Bought __July 8, 20X2__    Serial Number __02-63232-6432__    Original Cost __$800.00__

Estimated Useful Life __7 years__    Estimated Salvage Value __$100.00__    Depreciation Method __Straight-line__

Disposed of:    Discarded _____    Sold _____    Traded _____

Date _____      Disposal Amount _____

| Year | Annual Depreciation Expense | Accumulated Depreciation | Ending Book Value |
|---|---|---|---|
| 20X2 | $ 50.00 | $ 50.00 | $750.00 |
| 20X3 | 100.00 | 150.00 | 650.00 |
| 20X4 | 100.00 | 250.00 | 550.00 |
| | | | |
| | | | |
| | | | |

## 7-4 WORK TOGETHER, p. 223

**Computing depreciation using various depreciation methods and calculating depletion**

**1.**

| Plant asset: | Machine | Original cost: | $24,000.00 |
| Depreciation method: | Double declining-balance | Estimated salvage value: | $3,000.00 |
| | | Estimated useful life: | 5 years |

| Year | Beginning Book Value | Declining-Balance Rate | Annual Depreciation | Ending Book Value |
|------|----------------------|------------------------|---------------------|-------------------|
| 1 | | | | |
| 2 | | | | |
| 3 | | | | |
| 4 | | | | |
| 5 | | | | |
| 6 | | | | |
| 7 | | | | |
| 8 | | | | |
| 9 | | | | |

| Plant asset: | Machine | Original cost: | $24,000.00 |
| Depreciation method: | Units-of-production | Estimated salvage value: | $3,000.00 |
| | | Estimated useful life: | 16,000 hours |
| | | Depreciation rate: | |

| Year | Beginning Book Value | Production Hours | Annual Depreciation | Ending Book Value |
|------|----------------------|------------------|---------------------|-------------------|
| 1 | | | | |
| 2 | | | | |
| 3 | | | | |
| 4 | | | | |
| 5 | | | | |
| 6 | | | | |
| 7 | | | | |
| 8 | | | | |
| 9 | | | | |

**Computing depreciation using various depreciation methods and calculating depletion**

| Plant asset: | Machine | | Original cost: | $24,000.00 |
|---|---|---|---|---|
| Depreciation method: | MACRS | | Estimated salvage value: | 5-year |

| Year | Beginning Book Value | Depreciation Rate | Annual Depreciation | Ending Book Value |
|---|---|---|---|---|
| 1 | | | | |
| 2 | | | | |
| 3 | | | | |
| 4 | | | | |
| 5 | | | | |
| 6 | | | | |
| 7 | | | | |
| 8 | | | | |
| 9 | | | | |

**2.**

| Plant asset: | Gas well | Original cost: | $840,000.00 |
|---|---|---|---|
| Depreciation method: | Units-of-production | Estimated salvage value: | $60,000.00 |
| | | Estimated total depletion: | |
| | | Estimated useful life: | 800,000 MCF |
| | | Depletion rate: | |

| Year | Beginning Book Value | MCF Recovered | Annual Depletion | Ending Book Value |
|---|---|---|---|---|
| 1 | | | | |
| 2 | | | | |
| 3 | | | | |
| 4 | | | | |
| 5 | | | | |
| 6 | | | | |
| 7 | | | | |
| 8 | | | | |
| 9 | | | | |

**7-4** ON YOUR OWN, p. 224

**Computing depreciation using various depreciation methods and calculating depletion**

**1.**

| Plant asset: | Truck | Original cost: | $38,000.00 |
| Depreciation method: | Double declining-balance | Estimated salvage value: | $3,000.00 |
| | | Estimated useful life: | 3 years |

| Year | Beginning Book Value | Declining-Balance Rate | Annual Depreciation | Ending Book Value |
|------|----------------------|------------------------|---------------------|-------------------|
| 1 | | | | |
| 2 | | | | |
| 3 | | | | |
| 4 | | | | |
| 5 | | | | |
| 6 | | | | |
| 7 | | | | |
| 8 | | | | |
| 9 | | | | |

| Plant asset: | Truck | Original cost: | $38,000.00 |
| Depreciation method: | Units-of-production | Estimated salvage value: | $3,000.00 |
| | | Estimated useful life: | 300,000 miles |
| | | Depreciation rate: | |

| Year | Beginning Book Value | Miles Driven | Annual Depreciation | Ending Book Value |
|------|----------------------|--------------|---------------------|-------------------|
| 1 | | | | |
| 2 | | | | |
| 3 | | | | |
| 4 | | | | |
| 5 | | | | |
| 6 | | | | |
| 7 | | | | |
| 8 | | | | |
| 9 | | | | |

| | | | | |
|---|---|---|---|---|
| Plant asset: | Truck | | Original cost: | $38,000.00 |
| Depreciation method: | MACRS | | Property class: | 5-year |

| Year | Beginning Book Value | Depreciation Rate | Annual Depreciation | Ending Book Value |
|---|---|---|---|---|
| 1 | | | | |
| 2 | | | | |
| 3 | | | | |
| 4 | | | | |
| 5 | | | | |
| 6 | | | | |
| 7 | | | | |
| 8 | | | | |
| 9 | | | | |

**2.**

| | | | |
|---|---|---|---|
| Plant asset: | Mineral mine | Original cost: | $420,000.00 |
| Depreciation method: | Units-of-production | Estimated salvage value: | $80,000.00 |
| | | Estimated total depletion: | |
| | | Estimated useful life: | 120,000 tons |
| | | Depletion rate: | |

| Year | Beginning Book Value | Tons Mined | Annual Depletion | Ending Book Value |
|---|---|---|---|---|
| 1 | | | | |
| 2 | | | | |
| 3 | | | | |
| 4 | | | | |
| 5 | | | | |
| 6 | | | | |
| 7 | | | | |
| 8 | | | | |
| 9 | | | | |

**7-1** **APPLICATION PROBLEM (LO1), p. 228**

**Journalizing asset purchase transactions**

**1.**

## CASH PAYMENTS JOURNAL

PAGE 1

| DATE | ACCOUNT TITLE | CK. NO. | POST. REF. | GENERAL DEBIT (1) | GENERAL CREDIT (2) | ACCOUNTS PAYABLE DEBIT (3) | PURCHASES DISCOUNT CREDIT (4) | CASH CREDIT (5) | |
|---|---|---|---|---|---|---|---|---|---|
| | | | | | | | | | 1 |
| | | | | | | | | | 2 |
| | | | | | | | | | 3 |
| | | | | | | | | | 4 |
| | | | | | | | | | 5 |
| | | | | | | | | | 6 |
| | | | | | | | | | 7 |
| | | | | | | | | | 8 |
| | | | | | | | | | 9 |

**1.**

## GENERAL JOURNAL

PAGE 8

| DATE | ACCOUNT TITLE | DOC. NO. | POST. REF. | DEBIT | CREDIT | |
|---|---|---|---|---|---|---|
| | | | | | | 1 |
| | | | | | | 2 |
| | | | | | | 3 |
| | | | | | | 4 |
| | | | | | | 5 |
| | | | | | | 6 |
| | | | | | | 7 |
| | | | | | | 8 |
| | | | | | | 9 |

**2.**

PLANT ASSET RECORD No. _____        General Ledger Account No. _____

Description _____        General Ledger Account _____

Date Bought _____   Serial Number _____    Original Cost _____

Estimated Useful Life _____   Estimated Salvage Value _____    Depreciation Method _____

Disposed of:     Discarded _____    Sold _____   Traded _____

Date _____     Disposal Amount _____

| Year | Annual Depreciation Expense | Accumulated Depreciation | Ending Book Value |
|------|------------------------------|---------------------------|-------------------|
|      |                              |                           |                   |
|      |                              |                           |                   |
|      |                              |                           |                   |
|      |                              |                           |                   |
|      |                              |                           |                   |
|      |                              |                           |                   |

PLANT ASSET RECORD No. _____        General Ledger Account No. _____

Description _____        General Ledger Account _____

Date Bought _____   Serial Number _____    Original Cost _____

Estimated Useful Life _____   Estimated Salvage Value _____    Depreciation Method _____

Disposed of:     Discarded _____    Sold _____   Traded _____

Date _____     Disposal Amount _____

| Year | Annual Depreciation Expense | Accumulated Depreciation | Ending Book Value |
|------|------------------------------|---------------------------|-------------------|
|      |                              |                           |                   |
|      |                              |                           |                   |
|      |                              |                           |                   |
|      |                              |                           |                   |
|      |                              |                           |                   |
|      |                              |                           |                   |

**7-1** **APPLICATION PROBLEM (continued)**

PLANT ASSET RECORD No. _____          General Ledger Account No. _____

Description _____          General Ledger Account _____

Date
Bought _____     Serial
Number _____ Original Cost _____

Estimated
Useful Life _____     Estimated
Salvage
Value _____     Depreciation
Method _____

Disposed of:          Discarded _____ Sold _____ Traded _____
Date _____          Disposal Amount _____

| Year | Annual Depreciation Expense | Accumulated Depreciation | Ending Book Value |
|------|------------------------------|---------------------------|--------------------|
|      |                              |                           |                    |
|      |                              |                           |                    |
|      |                              |                           |                    |
|      |                              |                           |                    |
|      |                              |                           |                    |
|      |                              |                           |                    |
|      |                              |                           |                    |
|      |                              |                           |                    |

PLANT ASSET RECORD No. _____          General Ledger Account No. _____

Description _____          General Ledger Account _____

Date                    Serial
Bought _____    Number _____    Original Cost _____

Estimated               Estimated
                        Salvage             Depreciation
Estimated               Value _____     Method _____
Useful Life _____

Disposed of:          Discarded _____  Sold _____  Traded _____
Date _____          Disposal Amount _____

| Year | Annual Depreciation Expense | Accumulated Depreciation | Ending Book Value |
|------|------------------------------|---------------------------|--------------------|
|      |                              |                           |                    |
|      |                              |                           |                    |
|      |                              |                           |                    |
|      |                              |                           |                    |
|      |                              |                           |                    |
|      |                              |                           |                    |

|  | Appraised Value | Percentage of Total Appraised Value | Assigned Cost |
|--|------------------|--------------------------------------|----------------|
| Building ........................... |  |  |  |
| Land .................................. |  |  |  |
| Total ................................. |  |  |  |

**3.**

|  | Appraised Value | Percentage of Total Appraised Value | Assigned Cost |
|--|------------------|--------------------------------------|----------------|
| Engine ............................. |  |  |  |
| Transmission ................... |  |  |  |
| Tires ................................. |  |  |  |
| Frame ............................... |  |  |  |
| Total ................................. |  |  |  |

## 7-2 APPLICATION PROBLEM (LO2), p. 228

**Calculating and journalizing depreciation**

**1.**

| Plant asset: | Copy machine | Date bought: | January 12, 20X1 |
| Depreciation method: | Straight-line | Original cost: | $2,400.00 |
| | | Estimated salvage value: | $200.00 |
| | | Estimated useful life: | 5 years |

| Year | Beginning Book Value | Annual Depreciation | Accumulated Depreciation | Ending Book Value |
|------|---------------------|---------------------|--------------------------|-------------------|
| | | | | |
| | | | | |
| | | | | |
| | | | | |
| | | | | |

| Plant asset: | Shelving unit | Date bought: | August 22, 20X1 |
| Depreciation method: | Straight-line | Original cost: | $4,800.00 |
| | | Estimated salvage value: | $1,000.00 |
| | | Estimated useful life: | 5 years |

| Year | Beginning Book Value | Annual Depreciation | Accumulated Depreciation | Ending Book Value |
|------|---------------------|---------------------|--------------------------|-------------------|
| | | | | |
| | | | | |
| | | | | |
| | | | | |
| | | | | |
| | | | | |

| Plant asset: | Warehouse | Date bought: | September 27, 20X1 |
| Depreciation method: | Straight-line | Original cost: | |
| | | Estimated salvage value: | $60,000.00 |
| | | Estimated useful life: | 25 years |

| Year | Beginning Book Value | Annual Depreciation | Accumulated Depreciation | Ending Book Value |
|------|---------------------|---------------------|--------------------------|-------------------|
| | | | | |
| | | | | |
| | | | | |
| | | | | |
| | | | | |
| | | | | |

**3.**

GENERAL JOURNAL PAGE 15

| | DATE | ACCOUNT TITLE | DOC. NO. | POST. REF. | DEBIT | CREDIT | |
|---|---|---|---|---|---|---|---|
| 1 | | | | | | | 1 |
| 2 | | | | | | | 2 |
| 3 | | | | | | | 3 |
| 4 | | | | | | | 4 |
| 5 | | | | | | | 5 |
| 6 | | | | | | | 6 |
| 7 | | | | | | | 7 |
| 8 | | | | | | | 8 |
| 9 | | | | | | | 9 |
| 10 | | | | | | | 10 |
| 11 | | | | | | | 11 |
| 12 | | | | | | | 12 |
| 13 | | | | | | | 13 |
| 14 | | | | | | | 14 |
| 15 | | | | | | | 15 |
| 16 | | | | | | | 16 |
| 17 | | | | | | | 17 |
| 18 | | | | | | | 18 |
| 19 | | | | | | | 19 |
| 20 | | | | | | | 20 |
| 21 | | | | | | | 21 |
| 22 | | | | | | | 22 |
| 23 | | | | | | | 23 |
| 24 | | | | | | | 24 |
| 25 | | | | | | | 25 |
| 26 | | | | | | | 26 |
| 27 | | | | | | | 27 |
| 28 | | | | | | | 28 |
| 29 | | | | | | | 29 |
| 30 | | | | | | | 30 |
| 31 | | | | | | | 31 |
| 32 | | | | | | | 32 |

**7-3** **APPLICATION PROBLEM (LO3), p. 228**

**Recording the disposal of plant assets**

**1.**

## CASH RECEIPTS JOURNAL

PAGE 1

| | DATE | ACCOUNT TITLE | DOC. NO. | POST. REF. | GENERAL DEBIT | GENERAL CREDIT | ACCOUNTS RECEIVABLE CREDIT | SALES CREDIT | SALES TAX PAYABLE CREDIT | SALES DISCOUNT DEBIT | CASH DEBIT | |
|---|---|---|---|---|---|---|---|---|---|---|---|---|
| 1 | | | | | | | | | | | | 1 |
| 2 | | | | | | | | | | | | 2 |
| 3 | | | | | | | | | | | | 3 |
| 4 | | | | | | | | | | | | 4 |
| 5 | | | | | | | | | | | | 5 |
| 6 | | | | | | | | | | | | 6 |
| 7 | | | | | | | | | | | | 7 |
| 8 | | | | | | | | | | | | 8 |
| 9 | | | | | | | | | | | | 9 |
| 10 | | | | | | | | | | | | 10 |
| 11 | | | | | | | | | | | | 11 |
| 12 | | | | | | | | | | | | 12 |
| 13 | | | | | | | | | | | | 13 |
| 14 | | | | | | | | | | | | 14 |

## CASH PAYMENTS JOURNAL

PAGE 18

**1.**

| | DATE | ACCOUNT TITLE | CK. NO. | POST. REF. | GENERAL DEBIT | GENERAL CREDIT | ACCOUNTS PAYABLE DEBIT | PURCHASES DISCOUNT CREDIT | CASH CREDIT | |
|---|---|---|---|---|---|---|---|---|---|---|
| 1 | | | | | | | | | | 1 |
| 2 | | | | | | | | | | 2 |
| 3 | | | | | | | | | | 3 |
| 4 | | | | | | | | | | 4 |

**1.**

GENERAL JOURNAL

| | DATE | | ACCOUNT TITLE | DOC. NO. | POST. REF. | DEBIT | CREDIT | |
|---|---|---|---|---|---|---|---|---|
| 1 | | | | | | | | 1 |
| 2 | | | | | | | | 2 |
| 3 | | | | | | | | 3 |
| 4 | | | | | | | | 4 |
| 5 | | | | | | | | 5 |
| 6 | | | | | | | | 6 |
| 7 | | | | | | | | 7 |
| 8 | | | | | | | | 8 |
| 9 | | | | | | | | 9 |
| 10 | | | | | | | | 10 |
| 11 | | | | | | | | 11 |
| 12 | | | | | | | | 12 |
| 13 | | | | | | | | 13 |
| 14 | | | | | | | | 14 |
| 15 | | | | | | | | 15 |
| 16 | | | | | | | | 16 |
| 17 | | | | | | | | 17 |
| 18 | | | | | | | | 18 |
| 19 | | | | | | | | 19 |
| 20 | | | | | | | | 20 |
| 21 | | | | | | | | 21 |
| 22 | | | | | | | | 22 |
| 23 | | | | | | | | 23 |
| 24 | | | | | | | | 24 |
| 25 | | | | | | | | 25 |
| 26 | | | | | | | | 26 |
| 27 | | | | | | | | 27 |
| 28 | | | | | | | | 28 |
| 29 | | | | | | | | 29 |
| 30 | | | | | | | | 30 |
| 31 | | | | | | | | 31 |
| 32 | | | | | | | | 32 |

**7-3**    **APPLICATION PROBLEM (concluded)**

**2.**

---

PLANT ASSET RECORD No. __289__      General Ledger Account No. __1230__

Description __Desk__      General Ledger Account __Office Equipment__

Date Bought __January 14, 20X0__   Serial Number __6-33264-36__   Original Cost __$1,500.00__

Estimated Useful Life __7 years__   Estimated Salvage Value __$100.00__   Depreciation Method __Straight-line__

Disposed of:    Discarded _____   Sold _____   Traded _____

Date _____    Disposal Amount _____

| Year | Annual Depreciation Expense | Accumulated Depreciation | Ending Book Value |
|------|------|------|------|
| 20X0 | $200.00 | $ 200.00 | $1,300.00 |
| 20X1 | 200.00 | 400.00 | 1,100.00 |
| 20X2 | 200.00 | 600.00 | 900.00 |
| 20X3 | 200.00 | 800.00 | 700.00 |
| 20X4 | 200.00 | 1,000.00 | 500.00 |
|  |  |  |  |

---

PLANT ASSET RECORD No. __332__      General Ledger Account No. __1250__

Description __Truck__      General Ledger Account __Transportation Equipment__

Date Bought __July 8, 20X2__   Serial Number __02-63232-6432__   Original Cost __$32,000.00__

Estimated Useful Life __5 years__   Estimated Salvage Value __$5,000.00__   Depreciation Method __Straight-line__

Disposed of:    Discarded _____   Sold _____   Traded _____

Date _____    Disposal Amount _____

| Year | Annual Depreciation Expense | Accumulated Depreciation | Ending Book Value |
|------|------|------|------|
| 20X2 | $2,700.00 | $ 2,700.00 | $29,300.00 |
| 20X3 | 5,400.00 | 8,100.00 | 23,900.00 |
| 20X4 | 5,400.00 | 13,500.00 | 18,500.00 |
|  |  |  |  |
|  |  |  |  |
|  |  |  |  |

**Computing depreciation using various depreciation methods and calculating depletion**

**1.**

| Plant asset: | Car | Original cost: | $30,000.00 |
| --- | --- | --- | --- |
| Depreciation method: | Double declining-balance | Estimated salvage value: | $3,000.00 |
| | | Estimated useful life: | 5 years |

| Year | Beginning Book Value | Declining-Balance Rate | Annual Depreciation | Ending Book Value |
| --- | --- | --- | --- | --- |
| 1 | | | | |
| 2 | | | | |
| 3 | | | | |
| 4 | | | | |
| 5 | | | | |
| 6 | | | | |
| 7 | | | | |
| 8 | | | | |
| 9 | | | | |

| Plant asset: | Car | Original cost: | $30,000.00 |
| --- | --- | --- | --- |
| Depreciation method: | Units-of-production | Estimated salvage value: | $3,000.00 |
| | | Estimated useful life: | 100,000 miles |
| | | Depreciation rate: | |

| Year | Beginning Book Value | Miles Driven | Annual Depreciation | Ending Book Value |
| --- | --- | --- | --- | --- |
| 1 | | | | |
| 2 | | | | |
| 3 | | | | |
| 4 | | | | |
| 5 | | | | |
| 6 | | | | |
| 7 | | | | |
| 8 | | | | |
| 9 | | | | |

**7-4** **APPLICATION PROBLEM (concluded)**

| Plant asset: | Car | | Original cost: | $30,000.00 |
| Depreciation method: | MACRS | | Property class: | 5-year |

| Year | Beginning Book Value | Depreciation Rate | Annual Depreciation | Ending Book Value |
|------|----------------------|-------------------|---------------------|-------------------|
| 1 | | | | |
| 2 | | | | |
| 3 | | | | |
| 4 | | | | |
| 5 | | | | |
| 6 | | | | |
| 7 | | | | |
| 8 | | | | |
| 9 | | | | |

**2.**

| Plant asset: | Mineral mine | Original cost: | $925,000.00 |
| Depreciation method: | Units-of-production | Estimated salvage value: | $100,000.00 |
| | | Estimated total depletion: | |
| | | Estimated useful life: | 900,000 tons |
| | | Depletion rate: | |

| Year | Beginning Book Value | Tons Mined | Annual Depletion | Ending Book Value |
|------|----------------------|------------|------------------|-------------------|
| 1 | | | | |
| 2 | | | | |
| 3 | | | | |
| 4 | | | | |
| 5 | | | | |
| 6 | | | | |
| 7 | | | | |
| 8 | | | | |
| 9 | | | | |

**Recording entries for plant assets**

**1.**

## CASH RECEIPTS JOURNAL

PAGE 9

| | DATE | ACCOUNT TITLE | DOC. NO. | POST. REF. | 1 GENERAL DEBIT | 2 GENERAL CREDIT | 3 ACCOUNTS RECEIVABLE CREDIT | 4 SALES CREDIT | 5 SALES TAX PAYABLE CREDIT | 6 SALES DISCOUNT DEBIT | 7 CASH DEBIT | |
|---|---|---|---|---|---|---|---|---|---|---|---|---|
| 1 | | | | | | | | | | | | 1 |
| 2 | | | | | | | | | | | | 2 |
| 3 | | | | | | | | | | | | 3 |
| 4 | | | | | | | | | | | | 4 |
| 5 | | | | | | | | | | | | 5 |
| 6 | | | | | | | | | | | | 6 |
| 7 | | | | | | | | | | | | 7 |
| 8 | | | | | | | | | | | | 8 |
| 9 | | | | | | | | | | | | 9 |
| 10 | | | | | | | | | | | | 10 |
| 11 | | | | | | | | | | | | 11 |

**1.**

## CASH PAYMENTS JOURNAL

PAGE 3

| | DATE | ACCOUNT TITLE | CK. NO. | POST. REF. | 1 GENERAL DEBIT | 2 GENERAL CREDIT | 3 ACCOUNTS PAYABLE DEBIT | 4 PURCHASES DISCOUNT CREDIT | 5 CASH CREDIT | |
|---|---|---|---|---|---|---|---|---|---|---|
| 1 | | | | | | | | | | 1 |
| 2 | | | | | | | | | | 2 |
| 3 | | | | | | | | | | 3 |
| 4 | | | | | | | | | | 4 |
| 5 | | | | | | | | | | 5 |
| 6 | | | | | | | | | | 6 |
| 7 | | | | | | | | | | 7 |

**7-M** **MASTERY PROBLEM (continued)**

**1.**

GENERAL JOURNAL PAGE 3

| | DATE | ACCOUNT TITLE | DOC. NO. | POST. REF. | DEBIT | CREDIT | |
|---|---|---|---|---|---|---|---|
| 1 | | | | | | | 1 |
| 2 | | | | | | | 2 |
| 3 | | | | | | | 3 |
| 4 | | | | | | | 4 |
| 5 | | | | | | | 5 |
| 6 | | | | | | | 6 |
| 7 | | | | | | | 7 |
| 8 | | | | | | | 8 |
| 9 | | | | | | | 9 |
| 10 | | | | | | | 10 |
| 11 | | | | | | | 11 |
| 12 | | | | | | | 12 |
| 13 | | | | | | | 13 |
| 14 | | | | | | | 14 |
| 15 | | | | | | | 15 |
| 16 | | | | | | | 16 |
| 17 | | | | | | | 17 |
| 18 | | | | | | | 18 |
| 19 | | | | | | | 19 |
| 20 | | | | | | | 20 |
| 21 | | | | | | | 21 |
| 22 | | | | | | | 22 |
| 23 | | | | | | | 23 |
| 24 | | | | | | | 24 |
| 25 | | | | | | | 25 |
| 26 | | | | | | | 26 |
| 27 | | | | | | | 27 |
| 28 | | | | | | | 28 |
| 29 | | | | | | | 29 |
| 30 | | | | | | | 30 |
| 31 | | | | | | | 31 |
| 32 | | | | | | | 32 |

**1., 2.**

PLANT ASSET RECORD No. __233__

General Ledger Account No. __1230__

Description __Computer__

General Ledger Account __Office Equipment__

Date Bought __June 23, 19X9__

Serial Number __C16443P__

Original Cost __$2,300.00__

Estimated Useful Life __3 years__

Estimated Salvage Value __$500.00__

Depreciation Method __Straight-line__

Disposed of:   Discarded _____ Sold _____ Traded _____

Date _____   Disposal Amount _____

| Year | Annual Depreciation Expense | Accumulated Depreciation | Ending Book Value |
|------|------------------------------|---------------------------|--------------------|
| 19X9 | $300.00 | $ 300.00 | $2,000.00 |
| 20X0 | 600.00 | 900.00 | 1,400.00 |
| 20X1 | | | |
| | | | |
| | | | |
| | | | |

PLANT ASSET RECORD No. _____

General Ledger Account No. _____

Description _____

General Ledger Account _____

Date Bought _____

Serial Number _____

Original Cost _____

Estimated Useful Life _____

Estimated Salvage Value _____

Depreciation Method _____

Disposed of:   Discarded _____ Sold _____ Traded _____

Date _____   Disposal Amount _____

| Year | Annual Depreciation Expense | Accumulated Depreciation | Ending Book Value |
|------|------------------------------|---------------------------|--------------------|
| | | | |
| | | | |
| | | | |
| | | | |
| | | | |
| | | | |

## 7-M MASTERY PROBLEM (concluded)

**3.**

| Plant asset: | Office desk | Original cost: | $2,600.00 |
|---|---|---|---|
| Depreciation method: | Double declining-balance | Estimated salvage value: | $400.00 |
| | | Estimated useful life: | 7 years |

| Year | Beginning Book Value | Declining-Balance Rate | Annual Depreciation | Ending Book Value |
|---|---|---|---|---|
| 1 | | | | |
| 2 | | | | |
| 3 | | | | |
| 4 | | | | |
| 5 | | | | |
| 6 | | | | |
| 7 | | | | |
| 8 | | | | |

| Plant asset: | Office desk | Original cost: | $2,600.00 |
|---|---|---|---|
| Depreciation method: | MACRS | Property class: | 7-year |

| Year | Beginning Book Value | Depreciation Rate | Annual Depreciation | Ending Book Value |
|---|---|---|---|---|
| 1 | | | | |
| 2 | | | | |
| 3 | | | | |
| 4 | | | | |
| 5 | | | | |
| 6 | | | | |
| 7 | | | | |
| 8 | | | | |
| 9 | | | | |

**4.**

| | Percentage of Total Appraised Value | Assigned Cost |
|---|---|---|
| Land | 45% | |
| Warehouse | | |
| Structure | 35% | |
| Electrical systems | 12% | |
| Roof | 5% | |
| Landscaping | 3% | |
| Total Cost | | |

**Calculating depletion with a change in estimates**

**1., 2.**

| | | | | | |
|---|---|---|---|---|---|
| Plant asset: | Coal mine | | Original cost: | | $650,000.00 |
| Depreciation method: | Units-of-production | | Estimated salvage value: | | $50,000.00 |
| | | | Estimated total depletion: | | |
| | | | Estimated tons: | | 326,000 tons |

| Year | Beginning Book Value | Tons Mined | Depletion Rate | Annual Depletion | Ending Book Value |
|------|----------------------|------------|----------------|------------------|-------------------|
| 1 | | | | | |
| 2 | | | | | |
| 3 | | | | | |
| 4 | | | | | |
| 5 | | | | | |
| 6 | | | | | |
| 7 | | | | | |
| 8 | | | | | |
| 9 | | | | | |

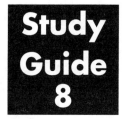
| Name | Perfect Score | Your Score |
|---|---|---|
| Identifying Accounting Terms | 18 Pts. | |
| Analyzing Procedures for Notes Payable, Prepaid Expenses, and Accrued Expenses | 10 Pts. | |
| Analyzing Entries for Notes Payable, Prepaid Expenses, and Accrued Expenses | 22 Pts. | |
| **Total** | 50 Pts. | |

## Part One—Identifying Accounting Terms

**Directions:** Select the one term in Column I that best fits each definition in Column II. Print the letter identifying your choice in the Answers column.

| Column I | Column II | Answers |
|---|---|---|
| A. accrued expenses | 1. Obtaining capital by borrowing money for a period of time. (p. 236) | 1. _____ |
| B. current liabilities | 2. A written and signed promise to pay a sum of money at a specified time. (p. 236) | 2. _____ |
| C. date of a note | 3. Promissory notes signed by a business and given to a creditor. (p. 236) | 3. _____ |
| D. debt financing | | |
| E. interest | 4. The day a note is issued. (p. 236) | 4. _____ |
| F. interest expense | 5. The original amount of a note. (p. 236) | 5. _____ |
| G. interest rate | 6. The date on which the principal of a note is due to be repaid. (p. 236) | 6. _____ |
| H. interest-bearing note | | |
| I. line of credit | 7. An amount paid for the use of money for a period of time. (p. 236) | 7. _____ |
| J. maturity date | 8. The percentage of the principal that is due for the use of the funds secured by a note. (p. 236) | 8. _____ |
| K. maturity value | | |
| L. noninterest-bearing note | 9. Liabilities due within a short time, usually within a year. (p. 237) | 9. _____ |
| M. notes payable | 10. Interest accrued on borrowed funds. (p. 239) | 10. _____ |
| N. prepaid expense | 11. The amount that is due on the maturity date of a note. (p. 239) | 11. _____ |
| O. prime interest rate | 12. A note having a stated interest rate. (p. 239) | 12. _____ |
| P. principal | 13. A note that deducts interest from the face value of the note. (p. 239) | 13. _____ |
| Q. promissory note | | |
| R. reversing entry | 14. A bank loan agreement that provides immediate short-term access to cash. (p. 240) | 14. _____ |
| | 15. The interest rate charged to a bank's most creditworthy customers. (p. 240) | 15. _____ |
| | 16. Cash paid for an expense in one fiscal period that is not used until a later period. (p. 242) | 16. _____ |
| | 17. An entry made at the beginning of one fiscal period to reverse an adjusting entry made in the previous fiscal period. (p. 244) | 17. _____ |
| | 18. Expenses incurred in one fiscal period but not paid until a later fiscal period. (p. 248) | 18. _____ |

## Part Two—Analyzing Procedures for Notes Payable, Prepaid Expenses, and Accrued Expenses

**Directions:** Place a *T* for True or an *F* for False in the Answers column to show whether each of the following statements is true or false.

1. The amount of note interest is slightly higher using a 360-day year compared to a 365-day year. (p. 238)

   1. _____

2. Interest expense is reported as an operating expense. (p. 239)

   2. _____

3. The proceeds of a noninterest-bearing note are less than its maturity value. (p. 239)

   3. _____

4. The interest rate on a credit line can change, based on market interest rates. (p. 240)

   4. _____

5. When prepaid expenses are initially recorded as expenses, no adjusting entry is required prior to preparing financial statements. (p. 243)

   5. _____

6. If an adjusting entry creates a balance in an asset or a liability account, the adjusting entry is reversed. (p. 244)

   6. _____

7. A reversing entry is usually the opposite of the adjusting entry made to the same accounts. (p. 244)

   7. _____

8. The reversing entry for an accrued expense results in a temporary credit balance in the expense account. (p. 249)

   8. _____

9. Recording repair costs during a warranty period as an expense in the same period the merchandise is sold is an application of the accounting concept Matching Expenses with Revenue. (p. 252)

   9. _____

10. Accrued Warranty Liability and Allowance for Uncollectible Accounts each have natural credit balances. (p. 253)

    10. _____

## Part Three—Analyzing Entries for Notes Payable, Prepaid Expenses, and Accrued Expenses

**Directions:** For each transaction below, print in the proper Answers columns the identifying letter of the accounts to be debited and credited. The company initially records prepaid expenses as expenses.

| Account Titles | Transactions | Answers Debit | Credit |
|---|---|---|---|
| **A.** Accrued Warranty Liability | **1.** Issued a 90-day note to the bank. (p. 237) | **1.** _____ | **2.** _____ |
| **B.** Cash | **2.** Paid cash for the maturity value of a note payable. (p. 239) | **3.** _____ | **4.** _____ |
| **C.** Insurance Expense | **3.** Drew from a line of credit. (p. 240) | **5.** _____ | **6.** _____ |
| **D.** Interest Expense | **4.** Paid a line of credit. (p. 240) | **7.** _____ | **8.** _____ |
| **E.** Interest Payable | **5.** Adjusting entry for prepaid insurance initially recorded as an expense. (p. 243) | **9.** _____ | **10.** _____ |
| **F.** Line of Credit | **6.** Reversing entry for supplies expense. (p. 244) | **11.** _____ | **12.** _____ |
| **G.** Notes Payable | **7.** Adjusting entry for accrued interest expense. (p. 248) | **13.** _____ | **14.** _____ |
| **H.** Prepaid Insurance | **8.** Reversing entry for accrued interest expense. (p. 249) | **15.** _____ | **16.** _____ |
| **I.** Supplies | **9.** Payment of a note at maturity. (p 250) | **17.** _____ | **18.** _____ |
| **J.** Supplies Expense | **10.** Adjusting entry for warranty expense. (p. 252) | **19.** _____ | **20.** _____ |
| **K.** Warranty Expense | **11.** Paid for a repair on an item under warranty. (p. 253) | **21.** _____ | **22.** _____ |

**8-1** **WORK TOGETHER, p. 241**

**Journalizing notes payable transactions**

**1.**

**CASH RECEIPTS JOURNAL** PAGE 6

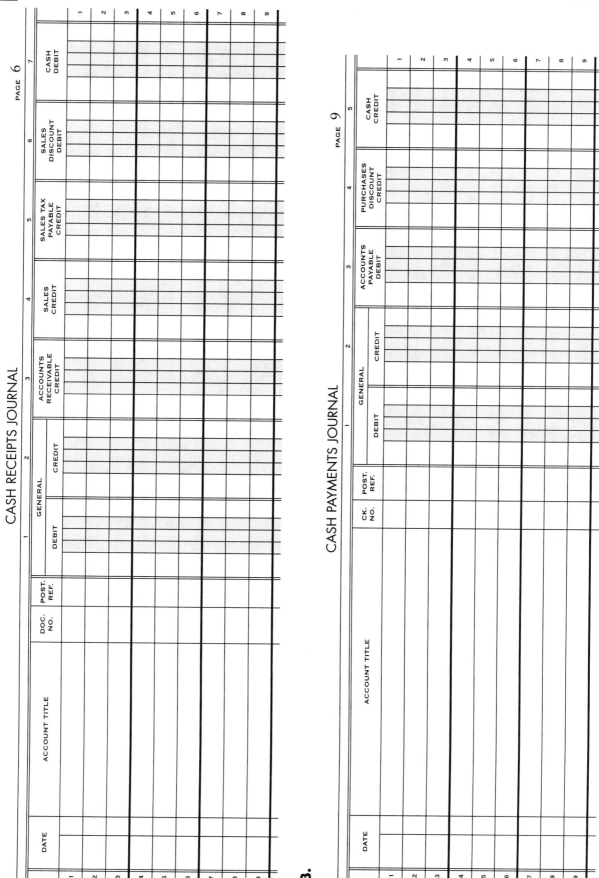

**3.**

**CASH PAYMENTS JOURNAL** PAGE 9

Chapter 8 Accounting for Notes Payable, Prepaid Expenses, and Accrued Expenses • **311**

**2.**

**Maturity dates:**

| June 4, $5,000.00 Note | | |
|---|---|---|
| | Days from the Month | Days Remaining |
| Term of the Note | | |
| | | |
| | | |
| | | |
| | | |
| | | |
| | | |
| | | |

| July 15, $8,000.00 Note | | |
|---|---|---|
| | Days from the Month | Days Remaining |
| Term of the Note | | |
| | | |
| | | |
| | | |
| | | |
| | | |
| | | |
| | | |

**2.**

**Interest due at maturity:**

June 4, $5,000.00 Note

| Principal | × | Interest Rate | × | Time as a Fraction of Year | = | Interest for Fraction of Year |
|---|---|---|---|---|---|---|
| | | | | /365 | | |

July 15, $8,000.00 Note

| Principal | × | Interest Rate | × | Time as a Fraction of Year | = | Interest for Fraction of Year |
|---|---|---|---|---|---|---|
| | | | | /365 | | |

**8-1** **ON YOUR OWN, p. 241**

**Journalizing notes payable transactions**

**1.**

PAGE 5

## CASH RECEIPTS JOURNAL

| | | | | GENERAL | | ACCOUNTS RECEIVABLE CREDIT | SALES CREDIT | SALES TAX PAYABLE CREDIT | SALES DISCOUNT DEBIT | CASH DEBIT |
|---|---|---|---|---|---|---|---|---|---|---|
| DATE | ACCOUNT TITLE | DOC. NO. | POST. REF. | DEBIT | CREDIT | | | | | |
| 1 | | | | | | | | | | |
| 2 | | | | | | | | | | |
| 3 | | | | | | | | | | |
| 4 | | | | | | | | | | |
| 5 | | | | | | | | | | |
| 6 | | | | | | | | | | |
| 7 | | | | | | | | | | |
| 8 | | | | | | | | | | |
| 9 | | | | | | | | | | |

**3.**

PAGE 11

## CASH PAYMENTS JOURNAL

| | | | | GENERAL | | ACCOUNTS PAYABLE DEBIT | PURCHASES DISCOUNT CREDIT | CASH CREDIT |
|---|---|---|---|---|---|---|---|---|
| DATE | ACCOUNT TITLE | CK. NO. | POST. REF. | DEBIT | CREDIT | | | |
| 1 | | | | | | | | |
| 2 | | | | | | | | |
| 3 | | | | | | | | |
| 4 | | | | | | | | |
| 5 | | | | | | | | |
| 6 | | | | | | | | |
| 7 | | | | | | | | |
| 8 | | | | | | | | |
| 9 | | | | | | | | |

**2.**

**Maturity dates:**

| May 16, $16,000.00 Note | | |
|---|---|---|
| | Days from the Month | Days Remaining |
| Term of the Note | | |
| | | |
| | | |
| | | |
| | | |
| | | |
| | | |
| | | |

| August 8, $20,000.00 Note | | |
|---|---|---|
| | Days from the Month | Days Remaining |
| Term of the Note | | |
| | | |
| | | |
| | | |
| | | |
| | | |
| | | |

**2.**

**Interest due at maturity:**

May 16, $16,000.00 Note

| Principal | × | Interest Rate | × | Time as a Fraction of Year | = | Interest for Fraction of Year |
|---|---|---|---|---|---|---|
| | | | | /365 | | |

August 8, $20,000.00 Note

| Principal | × | Interest Rate | × | Time as a Fraction of Year | = | Interest for Fraction of Year |
|---|---|---|---|---|---|---|
| | | | | /365 | | |

## 8-2 WORK TOGETHER, p. 247

**Journalizing adjusting and reversing entries for prepaid expenses**

**1.**

GENERAL JOURNAL

| | DATE | ACCOUNT TITLE | DOC. NO. | POST. REF. | DEBIT | CREDIT | |
|---|---|---|---|---|---|---|---|
| 1 | | | | | | | 1 |
| 2 | | | | | | | 2 |
| 3 | | | | | | | 3 |
| 4 | | | | | | | 4 |
| 5 | | | | | | | 5 |
| 6 | | | | | | | 6 |
| 7 | | | | | | | 7 |
| 8 | | | | | | | 8 |
| 9 | | | | | | | 9 |
| 10 | | | | | | | 10 |
| 11 | | | | | | | 11 |
| 12 | | | | | | | 12 |
| 13 | | | | | | | 13 |

**2.**

GENERAL JOURNAL

| | DATE | ACCOUNT TITLE | DOC. NO. | POST. REF. | DEBIT | CREDIT | |
|---|---|---|---|---|---|---|---|
| 1 | | | | | | | 1 |
| 2 | | | | | | | 2 |
| 3 | | | | | | | 3 |
| 4 | | | | | | | 4 |
| 5 | | | | | | | 5 |
| 6 | | | | | | | 6 |
| 7 | | | | | | | 7 |
| 8 | | | | | | | 8 |
| 9 | | | | | | | 9 |
| 10 | | | | | | | 10 |
| 11 | | | | | | | 11 |
| 12 | | | | | | | 12 |
| 13 | | | | | | | 13 |

**Journalizing adjusting and reversing entries for prepaid expenses**

**1.**

GENERAL JOURNAL                                                    PAGE 13

| | DATE | ACCOUNT TITLE | DOC. NO. | POST. REF. | DEBIT | CREDIT | |
|---|---|---|---|---|---|---|---|
| 1 | | | | | | | 1 |
| 2 | | | | | | | 2 |
| 3 | | | | | | | 3 |
| 4 | | | | | | | 4 |
| 5 | | | | | | | 5 |
| 6 | | | | | | | 6 |
| 7 | | | | | | | 7 |
| 8 | | | | | | | 8 |
| 9 | | | | | | | 9 |
| 10 | | | | | | | 10 |
| 11 | | | | | | | 11 |
| 12 | | | | | | | 12 |
| 13 | | | | | | | 13 |

**2.**

GENERAL JOURNAL                                                    PAGE 1

| | DATE | ACCOUNT TITLE | DOC. NO. | POST. REF. | DEBIT | CREDIT | |
|---|---|---|---|---|---|---|---|
| 1 | | | | | | | 1 |
| 2 | | | | | | | 2 |
| 3 | | | | | | | 3 |
| 4 | | | | | | | 4 |
| 5 | | | | | | | 5 |
| 6 | | | | | | | 6 |
| 7 | | | | | | | 7 |
| 8 | | | | | | | 8 |
| 9 | | | | | | | 9 |
| 10 | | | | | | | 10 |
| 11 | | | | | | | 11 |
| 12 | | | | | | | 12 |
| 13 | | | | | | | 13 |

**8-3** **WORK TOGETHER, p. 254**

## Journalizing adjusting and reversing entries for accrued expenses

**1.**

**GENERAL JOURNAL**                                                    PAGE 16

| DATE | ACCOUNT TITLE | DOC. NO. | POST. REF. | DEBIT | CREDIT | |
|------|---------------|----------|------------|-------|--------|---|
| | | | | | | 1 |
| | | | | | | 2 |
| | | | | | | 3 |
| | | | | | | 4 |
| | | | | | | 5 |
| | | | | | | 6 |
| | | | | | | 7 |
| | | | | | | 8 |
| | | | | | | 9 |
| | | | | | | 10 |
| | | | | | | 11 |
| | | | | | | 12 |
| | | | | | | 13 |
| | | | | | | 14 |
| | | | | | | 15 |

**3.**

**CASH PAYMENTS JOURNAL**                                             PAGE 2

| | | | | GENERAL | | ACCOUNTS PAYABLE DEBIT | PURCHASES DISCOUNT CREDIT | CASH CREDIT | |
|---|---|---|---|---|---|---|---|---|---|
| DATE | ACCOUNT TITLE | CK. NO. | POST. REF. | DEBIT | CREDIT | | | | |
| | | | | | | | | | 1 |
| | | | | | | | | | 2 |
| | | | | | | | | | 3 |
| | | | | | | | | | 4 |
| | | | | | | | | | 5 |

**2.**

GENERAL JOURNAL

PAGE 1

| | DATE | ACCOUNT TITLE | DOC. NO. | POST. REF. | DEBIT | CREDIT | |
|---|---|---|---|---|---|---|---|
| 1 | | | | | | | 1 |
| 2 | | | | | | | 2 |
| 3 | | | | | | | 3 |
| 4 | | | | | | | 4 |
| 5 | | | | | | | 5 |
| 6 | | | | | | | 6 |
| 7 | | | | | | | 7 |
| 8 | | | | | | | 8 |
| 9 | | | | | | | 9 |
| 10 | | | | | | | 10 |
| 11 | | | | | | | 11 |
| 12 | | | | | | | 12 |
| 13 | | | | | | | 13 |
| 14 | | | | | | | 14 |
| 15 | | | | | | | 15 |
| 16 | | | | | | | 16 |
| 17 | | | | | | | 17 |
| 18 | | | | | | | 18 |
| 19 | | | | | | | 19 |
| 20 | | | | | | | 20 |
| 21 | | | | | | | 21 |
| 22 | | | | | | | 22 |
| 23 | | | | | | | 23 |
| 24 | | | | | | | 24 |
| 25 | | | | | | | 25 |
| 26 | | | | | | | 26 |
| 27 | | | | | | | 27 |
| 28 | | | | | | | 28 |
| 29 | | | | | | | 29 |
| 30 | | | | | | | 30 |
| 31 | | | | | | | 31 |
| 32 | | | | | | | 32 |

**Journalizing adjusting and reversing entries for accrued expenses**

**1.**

GENERAL JOURNAL                                                    PAGE 13

| DATE | ACCOUNT TITLE | DOC. NO. | POST. REF. | DEBIT | CREDIT | |
|------|--------------|----------|------------|-------|--------|---|
| | | | | | | 1 |
| | | | | | | 2 |
| | | | | | | 3 |
| | | | | | | 4 |
| | | | | | | 5 |
| | | | | | | 6 |
| | | | | | | 7 |
| | | | | | | 8 |
| | | | | | | 9 |
| | | | | | | 10 |
| | | | | | | 11 |
| | | | | | | 12 |
| | | | | | | 13 |
| | | | | | | 14 |
| | | | | | | 15 |

**3.**

CASH PAYMENTS JOURNAL                                              PAGE 2

| | | | | GENERAL | | ACCOUNTS PAYABLE DEBIT | PURCHASES DISCOUNT CREDIT | CASH CREDIT | |
|---|---|---|---|---|---|---|---|---|---|
| DATE | ACCOUNT TITLE | CK. NO. | POST. REF. | DEBIT | CREDIT | | | | |
| | | | | | | | | | 1 |
| | | | | | | | | | 2 |
| | | | | | | | | | 3 |
| | | | | | | | | | 4 |
| | | | | | | | | | 5 |

**2.**

## GENERAL JOURNAL

PAGE 1

| | DATE | ACCOUNT TITLE | DOC. NO. | POST. REF. | DEBIT | CREDIT | |
|---|---|---|---|---|---|---|---|
| 1 | | | | | | | 1 |
| 2 | | | | | | | 2 |
| 3 | | | | | | | 3 |
| 4 | | | | | | | 4 |
| 5 | | | | | | | 5 |
| 6 | | | | | | | 6 |
| 7 | | | | | | | 7 |
| 8 | | | | | | | 8 |
| 9 | | | | | | | 9 |
| 10 | | | | | | | 10 |
| 11 | | | | | | | 11 |
| 12 | | | | | | | 12 |
| 13 | | | | | | | 13 |
| 14 | | | | | | | 14 |
| 15 | | | | | | | 15 |
| 16 | | | | | | | 16 |
| 17 | | | | | | | 17 |
| 18 | | | | | | | 18 |
| 19 | | | | | | | 19 |
| 20 | | | | | | | 20 |
| 21 | | | | | | | 21 |
| 22 | | | | | | | 22 |
| 23 | | | | | | | 23 |
| 24 | | | | | | | 24 |
| 25 | | | | | | | 25 |
| 26 | | | | | | | 26 |
| 27 | | | | | | | 27 |
| 28 | | | | | | | 28 |
| 29 | | | | | | | 29 |
| 30 | | | | | | | 30 |
| 31 | | | | | | | 31 |
| 32 | | | | | | | 32 |

**8-1**  **APPLICATION PROBLEM (LO1), p. 258**

**Journalizing notes payable transactions**

**1.**

## CASH RECEIPTS JOURNAL

PAGE 5

| | | | | GENERAL | | ACCOUNTS RECEIVABLE CREDIT | SALES CREDIT | SALES TAX PAYABLE CREDIT | SALES DISCOUNT DEBIT | CASH DEBIT |
|---|---|---|---|---|---|---|---|---|---|---|
| DATE | ACCOUNT TITLE | DOC. NO. | POST. REF. | DEBIT | CREDIT | | | | | |
| | | | | 1 | 2 | 3 | 4 | 5 | 6 | 7 |

**3.**

## CASH PAYMENTS JOURNAL

PAGE 9

| | | | | GENERAL | | ACCOUNTS PAYABLE DEBIT | PURCHASES DISCOUNT CREDIT | CASH CREDIT |
|---|---|---|---|---|---|---|---|---|
| DATE | ACCOUNT TITLE | CK. NO. | POST. REF. | DEBIT | CREDIT | | | |
| | | | | 1 | 2 | 3 | 4 | 5 |

**2.**

**Maturity dates:**

| May 16, $10,000.00 Note | | |
|---|---|---|
| | Days from the Month | Days Remaining |
| Term of the Note | | |
| | | |
| | | |
| | | |
| | | |
| | | |
| | | |
| | | |

| June 23, $4,500.00 Note | | |
|---|---|---|
| | Days from the Month | Days Remaining |
| Term of the Note | | |
| | | |
| | | |
| | | |
| | | |
| | | |
| | | |

**2.**

**Interest due at maturity:**

May 16, $10,000.00 Note

| Principal | × | Interest Rate | × | Time as a Fraction of Year | = | Interest for Fraction of Year |
|---|---|---|---|---|---|---|
| | | | | /365 | | |

June 23, $4,500.00 Note

| Principal | × | Interest Rate | × | Time as a Fraction of Year | = | Interest for Fraction of Year |
|---|---|---|---|---|---|---|
| | | | | /365 | | |

**8-2** **APPLICATION PROBLEM (LO2), p. 258**

### Journalizing adjusting and reversing entries for prepaid expenses

**1.**

GENERAL JOURNAL

PAGE 13

| | DATE | ACCOUNT TITLE | DOC. NO. | POST. REF. | DEBIT | CREDIT | |
|---|---|---|---|---|---|---|---|
| 1 | | | | | | | 1 |
| 2 | | | | | | | 2 |
| 3 | | | | | | | 3 |
| 4 | | | | | | | 4 |
| 5 | | | | | | | 5 |
| 6 | | | | | | | 6 |
| 7 | | | | | | | 7 |
| 8 | | | | | | | 8 |
| 9 | | | | | | | 9 |
| 10 | | | | | | | 10 |
| 11 | | | | | | | 11 |
| 12 | | | | | | | 12 |
| 13 | | | | | | | 13 |

**2.**

GENERAL JOURNAL

PAGE 1

| | DATE | ACCOUNT TITLE | DOC. NO. | POST. REF. | DEBIT | CREDIT | |
|---|---|---|---|---|---|---|---|
| 1 | | | | | | | 1 |
| 2 | | | | | | | 2 |
| 3 | | | | | | | 3 |
| 4 | | | | | | | 4 |
| 5 | | | | | | | 5 |
| 6 | | | | | | | 6 |
| 7 | | | | | | | 7 |
| 8 | | | | | | | 8 |
| 9 | | | | | | | 9 |
| 10 | | | | | | | 10 |
| 11 | | | | | | | 11 |
| 12 | | | | | | | 12 |
| 13 | | | | | | | 13 |

**Journalizing adjusting and reversing entries for accrued expenses**

**1.**

GENERAL JOURNAL

PAGE 16

| DATE | ACCOUNT TITLE | DOC. NO. | POST. REF. | DEBIT | CREDIT | |
|---|---|---|---|---|---|---|
| | | | | | | 1 |
| | | | | | | 2 |
| | | | | | | 3 |
| | | | | | | 4 |
| | | | | | | 5 |
| | | | | | | 6 |
| | | | | | | 7 |
| | | | | | | 8 |
| | | | | | | 9 |
| | | | | | | 10 |
| | | | | | | 11 |
| | | | | | | 12 |
| | | | | | | 13 |
| | | | | | | 14 |
| | | | | | | 15 |
| | | | | | | 16 |
| | | | | | | 17 |

**3.**

CASH PAYMENTS JOURNAL

PAGE 2

| | | | | 1 GENERAL | | 3 ACCOUNTS PAYABLE DEBIT | 4 PURCHASES DISCOUNT CREDIT | 5 CASH CREDIT | |
|---|---|---|---|---|---|---|---|---|---|
| DATE | ACCOUNT TITLE | CK. NO. | POST. REF. | DEBIT | CREDIT | | | | |
| | | | | | | | | | 1 |
| | | | | | | | | | 2 |
| | | | | | | | | | 3 |

**8-3** **APPLICATION PROBLEM (concluded)**

**2.**

### GENERAL JOURNAL

PAGE 1

| | DATE | | ACCOUNT TITLE | DOC. NO. | POST. REF. | DEBIT | CREDIT | |
|---|---|---|---|---|---|---|---|---|
| 1 | | | | | | | | 1 |
| 2 | | | | | | | | 2 |
| 3 | | | | | | | | 3 |
| 4 | | | | | | | | 4 |
| 5 | | | | | | | | 5 |
| 6 | | | | | | | | 6 |
| 7 | | | | | | | | 7 |
| 8 | | | | | | | | 8 |
| 9 | | | | | | | | 9 |
| 10 | | | | | | | | 10 |
| 11 | | | | | | | | 11 |
| 12 | | | | | | | | 12 |
| 13 | | | | | | | | 13 |
| 14 | | | | | | | | 14 |
| 15 | | | | | | | | 15 |
| 16 | | | | | | | | 16 |
| 17 | | | | | | | | 17 |
| 18 | | | | | | | | 18 |
| 19 | | | | | | | | 19 |
| 20 | | | | | | | | 20 |
| 21 | | | | | | | | 21 |
| 22 | | | | | | | | 22 |
| 23 | | | | | | | | 23 |
| 24 | | | | | | | | 24 |
| 25 | | | | | | | | 25 |
| 26 | | | | | | | | 26 |
| 27 | | | | | | | | 27 |
| 28 | | | | | | | | 28 |
| 29 | | | | | | | | 29 |
| 30 | | | | | | | | 30 |
| 31 | | | | | | | | 31 |
| 32 | | | | | | | | 32 |

**Journalizing notes payable transactions and adjusting and reversing entries**

**1.**

CASH RECEIPTS JOURNAL

PAGE 10

| | | | | | 1 GENERAL | | 2 GENERAL | 3 ACCOUNTS RECEIVABLE CREDIT | 4 SALES CREDIT | 5 SALES TAX PAYABLE CREDIT | 6 SALES DISCOUNT DEBIT | 7 CASH DEBIT |
|---|---|---|---|---|---|---|---|---|---|---|---|---|
| DATE | ACCOUNT TITLE | DOC. NO. | POST. REF. | | DEBIT | CREDIT | | | | | | |

**5.**

CASH PAYMENTS JOURNAL

PAGE 9

| | | | | | 1 GENERAL | 2 GENERAL | 3 ACCOUNTS PAYABLE DEBIT | 4 PURCHASES DISCOUNT CREDIT | 5 CASH CREDIT |
|---|---|---|---|---|---|---|---|---|---|
| DATE | ACCOUNT TITLE | CK. NO. | POST. REF. | | DEBIT | CREDIT | | | |

## 8-M MASTERY PROBLEM (continued)

**4.**

| August 10, $20,000 Note | | |
|---|---|---|
| | Days from the Month | Days Remaining |
| Term of the Note | | |
| | | |
| | | |
| | | |
| | | |
| | | |
| | | |
| | | |

| October 20, $25,000 Note | | |
|---|---|---|
| | Days from the Month | Days Remaining |
| Term of the Note | | |
| | | |
| | | |
| | | |
| | | |
| | | |
| | | |
| | | |

| November 5, $13,000 Note | | |
|---|---|---|
| | Days from the Month | Days Remaining |
| Term of the Note | | |
| | | |
| | | |
| | | |
| | | |
| | | |
| | | |
| | | |

**4.**

**Interest due at maturity:**

August 10, $20,000 Note

| Principal | × | Interest Rate | × | Time as a Fraction of Year | = | Interest for Fraction of Year |
|-----------|---|---------------|---|----------------------------|---|-------------------------------|
| | | | | /365 | | |

October 20, $25,000 Note

| Principal | × | Interest Rate | × | Time as a Fraction of Year | = | Interest for Fraction of Year |
|-----------|---|---------------|---|----------------------------|---|-------------------------------|
| | | | | /365 | | |

November 5, $13,000 Note

| Principal | × | Interest Rate | × | Time as a Fraction of Year | = | Interest for Fraction of Year |
|-----------|---|---------------|---|----------------------------|---|-------------------------------|
| | | | | /365 | | |

**2.**

**Supporting calculations for interest accrual:**

August 10, $20,000 Note

| Principal | × | Interest Rate | × | Time as a Fraction of Year | = | Interest for Fraction of Year |
|-----------|---|---------------|---|----------------------------|---|-------------------------------|
| | | | | /365 | | |

October 20, $25,000 Note

| Principal | × | Interest Rate | × | Time as a Fraction of Year | = | Interest for Fraction of Year |
|-----------|---|---------------|---|----------------------------|---|-------------------------------|
| | | | | /365 | | |

November 5, $13,000 Note

| Principal | × | Interest Rate | × | Time as a Fraction of Year | = | Interest for Fraction of Year |
|-----------|---|---------------|---|----------------------------|---|-------------------------------|
| | | | | /365 | | |

**8-M** **MASTERY PROBLEM (concluded)**

**2.**

GENERAL JOURNAL                                   PAGE 13

| | DATE | ACCOUNT TITLE | DOC. NO. | POST. REF. | DEBIT | CREDIT | |
|---|---|---|---|---|---|---|---|
| 1 | | | | | | | 1 |
| 2 | | | | | | | 2 |
| 3 | | | | | | | 3 |
| 4 | | | | | | | 4 |
| 5 | | | | | | | 5 |
| 6 | | | | | | | 6 |
| 7 | | | | | | | 7 |
| 8 | | | | | | | 8 |
| 9 | | | | | | | 9 |
| 10 | | | | | | | 10 |
| 11 | | | | | | | 11 |
| 12 | | | | | | | 12 |
| 13 | | | | | | | 13 |

**3.**

GENERAL JOURNAL                                   PAGE 1

| | DATE | ACCOUNT TITLE | DOC. NO. | POST. REF. | DEBIT | CREDIT | |
|---|---|---|---|---|---|---|---|
| 1 | | | | | | | 1 |
| 2 | | | | | | | 2 |
| 3 | | | | | | | 3 |
| 4 | | | | | | | 4 |
| 5 | | | | | | | 5 |
| 6 | | | | | | | 6 |
| 7 | | | | | | | 7 |
| 8 | | | | | | | 8 |
| 9 | | | | | | | 9 |
| 10 | | | | | | | 10 |
| 11 | | | | | | | 11 |
| 12 | | | | | | | 12 |
| 13 | | | | | | | 13 |

**Accruing for self-insurance losses**

**3.**

|  | 20X1 | 20X2 | 20X3 | 20X4 | 20X5 |
|---|---|---|---|---|---|
| Product claims |  |  |  |  |  |
| Sales |  |  |  |  |  |
| Claim ratio |  |  |  |  |  |

**1., 2., 3.**

| Name | | Perfect Score | Your Score |
|------|---|---|---|
| Analyzing Procedures for Unearned Revenue, Accrued Revenue, and Installment Notes Receivable | | 20 Pts. | |
| Identifying Accounting Terms | | 6 Pts. | |
| Analyzing Entries for Unearned Revenue, Accrued Revenue, and Installment Notes Receivable | | 20 Pts. | |
| | **Total** | 46 Pts. | |

## Part One—Analyzing Procedures for Unearned Revenue, Accrued Revenue, and Installment Notes Receivable

**Directions:** Place a *T* for True or an *F* for False in the Answers column to show whether each of the following statements is true or false.

**Answers**

1. Unearned revenue is also known as deferred revenue. (p. 264)

   1. _____

2. Unearned Rent is classified as a long-term liability. (p. 265)

   2. _____

3. A business not in the business of renting buildings should classify rental income in the Other Revenue section of the income statement. (p. 265)

   3. _____

4. If an adjusting entry creates a balance in an asset or liability account, the adjusting entry is normally reversed. (p. 266)

   4. _____

5. When making end-of-period adjusting entries, accrued interest on a note receivable is calculated from the date of the note through the maturity date of the note. (p. 267)

   5. _____

6. Interest Income is reported in the Other Revenue section of the income statement. (p. 267)

   6. _____

7. Interest Receivable is reported in the Long-Term Assets section of the balance sheet. (p. 267)

   7. _____

8. Retailers often issue a gift card to a customer returning merchandise. (p. 270)

   8. _____

9. Gift cards have a magnetic strip where the amount of the card balance is stored. (p. 270)

   9. _____

10. The sale of a gift card results in the recognition of revenue when payment for the card is received. (p. 270)

    10. _____

11. Until a gift card is redeemed, the outstanding balance of the card is unearned revenue. (p. 270)

    11. _____

12. Laws allow retailers to charge monthly fees every month gift cards are not redeemed. (p. 270)

    12. _____

13. The redemption of a gift card reduces the amount of gift cards outstanding. (p. 271)

    13. _____

14. When a business concludes that a gift card will never be redeemed, the value of the card is no longer an asset. (p. 272)

    14. _____

15. The account Sales Returns and Allowances is often used to record the value of unredeemed cards. (p. 272)

    15. _____

16. The amount of Breakage Revenue is an estimate. (p. 272)

    16. _____

17. The total sales from gift cards is listed separately on the income statement to allow users to compare the amount of revenue from sales with the related cost of merchandise sold. (p. 272)

17. _____

18. The amount of revenue recognized each month from the receipt of an installment note payment is equal to the principal portion of the payment. (p. 275)

18. _____

19. When a balance sheet is prepared, the amount presented as the Current Portion of Notes Receivable is equal to the total payments the business expects to collect during the next fiscal period. (p. 276)

19. _____

20. The Current Portion of Notes Receivable appears in the Current Assets section of the balance sheet. (p. 276)

20. _____

## Part Two—Identifying Accounting Terms

**Directions:** Select the one term in Column I that best fits each definition in Column II. Print the letter identifying your choice in the Answers column.

| Column I | Column II | Answers |
|---|---|---|
| A. Accrued Revenue | 1. Cash received for goods and services which have not been provided. (p. 264) | 1. _____ |
| B. Amortization Schedule | | |
| C. Breakage | 2. Revenue earned in one fiscal period but not received until a later fiscal period. (p. 267) | 2. _____ |
| D. Installment Note | 3. The value of unredeemed gift cards. (p. 272) | 3. _____ |
| E. Reclassification Entry | 4. A note resulting from a sale that requires monthly payments of principal and interest. (p. 274) | 4. _____ |
| F. Unearned Revenue | | |
| | 5. A schedule of the periodic payments on a note. (p. 275) | 5. _____ |
| | 6. An entry that transfers account balances between accounts on one financial statement. (p. 276) | 6. _____ |

# Part Three—Analyzing Entries for Unearned Revenue, Accrued Revenue, and Installment Notes Receivable

**Directions:** For each transaction below, print in the proper Answers columns the identifying letter of the accounts to be debited and credited.

| Account Titles | Transactions | Answers Debit | Credit |
|---|---|---|---|
| **A.** Breakage Revenue | **1-2.** Adjusting entry to recognize one month of rental use owed to the lessee. The business recognizes rental payments as revenue when payment is received. (p. 264) | 1._____ | 2._____ |
| **B.** Cash | | | |
| **C.** Current Portion of Notes Receivable | **3-4.** Reversing entry required for unearned rent. (p. 266) | 3._____ | 4._____ |
| **D.** Gift Cards Outstanding | **5-6.** Adjusting entry for interest earned that will be received in the next fiscal period. (p. 267) | 5._____ | 6._____ |
| **E.** Interest Income | | | |
| **F.** Interest Receivable | **7-8.** Reversing entry required for accrued interest income. (p. 268) | 7._____ | 8._____ |
| **G.** Notes Receivable | **9-10.** Received cash for the sale of gift cards. (p. 270) | 9._____ | 10._____ |
| **H.** Rent Income | | | |
| **I.** Sales | **11-12.** Customers redeemed gift cards for the sale of merchandise (ignore sales taxes). (p. 271) | 11._____ | 12._____ |
| **J.** Unearned Rent | **13-14.** Adjusting entry to recognize the value of gift cards that will never be redeemed. (p. 272) | 13._____ | 14._____ |
| | **15-16.** Sold merchandise, receiving a down payment and accepting an installment note receivable. (p. 274). | 15._____ | 16._____ |
| | **17-18.** Received cash for the monthly payment of an installment note receivable. (p. 275) | 17._____ | 18._____ |
| | **19-20.** Reclassify the value of notes receivable to be received during the next fiscal period. (p. 276) | 19._____ | 20._____ |

**9-1** **WORK TOGETHER, p. 269**

## Journalizing adjusting and reversing entries for unearned and accrued revenue

**1.**

GENERAL JOURNAL      PAGE 13

| | DATE | ACCOUNT TITLE | DOC. NO. | POST. REF. | DEBIT | CREDIT | |
|---|---|---|---|---|---|---|---|
| 1 | | | | | | | 1 |
| 2 | | | | | | | 2 |
| 3 | | | | | | | 3 |
| 4 | | | | | | | 4 |
| 5 | | | | | | | 5 |
| 6 | | | | | | | 6 |
| 7 | | | | | | | 7 |
| 8 | | | | | | | 8 |

**2.**

GENERAL JOURNAL      PAGE 14

| | DATE | ACCOUNT TITLE | DOC. NO. | POST. REF. | DEBIT | CREDIT | |
|---|---|---|---|---|---|---|---|
| 1 | | | | | | | 1 |
| 2 | | | | | | | 2 |
| 3 | | | | | | | 3 |
| 4 | | | | | | | 4 |
| 5 | | | | | | | 5 |
| 6 | | | | | | | 6 |
| 7 | | | | | | | 7 |
| 8 | | | | | | | 8 |

Note: Calculation not a required part of solution.

| Note | Principal | × | Interest Rate | × | Fraction of Year | = | Accrued Interest Income |
|---|---|---|---|---|---|---|---|
| | | | | | /365 | | |
| | | | | | /365 | | |

**Journalizing adjusting and reversing entries for unearned and accrued revenue**

**1.**

GENERAL JOURNAL

| | DATE | | ACCOUNT TITLE | DOC. NO. | POST. REF. | DEBIT | CREDIT | |
|---|---|---|---|---|---|---|---|---|
| 1 | | | | | | | | 1 |
| 2 | | | | | | | | 2 |
| 3 | | | | | | | | 3 |
| 4 | | | | | | | | 4 |
| 5 | | | | | | | | 5 |
| 6 | | | | | | | | 6 |
| 7 | | | | | | | | 7 |
| 8 | | | | | | | | 8 |

**2.**

GENERAL JOURNAL

| | DATE | | ACCOUNT TITLE | DOC. NO. | POST. REF. | DEBIT | CREDIT | |
|---|---|---|---|---|---|---|---|---|
| 1 | | | | | | | | 1 |
| 2 | | | | | | | | 2 |
| 3 | | | | | | | | 3 |
| 4 | | | | | | | | 4 |
| 5 | | | | | | | | 5 |
| 6 | | | | | | | | 6 |
| 7 | | | | | | | | 7 |
| 8 | | | | | | | | 8 |

Note: Calculation not a required part of solution.

| Note | Principal | × | Interest Rate | × | Fraction of Year | = | Accrued Interest Income |
|---|---|---|---|---|---|---|---|
| | | | | | /365 | | |
| | | | | | /365 | | |

**9-2**   **WORK TOGETHER, p. 273**

**Journalizing gift card transactions**

**1.**

CASH RECEIPTS JOURNAL

| DATE | ACCOUNT TITLE | DOC. NO. | POST. REF. | GENERAL DEBIT | GENERAL CREDIT | ACCOUNTS RECEIVABLE CREDIT | SALES CREDIT | SALES TAX PAYABLE CREDIT | SALES DISCOUNT DEBIT | CASH DEBIT |
|---|---|---|---|---|---|---|---|---|---|---|
| | | | | | | | | | | |
| | | | | | | | | | | |
| | | | | | | | | | | |
| | | | | | | | | | | |
| | | | | | | | | | | |
| | | | | | | | | | | |
| | | | | | | | | | | |
| | | | | | | | | | | |
| | | | | | | | | | | |
| | | | | | | | | | | |
| | | | | | | | | | | |
| | | | | | | | | | | |
| | | | | | | | | | | |
| | | | | | | | | | | |
| | | | | | | | | | | |
| | | | | | | | | | | |
| | | | | | | | | | | |
| | | | | | | | | | | |
| | | | | | | | | | | |
| | | | | | | | | | | |
| | | | | | | | | | | |
| | | | | | | | | | | |

**1.**

GENERAL JOURNAL                                                                    PAGE 18

| | DATE | ACCOUNT TITLE | DOC. NO. | POST. REF. | DEBIT | CREDIT | |
|---|---|---|---|---|---|---|---|
| 1 | | | | | | | 1 |
| 2 | | | | | | | 2 |
| 3 | | | | | | | 3 |
| 4 | | | | | | | 4 |
| 5 | | | | | | | 5 |
| 6 | | | | | | | 6 |
| 7 | | | | | | | 7 |
| 8 | | | | | | | 8 |
| 9 | | | | | | | 9 |
| 10 | | | | | | | 10 |
| 11 | | | | | | | 11 |
| 12 | | | | | | | 12 |
| 13 | | | | | | | 13 |

**2.**

GENERAL JOURNAL                                                                    PAGE 19

| | DATE | ACCOUNT TITLE | DOC. NO. | POST. REF. | DEBIT | CREDIT | |
|---|---|---|---|---|---|---|---|
| 1 | | | | | | | 1 |
| 2 | | | | | | | 2 |
| 3 | | | | | | | 3 |
| 4 | | | | | | | 4 |
| 5 | | | | | | | 5 |
| 6 | | | | | | | 6 |
| 7 | | | | | | | 7 |
| 8 | | | | | | | 8 |
| 9 | | | | | | | 9 |
| 10 | | | | | | | 10 |
| 11 | | | | | | | 11 |
| 12 | | | | | | | 12 |
| 13 | | | | | | | 13 |

## 9-2 ON YOUR OWN, p. 273

**Journalizing gift card transactions**

**1.**

CASH RECEIPTS JOURNAL

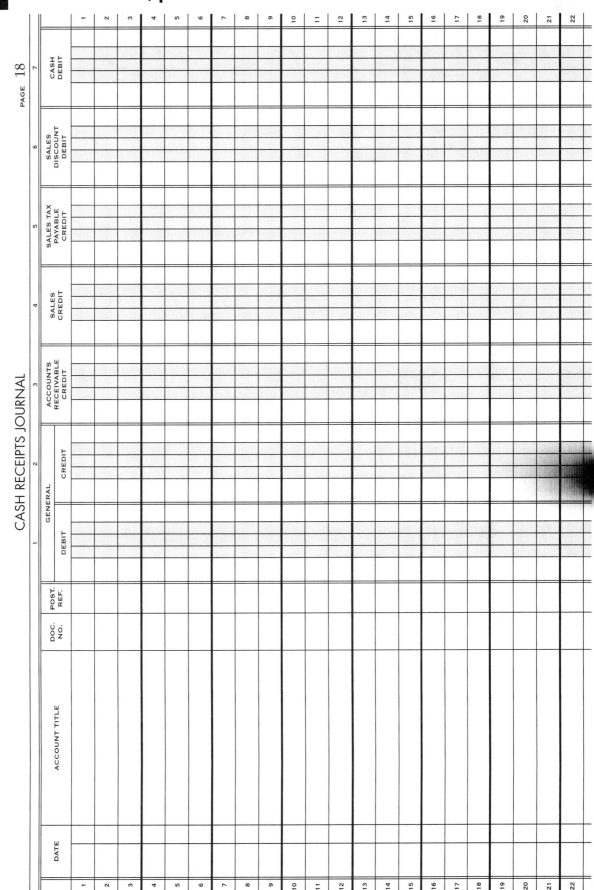

| DATE | ACCOUNT TITLE | DOC. NO. | POST. REF. | GENERAL DEBIT | GENERAL CREDIT | ACCOUNTS RECEIVABLE CREDIT | SALES CREDIT | SALES TAX PAYABLE CREDIT | SALES DISCOUNT DEBIT | CASH DEBIT |
|---|---|---|---|---|---|---|---|---|---|---|
| | | | | | | | | | | |
| | | | | | | | | | | |
| | | | | | | | | | | |
| | | | | | | | | | | |
| | | | | | | | | | | |
| | | | | | | | | | | |
| | | | | | | | | | | |
| | | | | | | | | | | |
| | | | | | | | | | | |
| | | | | | | | | | | |
| | | | | | | | | | | |
| | | | | | | | | | | |
| | | | | | | | | | | |
| | | | | | | | | | | |
| | | | | | | | | | | |
| | | | | | | | | | | |
| | | | | | | | | | | |
| | | | | | | | | | | |
| | | | | | | | | | | |
| | | | | | | | | | | |
| | | | | | | | | | | |
| | | | | | | | | | | |

Chapter 9 Accounting for Unearned Revenue, Accrued Revenue, and Installment Notes Receivable • **339**

**1.**

GENERAL JOURNAL

PAGE 14

| | DATE | | ACCOUNT TITLE | DOC. NO. | POST. REF. | DEBIT | CREDIT | |
|---|---|---|---|---|---|---|---|---|
| 1 | | | | | | | | 1 |
| 2 | | | | | | | | 2 |
| 3 | | | | | | | | 3 |
| 4 | | | | | | | | 4 |
| 5 | | | | | | | | 5 |
| 6 | | | | | | | | 6 |
| 7 | | | | | | | | 7 |
| 8 | | | | | | | | 8 |
| 9 | | | | | | | | 9 |
| 10 | | | | | | | | 10 |
| 11 | | | | | | | | 11 |
| 12 | | | | | | | | 12 |
| 13 | | | | | | | | 13 |

**2.**

GENERAL JOURNAL

PAGE 15

| | DATE | | ACCOUNT TITLE | DOC. NO. | POST. REF. | DEBIT | CREDIT | |
|---|---|---|---|---|---|---|---|---|
| 1 | | | | | | | | 1 |
| 2 | | | | | | | | 2 |
| 3 | | | | | | | | 3 |
| 4 | | | | | | | | 4 |
| 5 | | | | | | | | 5 |
| 6 | | | | | | | | 6 |
| 7 | | | | | | | | 7 |
| 8 | | | | | | | | 8 |
| 9 | | | | | | | | 9 |
| 10 | | | | | | | | 10 |
| 11 | | | | | | | | 11 |
| 12 | | | | | | | | 12 |
| 13 | | | | | | | | 13 |

**9-3** **WORK TOGETHER, p. 279**

**Journalizing installment notes receivable transactions**

**1.**

CASH RECEIPTS JOURNAL

PAGE 5

| | | | | 1 | 2 | 3 | 4 | 5 | 6 | 7 |
|---|---|---|---|---|---|---|---|---|---|---|
| | | | | GENERAL | | ACCOUNTS RECEIVABLE CREDIT | SALES CREDIT | SALES TAX PAYABLE CREDIT | SALES DISCOUNT DEBIT | CASH DEBIT |
| DATE | ACCOUNT TITLE | DOC. NO. | POST. REF. | DEBIT | CREDIT | | | | | |
| 1 | | | | | | | | | | |
| 2 | | | | | | | | | | |
| 3 | | | | | | | | | | |
| 4 | | | | | | | | | | |
| 5 | | | | | | | | | | |
| 6 | | | | | | | | | | |

**Illustration for 1.**

| Borrower | Daniel Toney |
|---|---|
| Amount Borrowed | $12,000.00 |
| Term of Note (Months) | 60 |
| Annual Interest Rate | 8% |
| Monthly Payment | $243.32 |
| Monthly Due Date | 10th |

| Payment Number | Month | Beginning Balance | Interest | Principal | Ending Balance |
|---|---|---|---|---|---|
| 1 | January | $12,000.00 | $80.00 | $163.32 | $11,836.68 |
| 2 | February | $11,836.68 | $78.91 | $164.41 | $11,672.27 |
| 3 | March | $11,672.27 | $77.82 | $165.50 | $11,506.77 |
| 4 | April | $11,506.77 | $76.71 | $166.61 | $11,340.16 |
| 5 | May | $11,340.16 | $75.60 | $167.72 | $11,172.44 |
| 6 | June | $11,172.44 | $74.48 | $168.84 | $11,003.60 |
| 7 | July | $11,003.60 | $73.36 | $169.96 | $10,833.64 |
| 8 | August | $10,833.64 | $72.22 | $171.10 | $10,662.54 |

Chapter 9 Accounting for Unearned Revenue, Accrued Revenue, and Installment Notes Receivable • **341**

**2.**

GENERAL JOURNAL

PAGE 15

| | DATE | ACCOUNT TITLE | DOC. NO. | POST. REF. | DEBIT | CREDIT | |
|---|---|---|---|---|---|---|---|
| 1 | | | | | | | 1 |
| 2 | | | | | | | 2 |
| 3 | | | | | | | 3 |
| 4 | | | | | | | 4 |
| 5 | | | | | | | 5 |
| 6 | | | | | | | 6 |
| 7 | | | | | | | 7 |
| 8 | | | | | | | 8 |
| 9 | | | | | | | 9 |
| 10 | | | | | | | 10 |
| 11 | | | | | | | 11 |
| 12 | | | | | | | 12 |
| 13 | | | | | | | 13 |

**3.**

GENERAL JOURNAL

PAGE 16

| | DATE | ACCOUNT TITLE | DOC. NO. | POST. REF. | DEBIT | CREDIT | |
|---|---|---|---|---|---|---|---|
| 1 | | | | | | | 1 |
| 2 | | | | | | | 2 |
| 3 | | | | | | | 3 |
| 4 | | | | | | | 4 |
| 5 | | | | | | | 5 |
| 6 | | | | | | | 6 |
| 7 | | | | | | | 7 |
| 8 | | | | | | | 8 |
| 9 | | | | | | | 9 |
| 10 | | | | | | | 10 |
| 11 | | | | | | | 11 |
| 12 | | | | | | | 12 |
| 13 | | | | | | | 13 |

**9-3** **ON YOUR OWN, p. 279**

Journalizing installment notes receivable transactions

**1.**

CASH RECEIPTS JOURNAL

PAGE 6

| DATE | ACCOUNT TITLE | DOC. NO. | POST. REF. | GENERAL DEBIT | GENERAL CREDIT | ACCOUNTS RECEIVABLE CREDIT | SALES CREDIT | SALES TAX PAYABLE CREDIT | SALES DISCOUNT DEBIT | CASH DEBIT |
|---|---|---|---|---|---|---|---|---|---|---|
| | | | | 1 | 2 | 3 | 4 | 5 | 6 | 7 |
| | | | | | | | | | | |
| | | | | | | | | | | |
| | | | | | | | | | | |
| | | | | | | | | | | |
| | | | | | | | | | | |
| | | | | | | | | | | |
| | | | | | | | | | | |
| | | | | | | | | | | |
| | | | | | | | | | | |
| | | | | | | | | | | |
| | | | | | | | | | | |
| | | | | | | | | | | |
| | | | | | | | | | | |
| | | | | | | | | | | |
| | | | | | | | | | | |
| | | | | | | | | | | |
| | | | | | | | | | | |
| | | | | | | | | | | |
| | | | | | | | | | | |
| | | | | | | | | | | |
| | | | | | | | | | | |

**Illustrations for 1.**

| Borrower | Wayne Wood |
|---|---|
| Amount Borrowed | $3,800.00 |
| Term of Note (Months) | 36 |
| Annual Interest Rate | 9% |
| Monthly Payment | $120.84 |
| Monthly Due Date | 6th |

| Payment Number | Month | Beginning Balance | Interest | Principal | Ending Balance |
|---|---|---|---|---|---|
| 1 | December | $3,800.00 | $28.50 | $92.34 | $3,707.66 |
| 2 | January | $3,707.66 | $27.81 | $93.03 | $3,614.63 |
| 3 | February | $3,614.63 | $27.11 | $93.73 | $3,520.90 |
| 4 | March | $3,520.90 | $26.41 | $94.43 | $3,426.47 |
| 5 | April | $3,426.47 | $25.70 | $95.14 | $3,331.33 |
| 6 | May | $3,331.33 | $24.98 | $95.86 | $3,235.47 |
| 7 | June | $3,235.47 | $24.27 | $96.57 | $3,138.90 |
| 8 | July | $3,138.90 | $23.54 | $97.30 | $3,041.60 |

| Borrower | Patrick Morgan |
|---|---|
| Amount Borrowed | $4,000.00 |
| Term of Note (Months) | 36 |
| Annual Interest Rate | 9% |
| Monthly Payment | $127.20 |
| Monthly Due Date | 22nd |

| Payment Number | Month | Beginning Balance | Interest | Principal | Ending Balance |
|---|---|---|---|---|---|
| 1 | April | $4,000.00 | $30.00 | $ 97.20 | $3,902.80 |
| 2 | May | $3,902.80 | $29.27 | $ 97.93 | $3,804.87 |
| 3 | June | $3,804.87 | $28.54 | $ 98.66 | $3,706.21 |
| 4 | July | $3,706.21 | $27.80 | $ 99.40 | $3,606.81 |
| 5 | August | $3,606.81 | $27.05 | $100.15 | $3,506.66 |
| 6 | September | $3,506.66 | $26.30 | $100.90 | $3,405.76 |
| 7 | October | $3,405.76 | $25.54 | $101.66 | $3,304.10 |
| 8 | November | $3,304.10 | $24.78 | $102.42 | $3,201.68 |

**9-3**  **ON YOUR OWN (concluded)**

**2.**

GENERAL JOURNAL

| | DATE | ACCOUNT TITLE | DOC. NO. | POST. REF. | DEBIT | CREDIT | |
|---|---|---|---|---|---|---|---|
| 1 | | | | | | | 1 |
| 2 | | | | | | | 2 |
| 3 | | | | | | | 3 |
| 4 | | | | | | | 4 |
| 5 | | | | | | | 5 |
| 6 | | | | | | | 6 |
| 7 | | | | | | | 7 |
| 8 | | | | | | | 8 |
| 9 | | | | | | | 9 |
| 10 | | | | | | | 10 |
| 11 | | | | | | | 11 |
| 12 | | | | | | | 12 |
| 13 | | | | | | | 13 |

**3.**

GENERAL JOURNAL

| | DATE | ACCOUNT TITLE | DOC. NO. | POST. REF. | DEBIT | CREDIT | |
|---|---|---|---|---|---|---|---|
| 1 | | | | | | | 1 |
| 2 | | | | | | | 2 |
| 3 | | | | | | | 3 |
| 4 | | | | | | | 4 |
| 5 | | | | | | | 5 |
| 6 | | | | | | | 6 |
| 7 | | | | | | | 7 |
| 8 | | | | | | | 8 |
| 9 | | | | | | | 9 |
| 10 | | | | | | | 10 |
| 11 | | | | | | | 11 |
| 12 | | | | | | | 12 |
| 13 | | | | | | | 13 |

**APPLICATION PROBLEM (LO1, 2), p. 283**

**Journalizing adjusting and reversing entries for unearned and accrued revenue**

**1., 3.**

GENERAL JOURNAL

PAGE 16

| | DATE | ACCOUNT TITLE | DOC. NO. | POST. REF. | DEBIT | CREDIT | |
|---|------|---------------|----------|------------|-------|--------|---|
| 1 | | | | | | | 1 |
| 2 | | | | | | | 2 |
| 3 | | | | | | | 3 |
| 4 | | | | | | | 4 |
| 5 | | | | | | | 5 |
| 6 | | | | | | | 6 |
| 7 | | | | | | | 7 |
| 8 | | | | | | | 8 |

**2., 4.**

GENERAL JOURNAL

PAGE 17

| | DATE | ACCOUNT TITLE | DOC. NO. | POST. REF. | DEBIT | CREDIT | |
|---|------|---------------|----------|------------|-------|--------|---|
| 1 | | | | | | | 1 |
| 2 | | | | | | | 2 |
| 3 | | | | | | | 3 |
| 4 | | | | | | | 4 |
| 5 | | | | | | | 5 |
| 6 | | | | | | | 6 |
| 7 | | | | | | | 7 |
| 8 | | | | | | | 8 |

Note: Calculation not a required part of solution.

| Note | Principal | × | Interest Rate | × | Fraction of Year | = | Accrued Interest Income |
|------|-----------|---|---------------|---|------------------|---|-------------------------|
| | | | | | /365 | | |
| | | | | | /365 | | |

**9-2**    **APPLICATION PROBLEM (LO3, 4), p. 283**

**Journalizing gift card transactions**

**1.**

**CASH RECEIPTS JOURNAL**      PAGE 16

| | | | | GENERAL | | ACCOUNTS RECEIVABLE CREDIT | SALES CREDIT | SALES TAX PAYABLE CREDIT | SALES DISCOUNT DEBIT | CASH DEBIT |
|---|---|---|---|---|---|---|---|---|---|---|
| DATE | ACCOUNT TITLE | DOC. NO. | POST. REF. | DEBIT | CREDIT | | | | | |
| | | | | 1 | 2 | 3 | 4 | 5 | 6 | 7 |
| 1 | | | | | | | | | | |
| 2 | | | | | | | | | | |
| 3 | | | | | | | | | | |
| 4 | | | | | | | | | | |
| 5 | | | | | | | | | | |
| 6 | | | | | | | | | | |
| 7 | | | | | | | | | | |
| 8 | | | | | | | | | | |
| 9 | | | | | | | | | | |
| 10 | | | | | | | | | | |
| 11 | | | | | | | | | | |
| 12 | | | | | | | | | | |
| 13 | | | | | | | | | | |
| 14 | | | | | | | | | | |
| 15 | | | | | | | | | | |
| 16 | | | | | | | | | | |
| 17 | | | | | | | | | | |
| 18 | | | | | | | | | | |
| 19 | | | | | | | | | | |
| 20 | | | | | | | | | | |
| 21 | | | | | | | | | | |
| 22 | | | | | | | | | | |

**1.**

GENERAL JOURNAL                                    PAGE 12

| | DATE | | ACCOUNT TITLE | DOC. NO. | POST. REF. | DEBIT | CREDIT | |
|---|---|---|---|---|---|---|---|---|
| 1 | | | | | | | | 1 |
| 2 | | | | | | | | 2 |
| 3 | | | | | | | | 3 |
| 4 | | | | | | | | 4 |
| 5 | | | | | | | | 5 |
| 6 | | | | | | | | 6 |
| 7 | | | | | | | | 7 |
| 8 | | | | | | | | 8 |
| 9 | | | | | | | | 9 |
| 10 | | | | | | | | 10 |
| 11 | | | | | | | | 11 |
| 12 | | | | | | | | 12 |
| 13 | | | | | | | | 13 |

**2.**

GENERAL JOURNAL                                    PAGE 13

| | DATE | | ACCOUNT TITLE | DOC. NO. | POST. REF. | DEBIT | CREDIT | |
|---|---|---|---|---|---|---|---|---|
| 1 | | | | | | | | 1 |
| 2 | | | | | | | | 2 |
| 3 | | | | | | | | 3 |
| 4 | | | | | | | | 4 |
| 5 | | | | | | | | 5 |
| 6 | | | | | | | | 6 |
| 7 | | | | | | | | 7 |
| 8 | | | | | | | | 8 |
| 9 | | | | | | | | 9 |
| 10 | | | | | | | | 10 |
| 11 | | | | | | | | 11 |
| 12 | | | | | | | | 12 |
| 13 | | | | | | | | 13 |

## 9-3 APPLICATION PROBLEM (LO6, 7), p. 284

**Journalizing installment notes receivable transactions**

**1.**

**CASH RECEIPTS JOURNAL**

PAGE 7

| DATE | ACCOUNT TITLE | DOC. NO. | POST. REF. | GENERAL DEBIT | GENERAL CREDIT | ACCOUNTS RECEIVABLE CREDIT | SALES CREDIT | SALES TAX PAYABLE CREDIT | SALES DISCOUNT DEBIT | CASH DEBIT |
|------|---------------|----------|------------|---------------|----------------|----------------------------|--------------|--------------------------|----------------------|------------|
| | | | | 1 | 2 | 3 | 4 | 5 | 6 | 7 |
| | | | | | | | | | | |

Illustrations for 1.

| Borrower | Berk Hyde |
|---|---|
| Amount Borrowed | $62,350.00 |
| Term of Note (Months) | 60 |
| Annual Interest Rate | 8% |
| Monthly Payment | $1,264.23 |
| Monthly Due Date | 5th |

| Payment Number | Month | Beginning Balance | Interest | Principal | Ending Balance |
|---|---|---|---|---|---|
| 1 | March | $62,350.00 | $415.67 | $848.56 | $61,501.44 |
| 2 | April | $61,501.44 | $410.01 | $854.22 | $60,647.22 |
| 3 | May | $60,647.22 | $404.31 | $859.92 | $59,787.30 |
| 4 | June | $59,787.30 | $398.58 | $865.65 | $58,921.65 |
| 5 | July | $58,921.65 | $392.81 | $871.42 | $58,050.23 |
| 6 | August | $58,050.23 | $387.00 | $877.23 | $57,173.00 |
| 7 | September | $57,173.00 | $381.15 | $883.08 | $56,289.92 |
| 8 | October | $56,289.92 | $375.27 | $888.96 | $55,400.96 |

| Borrower | Altoria Johnwick |
|---|---|
| Amount Borrowed | $48,620.00 |
| Term of Note (Months) | 60 |
| Annual Interest Rate | 8% |
| Monthly Payment | $985.84 |
| Monthly Due Date | 12th |

| Payment Number | Month | Beginning Balance | Interest | Principal | Ending Balance |
|---|---|---|---|---|---|
| 1 | February | $48,620.00 | $324.13 | $661.71 | $47,958.29 |
| 2 | March | $47,958.29 | $319.72 | $666.12 | $47,292.17 |
| 3 | April | $47,292.17 | $315.28 | $670.56 | $46,621.61 |
| 4 | May | $46,621.61 | $310.81 | $675.03 | $45,946.58 |
| 5 | June | $45,946.58 | $306.31 | $679.53 | $45,267.05 |
| 6 | July | $45,267.05 | $301.78 | $684.06 | $44,582.99 |
| 7 | August | $44,582.99 | $297.22 | $688.62 | $43,894.37 |
| 8 | September | $43,894.37 | $292.63 | $693.21 | $43,201.16 |
| 9 | October | $43,201.16 | $288.01 | $697.83 | $42,503.33 |
| 10 | November | $42,503.33 | $283.36 | $702.48 | $41,800.85 |

**9-3** APPLICATION PROBLEM (concluded)

**2.**

GENERAL JOURNAL                                                                PAGE 20

| | DATE | ACCOUNT TITLE | DOC. NO. | POST. REF. | DEBIT | CREDIT | |
|---|---|---|---|---|---|---|---|
| 1 | | | | | | | 1 |
| 2 | | | | | | | 2 |
| 3 | | | | | | | 3 |
| 4 | | | | | | | 4 |
| 5 | | | | | | | 5 |
| 6 | | | | | | | 6 |
| 7 | | | | | | | 7 |
| 8 | | | | | | | 8 |
| 9 | | | | | | | 9 |
| 10 | | | | | | | 10 |
| 11 | | | | | | | 11 |
| 12 | | | | | | | 12 |
| 13 | | | | | | | 13 |

**3.**

GENERAL JOURNAL                                                                PAGE 21

| | DATE | ACCOUNT TITLE | DOC. NO. | POST. REF. | DEBIT | CREDIT | |
|---|---|---|---|---|---|---|---|
| 1 | | | | | | | 1 |
| 2 | | | | | | | 2 |
| 3 | | | | | | | 3 |
| 4 | | | | | | | 4 |
| 5 | | | | | | | 5 |
| 6 | | | | | | | 6 |
| 7 | | | | | | | 7 |
| 8 | | | | | | | 8 |
| 9 | | | | | | | 9 |
| 10 | | | | | | | 10 |
| 11 | | | | | | | 11 |
| 12 | | | | | | | 12 |
| 13 | | | | | | | 13 |

**Journalizing unearned revenue, accrued revenue, and gift card and installment note receivable transactions**

**1.**

## GENERAL JOURNAL

PAGE 20

| DATE | ACCOUNT TITLE | DOC. NO. | POST. REF. | DEBIT | CREDIT | |
|------|---------------|----------|------------|-------|--------|---|
| | | | | | | 1 |
| | | | | | | 2 |
| | | | | | | 3 |
| | | | | | | 4 |
| | | | | | | 5 |
| | | | | | | 6 |

## CASH RECEIPTS JOURNAL

PAGE 24

| | | | | 1 | 2 | 3 | 4 | 5 | 6 | 7 |
|---|---|---|---|---|---|---|---|---|---|---|
| DATE | ACCOUNT TITLE | DOC. NO. | POST. REF. | GENERAL DEBIT | GENERAL CREDIT | ACCOUNTS RECEIVABLE CREDIT | SALES CREDIT | SALES TAX PAYABLE CREDIT | SALES DISCOUNT DEBIT | CASH DEBIT |
| | | | | | | | | | | 1 |
| | | | | | | | | | | 2 |
| | | | | | | | | | | 3 |
| | | | | | | | | | | 4 |
| | | | | | | | | | | 5 |
| | | | | | | | | | | 6 |
| | | | | | | | | | | 7 |
| | | | | | | | | | | 8 |
| | | | | | | | | | | 9 |
| | | | | | | | | | | 10 |
| | | | | | | | | | | 11 |
| | | | | | | | | | | 12 |
| | | | | | | | | | | 13 |

**9-M MASTERY PROBLEM (continued)**

**Illustrations for 1.**

| Borrower | Lisa Renfroe |
|---|---|
| Amount Borrowed | $2,650.00 |
| Term of Note (Months) | 36 |
| Annual Interest Rate | 12% |
| Monthly Payment | $88.02 |
| Monthly Due Date | 24th |

| Payment Number | Month | Beginning Balance | Interest | Principal | Ending Balance |
|---|---|---|---|---|---|
| 1 | September | $2,650.00 | $26.50 | $61.52 | $2,588.48 |
| 2 | October | $2,588.48 | $25.88 | $62.14 | $2,526.34 |
| 3 | November | $2,526.34 | $25.26 | $62.76 | $2,463.58 |
| 4 | December | $2,463.58 | $24.64 | $63.38 | $2,400.20 |
| 5 | January | $2,400.20 | $24.00 | $64.02 | $2,336.18 |
| 6 | February | $2,336.18 | $23.36 | $64.66 | $2,271.52 |
| 7 | March | $2,271.52 | $22.72 | $65.30 | $2,206.22 |
| 8 | April | $2,206.22 | $22.06 | $65.96 | $2,140.26 |

| Borrower | Rose Cribbs |
|---|---|
| Amount Borrowed | $3,280.00 |
| Term of Note (Months) | 36 |
| Annual Interest Rate | 12% |
| Monthly Payment | $108.94 |
| Monthly Due Date | 31st |

| Payment Number | Month | Beginning Balance | Interest | Principal | Ending Balance |
|---|---|---|---|---|---|
| 1 | June | $3,280.00 | $32.80 | $76.14 | $3,203.86 |
| 2 | July | $3,203.86 | $32.04 | $76.90 | $3,126.96 |
| 3 | August | $3,126.96 | $31.27 | $77.67 | $3,049.29 |
| 4 | September | $3,049.29 | $30.49 | $78.45 | $2,970.84 |
| 5 | October | $2,970.84 | $29.71 | $79.23 | $2,891.61 |
| 6 | November | $2,891.61 | $28.92 | $80.02 | $2,811.59 |
| 7 | December | $2,811.59 | $28.12 | $80.82 | $2,730.77 |
| 8 | January | $2,730.77 | $27.31 | $81.63 | $2,649.14 |

**2.**

GENERAL JOURNAL

PAGE 21

| | DATE | | ACCOUNT TITLE | DOC. NO. | POST. REF. | DEBIT | CREDIT | |
|---|---|---|---|---|---|---|---|---|
| 1 | | | | | | | | 1 |
| 2 | | | | | | | | 2 |
| 3 | | | | | | | | 3 |
| 4 | | | | | | | | 4 |
| 5 | | | | | | | | 5 |
| 6 | | | | | | | | 6 |
| 7 | | | | | | | | 7 |

**3.**

GENERAL JOURNAL

PAGE 22

| | DATE | | ACCOUNT TITLE | DOC. NO. | POST. REF. | DEBIT | CREDIT | |
|---|---|---|---|---|---|---|---|---|
| 1 | | | | | | | | 1 |
| 2 | | | | | | | | 2 |
| 3 | | | | | | | | 3 |

**4.**

GENERAL JOURNAL

PAGE 23

| | DATE | | ACCOUNT TITLE | DOC. NO. | POST. REF. | DEBIT | CREDIT | |
|---|---|---|---|---|---|---|---|---|
| 1 | | | | | | | | 1 |
| 2 | | | | | | | | 2 |
| 3 | | | | | | | | 3 |
| 4 | | | | | | | | 4 |
| 5 | | | | | | | | 5 |
| 6 | | | | | | | | 6 |
| 7 | | | | | | | | 7 |

Note: Calculation not a required part of solution.

| Note | Principal | × | Interest Rate | × | Fraction of Year | = | Accrued Interest Income |
|---|---|---|---|---|---|---|---|
| | | | | | /365 | | |
| | | | | | /365 | | |

**9-C** **CHALLENGE PROBLEM (LO3), p. 285**

Journalizing sales and gift card transactions from a point-of-sale system

CASH RECEIPTS JOURNAL

PAGE 5

| | | | | | 1 | 2 | | 3 | 4 | 5 | 6 | 7 |
|---|---|---|---|---|---|---|---|---|---|---|---|---|
| | | | | | GENERAL | | ACCOUNTS RECEIVABLE CREDIT | SALES CREDIT | SALES TAX PAYABLE CREDIT | SALES DISCOUNT DEBIT | CASH DEBIT |
| DATE | ACCOUNT TITLE | DOC. NO. | POST. REF. | | DEBIT | CREDIT | | | | | | |
| 1 | | | | | | | | | | | | |
| 2 | | | | | | | | | | | | |
| 3 | | | | | | | | | | | | |
| 4 | | | | | | | | | | | | |
| 5 | | | | | | | | | | | | |
| 6 | | | | | | | | | | | | |
| 7 | | | | | | | | | | | | |
| 8 | | | | | | | | | | | | |
| 9 | | | | | | | | | | | | |
| 10 | | | | | | | | | | | | |
| 11 | | | | | | | | | | | | |
| 12 | | | | | | | | | | | | |
| 13 | | | | | | | | | | | | |
| 14 | | | | | | | | | | | | |
| 15 | | | | | | | | | | | | |
| 16 | | | | | | | | | | | | |
| 17 | | | | | | | | | | | | |
| 18 | | | | | | | | | | | | |
| 19 | | | | | | | | | | | | |
| 20 | | | | | | | | | | | | |
| 21 | | | | | | | | | | | | |

# REINFORCEMENT ACTIVITY 2, p. 287

**Processing Accounting Data for a Corporation**

**1.**

GENERAL JOURNAL

PAGE 12

| | DATE | ACCOUNT TITLE | DOC. NO. | POST. REF. | DEBIT | CREDIT | |
|---|---|---|---|---|---|---|---|
| 1 | | | | | | | 1 |
| 2 | | | | | | | 2 |
| 3 | | | | | | | 3 |
| 4 | | | | | | | 4 |
| 5 | | | | | | | 5 |
| 6 | | | | | | | 6 |
| 7 | | | | | | | 7 |
| 8 | | | | | | | 8 |
| 9 | | | | | | | 9 |
| 10 | | | | | | | 10 |
| 11 | | | | | | | 11 |
| 12 | | | | | | | 12 |
| 13 | | | | | | | 13 |
| 14 | | | | | | | 14 |
| 15 | | | | | | | 15 |
| 16 | | | | | | | 16 |
| 17 | | | | | | | 17 |
| 18 | | | | | | | 18 |
| 19 | | | | | | | 19 |
| 20 | | | | | | | 20 |
| 21 | | | | | | | 21 |
| 22 | | | | | | | 22 |
| 23 | | | | | | | 23 |
| 24 | | | | | | | 24 |
| 25 | | | | | | | 25 |
| 26 | | | | | | | 26 |
| 27 | | | | | | | 27 |
| 28 | | | | | | | 28 |

# REINFORCEMENT ACTIVITY 2 (continued)

**2., 3., 4.**

GENERAL JOURNAL

| | DATE | | ACCOUNT TITLE | DOC. NO. | POST. REF. | DEBIT | CREDIT | |
|---|---|---|---|---|---|---|---|---|
| 1 | | | | | | | | 1 |
| 2 | | | | | | | | 2 |
| 3 | | | | | | | | 3 |
| 4 | | | | | | | | 4 |
| 5 | | | | | | | | 5 |
| 6 | | | | | | | | 6 |
| 7 | | | | | | | | 7 |
| 8 | | | | | | | | 8 |
| 9 | | | | | | | | 9 |
| 10 | | | | | | | | 10 |
| 11 | | | | | | | | 11 |
| 12 | | | | | | | | 12 |
| 13 | | | | | | | | 13 |
| 14 | | | | | | | | 14 |
| 15 | | | | | | | | 15 |
| 16 | | | | | | | | 16 |
| 17 | | | | | | | | 17 |
| 18 | | | | | | | | 18 |
| 19 | | | | | | | | 19 |
| 20 | | | | | | | | 20 |
| 21 | | | | | | | | 21 |
| 22 | | | | | | | | 22 |
| 23 | | | | | | | | 23 |
| 24 | | | | | | | | 24 |
| 25 | | | | | | | | 25 |
| 26 | | | | | | | | 26 |
| 27 | | | | | | | | 27 |
| 28 | | | | | | | | 28 |
| 29 | | | | | | | | 29 |
| 30 | | | | | | | | 30 |
| 31 | | | | | | | | 31 |
| 32 | | | | | | | | 32 |

# REINFORCEMENT ACTIVITY 2 (continued)

**1.**

## CASH RECEIPTS JOURNAL

| | DATE | ACCOUNT TITLE | DOC. NO. | POST. REF. | GENERAL DEBIT | GENERAL CREDIT | ACCOUNTS RECEIVABLE CREDIT | SALES CREDIT | SALES TAX PAYABLE CREDIT | SALES DISCOUNT DEBIT | CASH DEBIT | |
|---|---|---|---|---|---|---|---|---|---|---|---|---|
| | | | | | 1 | 2 | 3 | 4 | 5 | 6 | 7 | |
| 1 | | | | | | | | | | | | 1 |
| 2 | | | | | | | | | | | | 2 |
| 3 | | | | | | | | | | | | 3 |
| 4 | | | | | | | | | | | | 4 |
| 5 | | | | | | | | | | | | 5 |
| 6 | | | | | | | | | | | | 6 |
| 7 | | | | | | | | | | | | 7 |
| 8 | | | | | | | | | | | | 8 |
| 9 | | | | | | | | | | | | 9 |
| 10 | | | | | | | | | | | | 10 |
| 11 | | | | | | | | | | | | 11 |
| 12 | | | | | | | | | | | | 12 |
| 13 | | | | | | | | | | | | 13 |
| 14 | | | | | | | | | | | | 14 |
| 15 | | | | | | | | | | | | 15 |
| 16 | | | | | | | | | | | | 16 |
| 17 | | | | | | | | | | | | 17 |
| 18 | | | | | | | | | | | | 18 |
| 19 | | | | | | | | | | | | 19 |
| 20 | | | | | | | | | | | | 20 |
| 21 | | | | | | | | | | | | 21 |

**1.**

**CASH PAYMENTS JOURNAL**

PAGE 20

| | DATE | ACCOUNT TITLE | CK. NO. | POST. REF. | GENERAL DEBIT (1) | GENERAL CREDIT (2) | ACCOUNTS PAYABLE DEBIT (3) | PURCHASES DISCOUNT CREDIT (4) | CASH CREDIT (5) | |
|---|---|---|---|---|---|---|---|---|---|---|
| 1 | | | | | | | | | | 1 |
| 2 | | | | | | | | | | 2 |
| 3 | | | | | | | | | | 3 |
| 4 | | | | | | | | | | 4 |
| 5 | | | | | | | | | | 5 |
| 6 | | | | | | | | | | 6 |
| 7 | | | | | | | | | | 7 |
| 8 | | | | | | | | | | 8 |
| 9 | | | | | | | | | | 9 |
| 10 | | | | | | | | | | 10 |
| 11 | | | | | | | | | | 11 |
| 12 | | | | | | | | | | 12 |
| 13 | | | | | | | | | | 13 |
| 14 | | | | | | | | | | 14 |
| 15 | | | | | | | | | | 15 |
| 16 | | | | | | | | | | 16 |

| | Appraised Value | Percentage of Total Appraised Value | Assigned Cost |
|---|---|---|---|
| Land | | | |
| Building | | | |
| Total | | | |

## REINFORCEMENT ACTIVITY 2 (continued)

**3.**

**Stock Item: C-362**

| Date | Units Purchased | Unit Price | Units | Cost |
|------|------|------|------|------|
| | **Purchases** | | **FIFO Method** | |
| Beginning Inventory | 33 | $30.95 | | |
| May | 50 | 33.15 | | |
| August | 50 | 32.08 | | |
| September | 50 | 32.66 | | |
| November | 10 | 33.21 | | |
| December | 10 | 34.15 | | |
| Totals | | | | |

**Stock Item: A-342**

| Date | Units Purchased | Unit Price | Units | Cost |
|------|------|------|------|------|
| | **Purchases** | | **FIFO Method** | |
| Beginning Inventory | 16 | $82.50 | | |
| January | 25 | 82.50 | | |
| March | 25 | 84.50 | | |
| June | 30 | 84.75 | | |
| July | 30 | 85.15 | | |
| October | 30 | 86.50 | | |
| Totals | | | | |

**Stock Item: B-164**

| Date | Units Purchased | Unit Price | Units | Cost |
|------|------|------|------|------|
| | **Purchases** | | **FIFO Method** | |
| Beginning Inventory | 16 | $1,251.25 | | |
| January | 10 | 1,184.24 | | |
| February | 5 | 850.00 | | |
| Totals | | | | |

**3.**

| Stock Item | Quantity of Units on Hand | Market Price per Unit | Total Market Price | FIFO Cost | Lower of Cost of Market |
|------|------|------|------|------|------|
| C-362 | 26 | $ 35.50 | | | |
| A-342 | 42 | 84.50 | | | |
| B-164 | 16 | 1,062.25 | | | |
| | | | Totals | | |

**4.**

| | | Borrower | | David Lander | |
| | | Amount Borrowed | | $2,480.00 | |
| | | Term of Note (Months) | | 12 | |
| | | Annual Interest Rate | | 12% | |
| | | Monthly Payment | | $220.34 | |
| | | Monthly Due Date | | 31st | |

| Payment Number | Month | Beginning Balance | Interest | Principal | Ending Balance |
|---|---|---|---|---|---|
| 1 | September | $2,480.00 | $24.80 | $195.54 | $2,284.46 |
| 2 | October | $2,284.46 | $22.84 | $197.50 | $2,086.96 |
| 3 | November | $2,086.96 | $20.87 | $199.47 | $1,887.49 |
| 4 | December | $1,887.49 | $18.87 | $201.47 | $1,686.02 |
| 5 | January | $1,686.02 | $16.86 | $203.48 | $1,482.54 |
| 6 | February | $1,482.54 | $14.83 | $205.51 | $1,277.03 |
| 7 | March | $1,277.03 | $12.77 | $207.57 | $1,069.46 |
| 8 | April | $1,069.46 | $10.69 | $209.65 | $ 859.81 |

| | | Borrower | | Danielle Petrus | |
| | | Amount Borrowed | | $4,200.00 | |
| | | Term of Note (Months) | | 12 | |
| | | Annual Interest Rate | | 10% | |
| | | Monthly Payment | | $369.25 | |
| | | Monthly Due Date | | 23rd | |

| Payment Number | Month | Beginning Balance | Interest | Principal | Ending Balance |
|---|---|---|---|---|---|
| 1 | May | $4,200.00 | $35.00 | $334.25 | $3,865.75 |
| 2 | June | $3,865.75 | $32.21 | $337.04 | $3,528.71 |
| 3 | July | $3,528.71 | $29.41 | $339.84 | $3,188.87 |
| 4 | August | $3,188.87 | $26.57 | $342.68 | $2,846.19 |
| 5 | September | $2,846.19 | $23.72 | $345.53 | $2,500.66 |
| 6 | October | $2,500.66 | $20.84 | $348.41 | $2,152.25 |
| 7 | November | $2,152.25 | $17.94 | $351.31 | $1,800.94 |
| 8 | December | $1,800.94 | $15.01 | $354.24 | $1,446.70 |
| 9 | January | $1,446.70 | $12.06 | $357.19 | $1,089.51 |
| 10 | February | $1,089.51 | $ 9.08 | $360.17 | $ 729.34 |

# REINFORCEMENT ACTIVITY 2 (concluded)

| | | | | | |
|---|---|---|---|---|---|
| Lender | | | Platt Equipment | | |
| Borrower | | | Franklin Auto Parts, Inc. | | |
| Amount Borrowed | | | $40,000.00 | | |
| Term of Note (Months) | | | 60 | | |
| Annual Interest Rate | | | 8% | | |
| Monthly Payment | | | $811.06 | | |
| Monthly Due Date | | | 31st | | |

| Payment Number | Month | Beginning Balance | Interest | Principal | Ending Balance |
|---|---|---|---|---|---|
| 1 | June | $40,000.00 | $266.67 | $544.39 | $39,455.61 |
| 2 | July | $39,455.61 | $263.04 | $548.02 | $38,907.59 |
| 3 | August | $38,907.59 | $259.38 | $551.68 | $38,355.91 |
| 4 | September | $38,355.91 | $255.71 | $555.35 | $37,800.56 |
| 5 | October | $37,800.56 | $252.00 | $559.06 | $37,241.50 |
| 6 | November | $37,241.50 | $248.28 | $562.78 | $36,678.72 |
| 7 | December | $36,678.72 | $244.52 | $566.54 | $36,112.18 |
| 8 | January | $36,112.18 | $240.75 | $570.31 | $35,541.87 |
| 9 | February | $35,541.87 | $236.95 | $574.11 | $34,967.76 |
| 10 | March | $34,967.76 | $233.12 | $577.94 | $34,389.82 |
| 11 | April | $34,389.82 | $229.27 | $581.79 | $33,808.03 |
| 12 | May | $33,808.03 | $225.39 | $585.67 | $33,222.36 |
| 13 | June | $33,222.36 | $221.48 | $589.58 | $32,632.78 |
| 14 | July | $32,632.78 | $217.55 | $593.51 | $32,039.27 |

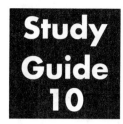

# Study Guide 10

| Name | Perfect Score | Your Score |
|---|---|---|
| Identifying Accounting Terms | 18 Pts. | |
| Analyzing Transactions for Organizing a Corporation | 12 Pts. | |
| Analyzing Concepts for Organizing a Corporation | 10 Pts. | |
| **Total** | 40 Pts. | |

## Part One—Identifying Accounting Terms

**Directions:** Select the one term in Column I that best fits each definition in Column II. Print the letter identifying your choice in the Answers column.

| Column I | Column II | Answers |
|---|---|---|
| **A.** articles of incorporation | **1.** The owner of one or more shares of stock. (p. 294) | 1._____ |
| **B.** board of directors | **2.** A group of persons elected by the stockholders to govern. (p. 295) | 2._____ |
| **C.** charter | | |
| **D.** conversion option | **3.** A legal document that identifies basic characteristics of a corporation, which is a part of the application submitted to a state to become a corporation. (p. 295) | 3._____ |
| **E.** conversion price | **4.** The legal right for a business to conduct operations as a corporation. (p. 295) | 4._____ |
| **F.** conversion ratio | | |
| **G.** convertible preferred stock | **5.** A class of stock that gives preferred shareholders preference over common shareholders in dividends along with other rights. (p. 296) | 5._____ |
| **H.** double taxation | | |
| **I.** initial public offering | **6.** Written evidence of the number of shares that each stockholder owns in a corporation. (p. 296) | 6._____ |
| **J.** limited liability corporation | **7.** A share of stock that has par value. (p. 296) | 7._____ |
| **K.** par-value stock | **8.** No-par-value stock that is assigned a value by a corporation. (p. 297) | 8._____ |
| **L.** preferred stock | | |
| **M.** privately held corporation | **9.** The taxation of earnings to the corporation and to the stockholders when they receive dividends. (p. 298) | 9._____ |
| **N.** publicly held corporation | **10.** A form of business organization that offers its owners (known as members) the limited liability afforded to corporate stockholders. (p. 298) | 10._____ |
| **O.** registration statement | **11.** A corporation owned by a small number of individuals. (p. 303) | 11._____ |
| **P.** stated-value stock | **12.** The initial issue of a security on a public exchange. (p. 303) | 12._____ |
| **Q.** stock certificate | **13.** A corporation having its stock traded on public exchanges. (p. 303) | 13._____ |
| **R.** stockholder | **14.** The document submitted to the SEC for permission to sell a security on a public exchange. (p. 303) | 14._____ |
| | **15.** The ability of a security to be traded for a specified number of shares of another security. (p. 307) | 15._____ |

| Column I | Column II | Answers |
|---|---|---|
| | 16. The number of shares of common stock received when a security is converted. (p. 307) | 16. _____ |
| | 17. Preferred stock that can be exchanged for a specified number of common shares. (p. 307) | 17. _____ |
| | 18. The par or stated value of the preferred stock divided by the conversion ratio. (p. 307) | 18. _____ |

# Part Two—Analyzing Transactions for Organizing a Corporation

**Directions:** For each transaction below, print in the proper Answers column the identifying letters of the accounts to be debited and credited.

| Account Titles | Transactions | Answers Debit | Credit |
|---|---|---|---|
| A. Capital Stock—Common | 1-2. Received $2,500 cash for 200 shares of $10.00 par-value common stock. (p. 299) | 1. _____ | 2. _____ |
| B. Capital Stock—Preferred | | | |
| C. Cash | 3-4. Received $6,000 cash for 1,000 shares of no-par-value common stock. (p. 300) | 3. _____ | 4. _____ |
| D. Inventory | 5-6. Received $5,000 cash for 40 shares of $10.00 stated-value common stock. (p. 301) | 5. _____ | 6. _____ |
| E. Paid-In Capital in Excess of Par Value—Common | | | |
| F. Paid-In Capital in Excess of Par Value—Preferred | 7-8. Received $2,000 cash for 20 shares of 6%, $100.00 par-value preferred stock at par value. (p. 304) | 7. _____ | 8. _____ |
| G. Paid-In Capital in Excess of Stated Value—Common | 9-10. Received $3,000 cash for 25 shares of 6%, $100.00 par-value preferred stock at $120 per share. (p. 305) | 9. _____ | 10. _____ |
| | 11-12. Issued 280 shares of 6%, $100.00 par-value preferred stock in exchange for inventory at an agreed value of $30,000. (p. 306) | 11. _____ | 12. _____ |

# Part Three—Analyzing Concepts for Organizing a Corporation

**Directions:** Place a *T* for True or an *F* for False in the Answers column to show whether each of the following statements is true or false.

**Answers**

1. Changing ownership of stock is referred to as a stock certificate. (p. 296)

1. _____

2. Double taxation is a disadvantage of organizing a business as an LLC. (p. 298)

2. _____

3. The credit to the capital stock account of no-par common stock equals the total cash or other assets received. (p. 300)

3. _____

4. The initial issue of a security on a public exchange is referred to as an IPO. (p. 303)

4. _____

5. The annual report a publicly held corporation submits to the SEC is the 10-K. (p. 303)

5. _____

6. Investors willing to accept a dividend rate higher than that offered by the preferred stock will pay more than the par value. (p. 305)

6. _____

7. The payment of dividends on preferred stock is guaranteed by the board of directors. (p. 305)

7. _____

8. The credit to the capital stock account always equals the total par or stated value of the stock issue. (p. 305)

8. _____

9. A conversion option adds value to preferred stock and enables the corporation to issue the stock with a lower dividend rate. (p. 307)

9. _____

10. A $100.00 par-value convertible preferred stock with a conversion ratio of 20 has a conversion price of $5.00. (p. 307 )

10. _____

# 10-1 WORK TOGETHER, p. 302

## Issuing common stock

### Assumption A: $1.00 par-value common stock

CASH RECEIPTS JOURNAL

PAGE 6

| | | | | 1 GENERAL | | 3 ACCOUNTS RECEIVABLE CREDIT | 4 SALES CREDIT | 5 SALES TAX PAYABLE CREDIT | 6 SALES DISCOUNT DEBIT | 7 CASH DEBIT |
|---|---|---|---|---|---|---|---|---|---|---|
| DATE | ACCOUNT TITLE | DOC. NO. | POST. REF. | DEBIT | CREDIT | | | | | |
| 1 | | | | | | | | | | |
| 2 | | | | | | | | | | |
| 3 | | | | | | | | | | |
| 4 | | | | | | | | | | |

### Assumption B: no-par-value common stock

CASH RECEIPTS JOURNAL

PAGE 6

| | | | | 1 GENERAL | | 3 ACCOUNTS RECEIVABLE CREDIT | 4 SALES CREDIT | 5 SALES TAX PAYABLE CREDIT | 6 SALES DISCOUNT DEBIT | 7 CASH DEBIT |
|---|---|---|---|---|---|---|---|---|---|---|
| DATE | ACCOUNT TITLE | DOC. NO. | POST. REF. | DEBIT | CREDIT | | | | | |
| 1 | | | | | | | | | | |
| 2 | | | | | | | | | | |
| 3 | | | | | | | | | | |
| 4 | | | | | | | | | | |

### Assumption C: $1.00 stated-value common stock

CASH RECEIPTS JOURNAL

PAGE 6

| | | | | 1 GENERAL | | 3 ACCOUNTS RECEIVABLE CREDIT | 4 SALES CREDIT | 5 SALES TAX PAYABLE CREDIT | 6 SALES DISCOUNT DEBIT | 7 CASH DEBIT |
|---|---|---|---|---|---|---|---|---|---|---|
| DATE | ACCOUNT TITLE | DOC. NO. | POST. REF. | DEBIT | CREDIT | | | | | |
| 1 | | | | | | | | | | |
| 2 | | | | | | | | | | |
| 3 | | | | | | | | | | |
| 4 | | | | | | | | | | |

**Issuing common stock**

Assumption A: $5.00 par-value common stock

## CASH RECEIPTS JOURNAL

PAGE 15

| | | | | 1 | 2 | 3 | 4 | 5 | 6 | 7 | |
|---|---|---|---|---|---|---|---|---|---|---|---|
| DATE | ACCOUNT TITLE | DOC. NO. | POST. REF. | GENERAL DEBIT | GENERAL CREDIT | ACCOUNTS RECEIVABLE CREDIT | SALES CREDIT | SALES TAX PAYABLE CREDIT | SALES DISCOUNT DEBIT | CASH DEBIT | |
| | | | | | | | | | | | 1 |
| | | | | | | | | | | | 2 |
| | | | | | | | | | | | 3 |
| | | | | | | | | | | | 4 |

Assumption B: no-par-value common stock

## CASH RECEIPTS JOURNAL

PAGE 15

| | | | | 1 | 2 | 3 | 4 | 5 | 6 | 7 | |
|---|---|---|---|---|---|---|---|---|---|---|---|
| DATE | ACCOUNT TITLE | DOC. NO. | POST. REF. | GENERAL DEBIT | GENERAL CREDIT | ACCOUNTS RECEIVABLE CREDIT | SALES CREDIT | SALES TAX PAYABLE CREDIT | SALES DISCOUNT DEBIT | CASH DEBIT | |
| | | | | | | | | | | | 1 |
| | | | | | | | | | | | 2 |
| | | | | | | | | | | | 3 |
| | | | | | | | | | | | 4 |

Assumption C: $5.00 stated-value common stock

## CASH RECEIPTS JOURNAL

PAGE 15

| | | | | 1 | 2 | 3 | 4 | 5 | 6 | 7 | |
|---|---|---|---|---|---|---|---|---|---|---|---|
| DATE | ACCOUNT TITLE | DOC. NO. | POST. REF. | GENERAL DEBIT | GENERAL CREDIT | ACCOUNTS RECEIVABLE CREDIT | SALES CREDIT | SALES TAX PAYABLE CREDIT | SALES DISCOUNT DEBIT | CASH DEBIT | |
| | | | | | | | | | | | 1 |
| | | | | | | | | | | | 2 |
| | | | | | | | | | | | 3 |
| | | | | | | | | | | | 4 |

**Journalizing preferred stock transactions**

## 10-2 WORK TOGETHER, p. 309

### CASH RECEIPTS JOURNAL

PAGE 14

| | DATE | ACCOUNT TITLE | DOC. NO. | POST. REF. | GENERAL DEBIT | GENERAL CREDIT | ACCOUNTS RECEIVABLE CREDIT | SALES CREDIT | SALES TAX PAYABLE CREDIT | SALES DISCOUNT DEBIT | CASH DEBIT | |
|---|---|---|---|---|---|---|---|---|---|---|---|---|
| 1 | | | | | | | | | | | | 1 |
| 2 | | | | | | | | | | | | 2 |
| 3 | | | | | | | | | | | | 3 |
| 4 | | | | | | | | | | | | 4 |
| 5 | | | | | | | | | | | | 5 |
| 6 | | | | | | | | | | | | 6 |
| 7 | | | | | | | | | | | | 7 |
| 8 | | | | | | | | | | | | 8 |
| 9 | | | | | | | | | | | | 9 |

### GENERAL JOURNAL

PAGE 12

| | DATE | ACCOUNT TITLE | DOC. NO. | POST. REF. | DEBIT | CREDIT | |
|---|---|---|---|---|---|---|---|
| 1 | | | | | | | 1 |
| 2 | | | | | | | 2 |
| 3 | | | | | | | 3 |
| 4 | | | | | | | 4 |
| 5 | | | | | | | 5 |
| 6 | | | | | | | 6 |
| 7 | | | | | | | 7 |
| 8 | | | | | | | 8 |
| 9 | | | | | | | 9 |

**Journalizing preferred stock transactions**

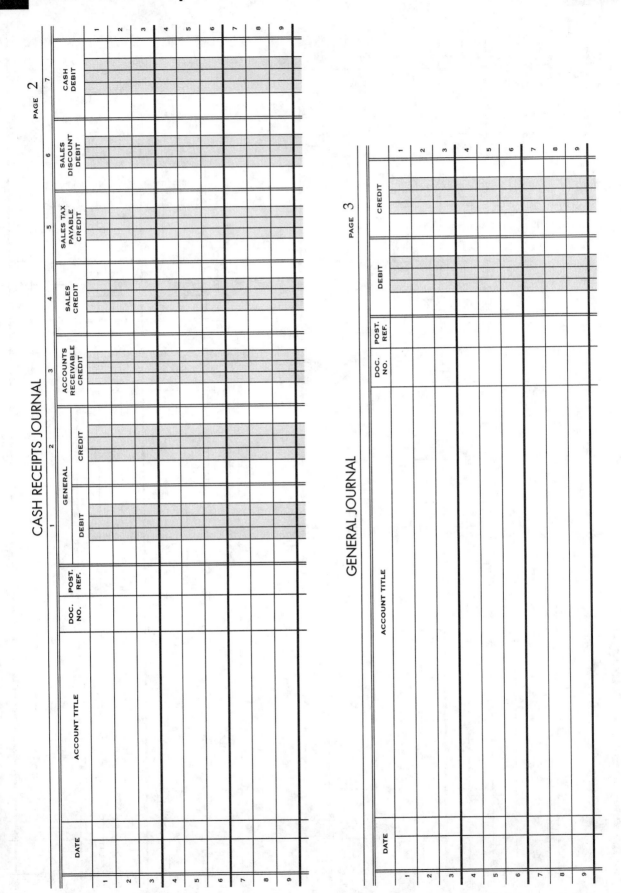

CASH RECEIPTS JOURNAL

PAGE 2

| | | | | 1 | 2 | 3 | 4 | 5 | 6 | 7 |
|---|---|---|---|---|---|---|---|---|---|---|
| | | | | GENERAL | | ACCOUNTS RECEIVABLE CREDIT | SALES CREDIT | SALES TAX PAYABLE CREDIT | SALES DISCOUNT DEBIT | CASH DEBIT |
| DATE | ACCOUNT TITLE | DOC. NO. | POST. REF. | DEBIT | CREDIT | | | | | |
| | | | | | | | | | | |

GENERAL JOURNAL

PAGE 3

| DATE | ACCOUNT TITLE | DOC. NO. | POST. REF. | DEBIT | CREDIT |
|---|---|---|---|---|---|
| | | | | | |

**10-1** **APPLICATION PROBLEM (LO4), p. 313**

**Issuing common stock**

Assumption A: $0.10 par-value common stock

## CASH RECEIPTS JOURNAL

PAGE 7

| DATE | ACCOUNT TITLE | DOC. NO. | POST. REF. | GENERAL DEBIT | GENERAL CREDIT | ACCOUNTS RECEIVABLE CREDIT | SALES CREDIT | SALES TAX PAYABLE CREDIT | SALES DISCOUNT DEBIT | CASH DEBIT |
|---|---|---|---|---|---|---|---|---|---|---|
| | | | | | | | | | | |
| | | | | | | | | | | |
| | | | | | | | | | | |
| | | | | | | | | | | |

Assumption B: no-par-value common stock

## CASH RECEIPTS JOURNAL

PAGE 7

| DATE | ACCOUNT TITLE | DOC. NO. | POST. REF. | GENERAL DEBIT | GENERAL CREDIT | ACCOUNTS RECEIVABLE CREDIT | SALES CREDIT | SALES TAX PAYABLE CREDIT | SALES DISCOUNT DEBIT | CASH DEBIT |
|---|---|---|---|---|---|---|---|---|---|---|
| | | | | | | | | | | |
| | | | | | | | | | | |
| | | | | | | | | | | |
| | | | | | | | | | | |

Assumption C: $0.10 stated-value common stock

## CASH RECEIPTS JOURNAL

PAGE 7

| DATE | ACCOUNT TITLE | DOC. NO. | POST. REF. | GENERAL DEBIT | GENERAL CREDIT | ACCOUNTS RECEIVABLE CREDIT | SALES CREDIT | SALES TAX PAYABLE CREDIT | SALES DISCOUNT DEBIT | CASH DEBIT |
|---|---|---|---|---|---|---|---|---|---|---|
| | | | | | | | | | | |
| | | | | | | | | | | |
| | | | | | | | | | | |
| | | | | | | | | | | |

Chapter 10 Organizing a Corporation • **373**

**Journalizing preferred stock transactions**

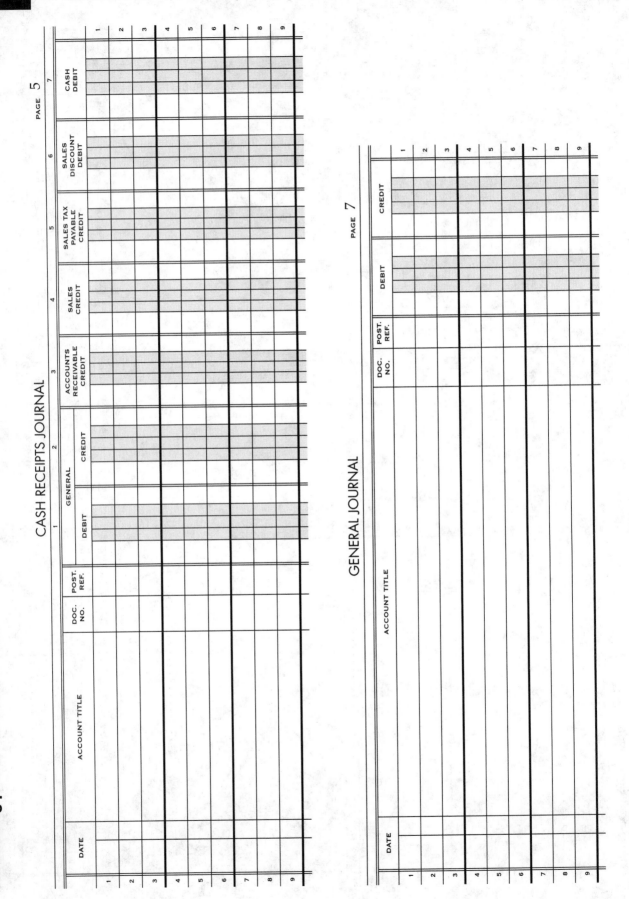

CASH RECEIPTS JOURNAL

PAGE 5

GENERAL JOURNAL

PAGE 7

## 10-M MASTERY PROBLEM (LO4, 5), p. 313

**Journalizing stock transactions**

### GENERAL JOURNAL

PAGE 4

| DATE | ACCOUNT TITLE | DOC. NO. | POST. REF. | DEBIT | CREDIT |
|------|--------------|----------|-----------|-------|--------|
| | | | | | |
| | | | | | |
| | | | | | |
| | | | | | |
| | | | | | |
| | | | | | |
| | | | | | |
| | | | | | |
| | | | | | |

### CASH RECEIPTS JOURNAL

PAGE 4

| | | | | GENERAL | | ACCOUNTS RECEIVABLE CREDIT | SALES CREDIT | SALES TAX PAYABLE CREDIT | SALES DISCOUNT DEBIT | CASH DEBIT |
|---|---|---|---|---|---|---|---|---|---|---|
| DATE | ACCOUNT TITLE | DOC. NO. | POST. REF. | DEBIT | CREDIT | | | | | |
| | | | | | | | | | | |
| | | | | | | | | | | |
| | | | | | | | | | | |
| | | | | | | | | | | |
| | | | | | | | | | | |
| | | | | | | | | | | |
| | | | | | | | | | | |
| | | | | | | | | | | |
| | | | | | | | | | | |
| | | | | | | | | | | |

**Journalizing stock transactions**

## GENERAL JOURNAL

PAGE 2

| | DATE | ACCOUNT TITLE | DOC. NO. | POST. REF. | DEBIT | CREDIT | |
|---|------|---------------|----------|------------|-------|--------|---|
| 1 | | | | | | | 1 |
| 2 | | | | | | | 2 |
| 3 | | | | | | | 3 |
| 4 | | | | | | | 4 |
| 5 | | | | | | | 5 |
| 6 | | | | | | | 6 |
| 7 | | | | | | | 7 |
| 8 | | | | | | | 8 |
| 9 | | | | | | | 9 |
| 10 | | | | | | | 10 |
| 11 | | | | | | | 11 |
| 12 | | | | | | | 12 |
| 13 | | | | | | | 13 |
| 14 | | | | | | | 14 |

## CASH RECEIPTS JOURNAL

PAGE 4

| | DATE | ACCOUNT TITLE | DOC. NO. | POST. REF. | 1 GENERAL DEBIT | 2 GENERAL CREDIT | 3 ACCOUNTS RECEIVABLE CREDIT | 4 SALES CREDIT | 5 SALES TAX PAYABLE CREDIT | 6 SALES DISCOUNT DEBIT | 7 CASH DEBIT | |
|---|------|---------------|----------|------------|-----------------|------------------|------------------------------|----------------|----------------------------|------------------------|--------------|---|
| 1 | | | | | | | | | | | | 1 |
| 2 | | | | | | | | | | | | 2 |
| 3 | | | | | | | | | | | | 3 |
| 4 | | | | | | | | | | | | 4 |
| 5 | | | | | | | | | | | | 5 |
| 6 | | | | | | | | | | | | 6 |
| 7 | | | | | | | | | | | | 7 |

| Name | Perfect Score | Your Score |
|---|---|---|
| Analyzing Transactions for Dividends, Treasury Stock, and Marketable Securities | 22 Pts. | |
| Identifying Accounting Terms | 7 Pts. | |
| Analyzing Concepts for Dividends, Treasury Stock, and Marketable Securities | 10 Pts. | |
| **Total** | 39 Pts. | |

## Part One—Analyzing Transactions for Dividends, Treasury Stock, and Marketable Securities

**Directions:** For each transaction below, print in the proper Answers column the identifying letters of the accounts to be debited and credited.

| Account Titles | Transactions | Answers Debit | Credit |
|---|---|---|---|
| **A.** Capital Stock—Common | Declared an annual cash dividend on common and preferred stock. (p. 320) | 1. _____ | 2. _____ |
| **B.** Cash | Paid cash for annual cash dividend previously declared. (p. 320) | 3. _____ | 4. _____ |
| **C.** Dividend Revenue | Declared a stock dividend payable next month. (p. 321) | 5. _____ | 6. _____ |
| **D.** Dividends—Common | | | |
| **E.** Dividends—Preferred | Issued common stock in payment of a previously declared stock dividend. (p. 322) | 7. _____ | 8. _____ |
| **F.** Dividends Payable | | | |
| **G.** Gain on Sale of Investments | Closed the Stock Dividends account. (p. 323) | 9. _____ | 10. _____ |
| **H.** Marketable Securities | Paid cash for 100 shares of the corporation's own par-value common stock. (p. 325) | 11. _____ | 12. _____ |
| **I.** Paid-In Capital from Sale of Treasury Stock | Received cash for 50 shares of treasury stock at $6.00 per share. Treasury stock was bought for $5.00 per share. (p. 326) | 13. _____ | 14. _____ |
| **J.** Paid-In Capital in Excess of Par Value—Common | Received cash for 50 shares of the remaining treasury stock at $4.00 per share. Treasury stock was bought for $5.00 per share. (p. 327) | 15. _____ | 16. _____ |
| **K.** Retained Earnings | | | |
| **L.** Stock Dividends | | | |
| **M.** Stock Dividends Distributable | Purchased 50 shares of another corporation's stock. (p. 330) | 17. _____ | 18. _____ |
| **N.** Treasury Stock | Received a cash dividend from an investment in the stock of another corporation. (p. 331) | 19. _____ | 20. _____ |
| | Sold stock of another corporation for $50.00 per share. The stock was purchased as an investment for $35.00 per share. (p. 332) | 21. _____ | 22. _____ |

Chapter 11 Corporate Dividends and Treasury Stock • **377**

## Part Two—Identifying Accounting Terms

**Directions:** Select the one term in Column I that best fits each definition in Column II. Print the letter identifying your choice in the Answers column.

| Column I | Column II | Answers |
|---|---|---|
| **A.** buyback | **1.** Action by a board of directors to distribute corporate earnings to stockholders. (p. 318) | **1.**_____ |
| **B.** date of declaration | **2.** The date on which a board of directors votes to distribute a dividend. (p. 318) | **2.**_____ |
| **C.** date of payment | **3.** The date that determines which stockholders are to receive dividends. (p. 318) | **3.**_____ |
| **D.** date of record | **4.** The date on which dividends are actually to be paid to stockholders. (p. 318) | **4.**_____ |
| **E.** declaring a dividend | **5.** The payment of a dividend with the stock of the corporation. (p. 321) | **5.**_____ |
| **F.** stock dividend | **6.** A corporation's own stock that has been issued and reacquired. (p. 325) | **6.**_____ |
| **G.** treasury stock | **7.** A program approved by a board of directors authorizing the corporation to repurchase its stock. (p. 325) | **7.**_____ |

## Part Three—Analyzing Concepts for Dividends, Treasury Stock, and Marketable Securities

**Directions:** Place a *T* for True or an *F* for False in the Answers column to show whether each of the following statements is true or false.

**Answers**

1. A corporation has no obligation to distribute retained earnings to stockholders until the board of directors has declared a dividend. (p. 318)

1. _____

2. A dividend is normally paid several weeks after the date of record. (p. 318)

2. _____

3. The total amount of dividends to be paid are allocated first to common stock, then to preferred stock. (p. 319)

3. _____

4. No journal entry is recorded on the date of record. (p. 320)

4. _____

5. The total amount of a stock dividend is calculated using the number of shares issued multiplied by the par or stated value of the stock. (p. 321)

5. _____

6. A stock dividend typically results in an increase in the market price per share. (p. 323)

6. _____

7. A buyback often occurs when a corporation believes that its stock is overvalued by the stock market. (p. 325)

7. _____

8. Treasury stock is not an asset of the corporation. (p. 326)

8. _____

9. Marketable securities are an asset of the corporation. (p. 330)

9. _____

10. Dividend Revenue is classified as other revenue on the income statement. (p. 331)

10. _____

**11-1** **WORK TOGETHER, p. 324**

**Journalizing dividend transactions**

GENERAL JOURNAL

PAGE 5

| DATE | ACCOUNT TITLE | DOC. NO. | POST. REF. | DEBIT | CREDIT | |
|------|---------------|----------|------------|-------|--------|---|
| | | | | | | 1 |
| | | | | | | 2 |
| | | | | | | 3 |
| | | | | | | 4 |
| | | | | | | 5 |
| | | | | | | 6 |
| | | | | | | 7 |
| | | | | | | 8 |
| | | | | | | 9 |
| | | | | | | 10 |
| | | | | | | 11 |
| | | | | | | 12 |
| | | | | | | 13 |
| | | | | | | 14 |
| | | | | | | 15 |

CASH PAYMENTS JOURNAL

PAGE 7

| | | | | 1 | 2 | 3 | 4 | 5 | |
|---|---|---|---|---|---|---|---|---|---|
| DATE | ACCOUNT TITLE | CK. NO. | POST. REF. | GENERAL DEBIT | GENERAL CREDIT | ACCOUNTS PAYABLE DEBIT | PURCHASES DISCOUNT CREDIT | CASH CREDIT | |
| | | | | | | | | | 1 |
| | | | | | | | | | 2 |
| | | | | | | | | | 3 |
| | | | | | | | | | 4 |
| | | | | | | | | | 5 |

**Supporting Calculations**

April 1 Cash Dividend

July 1 Stock Dividend

**11-1** ON YOUR OWN, p. 324

**Journalizing dividend transactions**

## GENERAL JOURNAL

PAGE 7

| | DATE | ACCOUNT TITLE | DOC. NO. | POST. REF. | DEBIT | CREDIT | |
|---|---|---|---|---|---|---|---|
| 1 | | | | | | | 1 |
| 2 | | | | | | | 2 |
| 3 | | | | | | | 3 |
| 4 | | | | | | | 4 |
| 5 | | | | | | | 5 |
| 6 | | | | | | | 6 |
| 7 | | | | | | | 7 |
| 8 | | | | | | | 8 |
| 9 | | | | | | | 9 |
| 10 | | | | | | | 10 |
| 11 | | | | | | | 11 |
| 12 | | | | | | | 12 |
| 13 | | | | | | | 13 |
| 14 | | | | | | | 14 |
| 15 | | | | | | | 15 |

## CASH PAYMENTS JOURNAL

PAGE 12

| | DATE | ACCOUNT TITLE | CK. NO. | POST. REF. | GENERAL DEBIT | GENERAL CREDIT | ACCOUNTS PAYABLE DEBIT | PURCHASES DISCOUNT CREDIT | CASH CREDIT | |
|---|---|---|---|---|---|---|---|---|---|---|
| 1 | | | | | | | | | | 1 |
| 2 | | | | | | | | | | 2 |
| 3 | | | | | | | | | | 3 |
| 4 | | | | | | | | | | 4 |
| 5 | | | | | | | | | | 5 |

**Supporting Calculations**

July 1 Cash Dividend

August 15 Stock Dividend

**11-2** **WORK TOGETHER, p. 329**

**Journalizing treasury stock transactions**

**CASH RECEIPTS JOURNAL**

PAGE 12

| | | | | | GENERAL | | ACCOUNTS RECEIVABLE CREDIT | SALES CREDIT | SALES TAX PAYABLE CREDIT | SALES DISCOUNT DEBIT | CASH DEBIT |
|---|---|---|---|---|---|---|---|---|---|---|---|
| DATE | ACCOUNT TITLE | DOC. NO. | POST. REF. | DEBIT | CREDIT | | | | | | |
| | | | | 1 | 2 | 3 | 4 | 5 | 6 | 7 | |
| 1 | | | | | | | | | | | |
| 2 | | | | | | | | | | | |
| 3 | | | | | | | | | | | |
| 4 | | | | | | | | | | | |
| 5 | | | | | | | | | | | |
| 6 | | | | | | | | | | | |
| 7 | | | | | | | | | | | |
| 8 | | | | | | | | | | | |
| 9 | | | | | | | | | | | |

**CASH PAYMENTS JOURNAL**

PAGE 2

| | | | | GENERAL | | ACCOUNTS PAYABLE DEBIT | PURCHASES DISCOUNT CREDIT | CASH CREDIT |
|---|---|---|---|---|---|---|---|---|
| DATE | ACCOUNT TITLE | CK. NO. | POST. REF. | DEBIT | CREDIT | | | |
| | | | | 1 | 2 | 3 | 4 | 5 |
| 1 | | | | | | | | |
| 2 | | | | | | | | |
| 3 | | | | | | | | |
| 4 | | | | | | | | |
| 5 | | | | | | | | |
| 6 | | | | | | | | |
| 7 | | | | | | | | |
| 8 | | | | | | | | |
| 9 | | | | | | | | |

**Journalizing treasury stock transactions**

## CASH RECEIPTS JOURNAL

PAGE 16

| DATE | ACCOUNT TITLE | DOC. NO. | POST. REF. | GENERAL DEBIT | GENERAL CREDIT | ACCOUNTS RECEIVABLE CREDIT | SALES CREDIT | SALES TAX PAYABLE CREDIT | SALES DISCOUNT DEBIT | CASH DEBIT |
|---|---|---|---|---|---|---|---|---|---|---|
| | | | | | | | | | | |
| | | | | | | | | | | |
| | | | | | | | | | | |
| | | | | | | | | | | |
| | | | | | | | | | | |
| | | | | | | | | | | |
| | | | | | | | | | | |
| | | | | | | | | | | |
| | | | | | | | | | | |

## CASH PAYMENTS JOURNAL

PAGE 4

| DATE | ACCOUNT TITLE | CK. NO. | POST. REF. | GENERAL DEBIT | GENERAL CREDIT | ACCOUNTS PAYABLE DEBIT | PURCHASES DISCOUNT CREDIT | CASH CREDIT |
|---|---|---|---|---|---|---|---|---|
| | | | | | | | | |
| | | | | | | | | |
| | | | | | | | | |
| | | | | | | | | |
| | | | | | | | | |
| | | | | | | | | |
| | | | | | | | | |
| | | | | | | | | |
| | | | | | | | | |

**11-3** **WORK TOGETHER, p. 333**

**Journalizing the purchase and sale of the capital stock of other corporations**

## CASH PAYMENTS JOURNAL

PAGE 3

| DATE | ACCOUNT TITLE | CK. NO. | POST. REF. | GENERAL DEBIT | GENERAL CREDIT | ACCOUNTS PAYABLE DEBIT | PURCHASES DISCOUNT CREDIT | CASH CREDIT | |
|---|---|---|---|---|---|---|---|---|---|
| | | | | | | | | | 1 |
| | | | | | | | | | 2 |
| | | | | | | | | | 3 |
| | | | | | | | | | 4 |
| | | | | | | | | | 5 |
| | | | | | | | | | 6 |
| | | | | | | | | | 7 |
| | | | | | | | | | 8 |
| | | | | | | | | | 9 |

## CASH RECEIPTS JOURNAL

PAGE 8

| DATE | ACCOUNT TITLE | DOC. NO. | POST. REF. | GENERAL DEBIT | GENERAL CREDIT | ACCOUNTS RECEIVABLE CREDIT | SALES CREDIT | SALES TAX PAYABLE CREDIT | SALES DISCOUNT DEBIT | CASH DEBIT | |
|---|---|---|---|---|---|---|---|---|---|---|---|
| | | | | | | | | | | | 1 |
| | | | | | | | | | | | 2 |
| | | | | | | | | | | | 3 |
| | | | | | | | | | | | 4 |
| | | | | | | | | | | | 5 |
| | | | | | | | | | | | 6 |
| | | | | | | | | | | | 7 |
| | | | | | | | | | | | 8 |
| | | | | | | | | | | | 9 |

**Journalizing the purchase and sale of the capital stock of other corporations**

## CASH PAYMENTS JOURNAL

PAGE 1

| | | | | 1 GENERAL | 2 GENERAL | 3 ACCOUNTS PAYABLE DEBIT | 4 PURCHASES DISCOUNT CREDIT | 5 CASH CREDIT |
|---|---|---|---|---|---|---|---|---|
| DATE | ACCOUNT TITLE | CK. NO. | POST. REF. | DEBIT | CREDIT | | | |
| | | | | | | | | |

## CASH RECEIPTS JOURNAL

PAGE 6

| | | | | 1 GENERAL | 2 GENERAL | 3 ACCOUNTS RECEIVABLE CREDIT | 4 SALES CREDIT | 5 SALES TAX PAYABLE CREDIT | 6 SALES DISCOUNT DEBIT | 7 CASH DEBIT |
|---|---|---|---|---|---|---|---|---|---|---|
| DATE | ACCOUNT TITLE | DOC. NO. | POST. REF. | DEBIT | CREDIT | | | | | |
| | | | | | | | | | | |

**11-1** **APPLICATION PROBLEM (LO1, 2), p. 335**

**Journalizing dividend transactions**

GENERAL JOURNAL

PAGE 1

| DATE | ACCOUNT TITLE | DOC. NO. | POST. REF. | DEBIT | CREDIT | |
|------|---------------|----------|------------|-------|--------|---|
| | | | | | | 1 |
| | | | | | | 2 |
| | | | | | | 3 |
| | | | | | | 4 |
| | | | | | | 5 |
| | | | | | | 6 |
| | | | | | | 7 |
| | | | | | | 8 |
| | | | | | | 9 |
| | | | | | | 10 |
| | | | | | | 11 |
| | | | | | | 12 |
| | | | | | | 13 |
| | | | | | | 14 |
| | | | | | | 15 |

CASH PAYMENTS JOURNAL

PAGE 2

| | | | | 1 | 2 | 3 | 4 | 5 | |
|---|---|---|---|---|---|---|---|---|---|
| | | | | GENERAL | | ACCOUNTS PAYABLE DEBIT | PURCHASES DISCOUNT CREDIT | CASH CREDIT | |
| DATE | ACCOUNT TITLE | CK. NO. | POST. REF. | DEBIT | CREDIT | | | | |
| | | | | | | | | | 1 |
| | | | | | | | | | 2 |
| | | | | | | | | | 3 |
| | | | | | | | | | 4 |
| | | | | | | | | | 5 |

**Supporting Calculations**

January 1 Cash Dividend

April 1 Cash Dividend

May 15 Stock Dividend

**Journalizing treasury stock transactions**

## 11-2 APPLICATION PROBLEM (LO3, 4), p. 335

### CASH RECEIPTS JOURNAL

| DATE | ACCOUNT TITLE | DOC. NO. | POST. REF. | GENERAL DEBIT | GENERAL CREDIT | ACCOUNTS RECEIVABLE CREDIT | SALES CREDIT | SALES TAX PAYABLE CREDIT | SALES DISCOUNT DEBIT | CASH DEBIT |
|------|---------------|----------|------------|---------------|----------------|----------------------------|--------------|--------------------------|----------------------|------------|
| | | | | | | | | | | |
| | | | | | | | | | | |
| | | | | | | | | | | |
| | | | | | | | | | | |
| | | | | | | | | | | |
| | | | | | | | | | | |
| | | | | | | | | | | |
| | | | | | | | | | | |
| | | | | | | | | | | |

### CASH PAYMENTS JOURNAL

| DATE | ACCOUNT TITLE | CK. NO. | POST. REF. | GENERAL DEBIT | GENERAL CREDIT | ACCOUNTS PAYABLE DEBIT | PURCHASES DISCOUNT CREDIT | CASH CREDIT |
|------|---------------|---------|------------|---------------|----------------|------------------------|---------------------------|-------------|
| | | | | | | | | |
| | | | | | | | | |
| | | | | | | | | |
| | | | | | | | | |
| | | | | | | | | |
| | | | | | | | | |
| | | | | | | | | |
| | | | | | | | | |
| | | | | | | | | |

**Journalizing the purchase and sale of the capital stock of other corporations**

## CASH PAYMENTS JOURNAL

PAGE 15

| DATE | ACCOUNT TITLE | CK. NO. | POST. REF. | GENERAL DEBIT | GENERAL CREDIT | ACCOUNTS PAYABLE DEBIT | PURCHASES DISCOUNT CREDIT | CASH CREDIT |
|------|---------------|---------|------------|---------|----------|----------------|-------------------|------|
| | | | | | | | | |
| | | | | | | | | |
| | | | | | | | | |
| | | | | | | | | |
| | | | | | | | | |
| | | | | | | | | |
| | | | | | | | | |
| | | | | | | | | |
| | | | | | | | | |

## CASH RECEIPTS JOURNAL

PAGE 10

| DATE | ACCOUNT TITLE | DOC. NO. | POST. REF. | GENERAL DEBIT | GENERAL CREDIT | ACCOUNTS RECEIVABLE CREDIT | SALES CREDIT | SALES TAX PAYABLE CREDIT | SALES DISCOUNT DEBIT | CASH DEBIT |
|------|---------------|----------|------------|---------|----------|------------------|-------|-----------------|----------------|------|
| | | | | | | | | | | |
| | | | | | | | | | | |
| | | | | | | | | | | |
| | | | | | | | | | | |
| | | | | | | | | | | |
| | | | | | | | | | | |
| | | | | | | | | | | |
| | | | | | | | | | | |
| | | | | | | | | | | |

## 11-M MASTERY PROBLEM (LO1, 2, 3, 4, 5), p. 336

**Journalizing dividend, treasury stock, and investment transactions**

### GENERAL JOURNAL

PAGE 4

| DATE | ACCOUNT TITLE | DOC. NO. | POST. REF. | DEBIT | CREDIT | |
|------|---------------|----------|-----------|-------|--------|---|
| | | | | | | 1 |
| | | | | | | 2 |
| | | | | | | 3 |
| | | | | | | 4 |
| | | | | | | 5 |
| | | | | | | 6 |
| | | | | | | 7 |
| | | | | | | 8 |
| | | | | | | 9 |
| | | | | | | 10 |

### CASH RECEIPTS JOURNAL

PAGE 6

| | | | | GENERAL | | ACCOUNTS RECEIVABLE CREDIT | SALES CREDIT | SALES TAX PAYABLE CREDIT | SALES DISCOUNT DEBIT | CASH DEBIT | |
|------|---------------|----------|-----------|---------|---------|---------|-------|---------|---------|------|---|
| DATE | ACCOUNT TITLE | DOC. NO. | POST. REF. | DEBIT | CREDIT | | | | | | |
| | | | | 1 | 2 | 3 | 4 | 5 | 6 | 7 | |
| | | | | | | | | | | | 1 |
| | | | | | | | | | | | 2 |
| | | | | | | | | | | | 3 |
| | | | | | | | | | | | 4 |
| | | | | | | | | | | | 5 |
| | | | | | | | | | | | 6 |
| | | | | | | | | | | | 7 |
| | | | | | | | | | | | 8 |
| | | | | | | | | | | | 9 |

CASH PAYMENTS JOURNAL

| DATE | ACCOUNT TITLE | CK. NO. | POST. REF. | GENERAL DEBIT 1 | GENERAL CREDIT 2 | ACCOUNTS PAYABLE DEBIT 3 | PURCHASES DISCOUNT CREDIT 4 | CASH CREDIT 5 |
|------|---------------|---------|-----------|---------|---------|---------|---------|---------|
| | | | | | | | | | 1 |
| | | | | | | | | | 2 |
| | | | | | | | | | 3 |
| | | | | | | | | | 4 |
| | | | | | | | | | 5 |
| | | | | | | | | | 6 |
| | | | | | | | | | 7 |
| | | | | | | | | | 8 |
| | | | | | | | | | 9 |
| | | | | | | | | | 10 |
| | | | | | | | | | 11 |
| | | | | | | | | | 12 |
| | | | | | | | | | 13 |
| | | | | | | | | | 14 |
| | | | | | | | | | 15 |
| | | | | | | | | | 16 |
| | | | | | | | | | 17 |
| | | | | | | | | | 18 |
| | | | | | | | | | 19 |
| | | | | | | | | | 20 |
| | | | | | | | | | 21 |
| | | | | | | | | | 22 |
| | | | | | | | | | 23 |

# 11-M  MASTERY PROBLEM (concluded)

**Supporting Calculations**

July 1 Cash Dividend

August 6 Stock Dividend

**Journalizing stock and dividend transactions**

## GENERAL JOURNAL

PAGE 1

| DATE | ACCOUNT TITLE | DOC. NO. | POST. REF. | DEBIT | CREDIT | |
|------|--------------|----------|-----------|-------|--------|---|
| | | | | | | 1 |
| | | | | | | 2 |
| | | | | | | 3 |
| | | | | | | 4 |
| | | | | | | 5 |
| | | | | | | 6 |
| | | | | | | 7 |
| | | | | | | 8 |
| | | | | | | 9 |
| | | | | | | 10 |
| | | | | | | 11 |
| | | | | | | 12 |
| | | | | | | 13 |
| | | | | | | 14 |
| | | | | | | 15 |

## CASH RECEIPTS JOURNAL

PAGE 4

| | | | GENERAL | | ACCOUNTS RECEIVABLE CREDIT | SALES CREDIT | SALES TAX PAYABLE CREDIT | SALES DISCOUNT DEBIT | CASH DEBIT | |
|------|--------------|----------|-----------|-------------|------|------|-------|--------|---|---|
| DATE | ACCOUNT TITLE | DOC. NO. | POST. REF. | DEBIT | CREDIT | | | | | | |
| | | | | | | | | | | | 1 |
| | | | | | | | | | | | 2 |
| | | | | | | | | | | | 3 |
| | | | | | | | | | | | 4 |
| | | | | | | | | | | | 5 |

CASH PAYMENTS JOURNAL

PAGE 3

| | | CK. NO. | POST. REF. | GENERAL | | ACCOUNTS PAYABLE DEBIT | PURCHASES DISCOUNT CREDIT | CASH CREDIT |
|---|---|---|---|---|---|---|---|---|
| DATE | ACCOUNT TITLE | | | DEBIT | CREDIT | | | |
| | | | | 1 | 2 | 3 | 4 | 5 |
| 1 | | | | | | | | |
| 2 | | | | | | | | |
| 3 | | | | | | | | |
| 4 | | | | | | | | |
| 5 | | | | | | | | |
| 6 | | | | | | | | |
| 7 | | | | | | | | |
| 8 | | | | | | | | |
| 9 | | | | | | | | |
| 10 | | | | | | | | |
| 11 | | | | | | | | |
| 12 | | | | | | | | |
| 13 | | | | | | | | |
| 14 | | | | | | | | |
| 15 | | | | | | | | |
| 16 | | | | | | | | |
| 17 | | | | | | | | |
| 18 | | | | | | | | |
| 19 | | | | | | | | |
| 20 | | | | | | | | |
| 21 | | | | | | | | |
| 22 | | | | | | | | |
| 23 | | | | | | | | |

**Supporting Calculations**

January 5 Stock Dividend

**Supporting Calculations**

Preferred Dividend Payments

| Name | | Perfect Score | Your Score |
|---|---|---|---|
| | Identifying Accounting Terms | 13 Pts. | |
| | Analyzing Transactions for Bonds | 20 Pts. | |
| | Analyzing Concepts for Bonds | 10 Pts. | |
| | **Total** | 43 Pts. | |

## Part One—Identifying Accounting Terms

**Directions:** Select the one term in Column I that best fits each definition in Column II. Print the letter identifying your choice in the Answers column.

| Column I | Column II | Answers |
|---|---|---|
| **A.** bond | **1.** A long-term promise to pay a specified amount on a specified date and to pay interest at stated intervals. (p. 342) | 1._____ |
| **B.** bond amortization | **2.** All bonds representing the total amount of a loan. (p. 342) | 2._____ |
| **C.** bond issue | **3.** The amount to be paid to a bondholder at the bond maturity date. (p. 343) | 3._____ |
| **D.** call option | **4.** The rate of interest used to calculate periodic interest payments on a bond. (p. 343) | 4._____ |
| **E.** callable bond | | |
| **F.** carrying value | **5.** The market interest rate at the time bonds are issued. (p. 346) | 5._____ |
| **G.** effective interest rate | **6.** Reducing the amount of a bond discount or premium over time. (p. 347) | 6._____ |
| **H.** face value | **7.** The face value of a bond adjusted for any unamortized discount or premium. (p. 347) | 7._____ |
| **I.** institutional investors | **8.** Paying the amounts owed to bondholders for a bond issue. (p. 350) | 8._____ |
| **J.** retiring a bond issue | | |
| **K.** serial bonds | **9.** Bonds that all mature on the same date. (p. 350) | 9._____ |
| **L.** stated interest rate | **10.** Portions of a bond issue that mature on different dates. (p. 350) | 10._____ |
| **M.** term bonds | **11.** The right of a corporation to repurchase its security for a specified price. (p. 350) | 11._____ |
| | **12.** A bond that can be called before its maturity date. (p. 350) | 12._____ |
| | **13.** Organizations that manage the investments of individual investors. (p. 355) | 13._____ |

# Part Two—Analyzing Transactions for Bonds

**Directions:** For each transaction below, print in the proper Answers column the identifying letters of the accounts to be debited and credited.

| Account Titles | Transactions | Answers Debit | Answers Credit |
|---|---|---|---|
| **A.** Bonds Payable | Received cash for the issuance of 5%, $5,000 face-value bonds issued to yield 5.3%. (p. 343) | 1._____ | 2._____ |
| **B.** Cash | Received cash for the issuance of 5%, $5,000 face-value bonds issued to yield 4.8%. (p. 344) | 3._____ | 4._____ |
| **C.** Discount on Bonds Payable | | | |
| **D.** Gain on Sale of Investments | | | |
| **E.** Interest Expense | Paid cash for the semiannual interest payment for bonds issued at a discount. (p. 347) | 5._____ | 6._____ |
| **F.** Interest Revenue | Paid cash for the semiannual interest payment for bonds issued at a premium. (p. 348) | 7._____ | 8._____ |
| **G.** Investment Securities | Retired a bond at its face value. (p. 350) | 9._____ | 10._____ |
| **H.** Loss on Redemption of Bonds | Redeemed a $100,000 bond issue with a call option of 102%. The bonds had a carrying value of $94,000. (p. 351) | 11._____ | 12._____ |
| **I.** Premium on Bonds Payable | Purchased another corporation's $1,000 face-value bonds at $975. (p. 355) | 13._____ | 14._____ |
| | Received the semiannual interest payment on $5,000 bonds purchased for $4,875. (p. 357) | 15._____ | 16._____ |
| | Received the semiannual interest payment on $5,000 bonds purchased for $5,250. (p. 358) | 17._____ | 18._____ |
| | Received $215,000 cash from the sale of a $200,000 investment in the bonds of another corporation. (p. 359) | 19._____ | 20._____ |

**400** • Working Papers

## Part Three—Analyzing Concepts for Bonds

**Directions:** Place a *T* for True or an *F* for False in the Answers column to show whether each of the following statements is true or false.

1. An advantage of borrowing additional capital is that stockholders' equity is not spread over additional shares of stock. (p. 342)

   **1.** _____

2. The stated interest rate of a bond issue rarely equals the market interest rate on the day the bonds are issued. (p. 343)

   **2.** _____

3. If the market interest rate on a bond is below the stated interest rate, investors are not willing to pay full price for a bond that yields a below-market rate. (p. 343)

   **3.** _____

4. Interest expense is calculated based on the carrying value of the bonds, multiplied by the effective interest rate. (p. 347)

   **4.** _____

5. The amount of interest expense on bonds issued at a discount will decrease each year. (pp. 346, 348)

   **5.** _____

6. A call option protects a corporation from increases in market interest rates. (p. 351)

   **6.** _____

7. The redemption amount for a bond is almost always above the carrying value, resulting in a loss. (p. 351)

   **7.** _____

8. If the market price of the corporation's common stock rises above the conversion price, bondholders will not be willing to convert their bonds to common stock. (p. 352)

   **8.** _____

9. IFRS requires that the estimated value of the conversion option be recorded in a separate account from Bonds Payable. (p. 352)

   **9.** _____

10. The carrying value of the bonds purchased at a discount will gradually increase to equal the bonds' total face value. (p. 357)

   **10.** _____

**12-1** **WORK TOGETHER, p. 345**

**Journalizing bond transactions**

CASH RECEIPTS JOURNAL

| DATE | ACCOUNT TITLE | DOC. NO. | POST. REF. | GENERAL DEBIT | GENERAL CREDIT | ACCOUNTS RECEIVABLE CREDIT | SALES CREDIT | SALES TAX PAYABLE CREDIT | SALES DISCOUNT DEBIT | CASH DEBIT |
|------|---------------|----------|------------|---------------|----------------|-----------------------------|--------------|---------------------------|----------------------|------------|
| | | | | 1 | 2 | 3 | 4 | 5 | 6 | 7 |
| 1 | | | | | | | | | | |
| 2 | | | | | | | | | | |
| 3 | | | | | | | | | | |
| 4 | | | | | | | | | | |
| 5 | | | | | | | | | | |
| 6 | | | | | | | | | | |
| 7 | | | | | | | | | | |
| 8 | | | | | | | | | | |
| 9 | | | | | | | | | | |
| 10 | | | | | | | | | | |
| 11 | | | | | | | | | | |
| 12 | | | | | | | | | | |
| 13 | | | | | | | | | | |
| 14 | | | | | | | | | | |
| 15 | | | | | | | | | | |
| 16 | | | | | | | | | | |
| 17 | | | | | | | | | | |
| 18 | | | | | | | | | | |
| 19 | | | | | | | | | | |
| 20 | | | | | | | | | | |
| 21 | | | | | | | | | | |
| 22 | | | | | | | | | | |

**Journalizing bond transactions**

CASH RECEIPTS JOURNAL

| DATE | ACCOUNT TITLE | DOC. NO. | POST. REF. | GENERAL DEBIT | GENERAL CREDIT | ACCOUNTS RECEIVABLE CREDIT | SALES CREDIT | SALES TAX PAYABLE CREDIT | SALES DISCOUNT DEBIT | CASH DEBIT |
|---|---|---|---|---|---|---|---|---|---|---|
| | | | | | | | | | | |

## 12-2 WORK TOGETHER, p. 349

**Journalizing bond interest payments**

CASH PAYMENTS JOURNAL

| | DATE | ACCOUNT TITLE | CK. NO. | POST. REF. | GENERAL DEBIT | GENERAL CREDIT | ACCOUNTS PAYABLE DEBIT | PURCHASES DISCOUNT CREDIT | CASH CREDIT | |
|---|---|---|---|---|---|---|---|---|---|---|
| 1 | | | | | | | | | | 1 |
| 2 | | | | | | | | | | 2 |
| 3 | | | | | | | | | | 3 |
| 4 | | | | | | | | | | 4 |
| 5 | | | | | | | | | | 5 |
| 6 | | | | | | | | | | 6 |
| 7 | | | | | | | | | | 7 |
| 8 | | | | | | | | | | 8 |
| 9 | | | | | | | | | | 9 |
| 10 | | | | | | | | | | 10 |
| 11 | | | | | | | | | | 11 |
| 12 | | | | | | | | | | 12 |
| 13 | | | | | | | | | | 13 |
| 14 | | | | | | | | | | 14 |
| 15 | | | | | | | | | | 15 |
| 16 | | | | | | | | | | 16 |
| 17 | | | | | | | | | | 17 |
| 18 | | | | | | | | | | 18 |
| 19 | | | | | | | | | | 19 |
| 20 | | | | | | | | | | 20 |
| 21 | | | | | | | | | | 21 |

**Supporting Calculations**

June 30 Interest Payment

December 31 Interest Payment

## 12-2 ON YOUR OWN, p. 349

**Journalizing bond interest payments**

CASH PAYMENTS JOURNAL

PAGE 12

| DATE | ACCOUNT TITLE | CK. NO. | POST. REF. | GENERAL DEBIT | GENERAL CREDIT | ACCOUNTS PAYABLE DEBIT | PURCHASES DISCOUNT CREDIT | CASH CREDIT | |
|------|--------------|---------|-----------|-------|--------|-------|--------|------|---|
| | | | | | | | | | 1 |
| | | | | | | | | | 2 |
| | | | | | | | | | 3 |
| | | | | | | | | | 4 |
| | | | | | | | | | 5 |
| | | | | | | | | | 6 |
| | | | | | | | | | 7 |
| | | | | | | | | | 8 |
| | | | | | | | | | 9 |
| | | | | | | | | | 10 |
| | | | | | | | | | 11 |
| | | | | | | | | | 12 |
| | | | | | | | | | 13 |
| | | | | | | | | | 14 |
| | | | | | | | | | 15 |
| | | | | | | | | | 16 |
| | | | | | | | | | 17 |
| | | | | | | | | | 18 |
| | | | | | | | | | 19 |
| | | | | | | | | | 20 |
| | | | | | | | | | 21 |

**Supporting Calculations**

June 30 Interest Payment

December 31 Interest Payment

**12-3** **WORK TOGETHER, p. 354**

**Redeeming and calling a bond issue**

CASH PAYMENTS JOURNAL

PAGE 6

| | | | | GENERAL | | ACCOUNTS | PURCHASES | CASH |
| DATE | ACCOUNT TITLE | CK. NO. | POST. REF. | DEBIT | CREDIT | PAYABLE DEBIT | DISCOUNT CREDIT | CREDIT |
|---|---|---|---|---|---|---|---|---|
| | | | | 1 | 2 | 3 | 4 | 5 |
| 1 | | | | | | | | |
| 2 | | | | | | | | |
| 3 | | | | | | | | |
| 4 | | | | | | | | |
| 5 | | | | | | | | |
| 6 | | | | | | | | |
| 7 | | | | | | | | |
| 8 | | | | | | | | |
| 9 | | | | | | | | |
| 10 | | | | | | | | |
| 11 | | | | | | | | |
| 12 | | | | | | | | |
| 13 | | | | | | | | |
| 14 | | | | | | | | |
| 15 | | | | | | | | |
| 16 | | | | | | | | |
| 17 | | | | | | | | |
| 18 | | | | | | | | |
| 19 | | | | | | | | |
| 20 | | | | | | | | |
| 21 | | | | | | | | |

**Supporting Calculations**

July 1 Redemption

October 1 Redemption

**12-3** **ON YOUR OWN, p. 354**

**Redeeming and calling a bond issue**

CASH PAYMENTS JOURNAL

PAGE 10

| | | | | GENERAL | | ACCOUNTS PAYABLE DEBIT | PURCHASES DISCOUNT CREDIT | CASH CREDIT | |
|---|---|---|---|---|---|---|---|---|---|
| DATE | ACCOUNT TITLE | CK. NO. | POST. REF. | DEBIT | CREDIT | | | | |
| | | | | | | | | | 1 |
| | | | | | | | | | 2 |
| | | | | | | | | | 3 |
| | | | | | | | | | 4 |
| | | | | | | | | | 5 |
| | | | | | | | | | 6 |
| | | | | | | | | | 7 |
| | | | | | | | | | 8 |
| | | | | | | | | | 9 |
| | | | | | | | | | 10 |
| | | | | | | | | | 11 |
| | | | | | | | | | 12 |
| | | | | | | | | | 13 |
| | | | | | | | | | 14 |
| | | | | | | | | | 15 |
| | | | | | | | | | 16 |
| | | | | | | | | | 17 |
| | | | | | | | | | 18 |
| | | | | | | | | | 19 |
| | | | | | | | | | 20 |
| | | | | | | | | | 21 |

**Supporting Calculations**

October 1 Redemption

November 1 Redemption

**Journalizing bond investment transactions**

**12-4** **WORK TOGETHER, p. 360**

## CASH PAYMENTS JOURNAL

PAGE 5

| DATE | ACCOUNT TITLE | CK. NO. | POST. REF. | GENERAL DEBIT | GENERAL CREDIT | ACCOUNTS PAYABLE DEBIT | PURCHASES DISCOUNT CREDIT | CASH CREDIT |
|------|---------------|---------|-----------|---------------|----------------|------------------------|---------------------------|-------------|
| | | | | | | | | |

## CASH RECEIPTS JOURNAL

PAGE 3

| DATE | ACCOUNT TITLE | DOC. NO. | POST. REF. | GENERAL DEBIT | GENERAL CREDIT | ACCOUNTS RECEIVABLE CREDIT | SALES CREDIT | SALES TAX PAYABLE CREDIT | SALES DISCOUNT DEBIT | CASH DEBIT |
|------|---------------|----------|-----------|---------------|----------------|----------------------------|--------------|--------------------------|----------------------|------------|
| | | | | | | | | | | |

**Supporting Calculations**

PlatMat Corporation Interest Payment

OpeLin Industries Interest Payment

OpeLin Bond Sale

**12-4** **ON YOUR OWN, p. 360**

*Journalizing bond investment transactions*

## CASH PAYMENTS JOURNAL

PAGE 7

| DATE | ACCOUNT TITLE | CK. NO. | POST. REF. | GENERAL DEBIT | GENERAL CREDIT | ACCOUNTS PAYABLE DEBIT | PURCHASES DISCOUNT CREDIT | CASH CREDIT |
|---|---|---|---|---|---|---|---|---|
| | | | | | | | | |
| | | | | | | | | |
| | | | | | | | | |
| | | | | | | | | |
| | | | | | | | | |
| | | | | | | | | |
| | | | | | | | | |
| | | | | | | | | |
| | | | | | | | | |

## CASH RECEIPTS JOURNAL

PAGE 4

| DATE | ACCOUNT TITLE | DOC. NO. | POST. REF. | GENERAL DEBIT | GENERAL CREDIT | ACCOUNTS RECEIVABLE CREDIT | SALES CREDIT | SALES TAX PAYABLE CREDIT | SALES DISCOUNT DEBIT | CASH DEBIT |
|---|---|---|---|---|---|---|---|---|---|---|
| | | | | | | | | | | |
| | | | | | | | | | | |
| | | | | | | | | | | |
| | | | | | | | | | | |
| | | | | | | | | | | |
| | | | | | | | | | | |
| | | | | | | | | | | |
| | | | | | | | | | | |
| | | | | | | | | | | |

**Supporting Calculations**

Greatlin Industries Interest Payment

PESC Corporation Interest Payment

Pesc Corporation Bond Sale

**12-1** **APPLICATION PROBLEM (LO2), p. 362**

Journalizing bond transactions

CASH RECEIPTS JOURNAL

PAGE 8

| | | | | 1 | 2 | 3 | 4 | 5 | 6 | 7 |
|---|---|---|---|---|---|---|---|---|---|---|
| DATE | ACCOUNT TITLE | DOC. NO. | POST. REF. | GENERAL DEBIT | GENERAL CREDIT | ACCOUNTS RECEIVABLE CREDIT | SALES CREDIT | SALES TAX PAYABLE CREDIT | SALES DISCOUNT DEBIT | CASH DEBIT |
| | | | | | | | | | | |

**Journalizing bond interest payments**

CASH PAYMENTS JOURNAL

PAGE 18

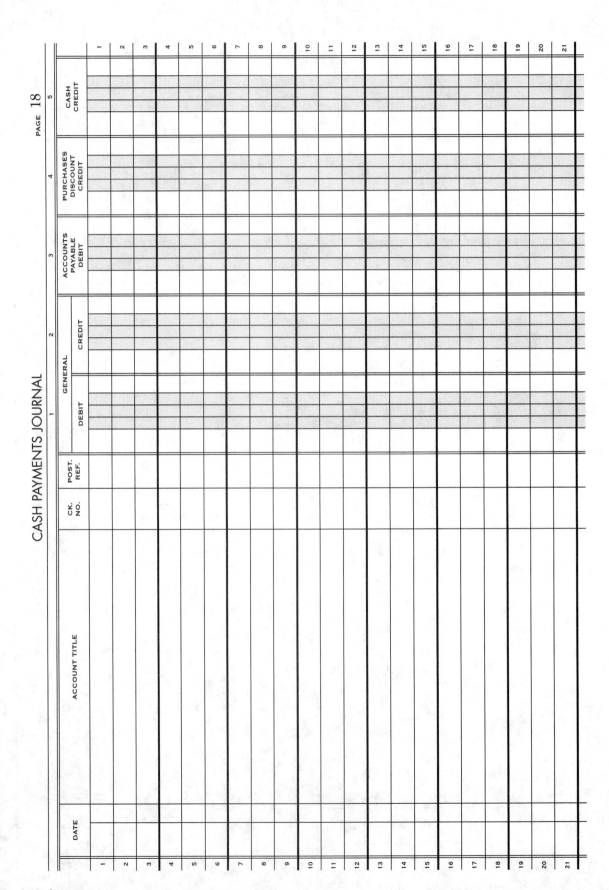

| | | | | GENERAL | | ACCOUNTS PAYABLE DEBIT | PURCHASES DISCOUNT CREDIT | CASH CREDIT |
|---|---|---|---|---|---|---|---|---|
| DATE | ACCOUNT TITLE | CK. NO. | POST. REF. | DEBIT | CREDIT | | | |
| | | | | 1 | 2 | 3 | 4 | 5 |

# 12-2 APPLICATION PROBLEM (concluded)

**Supporting Calculations**

July 1 Interest Payment

August 1 Interest Payment

**Redeeming and calling a bond issue**

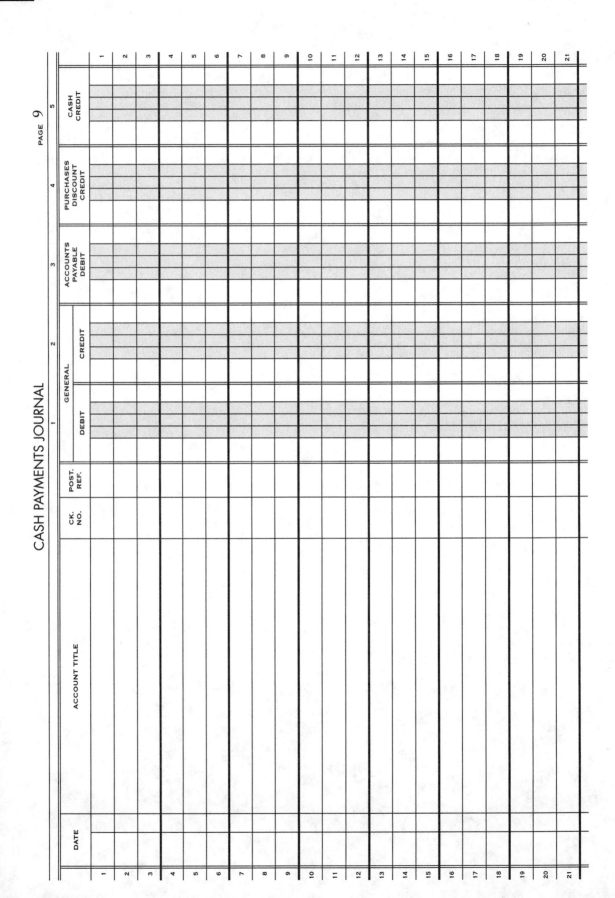

CASH PAYMENTS JOURNAL

PAGE 9

# 12-3 APPLICATION PROBLEM (concluded)

**Supporting Calculations**

April 1 Redemption

July 1 Redemption

**Journalizing bond investment transactions**

CASH PAYMENTS JOURNAL

PAGE 5

| | | | | 1 | 2 | 3 | 4 | 5 |
|---|---|---|---|---|---|---|---|---|
| | | | | GENERAL | | ACCOUNTS PAYABLE DEBIT | PURCHASES DISCOUNT CREDIT | CASH CREDIT |
| DATE | ACCOUNT TITLE | CK. NO. | POST. REF. | DEBIT | CREDIT | | | |
| | | | | | | | | |

CASH RECEIPTS JOURNAL

PAGE 3

| | | | | 1 | 2 | 3 | 4 | 5 | 6 | 7 |
|---|---|---|---|---|---|---|---|---|---|---|
| | | | | GENERAL | | ACCOUNTS RECEIVABLE CREDIT | SALES CREDIT | SALES TAX PAYABLE CREDIT | SALES DISCOUNT DEBIT | CASH DEBIT |
| DATE | ACCOUNT TITLE | DOC. NO. | POST. REF. | DEBIT | CREDIT | | | | | |
| | | | | | | | | | | |

## 12-4 APPLICATION PROBLEM (concluded)

**Supporting Calculations**

March 1 Interest Payment

April 1 Interest Payment

April 1 Bond Sale

**Journalizing bond transactions**

## CASH RECEIPTS JOURNAL

PAGE 6

| | | | | 1 | 2 | 3 | 4 | 5 | 6 | 7 |
|---|---|---|---|---|---|---|---|---|---|---|
| | | | GENERAL | | ACCOUNTS RECEIVABLE CREDIT | SALES CREDIT | SALES TAX PAYABLE CREDIT | SALES DISCOUNT DEBIT | CASH DEBIT | |
| DATE | ACCOUNT TITLE | DOC. NO. | POST. REF. | DEBIT | CREDIT | | | | | |
| 1 | | | | | | | | | | |
| 2 | | | | | | | | | | |
| 3 | | | | | | | | | | |
| 4 | | | | | | | | | | |
| 5 | | | | | | | | | | |
| 6 | | | | | | | | | | |

## CASH PAYMENTS JOURNAL

PAGE 3

| | | | | 1 | 2 | 3 | 4 | 5 |
|---|---|---|---|---|---|---|---|---|
| | | | GENERAL | | ACCOUNTS PAYABLE DEBIT | PURCHASES DISCOUNT CREDIT | CASH CREDIT | |
| DATE | ACCOUNT TITLE | CK. NO. | POST. REF. | DEBIT | CREDIT | | | |
| 1 | | | | | | | | |
| 2 | | | | | | | | |
| 3 | | | | | | | | |
| 4 | | | | | | | | |
| 5 | | | | | | | | |
| 6 | | | | | | | | |
| 7 | | | | | | | | |
| 8 | | | | | | | | |
| 9 | | | | | | | | |
| 10 | | | | | | | | |
| 11 | | | | | | | | |
| 12 | | | | | | | | |

# 12-M  MASTERY PROBLEM (continued)

**Supporting Calculations**

April 27 Interest Payment

July 1 Interest Payment

July 1 Redemption

October 1 Interest Revenue




October 1 Bond Sale

**12-C** **CHALLENGE PROBLEM (LO3, 5), p. 364**

**Journalizing bond transactions**

CASH PAYMENTS JOURNAL

PAGE 3

| DATE | ACCOUNT TITLE | CK. NO. | POST. REF. | GENERAL DEBIT | GENERAL CREDIT | ACCOUNTS PAYABLE DEBIT | PURCHASES DISCOUNT CREDIT | CASH CREDIT |
|------|---------------|---------|------------|-------|--------|-----------|------------|------|
| | | | | | | | | |
| | | | | | | | | |
| | | | | | | | | |
| | | | | | | | | |
| | | | | | | | | |
| | | | | | | | | |
| | | | | | | | | |
| | | | | | | | | |
| | | | | | | | | |
| | | | | | | | | |
| | | | | | | | | |
| | | | | | | | | |
| | | | | | | | | |
| | | | | | | | | |
| | | | | | | | | |
| | | | | | | | | |
| | | | | | | | | |
| | | | | | | | | |
| | | | | | | | | |
| | | | | | | | | |
| | | | | | | | | |

**Supporting Calculations**

April 1 Interest Payment

June 23 Interest Payment

June 23 Redemption

| Name | | Perfect Score | Your Score |
|---|---|---|---|
| | Identifying Accounting Terms | 24 Pts. | |
| | Analyzing Financial Analysis Practices | 20 Pts. | |
| | Analyzing Financial Information | 15 Pts. | |
| | **Total** | 59 Pts. | |

# Part One—Identifying Accounting Terms

**Directions:** Select the one term in Column I that best fits each definition in Column II. Print the letter identifying your choice in the Answers column.

| Column I | Column II | Answers |
|---|---|---|
| **A.** capital expenditures | **1.** Financial statements that provide information for multiple fiscal periods. (p. 368) | 1._____ |
| **B.** cash equivalents | **2.** Short-term, liquid investments that are readily convertible to cash and which mature in three months or less. (p. 371) | 2._____ |
| **C.** common equity per share | **3.** The amount of total current assets less total current liabilities. (p. 373) | 3._____ |
| **D.** comparative financial statements | **4.** A ratio that measures the relationship of current assets to current liabilities. (p. 374) | 4._____ |
| **E.** comprehensive income | **5.** Cash and other current assets that can be converted quickly into cash. (p. 374) | 5._____ |
| **F.** current ratio | | |
| **G.** debt ratio | **6.** A ratio that measures the relationship of quick assets to current liabilities. (p. 374) | 6._____ |
| **H.** dividend yield | **7.** Total liabilities divided by total assets. (p. 375) | 7._____ |
| **I.** earnings per share (EPS) | **8.** The ratio found by dividing stockholders' equity by total assets. (p. 375) | 8._____ |
| **J.** EBIT | | |
| **K.** equity ratio | **9.** The amount of common stockholders' equity belonging to a single share of common stock. (p. 376) | 9._____ |
| **L.** free cash flow | | |
| **M.** gross margin | **10.** Earnings before interest expense and taxes. (p. 376) | 10._____ |
| **N.** interest coverage ratio | **11.** The number of times a company can cover its interest expense with its earnings. (p. 376) | 11._____ |
| **O.** market value of a share of stock | **12.** Gross profit as a percent of net sales. (p. 378) | 12._____ |
| **P.** operating margin | **13.** Income from operations as a percent of net sales. (p. 379) | 13._____ |
| **Q.** permanent difference | **14.** The relationship between net income and average total assets. (p. 381) | 14._____ |
| | **15.** The relationship between net income and average stockholders' equity. (p. 382) | 15._____ |
| | **16.** Measure equal to cash flows from operations less cash used for capital expenditures. (p. 383) | 16._____ |
| | **17.** Purchases of plant assets used in the operation of a business. (p. 383) | 17._____ |

Chapter 13 Financial Reporting and Analysis for a Corporation • **429**

| Column I | Column II | Answers |
|---|---|---|
| R. price-earnings ratio | 18. Net income after federal income tax divided by the number of outstanding shares of stock. (p. 387) | 18._____ |
| S. quick assets | | |
| T. quick ratio | 19. The price at which a share of stock may be sold on the stock market at any given time. (p. 388) | 19._____ |
| U. rate earned on average stockholders' equity | 20. The relationship between the market value per share and earnings per share of a stock. (p. 388) | 20._____ |
| V. rate earned on average total assets | 21. The relationship between dividends per share and market price per share. (p. 389) | 21._____ |
| W. temporary difference | 22. A difference between net income and taxable income only for that year and that is never balanced out in a future year. (p. 391) | 22._____ |
| X. working capital | 23. A difference between net income and taxable income for more than one period that reverses out over the entire period. (p. 391) | 23._____ |
| | 24. All changes in equity for the period except changes caused by owner investments and owner distributions. (p. 392) | 24._____ |

# Part Two—Analyzing Financial Analysis Practices

**Directions:** Place a *T* for True or *F* for False in the Answers column to show whether each of the following statements is true or false.

**Answers**

1. The Securities and Exchange Commission requires public companies to submit quarterly and annual reports. (p. 368)

   1. _____

2. To be useful, financial statements must be prepared by using the same accounting principles in each period. (p. 368)

   2. _____

3. On a balance sheet, accounts receivable are listed at gross value. (p. 371)

   3. _____

4. A business can only get capital from owners' investments and retained earnings. (p. 373)

   4. _____

5. Plant assets are also known as working capital. (p. 373)

   5. _____

6. The current ratio can be too high, indicating more capital invested in current assets than is needed to run the business. (p. 374)

   6. _____

7. Quick assets include cash, inventory, and accounts receivable. (p. 374)

   7. _____

8. The debt ratio is a profitability ratio. (p. 375)

   8. _____

9. The debt and equity ratios show the mix of capital provided by capital borrowed and capital provided by stockholders. (p. 375)

   9. _____

10. The sum of the debt ratio and the equity ratio equals 100%. (p. 375)

    10. _____

11. Gross margin is a profitability ratio. (p. 378)

    11. _____

12. The ratio of the money earned relative to the amount of the investment is known as the *return on investment.* (p. 378)

    12. _____

13. Operating margin is a better measure of a company's profitability than a ratio using net income. (p. 379)

    13. _____

14. A decrease in the accounts receivable turnover ratio from 7.5 times to 6.0 times is considered a favorable trend. (p. 385)

    14. _____

15. An inventory turnover ratio considerably lower than the acceptable range would indicate that the company is at risk for lost sales because some items could be out of stock. (p. 386)

    15. _____

16. A low P/E ratio could mean that the stock is undervalued and would indicate a good time to buy the shares. (p. 388)

    16. _____

17. An example of a permanent difference between net income and taxable income is interest revenue on a tax-exempt bond. (p. 391)

    17. _____

18. Accrued items often lead to temporary differences between taxable income and net income. (p. 392)

    18. _____

19. The largest temporary difference is often associated with accounts receivable. (p. 392)

    19. _____

20. Companies must disclose comprehensive income only as a separate statement. (p. 392)

    20. _____

# Part Three—Analyzing Financial Information

**Directions:** For each of the following items, select the choice that best completes the statement. Print the letter identifying your choice in the Answers column.

1. If quick assets are $100,000.00, current assets are $200,000.00, and current liabilities are $50,000.00, the current ratio is (A) 4.0 times (B) 2.0 times (C) 1.0 time (D) none of the above. (p. 374)

   1. _____

2. If quick assets are $100,000.00, current assets are $200,000.00, and current liabilities are $50,000.00, the quick ratio is (A) 4.0 times (B) 2.0 times (C) 1.0 time (D) none of the above. (p. 374)

   2. _____

3. If total assets are $200,000.00, total stockholders' equity is $120,000.00, and total liabilities are $80,000.00, the debt ratio is (A) 250% (B) 60% (C) 40% (D) none of the above. (p. 375)

   3. _____

4. If total assets are $200,000.00, total stockholders' equity is $120,000.00, and total liabilities are $80,000.00, the equity ratio is (A) 250% (B) 60% (C) 40% (D) none of the above. (p. 375)

   4. _____

5. If the preferred stockholders' share of total stockholders' equity is $50,000.00, total stockholders' equity is $200,000.00, and there are 60,000 shares of common stock outstanding, the common equity per share is (A) $3.33 (B) $3.00 (C) $2.50 (D) $0.83. (p. 376)

   5. _____

6. If net income is $100,000.00, interest expense is $25,000.00, tax expense is $13,000.00, and gross profit is $75,000.00, EBIT is (A) $213,333.33 (B) $200,000.00 (C) $175,000.00 (D) $138,000.00. (p. 376)

   6. _____

7. If EBIT is $200,000.00 and interest expense is $25,000.00, the interest coverage ratio is (A) 9.0 (B) 8.0 (C) 1.0 (D) 0.125. (p. 376)

   7. _____

8. If gross profit is $200,000.00, income from operations is $150,000.00, net income is $50,000,00, and net sales are $250,000,00, the operating margin is (A) 80.0% (B) 60.0% (C) 40.0% (D) 20.0%. (p. 379)

   8. _____

9. If the beginning total assets are $225,000.00, ending total assets are $175,000.00, and net income is $26,000.00, the rate earned on average total assets is (A) 14.9% (B) 13.0% (C) 11.6% (D) 6.5%. (p. 381)

   9. _____

10. If cash flow from operating activities is $150,000.00, cash flow from investing activities is $225,000.00, cash flow from financing activities is $200,000.00, and capital expenditures are $50,000.00, free cash flow is (A) $525,000.00 (B) $175,000.00 (C) $150,000.00 (D) $100,000.00. (p. 383)

    10. _____

11. If average accounts receivable are $80,000.00 and net sales are $200,000.00, the accounts receivable turnover ratio is (A) 2.5 (B) 0.6 (C) 0.4 (D) none of the above. (p. 385)

    11. _____

12. If average merchandise inventory is $40,000.00, net sales are $100,000.00, and the cost of merchandise sold is $80,000.00, the inventory turnover ratio is (A) 2.5 (B) 0.8 (C) 0.5 (D) none of the above. (p. 386)

    12. _____

13. If a company has no outstanding preferred stock, net income after income tax is $75,000.00, and shares of stock outstanding are 25,000, the earnings per share is (A) $25.00 (B) $3.00 (C) 30 cents (D) none of the above. (p. 386)

    13. _____

14. If earnings per share are $10.00 and the market price of stock is $100.00 per share, the price-earnings ratio is (A) 20 times (B) 10 times (C) 0.1 time (D) none of the above. (p. 388)

    14. _____

15. If the common dividend per share is $0.30 and the market price per share is $10.00, the dividend yield is (A) 33.3% (B) 30.0% (C) 3.0% (D) 0.03%. (p. 389)

    15. _____

## 13-1 WORK TOGETHER, p. 377

**Analyzing short- and long-term financial strength**

| | Current Year | Prior Year |
|---|---|---|
| Total current assets | $1,610,000.00 | $1,425,000.00 |
| Total quick assets | 485,000.00 | 502,000.00 |
| Total assets | 2,409,000.00 | 2,222,000.00 |
| Total current liabilities | 624,000.00 | 678,000.00 |
| Total liabilities | 1,004,000.00 | 994,500.00 |
| Total stockholders' equity | 1,405,000.00 | 1,227,500.00 |
| Total interest expense | 9,500.00 | 7,800.00 |
| Total federal income tax | 39,332.00 | 26,930.00 |
| Net income | 104,468.00 | 85,070.00 |
| Shares of common stock outstanding | 90,000 | 84,750 |
| Shares of preferred stock outstanding, $100 par | 1,200 | 1,000 |

**1a. Working capital:**

**1b. Current ratio:**

**1c. Quick ratio:**

**1d. Debt ratio:**

**1e. Equity ratio:**

**1f. Common equity per share:**

**1g. Interest coverage ratio:**

**2.**

_____

_____

_____

# 13-1 ON YOUR OWN, p. 377

**Analyzing short- and long-term financial strength**

| | Current Year | Prior Year |
|---|---|---|
| Total current assets | $1,210,000.00 | $1,100,000.00 |
| Total quick assets | 603,750.00 | 544,000.00 |
| Total assets | 1,837,500.00 | 1,537,500.00 |
| Total current liabilities | 465,000.00 | 308,000.00 |
| Total liabilities | 1,185,000.00 | 732,000.00 |
| Total stockholders' equity | 652,500.00 | 805,500.00 |
| Total interest expense | 22,600.00 | 16,750.00 |
| Total federal income tax | 36,134.00 | 35,510.00 |
| Net income | 99,466.00 | 98,490.00 |
| Shares of common stock outstanding | 90,000 | 84,750 |
| Shares of preferred stock outstanding, $100 par | 1,300 | 1,200 |

**1a. Working capital:**

**1b. Current ratio:**

**1c. Quick ratio:**

**1d. Debt ratio:**

**1e. Equity ratio:**

**1f. Common equity per share:**

**1g. Interest coverage ratio:**

**2.**

_____

_____

## 13-2 WORK TOGETHER, p. 384

**Calculating profitability measures**

| | Current Year | Prior Year |
|---|---|---|
| Gross profit | $401,900.00 | $284,925.00 |
| Net sales | 648,750.00 | 555,000.00 |
| Income from operations | 60,300.00 | 47,300.00 |
| Net income | 58,388.00 | 44,400.00 |
| Beginning total assets | 623,200.00 | 486,800.00 |
| Ending total assets | 647,000.00 | 623,200.00 |
| Beginning total stockholders' equity | 424,897.00 | 268,853.00 |
| Ending total stockholders' equity | 380,453.00 | 424,897.00 |
| Cash flow from operating activities | 75,250.000 | 72,550.000 |
| Capital expenditures | 28,350.000 | 25,500.000 |

**1a. Gross margin:**

**1b. Operating margin:**

**1c. Rate earned on average total assets:**

**1d. Rate earned on average stockholders' equity:**

**1e. Free cash flow:**

**2.**

_____

_____

_____

_____

_____

_____

## 13-2 ON YOUR OWN, p. 384

**Calculating profitability measures**

| | Current Year | Prior Year |
|---|---|---|
| Gross profit | $165,338.00 | $234,740.00 |
| Net sales | 685,920.00 | 781,485.00 |
| Income from operations | 83,910.00 | 137,453.00 |
| Net income | 56,400.00 | 87,990.00 |
| Beginning total assets | 408,278.00 | 764,922.00 |
| Ending total assets | 427,250.00 | 408,278.00 |
| Beginning total stockholders' equity | 625,200.00 | 853,622.00 |
| Ending total stockholders' equity | 429,006.00 | 625,200.00 |
| Cash flow from operating activities | 83,745.000 | 92,150.000 |
| Capital expenditures | 52,500.000 | 50,950.000 |

**1a. Gross margin:**

**1b. Operating margin:**

**1c. Rate earned on average total assets:**

**1d. Rate earned on average stockholders' equity:**

**1e. Free cash flow:**

**2.**

_____

_____

_____

_____

_____

_____

## 13-3 WORK TOGETHER, p. 390

### Calculating and analyzing efficiency measures and market ratios

| | Current Year | Prior Year |
|---|---|---|
| Net sales | $4,320,000.00 | $4,105,500.00 |
| Net income | 397,500.00 | 348,967.00 |
| Cost of merchandise sold | 2,857,500.00 | 2,721,947.00 |
| Beginning accounts receivable (book value) | 472,500.00 | 455,700.00 |
| Ending accounts receivable (book value) | 532,500.00 | 472,500.00 |
| Beginning inventory | 375,000.00 | 353,853.00 |
| Ending inventory | 412,500.00 | 375,000.00 |
| Preferred dividends | 60,000.00 | 60,000.00 |
| Common dividends | 90,000.00 | 93,125.00 |
| Market price, common stock | 39.50 | 45.00 |
| Market price, preferred stock | 100.00 | 100.00 |
| Shares of preferred stock outstanding ($50.00, 6%) | 20,000 | 20,000 |
| Shares of common stock outstanding | 75,000 | 74,500 |

### a. Accounts receivable turnover ratio:

### b. Days' sales in accounts receivable:

**c. Inventory turnover ratio:**

**d. Days' sales in inventory:**

**e. Earnings per share:**

**f. Price-earnings ratio:**

## 13-3 WORK TOGETHER (concluded)

**g. Dividend yield:**

Common stock:

Preferred stock:

**2.**

_____

_____

_____

_____

_____

_____

_____

_____

**Calculating and analyzing efficiency measures and market ratios**

| | Current Year | Prior Year |
|---|---|---|
| Net sales | $4,320,000.00 | $3,980,100.00 |
| Net income | 294,000.00 | 244,274.00 |
| Cost of merchandise sold | 2,100,000.00 | 1,990,500.00 |
| Beginning accounts receivable (book value) | 356,250.00 | 425,250.00 |
| Ending accounts receivable (book value) | 393,750.00 | 356,250.00 |
| Beginning inventory | 225,000.00 | 288,300.00 |
| Ending inventory | 210,000.00 | 225,000.00 |
| Preferred dividends | 30,000.00 | 28,500.00 |
| Common dividends | 33,750.000 | 30,000.000 |
| Market price, common stock | 36.00 | 35.00 |
| Market price, preferred stock | 75.00 | 75.00 |
| Shares of preferred stock outstanding ($50.00, 6%) | 10,000 | 9,500 |
| Shares of common stock outstanding | 56,250 | 60,000 |

**a. Accounts receivable turnover ratio:**

**b. Days' sales in accounts receivable:**

**13-3** ON YOUR OWN (continued)

**c. Inventory turnover ratio:**

**d. Days' sales in inventory:**

**e. Earnings per share:**

**f. Price-earnings ratio:**

**g. Dividend yield:**

Common stock:

Preferred stock:

**2.**

_____

_____

_____

_____

_____

_____

_____

## 13-4 WORK TOGETHER, p. 393

**Calculating permanent and temporary differences in net income and taxable income**

|  | Permanent | Temporary |
|---|---|---|
| **1.** Depreciation of office furniture | _____ | _____ |
| Interest income | _____ | _____ |

**2.**

**3.**

**4.**

**Calculating permanent and temporary differences in net income and taxable income**

|  | Permanent | Temporary |
|---|---|---|
| **1.** Rent revenue | _____ | _____ |
| Interest revenue | _____ | _____ |

**2.**

**3.**

# 13-1 APPLICATION PROBLEM (LO1), p. 395

## Analyzing short- and long-term financial strength

|  | Current Year | Prior Year |
|---|---|---|
| Total current assets | $436,760.00 | $357,040.00 |
| Total quick assets | 173,050.00 | 172,250.00 |
| Total assets | 639,150.00 | 536,540.00 |
| Total current liabilities | 209,250.00 | 176,500.00 |
| Total liabilities | 273,250.00 | 256,500.00 |
| Total stockholders' equity | 365,900.00 | 280,040.00 |
| Total interest expense | 14,720.00 | 12,600.00 |
| Total federal income tax | 32,502.00 | 13,475.00 |
| Net income | 93,786.00 | 60,425.00 |
| Shares of common stock outstanding | 50,000 | 40,000 |
| Shares of preferred stock outstanding, $50 par | 4,000 | 4,000 |

| | | |
|---|---|---|
| **1a.** | Working capital:<br><br>Current year:<br><br>Prior year: | Trend:<br><br>Reason: |
| **1b.** | Current ratio:<br><br>Current year:<br><br>Prior year: | Trend:<br><br>Reason: |
| **1c.** | Quick ratio:<br><br>Current year:<br><br>Prior year: | Trend:<br><br>Reason: |
| **1d.** | Debt ratio:<br><br>Current year:<br><br>Prior year: | Trend:<br><br>Reason: |

| | | | |
|---|---|---|---|
| **1e.** | Equity ratio:<br><br>Current year:<br><br>Prior year: | Trend:<br><br>Reason: | |
| **1f.** | Common equity per share:<br><br>Current year:<br><br><br>Prior year: | Trend:<br><br>Reason: | |
| **1g.** | Interest coverage ratio:<br><br>Current year:<br><br><br>Prior year: | Trend:<br><br>Reason: | |

**2.**

_____

_____

_____

_____

_____

_____

## 13-2 APPLICATION PROBLEM (LO2), p. 395

**Calculating profitability measures**

| | Current Year | Prior Year |
|---|---|---|
| Gross profit | $ 375,588.00 | $ 264,540.00 |
| Net sales | 1,249,176.00 | 1,097,472.00 |
| Income from operations | 231,098.00 | 155,250.00 |
| Net income | 58,388.00 | 44,400.00 |
| Beginning total assets | 804,804.00 | 795,300.00 |
| Ending total assets | 958,716.00 | 804,804.00 |
| Beginning total stockholders' equity | 420,048.00 | 418,241.00 |
| Ending total stockholders' equity | 548,832.00 | 420,048.00 |
| Cash flow from operating activities | 70,066.00 | 68,547.00 |
| Capital expenditures | 52,750.00 | 32,100.00 |

| | | |
|---|---|---|
| **1a.** | Gross margin:<br><br>Current year:<br><br>Prior year: | Trend:<br><br>Reason: |
| **1b.** | Operating margin:<br><br>Current year:<br><br>Prior year: | Trend:<br><br>Reason: |
| **1c.** | Rate earned on average total assets:<br><br>Current year:<br><br><br>Prior year: | Trend:<br><br>Reason: |

| | | | |
|---|---|---|---|
| **1d.** | Rate earned on average stockholders' equity:<br><br>Current year:<br><br>Prior year: | Trend:<br><br>Reason: | |
| **1e.** | Free cash flow:<br>Current year:<br>Prior year: | Trend:<br><br>Reason: | |

**2.**

_____
_____
_____
_____
_____
_____
_____
_____

## 13-3  APPLICATION PROBLEM (LO3, 4), p. 396

**Calculating and analyzing efficiency measures and market ratios**

| | Current Year | Prior Year |
|---|---|---|
| Net sales | $1,651,200.00 | $1,254,120.00 |
| Net income | 149,920.00 | 135,680.00 |
| Cost of merchandise sold | 987,480.00 | 792,424.00 |
| Beginning accounts receivable (book value) | 194,312.00 | 165,450.00 |
| Ending accounts receivable (book value) | 161,312.00 | 194,312.00 |
| Beginning inventory | 138,350.00 | 140,435.00 |
| Ending inventory | 155,384.00 | 138,350.00 |
| Preferred dividends | 80,000.00 | 80,000.00 |
| Common dividends | 21,000.000 | 21,600.000 |
| Market price, common stock | 30.00 | 25.50 |
| Market price, preferred stock | 85.00 | 86.00 |
| Shares of preferred stock outstanding ($100.00, 8%) | 10,000 | 10,000 |
| Shares of common stock outstanding | 21,000 | 18,000 |
| | | |

| | | |
|---|---|---|
| **1a.** | Accounts receivable turnover ratio:<br><br>Current year:<br><br><br>Prior year: | Trend:<br><br>Reason: |
| **1b.** | Days' sales in accounts receivable:<br><br>Current year:<br>Prior year: | Trend:<br><br>Reason: |
| **1c.** | Inventory turnover ratio:<br><br>Current year:<br><br><br>Prior year: | Trend:<br><br>Reason: |

| | | |
|---|---|---|
| **1d.** | Days' sales in inventory:<br><br>Current year:<br><br>Prior year: | Trend:<br><br>Reason: |
| **1e.** | Earnings per share:<br><br>Current year:<br><br>Prior year: | Trend:<br><br>Reason: |
| **1f.** | Price-earnings ratio:<br><br>Current year:<br><br>Prior year: | Trend:<br><br>Reason: |
| **1g.** | Dividend yield:<br><br><u>Common</u><br><br>Current year:<br><br>Prior year:<br><br><u>Preferred</u><br><br>Current year:<br><br>Prior year: | Trend:<br><br>Reason:<br><br><br><br>Trend:<br><br>Reason: |

**2.**

_____

_____

_____

_____

_____

_____

_____

# 13-4 APPLICATION PROBLEM (LO5), p. 396

**Calculating permanent and temporary differences in net income and taxable income**

|  | Permanent | Temporary |
|---|---|---|
| **1.** Depreciation of office furniture | _____ | _____ |
| Interest income | _____ | _____ |
| Rent expense | _____ | _____ |

**2.**

**3.**

**4.**

**Analyzing financial statements**

| | Current Year | Prior Year |
|---|---|---|
| Beginning accounts receivable (book value) | $ 84,400.00 | $ 86,320.00 |
| Ending accounts receivable (book value) | 70,792.00 | 84,400.00 |
| Beginning inventory | 259,648.00 | 256,278.00 |
| Ending inventory | 268,624.00 | 259,648.00 |
| Total current assets | 483,000.00 | 523,168.00 |
| Total quick assets | 97,712.00 | 163,416.00 |
| Beginning total assets | 783,728.00 | 785,445.00 |
| Ending total assets | 733,160.00 | 783,728.00 |
| Total current liabilities | 196,776.00 | 224,480.00 |
| Total liabilities | 376,776.00 | 410,080.00 |
| Beginning total stockholders' equity | 373,648.00 | 378,112.00 |
| Ending total stockholders' equity | 356,384.00 | 373,648.00 |
| Net sales | 1,030,320.00 | 1,225,864.00 |
| Cost of merchandise sold | 730,504.00 | 814,944.00 |
| Gross profit | 299,816.00 | 410,920.00 |
| Income from operations | 51,576.00 | 96,232.00 |
| Total interest expense | 24,824.00 | 21,120.00 |
| Total federal income tax | 4,013.00 | 13,178.00 |
| Net income | 22,736.00 | 59,529.00 |
| Cash flow from operating activities | 60,180.000 | 78,100.000 |
| Capital expenditures | 29,775.000 | 51,000.000 |
| Preferred dividends | 5,000.00 | 5,000.00 |
| Common dividends | 44,800.000 | 45,000.000 |
| Market price, common stock | 10.00 | 20.00 |
| Market price, preferred stock | 58.00 | 68.00 |
| Shares of preferred stock outstanding ($100.00, 5%) | 1,000 | 1,000 |
| Shares of common stock outstanding | 16,000 | 15,000 |

**13-M** **MASTERY PROBLEM (continued)**

| | | |
|---|---|---|
| **1.** | Working capital:<br><br>Current year:<br><br>Prior year: | Trend:<br><br>Reason: |
| **2.** | Current ratio:<br><br>Current year:<br><br>Prior year: | Trend:<br><br>Reason: |
| **3.** | Quick ratio:<br><br>Current year:<br><br>Prior year: | Trend:<br><br>Reason: |
| **4.** | Debt ratio:<br><br>Current year:<br><br>Prior year: | Trend:<br><br>Reason: |
| **5.** | Equity ratio:<br><br>Current year:<br><br>Prior year: | Trend:<br><br>Reason: |
| **6.** | Common equity per share:<br><br>Current year:<br><br><br>Prior year: | Trend:<br><br>Reason: |
| **7.** | Interest coverage ratio:<br><br>Current year:<br><br><br>Prior year: | Trend:<br><br>Reason: |

| | | |
|---|---|---|
| **8.** | Gross margin:<br><br>Current year:<br><br>Prior year: | Trend:<br><br>Reason: |
| **9.** | Operating margin:<br><br>Current year:<br><br>Prior year: | Trend:<br><br>Reason: |
| **10.** | Rate earned on average total assets:<br><br>Current year:<br><br>Prior year: | Trend:<br><br>Reason: |
| **11.** | Rate earned on average stockholders' equity:<br><br>Current year:<br><br>Prior year: | Trend:<br><br>Reason: |
| **12.** | Free cash flow:<br><br>Current year:<br><br>Prior year: | Trend:<br><br>Reason: |
| **13.** | Accounts receivable turnover ratio:<br><br>Current year:<br><br>Prior year: | Trend:<br><br>Reason: |

**13-M MASTERY PROBLEM (concluded)**

| | | |
|---|---|---|
| **14.** | Days' sales in accounts receivable:<br><br>Current year:<br><br>Prior year: | Trend:<br><br>Reason: |
| **15.** | Inventory turnover ratio:<br><br>Current year:<br><br><br>Prior year: | Trend:<br><br>Reason: |
| **16.** | Days' sales in inventory:<br><br>Current year:<br>Prior year: | Trend:<br><br>Reason: |
| **17.** | Earnings per share:<br><br>Current year:<br>Prior year: | Trend:<br><br>Reason: |
| **18.** | Price-earnings ratio:<br><br>Current year:<br>Prior year: | Trend:<br><br>Reason: |
| **19.** | Dividend yield:<br><br>Common<br><br>Current year:<br><br>Prior year:<br><br><br>Preferred<br><br>Current year:<br><br>Prior year: | Trend:<br><br>Reason:<br><br><br><br><br>Trend:<br><br>Reason: |

**Calculating the effect of transactions on the current ratio**

**1. a.**

**b.**

**c.**

**d.**

**e.**

**2.**

_____

_____

_____

_____

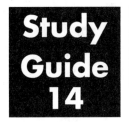

| Name | Perfect Score | Your Score |
|---|---|---|
| Analyzing Procedures and Concepts Related to the Statement of Cash Flows | 20 Pts. | |
| Analyzing a Statement of Cash Flows | 32 Pts. | |
| **Total** | 52 Pts. | |

# Part One—Analyzing Procedures and Concepts Related to the Statement of Cash Flows

**Directions:** Place a *T* for True or *F* for False in the Answers column to show whether each of the following statements is true or false.

**Answers**

1. Cash flow analysis helps owners, creditors, and other interested parties determine a company's potential to produce cash in the future. (p. 402) — 1. _____

2. The statement of cash flows is prepared on an accrual basis. (p. 402) — 2. _____

3. Only the cash flows from operating activities differ between the direct and indirect methods of preparing the statement of cash flows. (p. 403) — 3. _____

4. The total cash provided by (used for) operating activities equals the same amount, regardless of which method is used to prepare the statement of cash flows. (p. 403) — 4. _____

5. Activities in the operating activities section of the statement of cash flows can be indirectly determined by making adjustments to net income. (p. 403) — 5. _____

6. Depreciation expense is not recognized on the income statement, since no cash is used. (p. 404) — 6. _____

7. Amortization expense is a noncash expense and is treated in a manner similar to depreciation expense on the statement of cash flows. (p. 404) — 7. _____

8. An increase in a noncash current asset is a source of cash. (p. 405) — 8. _____

9. If Accounts Receivable declined during the year, it is considered a source of cash. (p. 405) — 9. _____

10. A decrease in a current liability represents a use of cash. (p. 407) — 10. _____

11. If cash from operating activities increases during the year, the statement of cash flows reports it as *Cash used by operating activities*. (p. 409) — 11. _____

12. Increases in accumulated depreciation are ignored when preparing the statement of cash flows. (p. 412) — 12. _____

13. Decreases in long-term assets are generally considered a *source of cash*. (p. 412) — 13. _____

14. Cash flows resulting from a company's financing activities are identified by analyzing changes in long-term assets presented on the comparative balance sheet. (p. 413) — 14. _____

15. One purpose of financing activities is to maintain an adequate balance in the cash account. (p. 413) — 15. _____

16. To analyze the financing activities of a corporation, the comparative balance sheet and comparative income statement must be analyzed. (p. 413) — 16. _____

17. Net income does not affect the financing activities of the business. (p. 413) — 17. _____

18. Decreases in long-term liabilities and the payment of cash dividends generally result in cash inflows. (p. 413)    18. _____

19. The net change in cash is determined by totaling the cash provided by (or used for) operating activities, investing activities, and financing activities. (p. 414)    19. _____

20. Similar to the current ratio, the operating cash flow ratio indicates how likely the company is to be able to pay off current liabilities with its cash flows from operations. (p. 415)    20. _____

## Part Two—Analyzing a Statement of Cash Flows

**Directions:** The parts of the statement of cash flows below are identified with capital letters. Decide the location of each of the following items. Print the letter identifying your choice in the Answers column.

A

B

C

**Answers**

|  |  |  |
|---|---|---|
| 1. | Date of the statement of cash flows. | 1. _____ |
| 2. | Heading of the investing activities section. | 2. _____ |
| 3. | Statement name. | 3. _____ |
| 4. | Explanation of first cash flow resulting from an investing activity. | 4. _____ |
| 5. | Amount of net increase or decrease in cash. | 5. _____ |
| 6. | The amount of net income/net loss. | 6. _____ |
| 7. | Words *Cash provided by/used for investing activities.* | 7. _____ |
| 8. | Words *Depreciation expense.* | 8. _____ |
| 9. | Words *Net increase/decrease in cash.* | 9. _____ |
| 10. | Words *Cash provided by/used for operating activities.* | 10. _____ |
| 11. | Business name. | 11. _____ |
| 12. | Amount of first cash flow resulting from an investing activity. | 12. _____ |
| 13. | Words *Cash balance, end of period.* | 13. _____ |
| 14. | Amount of ending Cash balance. | 14. _____ |
| 15. | Amount of cash provided by/used for investing activities. | 15. _____ |
| 16. | Heading of operating activities section. | 16. _____ |
| 17. | Amount of first cash flow resulting from a financing activity. | 17. _____ |
| 18. | Amount of depreciation expense. | 18. _____ |
| 19. | Heading of financing activities section. | 19. _____ |
| 20. | Words *Changes in current assets and liabilities.* | 20. _____ |
| 21. | Explanation of first change in current asset. | 21. _____ |
| 22. | Words *Net income* or *Net loss.* | 22. _____ |
| 23. | Words *Cash balance, beginning of period.* | 23. _____ |
| 24. | Amount of first change in current asset. | 24. _____ |
| 25. | Explanation of first cash flow resulting from a financing activity. | 25. _____ |
| 26. | Words *Adjustments to net income* or *Adjustments to net loss.* | 26. _____ |
| 27. | Amount of cash provided by/used for financing activities. | 27. _____ |
| 28. | Amount of total adjustments to net income/net loss. | 28. _____ |
| 29. | Amount of beginning Cash balance. | 29. _____ |
| 30. | Words *Total adjustments to net income* or *Total adjustments to net loss.* | 30. _____ |
| 31. | Words *Cash provided by/used for financing activities.* | 31. _____ |
| 32. | Amount of cash provided by/used for operating activities. | 32. _____ |

## 14-1 WORK TOGETHER, p. 410

**Preparing the operating activities section of a statement of cash flows**

Western Wear, Inc.

Comparative Balance Sheet

December 31, 20X2 and 20X1

| | 20X2 | 20X1 | Increase (Decrease) |
|---|---|---|---|
| **ASSETS** | | | |
| Current Assets: | | | |
| Cash | 49 3 8 0 00 | 20 5 0 0 00 | 28 8 8 0 00 |
| Accounts Receivable (book value) | 77 5 0 0 00 | 80 0 0 0 00 | (2 5 0 0 00) |
| Supplies | 3 0 0 0 00 | 2 7 5 0 00 | 2 5 0 00 |
| Merchandise Inventory | 49 0 0 0 00 | 46 0 0 0 00 | 3 0 0 0 00 |
| Total Current Assets | 178 8 8 0 00 | 149 2 5 0 00 | 29 6 3 0 00 |
| Plant Assets: | | | |
| Office Equipment | 22 5 0 0 00 | 19 5 0 0 00 | 3 0 0 0 00 |
| Store Furniture | 49 0 0 0 00 | 46 0 0 0 00 | 3 0 0 0 00 |
| Building | 70 0 0 0 00 | 70 0 0 0 00 | —— |
| Land | —— | 12 5 0 0 00 | (12 5 0 0 00) |
| Less Accum. Depr.—Equipment and Land | 20 4 5 0 00 | 6 8 0 0 00 | 13 6 5 0 00 |
| Total Plant Assets (book value) | 121 0 5 0 00 | 141 2 0 0 00 | (20 1 5 0 00) |
| Total Assets | 299 9 3 0 00 | 290 4 5 0 00 | 9 4 8 0 00 |
| **LIABILITIES** | | | |
| Current Liabilities: | | | |
| Notes Payable | 11 5 0 0 00 | 10 5 0 0 00 | 1 0 0 0 00 |
| Accounts Payable | 23 5 0 0 00 | 22 5 0 0 00 | 1 0 0 0 00 |
| Sales Tax Payable | 3 0 0 00 | 4 0 0 00 | (1 0 0 00) |
| Total Current Liabilities | 35 3 0 0 00 | 33 4 0 0 00 | 1 9 0 0 00 |
| Long-Term Liabilities: | | | |
| Mortgage Payable | 62 5 0 0 00 | 70 0 0 0 00 | (7 5 0 0 00) |
| Bonds Payable | 40 0 0 0 00 | 35 0 0 0 00 | 5 0 0 0 00 |
| Total Long-Term Liabilities | 102 5 0 0 00 | 105 0 0 0 00 | (2 5 0 0 00) |
| Total Liabilities | 137 8 0 0 00 | 138 4 0 0 00 | (6 0 0 00) |
| **STOCKHOLDERS' EQUITY** | | | |
| Total Stockholders' Equity | 162 1 3 0 00 | 152 0 5 0 00 | 10 0 8 0 00 |
| Total Liabilities and Stockholders' Equity | 299 9 3 0 00 | 290 4 5 0 00 | 9 4 8 0 00 |

**1. a., b., c.**

| Account | 20X2 | 20X1 | Current Asset or Current Liability | Increase (Decrease) | Source or Use of Cash |
|---|---|---|---|---|---|
| Accounts Receivable (book value) | | | | | |
| Supplies | | | | | |
| Merchandise Inventory | | | | | |
| Notes Payable | | | | | |
| Accounts Payable | | | | | |
| Sales Tax Payable | | | | | |

## 14-1 ON YOUR OWN, p. 410

### Preparing the operating activities section of a statement of cash flows

Southern Gulf Corporation

Comparative Balance Sheet

December 31, 20X2 and 20X1

| | 20X2 | 20X1 | Increase (Decrease) |
|---|---|---|---|
| **ASSETS** | | | |
| Current Assets: | | | |
| Cash | 132 6 0 0 00 | 140 0 0 0 00 | (7 4 0 0 00) |
| Accounts Receivable (book value) | 188 0 0 0 00 | 180 0 0 0 00 | 8 0 0 0 00 |
| Prepaid Insurance | 4 0 0 0 00 | 6 0 0 0 00 | (2 0 0 0 00) |
| Merchandise Inventory | 184 0 0 0 00 | 220 0 0 0 00 | (36 0 0 0 00) |
| Total Current Assets | 508 6 0 0 00 | 546 0 0 0 00 | (37 4 0 0 00) |
| Plant Assets: | | | |
| Office Equipment | 92 0 0 0 00 | 52 0 0 0 00 | 40 0 0 0 00 |
| Office Furniture | 36 0 0 0 00 | 24 0 0 0 00 | 12 0 0 0 00 |
| Building | 470 0 0 0 00 | 420 0 0 0 00 | 50 0 0 0 00 |
| Land | ——— | 24 0 0 0 00 | (24 0 0 0 00) |
| Less Accum. Depr.—Equipment and Land | 49 0 0 0 00 | 39 2 0 0 00 | 9 8 0 0 00 |
| Total Plant Assets (book value) | 549 0 0 0 00 | 480 8 0 0 00 | 68 2 0 0 00 |
| Total Assets | 1057 6 0 0 00 | 1026 8 0 0 00 | 30 8 0 0 00 |
| **LIABILITIES** | | | |
| Current Liabilities: | | | |
| Notes Payable | 33 0 0 0 00 | 36 0 0 0 00 | (3 0 0 0 00) |
| Accounts Payable | 76 0 0 0 00 | 68 0 0 0 00 | 8 0 0 0 00 |
| Total Current Liabilities | 109 0 0 0 00 | 104 0 0 0 00 | 5 0 0 0 00 |
| Long-Term Liabilities: | | | |
| Mortgage Payable | 356 0 0 0 00 | 372 0 0 0 00 | (16 0 0 0 00) |
| Bonds Payable | 80 0 0 0 00 | 100 0 0 0 00 | (20 0 0 0 00) |
| Total Long-Term Liabilities | 436 0 0 0 00 | 472 0 0 0 00 | (36 0 0 0 00) |
| Total Liabilities | 545 0 0 0 00 | 576 0 0 0 00 | (31 0 0 0 00) |
| **STOCKHOLDERS' EQUITY** | | | |
| Total Stockholders' Equity | 512 6 0 0 00 | 450 8 0 0 00 | 61 8 0 0 00 |
| Total Liabilities and Stockholders' Equity | 1057 6 0 0 00 | 1026 8 0 0 00 | 30 8 0 0 00 |

**1. a., b., c.**

| Account | 20X2 | 20X1 | Current Asset Current Liability | Increase (Decrease) | Source or Use of Cash |
|---|---|---|---|---|---|
| Accounts Receivable (book value) | | | | | |
| Prepaid Insurance | | | | | |
| Merchandise Inventory | | | | | |
| Notes Payable | | | | | |
| Accounts Payable | | | | | |

## 14-2 WORK TOGETHER, p. 417

**Completing the statement of cash flows**

**1.**

| Account | Current Year | Prior Year | Long-Term Asset or Long-Term Liability | Increase (Decrease) | Source or Use of Cash |
|---|---|---|---|---|---|
| Office Equipment | | | | | |
| Store Furniture | | | | | |
| Building | | | | | |
| Land (no gain on sale) | | | | | |
| Mortgage Payable | | | | | |
| Bonds Payable | | | | | |

**3.**

| Activity | Amount | Source or Use of Cash |
|---|---|---|
| Sale of additional common stock | $10,000.00 | |
| Payment of cash dividend | 5,000.00 | |

Western Wear, Inc.

Statement of Cash Flows

For Year Ended December 31, 20X2

**2.**

WT 14-1

**2.**

**4.**

WT 14-2

**5.**

**6.** Operating cash flow ratio   =

Cash flow margin ratio     =

## 14-2 ON YOUR OWN, p. 417

**Completing the statement of cash flows**

**1.**

| Account | 20X2 | 20X1 | Long-Term Asset or Long-Term Liability | Increase (Decrease) | Source or Use of Cash |
|---|---|---|---|---|---|
| Office Equipment | | | | | |
| Office Furniture | | | | | |
| Building | | | | | |
| Land (no gain on sale) | | | | | |
| Mortgage Payable | | | | | |
| Bonds Payable | | | | | |

**3.**

| Activity | Amount | Source or Use of Cash |
|---|---|---|
| Sale of additional common stock | $40,000.00 | |
| Payment of cash dividend | 20,000.00 | |

Southern Gulf Corporation

Statement of Cash Flows

For Year Ended December 31, 20X2

**2.**

OYO 14-1

**2.**

OYO 14-2

**4.**

**5.**

**6.** Operating cash flow ratio =

Cash flow margin ratio =

## 14-1 APPLICATION PROBLEM (LO1, 2), p. 419

**Preparing the operating activities section of a statement of cash flows**

**1.**

| Item | Amount | Source or Use of Cash |
|------|--------|-----------------------|
| Net income | | |

**2.**

| Item | Amount | Source or Use of Cash |
|------|--------|-----------------------|
| Depreciation expense | | |

**3.**

| Account | Current Year | Prior Year | Current Asset or Current Liability | Increase (Decrease) | Source or Use of Cash |
|---------|--------------|------------|------------------------------------|---------------------|-----------------------|
| Accounts Receivable (book value) | | | | | |
| Merchandise Inventory | | | | | |
| Supplies | | | | | |
| Accounts Payable | | | | | |

**Completing the statement of cash flows**

**1.**

| Account | Current Year | Prior Year | Long-Term Asset or Long-Term Liability | Increase (Decrease) | Source or Use of Cash |
|---|---|---|---|---|---|
| Office Equipment | | | | | |
| Office Furniture | | | | | |
| Land | | | | | |

| Account | Current Year | Prior Year | Long-Term Asset or Long-Term Liability | Increase (Decrease) | Source or Use of Cash |
|---|---|---|---|---|---|
| Mortgage Payable | | | | | |

**2.**

| Activity | Amount | Source or Use of Cash |
|---|---|---|
| Sale of additional common stock | | |
| Payment of cash dividend | | |

**5.**

| Item | Amount |
|---|---|
| Net increase in Cash | |

**6.**

| Item | Amount |
|---|---|
| Cash balance, beginning of period | |

**7.**

| Item | Amount |
|---|---|
| Cash balance, end of period | |

## 14-1/14-2 APPLICATION PROBLEM (concluded)

NLC Corporation

Statement of Cash Flows

For Year Ended December 31, 20X2

**4.** APPLICATION PROBLEM 14-1

**3.**

**4.** APPLICATION PROBLEM 14-2

**8., 9.**

**10.**  Operating cash flow ratio     =

Cash flow margin ratio     =

Preparing a statement of cash flows

Alpine Corporation

Comparative Income Statement

For Years Ended December 31, 20X2 and 20X1

| | 20X2 | 20X1 | Increase (Decrease) |
|---|---|---|---|
| Net Sales | 570 1 2 4 00 | 596 1 7 6 00 | (26 0 5 2 00) |
| Cost of Merchandise Sold | 233 6 2 8 00 | 240 8 9 9 00 | (7 2 7 1 00) |
| Gross Profit on Operations | 336 4 9 6 00 | 355 2 7 7 00 | (18 7 8 1 00) |
| Operating Expenses: | | | |
| Depreciation Expense | 12 0 5 7 00 | 11 4 0 9 00 | 6 4 8 00 |
| Other Operating Expenses | 293 5 8 3 00 | 282 3 8 0 00 | 11 2 0 3 00 |
| Total Operating Expenses | 305 6 4 0 00 | 293 7 8 9 00 | 11 8 5 1 00 |
| Net Income before Federal Income Tax Expense | 30 8 5 6 00 | 61 4 8 8 00 | (30 6 3 2 00) |
| Less Federal Income Tax Expense | 9 2 5 7 00 | 18 4 4 6 00 | (9 1 8 9 00) |
| Net Income after Federal Income Tax Expense | 21 5 9 9 00 | 43 0 4 2 00 | (21 4 4 3 00) |

Alpine Corporation

Comparative Statement of Stockholders' Equity

For Years Ended December 31, 20X2 and 20X1

| | 20X2 | 20X1 | Increase (Decrease) |
|---|---|---|---|
| Capital Stock: | | | |
| $15.00 Per Share | | | |
| Balance, January 1 | 120 0 0 0 00 | 120 0 0 0 00 | — |
| Additional Capital Stock Issued | 12 0 0 0 00 | — | 12 0 0 0 00 |
| Balance, December 31 | 132 0 0 0 00 | 120 0 0 0 00 | 12 0 0 0 00 |
| Retained Earnings: | | | |
| Balance, January 1 | 74 3 8 9 00 | 47 3 4 7 00 | 27 0 4 2 00 |
| Net Income after Federal Income Tax | 21 5 9 9 00 | 43 0 4 2 00 | (21 4 4 3 00) |
| Total | 95 9 8 8 00 | 90 3 8 9 00 | 5 5 9 9 00 |
| Less Dividend Payment | 22 0 0 0 00 | 16 0 0 0 00 | 6 0 0 0 00 |
| Balance, December 31 | 73 9 8 8 00 | 74 3 8 9 00 | (4 0 1 00) |
| Total Stockholders' Equity, December 31 | 205 9 8 8 00 | 194 3 8 9 00 | 11 5 9 9 00 |

**14-M MASTERY PROBLEM (continued)**

Alpine Corporation

Comparative Balance Sheet

December 31, 20X2 and 20X1

| | 20X2 | 20X1 | Increase (Decrease) |
|---|---|---|---|
| **ASSETS** | | | |
| Current Assets: | | | |
| Cash | 51 0 1 4 00 | 25 2 1 9 00 | 25 7 9 5 00 |
| Accounts Receivable (book value) | 207 1 7 4 00 | 231 0 1 0 00 | (23 8 3 6 00) |
| Supplies | 1 0 0 1 00 | 1 2 6 2 00 | ( 2 6 1 00) |
| Merchandise Inventory | 71 6 3 6 00 | 74 7 6 0 00 | (3 1 2 4 00) |
| Total Current Assets | 330 8 2 5 00 | 332 2 5 1 00 | (1 4 2 6 00) |
| Plant Assets: | | | |
| Equipment | 57 8 5 6 00 | 49 8 5 6 00 | 8 0 0 0 00 |
| Less Accum. Depreciation—Equipment | 26 2 0 0 00 | 14 1 4 3 00 | 12 0 5 7 00 |
| Total Plant Assets (book value) | 31 6 5 6 00 | 35 7 1 3 00 | (4 0 5 7 00) |
| Total Assets | 362 4 8 1 00 | 367 9 6 4 00 | (5 4 8 3 00) |
| **LIABILITIES** | | | |
| Current Liabilities: | | | |
| Notes Payable | 11 2 0 3 00 | 12 4 6 0 00 | (1 2 5 7 00) |
| Accounts Payable | 89 2 9 9 00 | 103 2 5 1 00 | (13 9 5 2 00) |
| Total Current Liabilities | 100 5 0 2 00 | 115 7 1 1 00 | (15 2 0 9 00) |
| Long-Term Liabilities: | | | |
| Mortgage Payable | 55 9 9 1 00 | 57 8 6 4 00 | (1 8 7 3 00) |
| Total Liabilities | 156 4 9 3 00 | 173 5 7 5 00 | (17 0 8 2 00) |
| **STOCKHOLDERS' EQUITY** | | | |
| Total Stockholders' Equity | 205 9 8 8 00 | 194 3 8 9 00 | 11 5 9 9 00 |
| Total Liabilities and Stockholders' Equity | 362 4 8 1 00 | 367 9 6 4 00 | (5 4 8 3 00) |

**1.**

| Item | Amount | Source or Use of Cash |
|------|--------|-----------------------|
| Net income | | |

| Item | Amount | Source or Use of Cash |
|------|--------|-----------------------|
| Depreciation expense | | |

**2.**

| Account | 20X2 | 20X1 | Current Asset or Current Liability | Increase (Decrease) | Source or Use of Cash |
|---------|------|------|-----------------------------------|---------------------|-----------------------|
| Accounts Receivable (book value) | | | | | |
| Supplies | | | | | |
| Merchandise Inventory | | | | | |
| Notes Payable | | | | | |
| Accounts Payable | | | | | |

**3., 4.**

| Account | 20X2 | 20X1 | Long-Term Asset or Long-Term Liability | Increase (Decrease) | Source or Use of Cash |
|---------|------|------|---------------------------------------|---------------------|-----------------------|
| Equipment | | | | | |
| Mortgage Payable | | | | | |

**5.**

| Activity | Amount | Source or Use of Cash |
|----------|--------|-----------------------|
| Sale of additional common stock | | |
| Payment of cash dividend | | |

**14-M** **MASTERY PROBLEM (continued)**

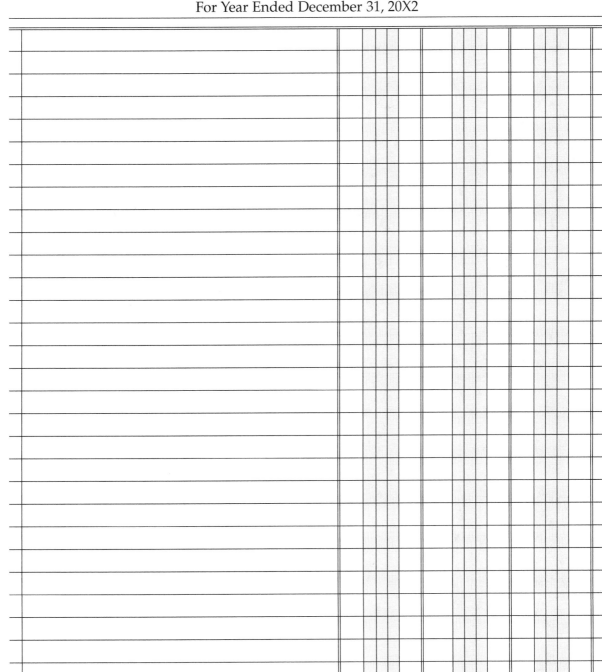

Alpine Corporation

Statement of Cash Flows

For Year Ended December 31, 20X2

**6.**

**7.**

**8.**

**10.** Operating cash flow ratio     =

Cash flow margin ratio      =

**11.**

_____

_____

_____

_____

_____

_____

_____

_____

_____

_____

## 14-C CHALLENGE PROBLEM (LO1, 2, 3), p. 421

**Preparing a statement of cash flows with amortization expense**

Southwest Electronics, Inc.

Comparative Income Statement

For Years Ended December 31, 20X2 and 20X1

| | 20X2 | 20X1 | Increase (Decrease) |
|---|---|---|---|
| Net Sales | 336 5 9 7 00 | 320 1 1 0 00 | 16 4 8 7 00 |
| Cost of Merchandise Sold | 154 2 1 8 00 | 135 5 3 7 00 | 18 6 8 1 00 |
| Gross Profit on Operations | 182 3 7 9 00 | 184 5 7 3 00 | (2 1 9 4 00) |
| Operating Expenses: | | | |
| Depreciation Expense | 13 6 5 0 00 | 4 7 0 0 00 | 8 9 5 0 00 |
| Other Operating Expenses | 168 7 4 4 00 | 172 1 7 8 00 | (3 4 3 4 00) |
| Amortization Expense | 4 7 1 0 00 | 4 7 1 0 00 | — |
| Total Operating Expenses | 187 1 0 4 00 | 181 5 8 8 00 | 5 5 1 6 00 |
| Net Income | (4 7 2 5 00) | 2 9 8 5 00 | (7 7 1 0 00) |

Southwest Electronics, Inc.

Comparative Statement of Stockholders' Equity

For Years Ended December 31, 20X2 and 20X1

| | 20X2 | 20X1 | Increase (Decrease) |
|---|---|---|---|
| Capital Stock: | | | |
| $10.00 Per Share | | | |
| Balance, January 1 | 153 5 6 5 00 | 153 5 6 5 00 | — |
| Additional Capital Stock Issued | 7 0 0 0 00 | — | 7 0 0 0 00 |
| Balance, December 31 | 160 5 6 5 00 | 153 5 6 5 00 | 7 0 0 0 00 |
| Retained Earnings: | | | |
| Balance, January 1 | 7 9 8 5 00 | 5 0 0 0 00 | 2 9 8 5 00 |
| Net Income (Net Loss) | (4 7 2 5 00) | 2 9 8 5 00 | (7 7 1 0 00) |
| Balance, December 31 | 3 2 6 0 00 | 7 9 8 5 00 | (4 7 2 5 00) |
| Total Stockholders' Equity, December 31 | 163 8 2 5 00 | 161 5 5 0 00 | 2 2 7 5 00 |

Southwest Electronics, Inc.

Comparative Balance Sheet

December 31, 20X2 and 20X1

| | 20X2 | 20X1 | Increase (Decrease) |
|---|---|---|---|
| **ASSETS** | | | |
| Current Assets: | | | |
| Cash | 23 355 00 | 20 385 00 | 2 970 00 |
| Notes Receivable | 10 130 00 | 6 325 00 | 3 805 00 |
| Accounts Receivable (book value) | 56 550 00 | 67 500 00 | (10 950 00) |
| Supplies | 2 500 00 | 800 00 | 1 700 00 |
| Merchandise Inventory | 91 050 00 | 46 600 00 | 44 450 00 |
| Total Current Assets | 183 585 00 | 141 610 00 | 41 975 00 |
| Plant Assets: | | | |
| Office Equipment | 27 810 00 | 22 660 00 | 5 150 00 |
| Office Furniture | 6 605 00 | 5 000 00 | 1 605 00 |
| Building | 32 500 00 | — | 32 500 00 |
| Land | 50 000 00 | 75 000 00 | (25 000 00) |
| Less Accum. Depreciation—Equipment | 20 450 00 | 6 800 00 | 13 650 00 |
| Total Plant Assets (book value) | 96 465 00 | 95 860 00 | 605 00 |
| Intangible Assets: | | | |
| Patents | 14 130 00 | 18 840 00 | (4 710 00) |
| Total Assets | 294 180 00 | 256 310 00 | 37 870 00 |
| **LIABILITIES** | | | |
| Current Liabilities: | | | |
| Notes Payable | 7 780 00 | 11 205 00 | (3 425 00) |
| Accounts Payable | 57 425 00 | 52 950 00 | 4 475 00 |
| Salaries Payable | 4 850 00 | 5 350 00 | (500 00) |
| Total Current Liabilities | 70 055 00 | 69 505 00 | 550 00 |
| Long-Term Liabilities: | | | |
| Mortgage Payable | 60 300 00 | 25 255 00 | 35 045 00 |
| Total Liabilities | 130 355 00 | 94 760 00 | 35 595 00 |
| **STOCKHOLDERS' EQUITY** | | | |
| Total Stockholders' Equity | 163 825 00 | 161 550 00 | 2 275 00 |
| Total Liabilities and Stockholders' Equity | 294 180 00 | 256 310 00 | 37 870 00 |

## 14-C CHALLENGE PROBLEM (concluded)

Southwest Electronics, Inc.

Statement of Cash Flows

For Year Ended December 31, 20X2

# REINFORCEMENT ACTIVITY 3, p. 424

**Processing and Analyzing Accounting Data for a Corporation**

**1.**

GENERAL JOURNAL                                                     PAGE 12

| | DATE | ACCOUNT TITLE | DOC. NO. | POST. REF. | DEBIT | CREDIT | |
|---|---|---|---|---|---|---|---|
| 17 | | | | | | | 17 |
| 18 | | | | | | | 18 |
| 19 | | | | | | | 19 |
| 20 | | | | | | | 20 |
| 21 | | | | | | | 21 |
| 22 | | | | | | | 22 |
| 23 | | | | | | | 23 |
| 24 | | | | | | | 24 |
| 25 | | | | | | | 25 |
| 26 | | | | | | | 26 |
| 27 | | | | | | | 27 |
| 28 | | | | | | | 28 |
| 29 | | | | | | | 29 |
| 30 | | | | | | | 30 |
| 31 | | | | | | | 31 |
| 32 | | | | | | | 32 |
| 33 | | | | | | | 33 |
| 34 | | | | | | | 34 |
| 35 | | | | | | | 35 |
| 36 | | | | | | | 36 |
| 37 | | | | | | | 37 |
| 38 | | | | | | | 38 |
| 39 | | | | | | | 39 |
| 40 | | | | | | | 40 |
| 41 | | | | | | | 41 |
| 42 | | | | | | | 42 |
| 43 | | | | | | | 43 |
| 44 | | | | | | | 44 |
| 45 | | | | | | | 45 |
| 46 | | | | | | | 46 |

# REINFORCEMENT ACTIVITY 3 (continued)

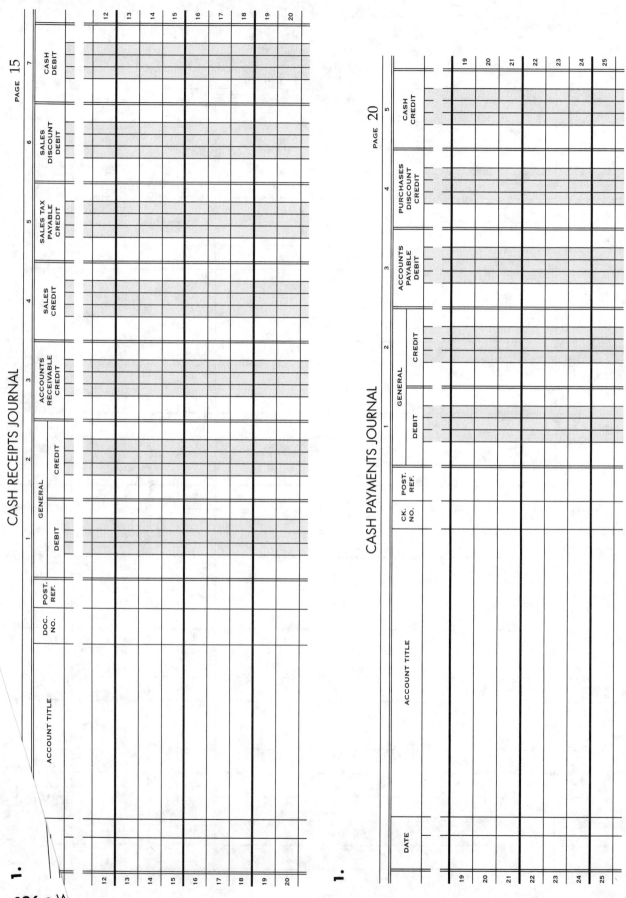

**CASH RECEIPTS JOURNAL**

PAGE 15

**1.**

**CASH PAYMENTS JOURNAL**

PAGE 20

**1.**

## REINFORCEMENT ACTIVITY 3 (continued)

**2.**

Peterson Pet Supply, Inc.

Income Statement

For Years Ended December 31, 20X3, 20X2, and 20X1

| | 20X3 | 20X2 | 20X1 |
|---|---|---|---|
| Net Sales | 625 5 5 5 22 | 597 5 4 6 78 | 545 2 1 0 10 |
| Cost of Merchandise Sold: | 396 3 2 1 84 | 387 4 6 5 98 | 360 0 0 0 00 |
| Gross Profit | 229 2 3 3 38 | 210 0 8 0 80 | 185 2 1 0 10 |
| | | | |
| Operating Expenses: | | | |
| Selling, General and Administrative | 129 5 5 5 55 | 116 5 4 4 41 | 101 3 6 5 36 |
| Depreciation | 40 0 0 0 00 | 38 0 0 0 00 | 35 0 0 0 00 |
| Total Operating Expenses | 169 5 5 5 55 | 154 5 4 4 41 | 136 3 6 5 36 |
| Income from Operations | 59 6 7 7 83 | 55 5 3 6 39 | 48 8 4 4 74 |
| | | | |
| Other Revenue and Expenses: | | | |
| Interest Income | 8 9 7 0 10 | 8 5 4 3 65 | 7 5 1 4 44 |
| Interest Expense | (9 6 6 8 33) | (7 8 5 0 00) | (5 5 5 4 15) |
| Total Other Revenue and Expenses | ( 6 9 8 23) | 6 9 3 65 | 1 9 6 0 29 |
| Net Income before Federal Income Tax | 58 9 7 9 60 | 56 2 3 0 04 | 50 8 0 5 03 |
| Less: Federal Income Tax Expense | 9 7 4 4 90 | 9 0 5 7 51 | 7 7 0 1 26 |
| Net Income | 49 2 3 4 70 | 47 1 7 2 53 | 43 1 0 3 77 |

**2.**

Peterson Pet Supply, Inc.

Statement of Stockholders' Equity

For Years Ended December 31, 20X3, 20X2, and 20X1

| | 20X3 | 20X2 | 20X1 |
|---|---|---|---|
| Paid-In Capital: | | | |
| Common Stock, $10.00 Par Value: | | | |
| Balance, January 1 | 750 0 0 0 00 | 650 0 0 0 00 | 650 0 0 0 00 |
| Additional Common Stock Issued | 250 0 0 0 00 | 100 0 0 0 00 | — |
| Balance, December 31 | 1000 0 0 0 00 | 750 0 0 0 00 | 650 0 0 0 00 |
| Preferred Stock, 8%, $100.00 Par Value: | | | |
| Balance, January 1 | 50 0 0 0 00 | 50 0 0 0 00 | 50 0 0 0 00 |
| Additional Preferred Stock Issued | 20 0 0 0 00 | — | — |
| Balance, December 31 | 70 0 0 0 00 | 50 0 0 0 00 | 50 0 0 0 00 |
| Total Capital Stock Issued | 1070 0 0 0 00 | 800 0 0 0 00 | 700 0 0 0 00 |
| Additional Paid-In Capital: | | | |
| Paid-In Capital in Excess of Par Value—Common | 210 0 0 0 00 | 150 0 0 0 00 | 100 0 0 0 00 |
| Paid-In Capital in Excess of Par Value—Preferred | 5 5 0 0 00 | 1 5 0 0 00 | 1 5 0 0 00 |
| Paid-In Capital from Sale of Treasury Stock | 15 2 0 0 00 | 15 0 0 0 00 | — |
| Total Additional Paid-In Capital | 230 7 0 0 00 | 166 5 0 0 00 | 101 5 0 0 00 |
| Total Paid-In Capital | 1300 7 0 0 00 | 966 5 0 0 00 | 801 5 0 0 00 |
| Retained Earnings: | | | |
| Balance, January 1, 20-- | 53 9 5 1 15 | 48 2 7 8 62 | 22 1 7 4 85 |
| Net Income after Federal Income Tax | 49 2 3 4 70 | 47 1 7 2 53 | 43 1 0 3 77 |
| Less Preferred Dividends Declared | (5 6 0 0 00) | (4 0 0 0 00) | (4 0 0 0 00) |
| Less Common Dividends Declared | (57 0 0 0 00) | (37 5 0 0 00) | (13 0 0 0 00) |
| Balance, December 31 | 40 5 8 5 85 | 53 9 5 1 15 | 48 2 7 8 62 |
| Treasury Stock | | | |
| Balance, December 31 | 29 0 0 0 00 | 30 0 0 0 00 | 20 0 0 0 00 |
| Total Stockholders' Equity, December 31, 20-- | 1312 2 8 5 85 | 990 4 5 1 15 | 829 7 7 8 62 |
| | | | |
| Common Shares Outstanding | 100 0 0 0 00 | 75 0 0 0 00 | 65 0 0 0 00 |
| Preferred Shares Outstanding | 7 0 0 00 | 5 0 0 00 | 5 0 0 00 |
| Treasury Shares | 2 9 0 0 00 | 3 0 0 0 00 | 2 0 0 0 00 |

# REINFORCEMENT ACTIVITY 3 (continued)

**2.**

Peterson Pet Supply, Inc.

Balance Sheet

December 31, 20X3 and 20X2

| | 20X3 | 20X2 |
|---|---|---|
| **Assets** | | |
| Current Assets: | | |
| Cash and Cash Equivalents | 47 2 7 7 30 | 45 3 7 8 52 |
| Marketable Securities | 73 6 2 6 38 | 69 7 4 6 36 |
| Accounts Receivable (book value) | 66 7 0 6 43 | 55 6 4 7 10 |
| Merchandise Inventory | 69 0 6 6 40 | 95 2 1 4 25 |
| Other Current Assets | 98 9 4 4 98 | 79 9 8 7 61 |
| Total Current Assets | 355 6 2 1 49 | 345 9 7 3 84 |
| Investment Securities | 438 4 0 0 00 | 120 0 0 0 00 |
| Land | 75 0 0 0 00 | 100 0 0 0 00 |
| Building | 300 0 0 0 00 | 300 0 0 0 00 |
| Accumulated Depreciation—Building | (50 0 0 0 00) | (40 0 0 0 00) |
| Office Equipment | 170 0 0 0 00 | 120 0 0 0 00 |
| Accumulated Depreciation—Office Equipment | (40 0 0 0 00) | (35 0 0 0 00) |
| Store Equipment | 385 0 0 0 00 | 350 0 0 0 00 |
| Accumulated Depreciation—Store Equipment | (75 0 0 0 00) | (50 0 0 0 00) |
| Total Assets | 1559 0 2 1 49 | 1210 9 7 3 84 |
| **Liabilities** | | |
| Current Liabilities: | | |
| Accounts Payable | 52 9 3 9 05 | 54 2 2 5 68 |
| Sales Tax Payable | 1 6 1 6 05 | 1 5 4 5 22 |
| Accrued Salaries and Related Expenses | 26 1 8 3 69 | 25 7 0 0 40 |
| Federal Income Tax Payable | 5 1 0 3 49 | 4 8 3 0 06 |
| Other Current Liabilities | 55 8 9 3 36 | 59 2 2 1 33 |
| Total Current Liabilities | 141 7 3 5 64 | 145 5 2 2 69 |
| Long-Term Liabilities: | | |
| Bonds Payable, net | 105 0 0 0 00 | 75 0 0 0 00 |
| Total Liabilities | 246 7 3 5 64 | 220 5 2 2 69 |
| **Stockholders' Equity** | | |
| Paid-In Capital | 1300 7 0 0 00 | 966 5 0 0 00 |
| Retained Earnings | 40 5 8 5 85 | 53 9 5 1 15 |
| Treasury Stock | (29 0 0 0 00) | (30 0 0 0 00) |
| Total Stockholders' Equity | 1312 2 8 5 85 | 990 4 5 1 15 |
| Total Liabilities and Stockholders' Equity | 1559 0 2 1 49 | 1210 9 7 3 84 |

## REINFORCEMENT ACTIVITY 3 (continued)

**3.**

| | | |
|---|---|---|
| **(a)** | **Profitability ratios:** | |
| **(1)** | Gross margin:<br><br>20X3:<br><br>20X2:<br><br>20X1: | Trend:<br><br>Reason: |
| **(2)** | Operating margin:<br><br>20X3:<br><br>20X2:<br><br>20X1: | Trend:<br><br>Reason: |
| **(3)** | Rate earned on average total assets:<br><br>20X3:<br><br><br>20X2: | Trend:<br><br>Reason: |
| **(4)** | Rate earned on average stockholders' equity:<br><br>20X3:<br><br><br>20X2: | Trend:<br><br>Reason: |
| **(b)** | **Efficiency ratios:** | |
| **(1)** | Accounts receivable turnover:<br><br>20X3:<br><br><br>20X2: | Trend:<br><br>Reason: |
| **(2)** | Inventory turnover:<br><br>20X3:<br><br><br>20X2: | Trend:<br><br>Reason: |

# REINFORCEMENT ACTIVITY 3 (continued)

**3.**

| | | |
|---|---|---|
| **(c)** | **Short-term financial strength ratios:** | |
| **(1)** | Working capital:<br><br>20X3:<br><br>20X2: | Trend:<br><br>Reason: |
| **(2)** | Current ratio:<br><br>20X3:<br><br>20X2: | Trend:<br><br>Reason: |
| **(3)** | Quick ratio:<br><br>20X3:<br><br>20X2: | Trend:<br><br>Reason: |
| **(d)** | **Long-term financial strength ratios:** | |
| **(1)** | Debt ratio:<br><br>20X3:<br><br>20X2: | Trend:<br><br>Reason: |
| **(2)** | Equity ratio:<br><br>20X3:<br><br>20X2: | Trend:<br><br>Reason: |
| **(3)** | Common equity per share:<br><br>20X3:<br><br>20X2:<br><br>20X1: | Trend:<br><br>Reason: |
| **(4)** | Interest coverage ratio:<br><br>20X3:<br><br>20X2:<br><br>20X1: | Trend:<br><br>Reason: |

## REINFORCEMENT ACTIVITY 3 (continued)

**3.**

| | | |
|---|---|---|
| **(e)** | **Market ratios:** | |
| **(1)** | Earnings per share:<br><br>20X3:<br><br>20X2:<br><br>20X1: | Trend:<br>Reason: |
| **(2)** | Price-earnings ratio:<br><br>20X3:<br><br>20X2:<br><br>20X1: | Trend:<br>Reason: |
| **(3)** | Dividend yield—common stock:<br><br>20X3:<br><br>20X2:<br><br>20X1: | Trend:<br>Reason: |
| **(f)** | **Cash ratios:** | |
| **(1)** | Free cash flow:<br>20X3:<br><br>20X2: | Trend:<br>Reason: |
| **(2)** | Operating cash flow ratio:<br><br>20X3:<br><br>20X2: | Trend:<br>Reason: |
| **(3)** | Cash flow margin ratio:<br>20X3:<br><br>20X2: | Trend:<br>Reason: |

# REINFORCEMENT ACTIVITY 3 (concluded)

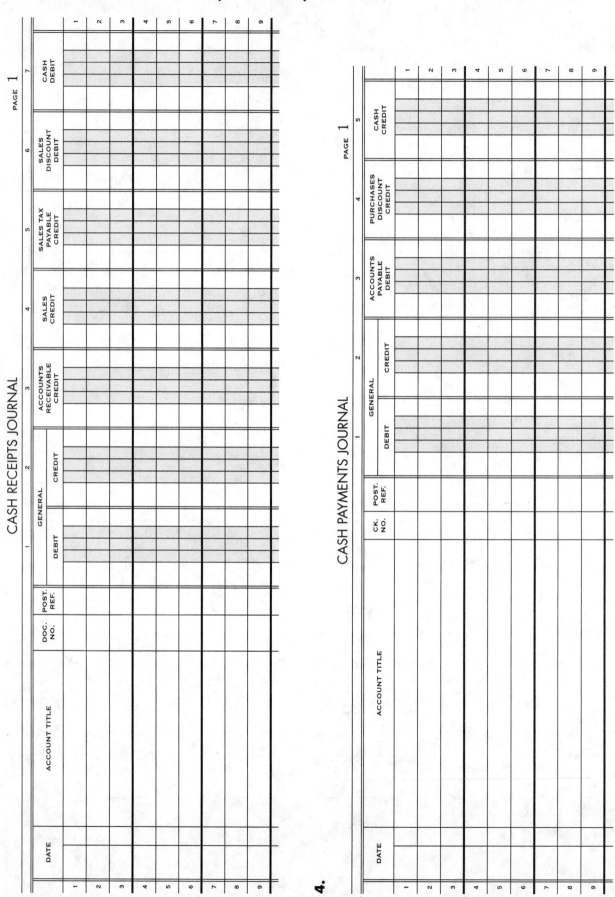

**4.**

**CASH RECEIPTS JOURNAL** — PAGE 1

**CASH PAYMENTS JOURNAL** — PAGE 1